ONE MUST NOT GO
ALTOGETHER WITH THE TIDE

One Must Not Go Altogether with the Tide

THE LETTERS OF EZRA POUND AND STANLEY NOTT

Edited and with Essays by Miranda B. Hickman

Annotations by Robin E. Feenstra
with Miranda B. Hickman

McGILL-QUEEN'S UNIVERSITY PRESS
MONTREAL & KINGSTON · LONDON · ITHACA

© McGill-Queen's University Press
ISBN 978-0-7735-3816-0

Legal deposit second quarter 2011
Bibliothèque nationale du Québec

Printed in Canada on acid-free paper that is 100% ancient forest free
(100% post-consumer recycled), processed chlorine free

This book has been published with the help of a grant from the
Canadian Federation for the Humanities and Social Sciences,
through the Aid to Scholarly Publications Program, using funds
provided by the Social Sciences and Humanities Research Council
of Canada.

McGill-Queen's University Press acknowledges the support of the
Canada Council for the Arts for our publishing program. We also
acknowledge the financial support of the Government of Canada
through the Canada Book Fund for our publishing activities.

LIBRARY AND ARCHIVES CANADA CATALOGUING IN PUBLICATION

Pound, Ezra, 1885–1972
One must not go altogether with the tide : the letters of Ezra
Pound and Stanley Nott / edited by Miranda B. Hickman ; essays
by Miranda B. Hickman ; annotations by Robin E. Feenstra with
Miranda B. Hickman.

Includes bibliographical references and index.
ISBN 978-0-7735-3816-0

1. Pound, Ezra, 1885–1972 – Correspondence.   2. Poets, American –
20th century – Correspondence.   3. Nott, C. S. – Correspondence.
4. Publishers and publishing – Great Britain – Correspondence.
5. Pound, Ezra, 1885–1972 – Political and social views.   I. Nott, C. S.
II. Hickman, Miranda B., 1969–   III. Title.

PS3531.O82Z4884 2011   811'.52   C2010-906919-6

Set in 10/13 Warnock Pro with Gill Sans
Book design & typesetting by Garet Markvoort, zijn digital

CONTENTS

ACKNOWLEDGMENTS

The detailed collaborative labour informing this edition has involved many individuals and organizations without whom the project would never have come to fruition. I acknowledge an immense debt of gratitude to them all. A three-year research grant from the Social Sciences and Humanities Research Council of Canada provided funding essential to the project, and SSHRCC's Aid to Scholarly Publications Programme supplied the subvention necessary to publication. Great thanks are due to the Beinecke Rare Book and Manuscript Library at Yale University, where the majority of this correspondence is housed; the expertise and patient support of the staff there offered an indispensable resource during the project's initial stages. We are also deeply indebted to the Harry Ransom Humanities Research Center at the University of Texas at Austin, where another considerable portion of the materials for the correspondence is located. The responsiveness and acuity of the HRC staff were likewise vital to the project.

Thanks also to staff at the Special Collections Library at McMaster University in Ontario, who provided important material on the correspondence between C.K. Ogden and Stanley Nott; the New York Public Library; the University of Victoria Special Collections Library; Archives and Rare Books at the London School of Economics; the British Library Newspaper Reading Room at Colindale, which offered valuable information on the *Morning Post*; and the UCLA Special Collections Library, where Jeff Rankin was especially helpful. The Lande-Arkin Canadiana Collection at McGill University's Rare Book and Special Collections Library also supplied information about Social Credit fundamental to the essays framing this edition.

Thanks to individuals are due, first, to members of the research team: above all, profound thanks to Robin E. Feenstra, primary researcher for the annotations and the glossaries, whose careful Herculean labour, tireless patience, and scholarly acumen are behind the apparatus for this edition. His generosity has been extraordinary and boundless. David N. Wright and Lindsay Holmgren contributed invaluable labour, leg-work, care, and insight to transcriptions of the letters. Noah Weisberg and Michael Lee provided astute, key research assistance at pivotal junctures.

We are deeply indebted also to Mary de Rachewiltz and Omar S. Pound, heirs of Ezra Pound, for their generous support of this project, as well as to Declan Spring, senior editor of New Directions Publishing Corporation, for his helpful and illuminating assistance with permissions. To Adam Nott and Rosemary Nott, likewise, we extend heartfelt thanks for their gracious support and crucial information. Gratitude goes also to the many people who provided much-needed information during various stages of research, including Pound scholars Barry Ahearn, Alec Marsh, Ira Nadel, Tim Redman, and Demetres Tryphonopoulos. My colleague Nathalie Cooke at McGill offered encouragement and guidance at a critical decision point. And Jad Adams steered me towards valuable commentary on British Fascism at just the right moment.

Last but certainly not least, a warm thanks to Jonathan Crago, editor at McGill-Queen's University Press, for his unflagging support, keen interest, and exceptionally helpful counsel during the final stages of the work.

Letters from Ezra Pound to Stanley Nott, Copyright © 2010 by Mary de Rachewiltz and Omar S. Pound. Used by permission of New Directions Publishing Corporation, agents.

Letters from Ezra Pound to A.S. Leese, Copyright © 2010 by Mary de Rachewiltz and Omar S. Pound. Used by permission of New Directions Publishing Corporation, agents.

Permission to publish the letters of Stanley Nott granted by Adam Nott.

Images from Ezra Pound's letter to Stanley Nott from 10 June 1937 published by permission of the Harry Ransom Humanities Research Center, the University of Texas at Austin.

Images from Stanley Nott's letter to Ezra Pound from 26 November 1934, as well as covers from *Social Credit: An Impact* and *Alfred Venison's Poems*, published by permission of the Beinecke Rare Book and Manuscript Library, Yale University.

I have made every effort to identify, credit appropriately, and obtain publication rights from copyright holders of material in this book. Notice of any errors or omissions in this regard will be gratefully received and correction made in any subsequent editions.

EDITORIAL MISCELLANY

ABBREVIATIONS IN LETTERS

ALS = autograph letter signed
AN = autograph note
APC = autograph postcard
APCS = autograph postcard signed
AS = autograph signature
ASC = autograph script
TL = typed letter
TLS = typed letter signed
TN = typed note
TPC = typed postcard
TPCS = typed postcard signed

HRHRC = This letter is housed at the Harry Ransom Humanities Research Center, the University of Texas at Austin, Ezra Pound Collection, series 2, box 7, folder 16.

All letters not marked HRHRC are housed at the Beinecke Rare Book and Manuscript Library, Yale University. Locations are indicated at the top of letters that begin a sequence located in a certain collection, series, box, and folder (e.g., YCAL MSS 43, series 1, box 37, folder 1579), which designation pertains to following letters until the designation changes at the top of a subsequent letter. Occasionally, there are exceptions to this in instances where letters were placed in folders out of sequence; when this is the case, the relevant folder for the letter is noted at the top of a letter. In letters following such exceptions, the resumption of the principal folder for this section of the correspondence is noted at the top of the letter.

ITALICS

Italics are generally used to designate autograph portions of letters. When italics are inserted within line of the letter, this indicates an ASC insertion. When the original letter was typed in italics, the letter also appears in italics, and this is noted at the head of the letter.

PENCIL INSERTIONS

Pencil insertions at the top of letters are surmises, likely from archivists, about dates of letters; these are not in EP's script unless this is explicitly noted (with EP).

LETTERHEAD ABBREVIATIONS

[Standard Nott Letterhead] (see Letter 1 for approximation; Illustration 1)
[Nott Postcard Letterhead] (see Letter 16 for approximation)
[EP, Gaudier-Brzeska Letterhead] (see Letter 76 for approximation; Illustration 2)
[EP, Postcard Letterhead] (see Letter 80 for approximation)
[EP, "A tax is not a share" Griffin Letterhead] (see Illustration 3)

EXPLANATION OF APPENDICES

Appendix 1. When an individual, book, journal, or movement is featured frequently, or plays an especially important role, in the correspondence, further information is supplied on this item in Appendix 1. If no additional information is provided in Appendix 1, fuller information will be available in the annotation itself. If the name of a person appears in Appendix 1, birth and death years are provided in parentheses in the first reference; otherwise, birth and death years are not supplied. Index entries for items in Appendix 1 appear in boldface.

Appendix 2. Appendix 2 provides a list of books and pamphlets published by Stanley Nott, along with fuller bibliographic information than is available in the annotations. The Pamphlets on the New Economics series is listed here.

ABBREVIATIONS IN ANNOTATIONS AND ESSAYS

[sic] Because the idiom Ezra Pound employs in his letters departs so consistently from conventions of spelling and punctuation, whereas Stanley Nott's epistolary idiom remains conventional, this abbreviation indicating departures from conventions of spelling and punctuation is used only in Stanley Nott's letters, not in Ezra Pound's.

C = Pound, *The Cantos of Ezra Pound*

Cxxxx = Abbreviations with capital letters and numbers in parentheses – for example, C1145 – derive from Donald Gallup's *Ezra Pound: A Bibliography*

CWC = Pound, *The Chinese Written Character as a Medium for Poetry*

EP = Ezra Pound

EPE = *The Ezra Pound Encyclopedia*, ed. Tryphonopoulos and Adams

G-B = Pound, *Gaudier-Brzeska*

GK = Pound, *Guide to Kulchur*

J/M = Pound, *Jefferson and/or Mussolini*

L = Pound, *Selected Letters of Ezra Pound*, ed. D.D. Paige

LE = Pound, *Literary Essays of Ezra Pound*, ed. T.S. Eliot

NEW = *New English Weekly*

P/A = Pound, *"I Cease Not to Yowl": Ezra Pound's Letters to Olivia Rossetti Agresti*

P/C = Pound, *Ezra Pound and Senator Bronson Cutting: A Political Correspondence, 1930–1935*

P/F = Pound, *Pound/Ford: The Story of a Literary Friendship*

P/J = Pound, *Pound/Joyce: The Letters of Ezra Pound to James Joyce*

P/L = Pound, *Ezra Pound and James Laughlin: Selected Letters*

P/W = Pound, *Pound/Williams: Selected Letters of Ezra Pound and William Carlos Williams*

P/WL = Pound, *Pound/Lewis: The Letters of Ezra Pound and Wyndham Lewis*

P/Z = Pound, *Pound/Zukofsky: Selected Letters of Ezra Pound and Louis Zukofsky*

P&P = *Ezra Pound's Poetry and Prose: Contributions to Periodicals*, eds. Baechler, Litz, and Longenbach

SP = Pound, *Selected Prose, 1909–1965*, ed. William Cookson

All other references are either complete in endnotes or are supplied in the Bibliography.

EDITORIAL PRINCIPLES

In its editorial principles, this project takes a cue from Lawrence Rainey's suggestion in *Ezra Pound and the Monument of Culture* – which is that, by considering the significance of a text's sociomaterial "inscriptures," we make an important kind of contact with history not otherwise available (7). Among documents that supply such sociomaterial inscriptures, letters – as ephemeral missives designed to report news, register developments, and seek information – are especially responsive to the fluidity of events surrounding a writer at the moment of inscription. Thus they provide a distinctively important way of accessing the trends in Pound's thought – for example, those that strengthened his support of Mussolini's fascism, the development of his antisemitism and his devotion to economic radicalism – by considering them *currente calamo* ("with running pen"), as inscribed in hastily written letters of the time as well as by way of the material features of those letters.

Accordingly, this edition of the Pound/Nott correspondence features documentary (also known as "diplomatic") editing, which, as William Proctor Williams and Craig Abbott note, "aims to reproduce a manuscript or printed text as a historical artifact. It presents a text as it was available at a particular time in a particular document" (55). This edition aims for reproduction that is as faithful as possible, in clear reading text, to the physical characteristics of Pound's letters – to his unorthodox spelling, punctuation, layout, and inter- and intra-linear spacing. This approach emerges from an epistemological conviction that, through such characteristics, we know something we otherwise do not, as we otherwise do not, about what Rainey terms the "homely contexts" (*Ezra Pound* 3) for the formation of Pound's thought, through evidence unique to the medium of correspondence. Pound's letters, in particular, provide such evidence through both the substance of his dashed-off communiqués and by way of the maverick epistolary idiom that he devised.

Accordingly, this edition seeks to maintain the greatest fidelity possible to Pound's idiom: to the "idiosyncratic positioning of paragraphs, sentences, and words on the page" (Spoo and Pound xi); to Pound's playful "misspellings" and "puns" (*P/L* xx), and to his "punctuation, word division, underlining and capitalization" (*Pound/Ford* xix). I am guided by a statement that Wyndham Lewis once made to D.D. Paige when Paige was preparing his now standard *Selected Letters of Ezra Pound*:

> My view – and I must ask your indulgence if I express it forcibly –
> is categoric. E.P.'s letters tidied up would no longer be E.P.'s
> letters. The "old hickory" flavour is essential. The more "Waal
> me deah Wyndamm" you have the better. Change this to "Well
> my dear Wyndham," and it is somebody else speaking–writing.
> It is not a Yankee-exoticism (its desirability, or otherwise) that
> is at issue. I prefer E.P. as he *is* – it is a question of portraiture
> and of accuracy. One cannot afford to jettison a single misplaced
> letter. E.P.'s correspondence is worth troubling about ... The
> publisher *who dulls these letters down* and deguts them will
> not only be doing a great disservice to Ezra but to the public of
> today and also tomorrow. (*Letters of Wyndham Lewis* 466)

In this spirit, I have aimed for a diplomatic rendering of Pound's bibliographic code, although rather than simply reproduce letters in facsimile (as do, for instance, the editions of Pound's letters to Joseph Ibbotson and Louis Dudek), our team has created from the copy-text a clear reading text that will facilitate access for both readers who are acquainted with Pound's work and those who are not. In this respect, we are following the need acknowledged by many editors of Pound's correspondences. Brita Lindberg-Seyersted, for example, rightly notes the "reader's legitimate concerns about a legible and pleasing text" (*Pound/Ford* xix). But whereas in many other cases, editorial practice issuing from this commitment has resulted in "silent" corrections of Pound's (often importantly loud) deviations from conventional practice, we have sought to display the letters in all their telling Poundian heterodoxy. George Bornstein has put into circulation the important concept of the "politics on the page": in this edition, which is devoted to illuminating the evolution of Pound's politics and its consequences, we seek to provide pages that indicate those politics as they take hold – through individual judgments, utterances, and actions.

INTRODUCTION

The name of American poet Ezra Pound (1885–1972) summons a host of unsettling associations: those who know of him usually think not only of his magnum opus, the *Cantos*, and his vital contributions to the development of twentieth-century modernist verse in English, but also of his troubling antisemitism and controversial ties to Italian Fascism. In the climate of political and economic upheaval of the 1930s, as an expatriate living in Italy, Pound became increasingly sympathetic to Mussolini's regime. In 1943, as a result of his broadcasts during the early 1940s via Rome Radio – which, both rhetorically eccentric and often intensely antisemitic, were also supportive of Fascist Italy – Pound was indicted for treason by the US government. Pound, however, always regarded himself as a loyal American committed to the principles of his country's founders and to the Jeffersonian tradition in particular:[1] as he saw it, his allegiance to Mussolini constituted an avenue for the expression of that commitment. To use a phrase from Pound's remarks read out before some of the broadcasts, he would say nothing "incompatible with his duties as a citizen of the United States of America" (Doob xiii). In this respect, Pound displayed a perspective analogous to that of William Joyce, widely known as "Lord Haw-Haw," who broadcast propaganda for the Nazis during the Second World War while believing himself an unshakeable British patriot, upholding the true British ideals that contemporary Britain, in his view, had betrayed.[2] While Joyce, however, was executed as a traitor to Britain, Pound was never convicted of treason by the United States, as he was ultimately deemed mentally unfit to stand trial. He was placed in St Elizabeths Hospital for the "criminally insane" in Washington, DC, where he remained from 1946 to 1958, confined in a city that stood for the kind of political power he had long tried to hold in his country of origin. Expressing typical disgust with the inability of the contemporary United States to reckon effectively with issues he held dear, Pound once commented that he could not have stood being anywhere in that country except an insane asylum (Farndale 340). In other words, he felt that he could only tolerate living in the United States if he were branded as mad by mainstream American standards and thus marked as a dissident with respect to the country's dominant values. Masked by this avant-gardist bravado, however, is that Pound had often sought to exert an impact on political decisions in the United States and regretted not being able to wield greater influence. As voluminous correspondence of the interwar period with several members of the US Congress suggests, although Pound remained largely away from American shores between 1925 and 1945 – there for only a brief visit in 1939 – he might well have spent more time in the United States had he been received as a distinguished visitor or, better yet, been assigned a significant political post.[3]

To this day, as attested not only by continuing scholarly work on Pound but also by plays about him such as Timothy Findley's *The Trials of Ezra Pound* (1990) and Billy Marshall Stoneking's *Sixteen Words for Water* (1991), as well as British economist Meghnad Desai's recent book on Pound's economic theories, *The Route of All Evil* (2006), many both inside and outside Pound studies, within and outside the academy, continue to wonder how a poet of Pound's titanic stature and erudition, as well as loyalty to what he construed as American ideals, could have arrived at such a pass.[4] Certainly Pound was not alone among writers of the time in being compelled by the example of fascism: as much scholarship of the last four decades has revealed, many modernist literary figures, including T.S. Eliot, Wyndham Lewis, and W.B. Yeats, were likewise drawn to varieties of interwar fascism.[5] Frank Kermode's now famous 1967 observation of the "correlation between early modernist literature and authoritarian politics which is more often noticed than explained" (108) led off a significant wave of commentary on the problem of the relationship between modernism and fascism – a problem that this edition addresses by examining the specifics of Pound's case.[6] But as compared to Yeats's, Lewis's, and Eliot's interest in fascism, Pound's attraction involved a more thoroughgoing commitment, sustained over two decades, and greater investment in the particulars of one regime, often verging on hero-worship.[7] Exceptional as well within the context of this circle of writers was Pound's eventual confidence in his own authority with regard to economic and political matters. As the Pound/Nott correspondence highlights, during the early 1930s, Pound sought to establish credentials as a commentator on both economics and politics – topics that, for him, together formed the locus for responsible work in a time of public crisis.[8] By the 1940s, when Pound was developing his speeches for Radio Rome, although his work on economics and politics had been received by most of the small public who knew of this dimension of his oeuvre as, at best, deplorably eccentric, and at worst, irresponsible and bigoted, Pound believed himself an economic and political commentator of importance.[9] One of this edition's major objectives is to shed further light on how he arrived at such a conviction.

One Must Not Go Altogether with the Tide presents a scholarly annotated edition of the 1930s correspondence between Ezra Pound and London-based publisher Stanley Nott (1887–1978). This correspondence, not yet addressed in either Pound scholarship or modernist literary studies, affords insight into the factors involved in Pound's still perplexing transformation from widely respected avant-garde poet and literary impresario into zealous economic reformer, virulent antisemite, and ardent supporter of Mussolini's regime. Pound's correspondence with Nott, who shared Pound's allegiance to the economic reform movement known as Social Credit, spanned the years from 1934 to 1939, reaching peak volume between 1935 and 1936. The portion of the Pound/Nott correspondence available in archives comprises 109 letters. While there are gaps in the available cor-pus – disruptions in continuity indicate that some letters are missing from our collection – there is nonetheless ample material to evoke a rich picture not only of the dynamic between Pound and Nott but also of the cultural activities and debates that their exchanges engage.

POUND'S INCURSION INTO "ECON/AND POLITICS"

The Pound/Nott correspondence spotlights Pound at a pivotal point in his career. At this juncture, out of a sense of civic responsibility during an interwar era of political and economic crisis, he averted his energies from the realm of literature and devoted himself chiefly to work in the domains of economics and politics, which, for him, were so intimately related that he often thought of them as components of one entity: "econ/and politics" (qtd. Kadlec 58).[10] He had begun this shift as early as the late 1910s, spurred by rage at the devastation of the First World War and, in particular, at the death of his comrade, the sculptor Henri Gaudier-Brzeska, on the front lines. In a 1921 piece (tellingly, a review of *Credit Power and Democracy* by C.H. Douglas, founder of Social Credit, indicating a commitment to economic reform that was already taking hold), Pound called upon artists to recognize their responsibility as public intellectuals to address urgent issues of the day: "The symbolist position, artistic aloofness from world affairs, is no good now."[11] As Leon Surette and Tim Redman observe, however, it was not until the early 1930s, partly in response to conditions of the Great Depression, that Pound would make his most pronounced swerve into political and economic work.[12] And as this book argues, Pound's relationship with Stanley Nott – although not through any intentional effort of Nott himself – supported Pound in his remarkable self-reinvention in arenas in which he had neither extensive background nor credentials. Pound's work with Nott both emerged from and helped to further this new stage of his career.[13]

Between 1934 and 1937, the years during which Nott's firm was active, Pound published five texts through Stanley Nott: two pamphlets focused on economic reform; two previously published books (*Ta Hio: The Great Learning* [1936], Pound's translation of the Confucian text into "the American language," and *The Chinese Written Character as a Medium for Poetry* [1936], the essay by sinologist Ernest Fenollosa that Pound had made it his mission to edit and publish); and *Jefferson and/or Mussolini* (1935), Pound's treatise justifying his support of Mussolini on the basis of what he read as essential similarities between fascist dictator and American founder.[14] Inter alia, this edition of the Pound/Nott correspondence addresses how Pound's outlandish *Jefferson and/or Mussolini* came to be published through Nott at a point when, as Pound noted in a comment on the copyright page to Nott's edition, "40 publishers" had already refused it. Over the years of their correspondence, given their overlapping interests, Nott and Pound sustained a robust conversation in letters not only about these publications and possible future joint ventures but also about many other topics: Pound's stature, reception, and aspirations; the Social Credit movement and economic radicalism more generally; figures in their mutual publishing and economic reform circles; contemporary political developments; and both Nott's firm and the world of publishing more widely.

This volume is particularly indebted to and in dialogue with two studies: Tim Redman's *Ezra Pound and Italian Fascism* (1991), which chronicles the evolution of Pound's allegiance to Mussolini, and Leon Surette's *Pound in Purgatory* (1999), which offers extensive commentary on the relationship between Pound's economic convictions and his investment in Italian Fascism. On the basis of the Pound/Nott correspondence, this volume offers further nuances to the rich accounts they have developed.

SPECIFICS OF THIS EDITION OF POUND'S LETTERS

One Must Not Go Altogether with the Tide: The Letters of Ezra Pound and Stanley Nott follows more than twenty published volumes of Pound's correspondences now in circulation, building upon the valuable work of editors who, over the past three decades, have made available many dimensions of Pound's astonishingly prolific epistolary corpus.[15] It offers a new contribution, first, by featuring a hitherto unpublished correspondence not addressed in existing scholarship. Moreover, it offers four critical essays on topics that the Pound/Nott correspondence highlights, drawing upon details of the letters to develop new arguments about Pound's involvement in radical economics, his engagement with fascism, his epistolary practice, and his work with Stanley Nott Ltd. during the 1930s – all of which, in turn, shed new light on his economically and politically oriented writing of the 1930s. The four essays thus provide (1) an overview of the evolution of Pound's relationship to Social Credit in the context of comparable contemporaneous efforts in economic radicalism; (2) a consideration of Pound's investment in Italian Fascism, which treats the role played therein by British Fascism; (3) a discussion of Pound's epistolary practice, focusing especially on the idiolect characteristic of Pound's letters; and (4) an account of the genesis and work of Stanley Nott Ltd.

This edition of Pound's letters aims for a new genre: while most editions of Pound's letters now available provide rich annotations, this edition ventures further by offering four framing essays that elaborate on topics central to the correspondence, elucidate the letters, and draw upon the material of the letters to advance new critical arguments about Pound's significant volta in the early 1930s. As no other edition has done, this one examines the role played by British Fascism in the development of Pound's economic and political work and, particularly, in the solidification of his support for Mussolini during the 1930s (see Essay 2). In addition, as both Pound and Stanley Nott were adherents (albeit self-styled heretical ones) of Social Credit – the economic reform movement that, during the 1930s, found considerable support in England, Canada, the United States, and Australia – the Pound/Nott correspondence illuminates the heterodox economic thought with which Pound engaged during this period and offers new information about the circles of economic reformers in which he moved (see Essay 1). As the economic radicalism Pound encountered often involved conspiracy theories about "Jewish international finance," this edition also considers the relationship between Pound's economic convictions and his antisemitism. It thereby enters an active debate within Pound studies regarding the nature and sources of Pound's antisemitism. Departing from the trend of recent commentary, I argue that Pound's correspondence with British Fascist Arnold Leese – invoked by the Pound/Nott correspondence – reveals a racially based antisemitism that, together with an economically based antisemitism, informed Pound's invective against Jews at this time.[16]

This edition of Pound's letters also moves into new territory by theorizing Pound's practice of writing letters – his epistolary conduct – as both infrastructure for his cultural evangelism and as epistemological strategy.

It also advances new claims about the significance of the playful idiolect Pound fashioned distinctively for his correspondence (see Essay 3). Finally, as this correspondence provides a wealth of information about Stanley Nott's firm and the publication of Pound's work – frequently right down to the material details of typeface, layout, binding, and prices that Jerome McGann recognizes as crucial aspects of the "textual condition" – it also reveals much about Pound's evolving convictions regarding publishing during this period, as well as about publishing culture more generally in Britain and, to some extent, in the United States at this time (see Essay 4). Together with annotations, informational appendices, and supporting essays, the Pound/Nott letters illuminate the complex trends of Pound's thought between the wars as well as the sociomaterial conditions of the environment that fostered his strongest allegiance to Mussolini, greatest involvement in economic reform, and most intensely antisemitic work.

A significant companion project to this edition is Roxana Preda's recent *Ezra Pound's Economic Correspondence, 1933–1940* (2007), which highlights Pound at the same juncture of his career, and, like this edition, features Pound's correspondence as it relates to his engagement with economic radicalism. The relationship between these two editions is complementary: whereas Preda's edition provides a wide array of Pound's economically oriented letters to various British and American correspondents during this period, this edition remains within the particulars of one economically inflected correspondence sustained during these years. It also focuses on the Pound/Nott correspondence of the 1930s for reasons that differ from those animating Preda's project: through the specifics of the Pound/Nott letters, it aims to shed light on the sociomaterial and psychological factors in Pound's environment that contribute to his surprising self-reinvention as an economic/political commentator in the early 1930s and on his confidence in a context in which, given his background, he was out of his depth. Admittedly, it was characteristic of Pound to display a propensity for improbable self-fashioning in unfamiliar contexts: this is what had enabled the young brash American, newly arrived in England, to establish himself rapidly in London literary circles. However, as this correspondence suggests, it was also a significantly robust collection of signals in his environment – from articles he was reading, movements of which he was learning, and, above all, correspondents with whom he was exchanging letters – that figured importantly in what Preda calls Pound's "economic turn" (25).

The relationship between these two editions of Pound's correspondence also calls to mind the figure of chiasmus: where Preda's emphasis is on illuminating Pound's economic involvements of this period, this edition ranges more widely, addressing several interrelated topics to which the Pound/Nott correspondence points – not only the evolution of Pound's economic thought but also his developing relationship to fascism, his epistolary idiom, and the significant impact of Nott's publishing firm on the development of his career. And whereas Preda develops her conclusions through the treatment of a group of Pound's economic correspondences, this edition achieves its arguments through sustained engagement with one correspondence. The economically accented correspondence with Stanley Nott, which Preda does not address, reveals a climate crucial to Pound's shift during this period, one that provides forms of external validation that enabled Pound to continue along his new path.

Moreover, although Preda's edition and this one share many points of reference, we also read the events of Pound's context somewhat differently, generating narratives with different emphases. For instance, whereas Preda rightly notes that, after 1937, Pound turned away from Social Credit and paid greater attention to fascism, both Italian and British, I read differently the role of Pound's economic "synthesis" (Preda, *Ezra Pound's Economic Correspondence*, 23) – his effort to unite Social Credit thought with the thought of economic reformer Silvio Gesell. Where Preda interprets this attempted synthesis as leading Pound away from Social Credit allies – who found his efforts to convert them to such combinations unconvincing – and towards fascism, I see Pound's conceptual "hybrids," both this one and others, as fostering stronger alliances with Social Crediters such as Nott (who, like Pound, were refusing Douglasite orthodoxy) as well as firmer ties with the British Fascists with whom he was corresponding and who sought comparable fusions between Social Credit and other varieties of economic reform.[17] Moreover, in my reading, this intensification of the exchange with British Fascists both strengthened Pound's belief that Social Credit was soon to be implemented in Fascist Italy and factored significantly into the heightening of his antisemitism during this period (see essays 1 and 2). In addition, one correspondence with a British Fascist to which the Pound/ Nott correspondence points – with Arnold Leese of the Imperial League of Fascists – mentioned only briefly in Preda's account, both reveals and, I argue, contributes significantly to the escalation of Pound's antisemitism after 1934. Both Leese and the growth of Pound's antisemitism through contact with Social Credit and British Fascism are accorded greater prominence in this edition than in Preda's.

Finally, in Essay 3, which theorizes Pound's epistolary practice, this edition of Pound's correspondence advances an argument about an aspect of Pound's propagandistic work during these years that Preda's edition does not address: his commitment to letters as a vital form of cultural work, emerging from his epistemological conviction that epistolary interchange could promote the construction of significantly collaborative forms of knowledge – knowledge whose value derives both from the robust pool of information developed through exchange and the networks of association thereby facilitated. Pound's letters to Nott both issued from and fuelled this commitment.

"TO OUR ... MUCHOEL ADVANTDG": STANLEY NOTT AND THE DEVELOPMENT OF POUND'S AUTHORITY

Significant to the milieu that helped Pound to develop his generative sense of command, urgency, and authority was access to circles of economic reformers in London of the 1930s, which his work of this time made possible. Important as well was Stanley Nott's receptivity to Pound's work in economics and politics. This is not to suggest that Stanley Nott was in any way responsible for Pound's ill-judged decisions during this period. The title of this edition of the Pound/Nott correspondence, *One Must Not Go Altogether with the Tide*, is drawn from a phrase of Nott's that captures his reasons (which include his admiration for what he read as Pound's independence of mind) for supporting Pound's maverick thought, even when he clearly did not agree with it. Nott could not have known that Pound's renegade political and intellectual eclecticism would eventually lead where it did. What I argue is that Nott's interchanges with Pound during the 1930s formed part of a larger environment that was hospitable to this new stage of Pound's work, which, in turn, spurred Pound to greater confidence and further work in directions that later led to trouble. Nott was an interlocutor whose opinions Pound valued, and whose tolerance of Pound's approach, together with the outlets he provided, helped Pound to build both his repertoire as an economic and political commentator and the courage to present himself as one.[18]

In one of the most compelling lines in the correspondence between Pound and Nott, one that crystallizes what held the two men together in a productive dynamic, Pound observes that the book he is publishing through Nott will likely serve as an "advertisement" for another of Nott's ventures – specifically, a pamphlet in a series on Social Credit, *Pamphlets on the New Economics*, that Nott had been publishing.

> I had forgotten that it was such an advt/ for the FIRST item in
> the pamphlet series/

> dare say you can indicate that on the jacket
> to our leZope muchoel advantdg. (Letter 26)

Here Pound indicates that the linkage readers are apt to perceive between his book and another publication of Nott's will, he hopes, be to his and Nott's "muchoel advantdg" – Poundese for "mutual advantage." Pound's phonetic heteroclite spelling here, typical of his epistolary idiom, indicates how "much" the association will likely benefit them both. On the one hand, the connection between Pound's book and Nott's series will be of help to Pound, who is seeking to build a reputation as an "kneeconymist" (Letter 30) (here the deviant spelling suggests both Pound's irreverence towards orthodox academic economists and the "knowledge" he seeks in order to assume this new role): association with a pamphlet series on economic reform places Pound in the company he wishes to keep, implying that he rightfully belongs among other commentators on economics. Moreover, since the context of this letter suggests that, by "pamphlet," Pound is in fact referring to his own pamphlet, *Social Credit: An Impact* (1935), he thereby gains publicity for his own work.[19] The connection will likewise help Nott – both because Pound's book points readers to the pamphlet and because the association with Pound's well-known name will bolster the image of Nott's firm. Nott evidently believed so, in any case. Although Pound's reputation as a renegade was deflecting many at this time,[20] Nott approached Pound for commentary on economics because he valued his work and his stature.[21] It was Nott's and Pound's shared understanding of the ways in which they could help each other that fuelled their relationship, one both registered in and maintained throughout their correspondence.

Charles Stanley Nott, born in Hertfordshire, lived much of his life in England, though he also resided for periods in the United States – in New York, Vermont, and Wisconsin – as well as in France. He enlisted in the Canadian Army during the First World War and, thereafter, turned to bookselling in New York in the 1920s. John Carswell, addressing Nott's involvement in circles of writers and artists in Britain and the United States in the 1920s and 1930s, comments that Nott was, "by turns," a soldier, a bookseller, a travelling salesman in felt hats, a farmer, and a publisher (214). It is on this last role that I focus: Nott's position as director of Stanley Nott Ltd., a firm devoted to publishing work on economic reform. While working at a bookshop in New York City during the 1920s, Nott met A.R. Orage, the critic and editor who had worked closely with Ezra Pound (see Essay 1). At the time, Orage was lecturing on the ideas of the mystic G.I. Gurdjieff, the spiritual teacher whose circle attracted many writers and artists of the early twentieth century, including Katherine Mansfield, Jean Toomer, Frank Lloyd Wright, Margaret Anderson, and Jane Heap. Inspired by Orage, Nott began to follow Gurdjieff. He would devote the rest of his life to Gurdjieffian teachings, writing two memoirs of his experiences with Gurdjieff and marrying one of Gurdjieff's pupils, Rosemary Lillard, in 1927. Nott's deepening friendship with Orage would give rise to other joint endeavours: as of the 1930s, Nott was prompted by Orage into the world of economic radicalism and developed the allegiance to Social Credit that would found the work of Stanley Nott Ltd. Essay 4 of this edition addresses the work of his firm in greater detail. It would be Orage's recommendation, along with Nott's knowledge of Pound's work through Orage's periodical the *New English Weekly*, that would spur Nott to approach Pound after Orage's death in 1934.

The book to which Pound refers in his "to our leZope muchoel advantdg" letter is his *Jefferson and/or Mussolini*, first written in 1933 and published through Nott in 1935. As the title implies, the book is premised on his discernment of a parallel – an example of what Pound conceives of as a "subject rhyme" or a "repeat in history" – between the American founder Pound keenly admired and the Italian leader in whose nation he had lived for a decade. Again, Nott agreed to publish *Jefferson and/or Mussolini* after, as Pound notes, forty other publishers had refused it. It is little wonder that they had (as a review at the time in *New Verse* maintains, the book was "refused very reasonably by forty publishers").[22] Like much of Pound's prose, the book is scattershot in its claims, largely devoid of sustained argument, and bizarrely off the expected conceptual keys. The wonder lies in Nott's willingness to publish such a text – and, in fact, the question of how Nott came to agree to do so formed one of the initial catalysts of this project. Through its essays, this edition of the Pound/Nott correspondence addresses how the climate in Britain of 1935 allowed for such a decision; how the nature of Nott's investments and values permitted him to welcome such a book; and how the relationship between Pound and Nott contributed to Nott's decision to publish *Jefferson and/or Mussolini*.

PUBLISHING *JEFFERSON AND/OR MUSSOLINI*

Among the elements that will likely strike readers as strange about *Jefferson and/or* Mussolini, first is that it asserts an essential congruency between the two men invoked in the title, beneath differences that Pound reads as merely superficial "top dressing" (11). In play here is Pound's typical tendency to read different historical figures as avatars of the same essential spirit. He yokes Jefferson and Mussolini together in a historical conceit that will strain the credulity of contemporary readers, although, in the early 1930s, before Mussolini's alliance with Hitler, as William Carlos Williams's review of the book suggests, for some, the parallel did not seem so implausible.[23] Another deep strangeness emerges from Pound's rhetoric. By this time, Pound exhibits in his prose a full-fledged version of what he terms the "ideogramic method" of rhetorical development (*Guide to Kulchur* 51) – alternatively spelled "ideogrammic" – derived, in part, from his work in the 1910s with the scholarship of sinologist Ernest Fenollosa, whose commentaries inspired the translations from Chinese poetry integral to Pound's early poetic work. This encounter with Fenollosa informed Pound's conviction that, to resensitize readers' faculties of perception and cognition, the best method entailed delivering clusters of apparently disparate ideas, paratactically arranged, the ligatures among which were – in what has now come to be recognized as a gambit typical of modernist difficulty – left for the reader to discern. This is the technique Pound begins to develop through his early labours in the Imagist vineyard in the 1910s; by the 1930s, he employs it with regularity in the *Cantos*. In *Jefferson and/or Mussolini*, Pound makes a clever case for this rhetorical approach, implying that to use a conventional argumentative strategy would be to engage in duplicity (28). "I am not putting these sentences into monolinear syllogistic arrangement," he notes, his adjectives indicating disdain for ordinary step-by-step prose, "and I have no intention of using that old form of trickery to fool the reader" (28). This approach reaches its fullest realization in the last extended prose treatise Pound would write: *Guide to Kulchur* (1938). Here, Pound suggests not only that this method forces readers to undertake the work of decipherment and, ultimately, provides a satisfying whole assembled from parts but also that this whole will enable better understanding of a familiar subject. The process of understanding promoted, moreover, will reinvigorate the reader's perceptual and conceptual abilities. As Pound notes: "That being the reason for presenting first one facet and then another – I mean to say the purpose of the writing is to reveal the subject. The ideogramic method consists of presenting one facet and then another until at some point one gets off the dead and desensitized surface of the reader's mind, onto a part that will register" (51). This method, Pound maintained, was the best avenue to a "real knowledge" of cultural phenomena.[24]

This is not to say that the wildness of Pound's rhetoric was always strategic – only that it accorded with his epistemological commitment to antisystematic, often ludic, prose designed to subvert ordinary rhetorical procedures and thereby to create more effective paths for relaying knowledge and modelling ways of knowing.[25] And some supportive readers responded favourably. Reviewing *J/M* in 1935 for *New Democracy*, for instance, William Carlos Williams (who, at this juncture, preferred maverick styles defiant of reason and logic) noted that "Pound's experience as a writer of prose is also of great value here. He has never done a better piece of writing" (61).[26]

What is on the page, however, will come across to many readers as mere eccentricity.[27] This impression is compounded by Pound's insistence on a congruency between Mussolini and Jefferson, which is likely perplexing as readers meet the text with a retrospective awareness of fascism, Mussolini's later alliance with Hitler, and the Holocaust. Of course also inevitably disturbing from this side of the historical divide of the Second World War is Pound's unequivocal celebration of Il Duce. One of the commitments of this edition, however, is to promote a heightened sensitivity to the difference between that which is perceptible in hindsight and that which was perceptible in the 1930s, between alignments that today seem inevitable but that, at that time, were anything but. As Samuel Hynes remarks in *The Auden Generation*:

> It is only when a period has passed that it solidifies and becomes history, and we begin to think of it as a set pattern of events, forces, and consequences. At the time, history feels fluid and uncertain, the forces that time will eventually confirm don't yet know that they *are* the significant ones; in studying the past, we must try by an act of imagination to recover that sense of fluidity. (12)

Addressing the case of Pound in the 1930s, Leon Surette likewise emphasizes such an "act of imagination" as he articulates a value that animates both his book, *Pound in Purgatory*, and this edition. Like Hynes, using a "must" construction, Surette notes that "we must make the imaginative effort to see what fascism looked like from the other side of WWII and the Holocaust" (18). This edition proceeds from the conviction that the Pound/ Nott letters can make an important contribution to such imaginative efforts to "recover the sense of fluidity" of the 1930s, to revisit what fascism "looked like" then.

To this end, again, this edition focuses on accounting for Stanley Nott's willingness to publish such a book as *Jefferson and/or Mussolini*.[28] What needs to be considered, first, is the fact that, until the time of Italy's imperialist designs on Abyssinia in 1935, Mussolini had enjoyed strong support in many quarters in Britain and North America. In the United States, where Mussolini had been a syndicated columnist for the Hearst newspapers (Surette, *Purgatory*, 6), as Philip Cannistraro and Brian Sullivan note, "Mussolini received overwhelmingly positive press coverage" from "conservative, moderate, and even a surprising number of liberal publications," largely because of his anti-communist campaigns and his tough stance on crime (350).[29] And in Britain, as G.C. Webber notes, among the political right of the early 1930s, fascism was still considered a "relatively 'respectable' alternative to liberal democracy" (2).[30] Following Nott's July and August 1935 publication of *Jefferson and/or Mussolini*, however, the tide of British public opinion began to turn against Mussolini in response to Italy's invasion of Abyssinia (present-day Ethiopia) in the autumn of 1935: for many, this was a clear indication of Mussolini's unwelcome imperialistic aspirations. Nott himself supported neither Mussolini nor the invasion; he noted to Pound that "Italy's excuses are an insult to any half intelligent person" and that "the invasion [of Abyssinia] belongs to gone and dead 19th century Imperialism" (Letter 63). But, he said, "one must not go altogether with the tide." Here Nott recognizes that, at this moment, much sentiment in England has turned against Mussolini; but in the interest of independent thought, he will resist following the prevailing trend in his decisions about what to publish. And what Nott demonstrates here is akin to a capacity he esteemed in Pound – his ability to defy and challenge settled assumptions and received thought (see Essay 4).[31] At this point, moreover, Italy was not yet linked with Hitler in the formal alliance that would be forged the following year; and, in fact, Italy's official invasion of Abyssinia would not occur until approximately two weeks after Nott's letter of 16 September, more than two months after the publication of *Jefferson and/or Mussolini*. The British response to these changing developments suggests that the door was open wider for Nott's publication of *J/M* in July 1935 than it would have been in late October of that year (by which time much British opinion had turned sharply against Italy) and certainly open much wider than it would have been after the Rome-Berlin Axis of October 1936.

Beyond the political and social climate in Britain in the summer of 1935, which was more favourable to pro-Mussolini work than it would have been just a few months later (and certainly more than it was after September 1939), what also made the publication of *Jefferson and/or Mussolini* possible was the nature of the connection that had by that point developed between Nott and Pound. In addition to reciprocal advantage, one of the forces sustaining their relationship was their shared commitment to the movement of Social Credit. Much of their discussion in the correspondence revolves around economic reform, and, in fact, Nott's firm was established in order to publish work on Social Credit – what Nott referred to as "The New Economics."

POUND AND SOCIAL CREDIT

Over the decades, this underconsumptionist effort in economic reform, which crucially informed Pound's thought and work during the 1930s, has often been read as merely a crank economic theory and fringe movement. As recent scholarship has begun to address, however, and as this edition argues, Social Credit in fact formed a vital part of a significant wave of economic radicalism during the interwar years (see Essay 1). More generally, the Pound/Nott correspondence provides a window on the larger cultural colloquy of this moment of economic reform, in which both Pound and Nott participated.

Pound was first introduced to Social Credit in the late 1910s through A.R. Orage, the journalist, critic, and editor with whom he had worked since shortly after his arrival in London from the United States in 1908. As of 1911, Pound had begun to write for Orage's reform-minded, eclectic journal of cultural commentary, the *New Age*. As Tim Redman notes, although he chiefly wrote articles about the arts for the periodical, Pound in fact received an extensive education in the realms of economics and politics through contact with Orage and groups of reformers gathered around him.[32] Nott, meanwhile, also became interested in Social Credit through Orage's influence. Although Nott recalls meeting Orage once during the 1910s when they both travelled in London literary circuits, he had his first memorable encounter with Orage in 1923 in New York, a year after Orage had turned away from journalism to devote himself to the teachings of the mystic G.I. Gurdjieff. Orage was in New York at the time to promote Gurdjieffian ideas: he gave a talk on Gurdjieff at the "Sunwise Turn" bookstore, where Nott was working at this point (Nott, *Teachings*, 1). Through close work with Orage, Nott steeped himself in both Gurdjieffian mysticism and, later, in the early 1930s, when both Nott and Orage returned to London, economic reform.[33] It was Nott's intimacy with Orage after years of having worked with him in Gurdjieffian communities ("instead of the father-mentor-teacher I had left in New York, he was now an elder brother and beloved friend" [Nott, *Further Teachings*, 13–14]) that made him so receptive to joining forces with Orage when the latter returned to England and renewed his dedication to Social Credit, which had lapsed upon his departure in 1922. Nott and Orage collaborated in founding a new journal, the *New English Weekly*, through which Orage sought to promote Social

Credit (Nott, *Further Teachings*, 29). Shortly afterward, Nott established his own publishing firm devoted to the same purpose (43).

INITIAL CONTACT BETWEEN POUND AND NOTT

Nott and Pound, however, did not make contact until November 1934, just after Orage's sudden and untimely death on the sixth of that month. In fact it was Orage's death that prompted their initial communication. In a 26 November letter to Pound, invoking Orage's name, Nott requested Pound's participation in a project to publish a series of pamphlets on the "New Economics." He also signalled that the genesis of the series had involved Orage.

> I am sending you a copy of a series of pamphlets we are doing. The series came about from an idea which I discussed with Orage about a year ago. They promise to be very popular.
>
> One further series will include pamphlets by Herbert Read, Storm Jameson, Will Dyson, Dean of Canterbury etc. and I was wondering if you would do one for me. The subject might be "The Writer in Regard to Social Credit" or "The Writer in the Age of Leisure" or some such subject. I will leave it to you to choose a suitable title. (Letter 1)

Nott knew of Pound's work through Orage, and he also knew of Pound's commitment to Social Credit. As Redman's account of the genesis of Pound's work in economics indicates, it was in the early 1930s that Pound made a pronounced move towards economics. In part, Pound's heightened interest was spurred by conditions of the Great Depression. Clearly, however, Orage's return to England after a decade's hiatus was also a factor. In 1932, unable to rejoin his former journal, the *New Age* (control of which the then current editor, Arthur Brenton, refused to surrender, largely because of his suspicion of Orage's occult interests; Finlay 173; Surette, *Purgatory*, 50–1), Orage founded the *NEW*, for which Pound began to write and of which Stanley Nott became manager. As Redman notes, "Orage's return to political and economic journalism, and Pound's turn to them, coincide perfectly. Pound was to contribute almost two hundred items to the *New English Weekly* during the thirties" (*Italian Fascism* 99n15).[34] By November 1934, Nott would have seen in the pages of the *NEW* a copious selection of Pound's work, including his review of economist Irving Fisher's *Stamp Scrip*; *Canto 38*, which features C.H. Douglas's ideas; and satirical poems on economics under the pseudonym of Alf Venison. Nott evidently liked what he saw: as he would later write to Pound, "I used to tell Orage that I enjoyed your writing and Dyson's next to his own, more than any I read in the New English Weekly" (Letter 11).

Nott's ties to Orage exerted pull with Pound. Also leading to a rapid solidification of the link between Pound and Nott was the fact that the project Nott invited Pound to join was not only economically minded (which, in itself, would have appealed at this point) but also continued the work with Orage that Nott had begun. It was thus the spirit of Orage that hovered over the initial dealings between Pound and Nott, strengthening their work together. Their rapport also emerged from the fact that, like Orage, both preferred to remove themselves from the fray of internecine quarrels among Social Crediters. As Nott observed:

> I hate almost all Social Creditors and so far I have kept clear of them.... They don't want to be united. Now that the movement is growing they want to form as many sects as possible and capitalise their interest in Social Credit....
>
> I have refused to be drawn into sect or club connected with Social Credit. I can do much better by remaining outside and keeping in touch with them all. (Letter 11)

In a similar spirit, Pound commented on the "fussing and quibbling, and mutuall [sic] biting social creditors" (Letter 10):

> The question is too serious, to let personal issue cloud it over. MUST find the points of AGREEMENTS, damn the difference.... (Letter 10)

Aware of the prospect of "mutual advantage," in his dealings with Pound, Nott saw not only a chance to build his publishing firm through association with Pound's cultural cachet but also someone whose work Orage had supported and who was equipped to continue in Orage's line. Pound, meanwhile, saw in Nott an opportunity to publish some of his new work on economics, which Orage's return to England had prompted, and thus a chance to begin establishing a reputation as an economic commentator. Nott offered ready access to an audience keenly interested in Social Credit.

POUND AS "KNEECONYMIST": CONSTRUCTING AUTHORITY

As Pound moved into a new arena for which his qualifications as poet, critic, and impresario were largely irrelevant, he found himself having to construct a new identity, to build credentials from the ground up. While he had been able to publish *ABC of Economics* through Faber and Faber in 1933,[35] Pound recognized that few doors would open to him easily as he sought to disseminate work in an entirely new field in which he had little cultural authority. Many of Pound's associates saw his effort to style himself an expert on economics as presumptuous. Even William Carlos Williams, an advocate of Social Credit who had clearly supported some of Pound's economic work, insisted by March 1935 that Pound had gone too far in his zeal to place himself as a pundit: "If you can't tell the difference between yourself and a trained economist, if you don't know your function as a poet, incidentally dealing with a messy situation re. money, then go sell your papers on some other corner" (*P/W* 171).

Pound was certainly aware of the need to construct authority: to Nott, he noted wryly that he had to develop a "grand reputation" as a "kneeconymist" (Letter 30).[36] While, given his scorn for establishment academic economists, Pound often revelled in his status as an untutored outsider, he nonetheless at times displayed anxiety about his lack of qualifications for economic commentary. He was acutely aware of the need to establish legitimacy.[37] This becomes evident through his repeated requests to Nott to include in his work a certain image – of paper money printed by his grandfather, Thaddeus Coleman Pound, at one time a partner in the Union Lumbering Company in Chippewa Falls, Wisconsin. Thaddeus Pound had paid his employees in scrip issued by the company, redeemable only at the company store, a practice whose moxie and independence Pound admired, and which he read as indicating economic savvy in his lineage.[38]

> I shall want the Chippewa Lumber Money, reproduced as frontispiece to   the pamphlet [sic], if that is not out of order. It is worth 500 words, in my philosophy ... and proves that there has been an economic background in the family. I   find those photos start people thinking a lot quicker than "remarks on the subject." (Letter 5)

Through this image, Pound thus presented himself as a descendant of smart entrepreneurs who knew how to bypass the corruptions of the existing economic system and to create superior alternative routes. The "Chippewa Lumber" block was ultimately included among the front matter for *Social Credit: An Impact* (1935), which Pound wrote in response to Nott's invitation to participate in the Pamphlets on the New Economics series. He then swiftly pressed Nott to publish much of his other work. He and Nott began to plan a second series that Pound would edit, the Ideogramic series – sometimes spelled "Ideogrammic" in the letters – intended to draw upon

Pound's background in culture and history.[39] While its overriding purpose remained inchoate, it seemed designed to provide readers with fundamental texts that Pound read as necessary to education; presumably, texts in the series would form part of a massive "ideogram" enabling cultural literacy.[40] Shortly after his first contact with him, Pound also found Nott willing to re-publish in pamphlet form the humorous verse he had published in the *NEW* under the pseudonym of Alfred Venison: these poems addressed economic and political matters in a facetious vein designed to make sport of the serious "expert" economists who were too entangled in arcane theories to see plain facts and realities.[41]

That Pound chose the persona of "Alf" Venison, a working-class bloke who expressed himself in a Cockney idiom, suggests the basic elements of his strategy for constructing economic authority. Although the verse is generally bad (apparently deliberately so, to suit the Venison persona), and even implicitly insulting to the working-class figures with whom Pound evidently sought to make common cause, it importantly signals Pound's desire for plainspoken, commonsensical dealings with economic problems; his effort to puncture the pretentiousness of snobbish economic expertise; and his conviction that, as non-expert and dissident, he had what it took to see through bunkum.[42] Redman concedes that Pound's lack of formal training in economics in some respects gave him an edge, enabling him to reach insights that those under the star of orthodoxy could not (*Italian Fascism* 124).

But if Pound's position as maverick in some ways offered an advantage, it was the rare publisher who saw matters this way; and Pound realized that Nott offered hospitality to his work where few others would.[43] Especially important to Pound was that his connection with Nott provided him with a chance to publish *Jefferson and/or Mussolini*, which he regarded as a crucial compendium of his ideas and a way to establish his authority as an economist. As he wrote to Nott in January of 1935:

> About the Jeff/Muss. I am simply held up the whol D/N time by not having it in print. (Letter 8)

Elsewhere, he notes in the same vein:

> I'm hamstrung, having to repeat and repeat in fragments, ALL the time, stuff that I have said in that book. (Letter 10)

Two months into their correspondence, Pound was agitating for its publication:

I want to know on what terms you cd/ do it. even if I have to advance part of the printing costs. I dont care about binding. (Letter 10)

Nott soon expressed serious businesslike interest in the book:

Re the Jefferson MS. Had I ample capital I would not hesitate to publish at once. Things are opening out with the firm in a most hopeful way.... I will get a cast-off done and let you know what it would cost to print. (Letter 11)

With this kind of practical responsiveness from Nott, we reach a pivotal element of the Pound/Nott interchange. Pound seeks to set himself up as an authoritative commentator in a new arena, and sensible encouragement from Nott plays an important role in affording Pound the confidence to continue.

THE CULTURAL WORK OF POUND'S LETTERS

This receptiveness from Nott thus became vital to the conditions that fostered Pound's turn to "econ/ and politics," promoted his increasing urgency, and fuelled his ability to believe, in the face of resistance and signals to the contrary, that he held a rightful place as an authority in these new zones: as Surette notes, Pound "flattered himself" that he 'was a major player in the historical drama' of the time" (*Purgatory* 88). In part, this was made possible out of what Wendy Flory identifies as Pound's "jeremiac" personality, which often fired him with a sense of mission that overrode doubt.[44] His ability to persist in the face of hostility also owed much to the avant-garde logic to which he was disposed and that he had pursued throughout his career. As theorists such as Poggioli and Bourdieu suggest, according to the avant-garde code, the position of being a rejected dissident in an area conferred a badge of honour. Beyond these factors, however, Pound's ability to continue with conviction also required an atmosphere in which he could maintain regular contact with interlocutors who were willing to exchange with him and engage seriously with what he had to impart. And for Pound, one of the best means of such interchange was epistolary.

As the sheer volume of his correspondence attests, Pound believed keenly in the value of letters: from his early career onward, he wrote letters prolifically and furiously. Essay 3 addresses in greater detail Pound's epistolary conduct: here I confine the discussion to a few brief claims about the reasons for Pound's investment in letters. In part he wrote them as he did because, given his cast of mind, nearly any idea that he supported became a cause for which he had to campaign. And in part, letters became his medium of choice because the avant-garde community of which he was a member was exilic and diasporic: contacts were scattered all over the globe. Moreover, Pound's vision of an international community of great minds made him delight in contact with people across the world. This ambit satisfied him as sufficiently large and important, as well as propitious for forming the kind of worldwide effort towards artistic growth that he sought.

Furthermore, as Redman notes, as a boy in Philadelphia, Pound had also been marked by the ideal of "committees of correspondence" such as those that the American founders had formed, and which had driven the inception of the American nation (*Italian Fascism* 107, 110; see also Essay 3). Inspired by the idea of such committees, Pound believed that the richest intellectual contact occurred among a small elite whose members were serious, committed to their causes, dedicated to sharing information and ideas and working out proposals through epistolary exchange. As he began his career as poet and artistic promoter, Pound carried this example with him into the sphere of the arts. It is not too much to maintain that he aspired to create a new nation in the domain of the arts: one that would transcend existing political national boundaries and follow what he conceived of as an "international standard" and an "ideal community" (Surette, *Purgatory*, 98). Here was the supranational nation, or imagined community, of modernism.

This edition argues that it is clearly not enough to regard Pound's letters as documents ancillary to his published work: they constitute a distinct corpus worthy of attention in its own right. Separate from his poetry and critical prose, letters offered Pound another crucial channel through which to express his ideas and to perform work as cultural arbiter, mentor, evangelist, and promoter. And in light of the eighteenth-century American example, epistolary exchange with a pamphleteering bent represented a means of both political efficacy and intellectual rigour. Pound's habit of avant-gardist campaigning primed him for debates about economic and political reform; the propagandistic strategies of position-taking that he had cultivated in the arts were structurally homologous with those he employed in politics and economic radicalism.

Thus in the early 1930s, as Pound adopted a new identity as advocate for Social Credit and Italian Fascism, his approach was congruent with that which he had enlisted in his previous involvement with the arts: to write letters, make contacts, drum up interest, persuade, cajole, flatter, badger, get the news out there. And letters were crucial to this cultural work of facilitating the exchange of ideas, keeping in touch with a live-minded elite, exerting influence. Beyond this, letters were also fundamental to the maintenance of Pound's belief that he was wielding influence; as Redman notes, Pound needed to "sustain the illusion that he was having an effect" (*Italian Fascism* 98).

To return to the impact of Stanley Nott specifically: Pound's correspondence with Nott during the 1930s formed one of the chief factors that helped him to "sustain" such an "illusion." Pound, I would argue, needed close dyadic epistolary exchanges to build his confidence – to help him maintain the thick skin that eventually translated into an imperviousness to certain forms of reality beyond his immediate ambit. He had sustained such dyadic relationships throughout his early career with friends such as Eliot, Joyce, Williams, and Lewis. He had achieved such exchanges with editors such as Harriet Monroe and Margaret Anderson. In the 1930s, his need for such epistolary sustenance was rendered especially acute by his remote location in Italy, which left him out of direct touch with many of the circles with which he had hitherto been involved on site, and which left letter-writing as his primary avenue for maintaining ties. But his group of correspondents had changed, as those compatriots with whom he was still in touch from earlier days often became suspicious of his new interests. Pound thus had to build a new circle of interlocutors, and Stanley Nott figured as a significant member of that new circle, one receptive to Pound's effort to make an important mark in a new domain.

Another dimension of Nott's influence on Pound derived from his status as publisher. Factoring significantly in Pound's trust in Nott was his liking for contact with those who could provide outlets for his new work, who possessed the awareness and resources to make real what was potential, to reach audiences with important news. Pound's avid letters to publishers throughout the 1910s and 1920s attest to his desire to facilitate and manage what he perceived as the right kind of information flow to the right readers. Spurred by long-standing disgust at mainstream commercial publishers for pandering to conventional tastes out of greed, by the early 1930s Pound sought and celebrated independent publishers who could "break" the "monopoly" of large firms such as Random House on the publishing world and "release communication" of live ideas from their "oppressive control" ("Individual in His Milieu" 273).[45] By the 1930s, then, Pound was consistently disposed to favour what he read as the purity of independent firms such as Nott's, which published out of idealism rather than out of a desire for commercial gain. Pound had supported such publication outlets from early in his career, when he had lauded little magazines such as *Poetry* and the *Little Review*, which gave risky and venturesome work a chance.

In the 1930s, in the realm of economics rather than literature, Nott's firm earned Pound's esteem for similar reasons.[46]

After the mid-1930s, Pound turned to James Laughlin, who, in 1936, on Pound's advice, devoted his resources as an independently wealthy heir to founding a publishing firm, New Directions – which in later years would champion Pound's work and that of many other modernist writers. But before Laughlin secured this niche as Pound's right-hand publisher, Stanley Nott exerted an important role in assuring Pound an outlet and developing his confidence, enabling him to assuage what Robert Spoo calls his tormenting "desire to be useful" (Spoo and Pound 9). Moreover, as Laughlin never did, Nott bestowed the reality of publication on much of Pound's fledgling economic work and provided a generative horizon of welcome to his economic writings that encouraged Pound's continued journey along this course.

POUND AND BRITISH FASCISM

During the period of his correspondence with Nott, as his letters indicate, Pound was also establishing sustaining ties with other figures associated with the *NEW* – not only Social Crediters but also a coalition of economic and political reformers who made common cause with Social Crediters against liberal democracy, communism, and statist socialism: these included Guild Socialists, Distributists, and British readers sympathetic to Italian Fascism and Nazism, some of them involved with British Fascist groups.[47]

This is certainly not to suggest that Social Credit was itself fascist. C.H. Douglas wrote vehemently against fascism; there was no official linkage between the fascists and the Social Crediters; and most Social Crediters refused fascism as too statist. Nott himself was certainly against fascism. But the affinity between Social Credit's animating refusals of big laissez-faire capitalism, liberal democracy, and statist socialism, and a similar constellation of rejections fuelling proto-fascist movements in Britain (see Essay 2), meant that there was notable proximity, and sometimes overlap, between Social Credit groups and proto-fascist and fascist circles. Also contributing to the propinquity between Social Crediters and British Fascists at this time was their shared desire to reform, rather than to reject, capitalism, as well as their common suspicion of international finance. As a result, some figures clearly belonged to both camps: Oswald Mosley, for example, in the 1920s a Social Crediter, founded the British Union of Fascists (BUF), the leading British Fascist movement from 1932 onward. And among the readers of the *NEW* were Antony Ludovici (a member of the proto-fascist "English Mistery"); Gerald Wallop, Viscount Lymington (also a member of the "Mistery," later of the pro-Nazi "Array"); and Arnold Leese of the Imperial League of Fascists. Essay 1 addresses in greater detail this difficult-to-read nexus between Social Credit and fascism.

As Essay 2 discusses, in many cases, Pound established contact with such British reformers sympathetic to British Fascism, Italian Fascism, and National Socialism – and exchanges with them, focused on economic reform, in several ways strengthened Pound's support for Mussolini. As I argue, this aspect of the development of Pound's allegiance to Mussolini, illuminated by the Pound/Nott correspondence, has not been sufficiently recognized: although during the 1930s Pound remained largely in Italy, he was able to carry out his campaign for Mussolini as well as to develop his own allegiance to the Italian regime partly and significantly through interchange with those in Britain invested in fascism.

"ONE MUST NOT GO ALTOGETHER WITH THE TIDE"

Again, the title of this edition derives from one of Nott's letters, in which he explains why he is ready to publish *Jefferson and/or Mussolini*, though he himself opposes Mussolini's imperialist ambitions and knows that many in Britain have turned against Italy:

> The book is the one stem against the flood of anti-Italian sentiment here. Feeling is strong against Mussolini.... And though I myself think that Italy's excuses are an insult to any half intelligent person, and that the invasion is [sic] belongs to gone and dead 19th century Imperialism, one must not go altogether with the tide. For that reason I am interested in pushing J/M. And it is a very good book. (Letter 63)

Through this comment, Nott indicates the attitude that renders him receptive to Pound's unconventional approach: while most Social Crediters "lack passion," in Nott's view, Pound handles economic reform with "vitality and emotional drive" (Letter 11); while most in Britain are against Mussolini, Pound defends him; even when many baulk at Pound's foray into economic work, Pound forges ahead with conviction nonetheless. For Nott, Pound thus shows the ability to resist the "tide," the main cultural currents in his environment, according to strong and principled currents of his own thought. It is an independence of mind that Nott both values and himself displays.

In this early twentieth-century environment, to "catch the tide" is to be able, perceptively, to ride a wave that is rising. One of Nott's fellow publishers in London at the time, Victor Gollancz, once observed in a letter that "the essence of publishing" was "to 'take the tide.'" Accordingly, this edition of the Pound/Nott correspondence investigates the "tides" at work in Pound's thought and environment with a view to accounting for how he arrived where he did. By the 1930s and 1940s, many of the choices Pound made out of his situation and projects indeed left him swimming upstream. Accordingly, this volume seeks, through both documentary editorial procedures and apparatus, to capture Pound and Nott with running pen, amid the running currents of the time, when, as Hynes memorably notes, circumstances displayed that "sense of fluidity," before the patterns of "events, forces, and consequences" we now commonly use to parse what occurred had been confirmed for the historical records. Revisiting that fluid time valuably illuminates cultural patterns against the dominant "tides" of the 1930s – both those of Pound himself and those of others of his cultural milieu.

Directors
Stanley Nott
Kenneth Gee

Telephone
Museum 3186
Cables
Newecon London

STANLEY NOTT LTD

Publishers

69 GRAFTON STREET · FITZROY SQUARE · LONDON · W·1

Ezra Pound Esq
Rapallo
Italy

November
Twenty-sixth
1934

Dear Ezra Pound:

I am sending you a copy of a series of pamphlets
we are doing. The series came about by an idea which
I discussed with Orage about a year ago. They promise
to be very popular.

Our futher series will include pamphlets by
Herbert Read, Storm Jameson, Will Dyson, Dean of Canterbury
etc. and I was wondering if you would do one for me.
The subject might be "The Writer in Regard to Social
Credit" or "The Writer in the Age of Leisure" or some
such subject. I would leave it to you to choose a
suitable title. We are paying a royalty of 10%. I
shall be interested to hear what you think of the idea.

You may remember that I helped Orage start the
"New English Weekly" and acted as his hon. manager for
a year or two. His death has been a bitter blow,
personally and otherwise, for we had planed quite a
number of publishing schemes together. He did suggest
my publishing your Alf Venison Poems and I said I would
like to do so. Would you agree to my doing this?

I shall be publishing 3 volumes of Orage's work
and I believe Butchart has written you about one of them.
They are :-
          His Political and Economic Writings
          His Literary and Critical Essays
          A collection of his Philisophical Essays & Writings

Illustration 1
Page 1 of a letter from Stanley Nott to Ezra Pound, 26 November 1934 (Letter 1)

Directors
Stanley Nott
Kenneth Gee

STANLEY NOTT LTD

Publishers

Telephone:
Museum 3186
Cables
Newecon London

69 GRAFTON STREET · FITZROY SQUARE · LONDON · W·1

2.

I hope that some day we may meet, but the
exchange makes it almost impossible for me to get
to Italy.

You may be interested to know that Jane Heap
is in London and that she and I are forming a
group in connection with the Gurdjieff ideas.

Yours sincerely

Stanley Nott

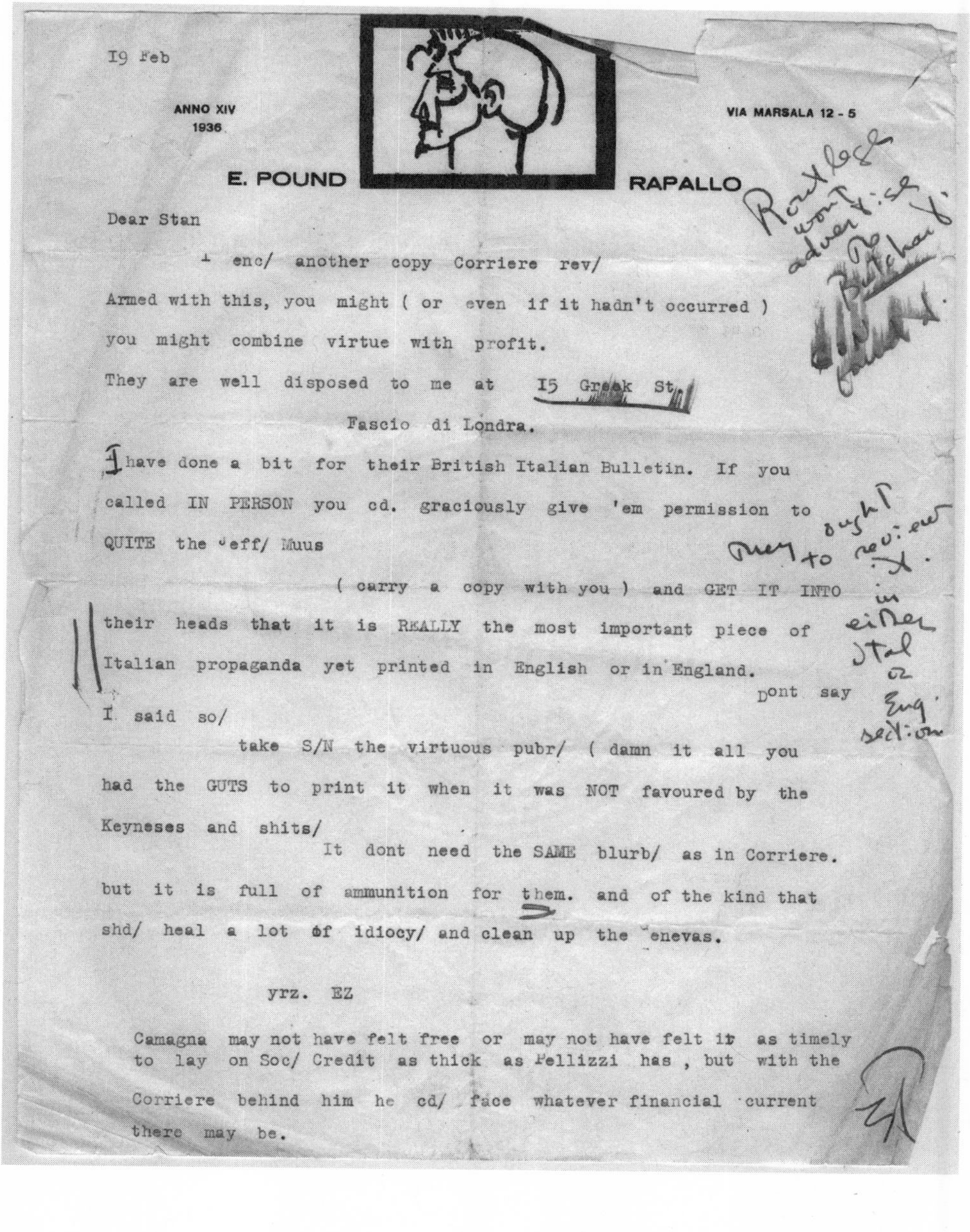

I9 Feb

ANNO XIV
1936

E. POUND   **RAPALLO**

VIA MARSALA 12 - 5

*Routledge
wont advice
[Bullshart?]* [handwritten]

Dear Stan

       ⊥ enc/ another copy Corriere rev/

Armed with this, you might (or even if it hadn't occurred)

you might combine virtue with profit.

They are well disposed to me at   I5 Greek St,

           Fascio di Londra.

I have done a bit for their British Italian Bulletin. If you

called IN PERSON you cd. graciously give 'em permission to

QUITE the Jeff/ Muus

[handwritten: they ought to review it.]

          (carry a copy with you) and GET IT INTO

their heads that it is REALLY the most important piece of

Italian propaganda yet printed in English or in England.

[handwritten: either Ital or Eng. section]

                               Dont say

I said so/

        take S/N the virtuous pubr/ (damn it all you

had the GUTS to print it when it was NOT favoured by the

Keyneses and shits/

            It dont need the SAME blurb/ as in Corriere.

but it is full of ammunition for them. and of the kind that

shd/ heal a lot of idiocy/ and clean up the Genevas.

        yrz. EZ

Camagna may not have felt free or may not have felt it as timely
to lay on Soc/ Credit as thick as Fellizzi has , but with the
Corriere behind him he cd/ face whatever financial current
there may be.

A tax is not a share
A nation need not and
should not pay rent for
its own credit.

10 June

1937
anno
XV

EZRA POUND
Via Marsala 12-5
RAPALLO

Dear Stan

Morley is well disposed toward you (very much so)
but hasn't a job open at the moment.

I can't make out ANYTHING much from yr/
letter. Nacherly I don't want money from you, especially
as you have none.

I want as MANY copies of the books as you can
save from the wreckage. And shd/ be prepared to put in as
big a bill as possible to keep 'em from less wortny creditors.

ANYTHING I can do to get you started again
in any way, I shall be glad to do. You turned out some
good books, and printed 'em extremely well. You deserve
well both of the public in general, and of the reformers ;
who (as I see it) have been damn'd snotty.

At any rate you got Butch's " Money " into print. and you have
not lived in vain. Very high % of real stuff printed,
and no trype printed intentionally (at least that is the
way I see it.)

I have NO idea which letters your letter
is intended to answer

Illustration 3
Page of letter from Ezra Pound to Stanley Nott, 10 June 1937 (Letter 101)

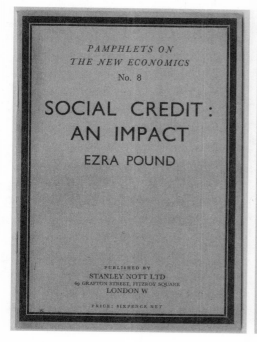

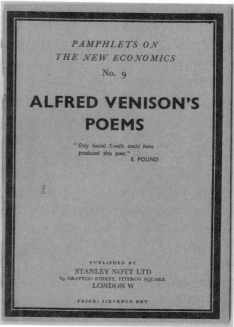

Illustration 4

left · Cover of Pound's *Social Credit: An Impact,* no. 8 in
the Pamphlets on the New Economics series

right · Cover of Pound's *Alfred Venison's Poems,* no. 9 in
the Pamphlets on the New Economics series

Illustration 5

right · Stanley with Adam, circa 1930

below · Stanley Nott with Rosemary, Adam, and Jim, circa 1933

Illustration 6
Ezra Pound, circa 1935

Illustration 7
Advertisement for E.S. Holter's *The ABC of Social Credit*, published by Stanley Nott Ltd., from the *New English Weekly*, 4 October 1934, 504.

THE LETTERS

{YCAL MSS 43, SERIES I, BOX 37, FOLDER 1579}
[LETTER I, TLS, SN TO EP]

Directors	**STANLEY NOTT LTD**	*Telephone*
Stanley Nott	*Publishers*	Museum 3186
Kenneth Gee		*Cables*
		Newecon London

69 GRAFTON STREET · FITZROY SQUARE · LONDON · W·1

Ezra Pound Esq
Rapallo
Italy

November
Twenty-sixth
1934

Dear Ezra Pound:

I am sending you a copy of a series of pamphlets[1] we are doing. The series came about ~~by~~ *from* an idea which I discussed with Orage[2] about a year ago. They promise to be very popular.

Our further series will include pamphlets by Herbert Read,[3] Storm Jameson,[4] Will Dyson,[5] Dean of Canterbury[6] etc. and I was wondering if you would do one for me. The subject might be "The Writer in Regard to Social Credit" or "The Writer in the Age of Leisure" or some such subject.[7] I would leave it to you to choose a suitable title. We are paying a royalty of 10%. I shall be interested to hear what you think of the idea.

1 Nott is referring to his Pamphlets on the New Economics series; nineteen numbers were printed between 1934 and 1936. See Appendix 2. The Stanley Nott Ltd. advertisement in the *New English Weekly* of 29 November 1934 claims that "5000 of these pamphlets were sold in the first six weeks," and it notes pamphlets by A.R. Orage, the Dean of Canterbury, Will Dyson, Storm Jameson, and William Ward.
2 Orage, Alfred Richard. Editor of the *New Age* (1907–22) and later the *New English Weekly* (1932–34).
3 Read, Sir Herbert. British poet, art critic.
4 Jameson, Margaret Storm. British novelist, critic.
5 Dyson, William Henry. Australian-born illustrator and cartoonist.
6 Johnson, Hewlett. Dean of Canterbury Cathedral.
7 EP eventually settled on the title *Social Credit: An Impact*. This pamphlet was published in May 1935 as no. 8 in the Pamphlets on the New Economics series.

You may remember that I helped Orage start the "New English Weekly"[8] and acted as his hon. manager for a year or two. His death[9] has been a bitter blow, personally and otherwise, for we had planed [sic] quite a number of publishing schemes together. He did suggest my publishing your Alf Venison Poems[10] and I said I would like to do so. Would you agree to my doing this?

I shall be publishing 3 volumes of Orage's work[11] and I believe Butchart[12] has written you about one of them. They are :-
    His Political and Economic Writings
    His Literary and Critical Essays
    A collection of his Philisophical [sic] Essays & Writings[13]

I hope that some day we may meet, but the exchange makes it almost impossible for me to get to Italy.

You may be interested to know that Jane Heap[14] is in London and that she and I are forming a group in connection with the Gurdjieff[15] ideas.

Yours sincerely
Stanley Nott [A S]

8 The *New English Weekly*. See Appendix 1.
9 Orage died on 6 November 1934, not long after a radio broadcast he gave the night before for the BBC Poverty in Plenty series. His final "Notes of the Week" column appeared in the 8 November 1934 issue of the *NEW*.
10 EP's *Alfred Venison's Poems: Social Credit Themes, by the Poet of Titchfield Street* would appear as no. 9 in the Pamphlets on the New Economics series.
11 Nott published Orage's *Political and Economic Writings* (1936), arranged by Montgomery Butchart, with the advice of Maurice Colbourne, Hilderic Cousins, Will Dyson, and others; *The B.B.C. Speech and the Fear of Leisure* (1935), no. 5 in the Pamphlets on the New Economics series; and *Selected Essays and Critical Writings* (1935), ed. Saurat and Read.
12 Butchart, Montgomery. Canadian writer and commentator on economics.
13 The projected third volume collecting Orage's philosophical writings did not come to press.
14 Heap, Jane. American artist, writer, and co-editor of the *Little Review*.
15 Gurdjieff, George Ivanovitch. Mystic; founder of the Institute for the Harmonious Development of Man. See Essay 4.

[LETTER 2, TLS, SN TO EP]
[STANDARD NOTT LETTERHEAD]

Ezra Pound Esq   December
Rapallo   Fifth
Italy   1934
via Marsala

Dear Ezra Pound:

Thanks for your letters of November 28th and 29th.[1] First of all
about the Alf Venison Poems.[2] I shall be delighted to publish them. The
pamphlet form would suit them very well. The important point is that
no one is interested in Alf Venison but they are interested in Ezra Pound.
How can we let them know? I would like to know what you think about it.
Meanwhile we are having copies of the New English Weekly sent to you so
you can arrange the poems as you think fit.

Yes we are publishing books other than Economics. When our
Spring Catalogue is ready you shall have a copy. We havn't [sic] published
anything important yet except a couple of cookery books and one on
Wine, but next year I think we shall have a few good things. A small
publishing firm must have a good foundation. Social Credit books will, I
hope, be our foundation.[3]

I am glad you like the pamphlet idea.[4] In two months we have sold a
total of 5000 to England and America. Almost none to Booksellers and
only to Groups. I have been discussing this pamphlet idea with Orage for
two years and now it has suddenly burst out.

1 Both letters are missing from the correspondence.
2 EP's *Alfred Venison's Poems*. See Appendix 1.
3 Stanley Nott Ltd. published primarily on the New Economics, but the firm produced
   a number of trade books as well. Nott may be referring to Joseph Davis's *A Beginner's
   Guide to Wines and Spirits* (1934), Mauduit's *Mauduit's Cookery Book* (1934), or *The
   Vicomte in the Kitchen* (1934). See Essay 4 and Appendix 2.
4 According to Nott, the idea for the Pamphlets on the New Economics series was
   devised with Orage (Letter 1).

"The Poet and Social Credit" is a good ~~title~~ *Subject* ~~The subject~~ though you may want to alter *the title*.[5]

The pamphlet series is a considered whole only as each pamphlet refers to the New Economics in some respect. Pamphlets, it seems to me, should represent points of view of people who count. As to length I think "The Use of Money"[6] by Douglas[7] is a good model.

Thanks for the address of Baker.[8]

I'll keep Jeffrey Mark[9] and McNair Wilson[10] in mind . I suppose they could come under the heading of "New Economics"

I see that you suggest "Poetic Angle". ~~The~~ *A* title[11] like "Social Credit and ^ *the* Poetic Angle" has possibilities.

What is the Winconsin note?[12]

Yours ever

Stanley Nott [A S]

[A N] *P. S. I've just discovered an exercise book at the office of the N.E.W. so I'm sending that instead of the copies of the paper.*

5 This refers to what would become Pound's pamphlet entitled *Social Credit: An Impact*, no. 8 in the series.
6 *The Use of Money* (1934). See Appendix 2.
7 Douglas, Major Clifford Hugh. Considered the founder of Social Credit, although some accounts credit A.R. Orage as co-founder. See Essay 1.
8 Likely Baker, Jacob. Administrator in the US Federal Emergency Relief Administration. Although this is less likely, Nott might instead be referring to Augustus Baker, who wrote *Money and Prices* (1931) and *The Control of Prices* (1934).
9 Mark, Jeffrey. British commentator on economics and history.
10 Wilson, Robert McNair. British commentator on history, medicine, and economics.
11 The letter in which EP suggests these titles is missing from the correspondence.
12 The Wisconsin note was reproduced as the frontispiece to *Social Credit: An Impact* and refers to the Chippewa Falls Union Lumbering Company, which was run by EP's grandfather, Thaddeus Coleman Pound, and which issued paper money to its employees.

[LETTER 3, TL, CARBON, EP TO SN]

[pencil: "Jan? 35"]

Dear Mr Nott

It wd/ be worse than useless for me to do a pamphlet that wd/ merely do what the others are doing.

With Mairet's Douglas Manuel,[1] etc/ with the cold and the technical stuff there ; I have of set purpose done the thing hot and molten. (as probably no one else will)

If anything puzzles you. I mean if you are puzzled as to why I choose to say it, or say it just where I do , I will explain my reasons. This is merely to say that there is reason behind the heat. There is , also , no reason why the pamphlet shd/ PLEASE the already converted.

I , naturally, want yr/ opinion on it/ and Newsomes,[2] but I also want / the opportunity to justify privately , anything that worries you in it.

Rereading what I have put together , complete except the details re/ Banco di Genova,[3] which I have written out so often that I can hardly bear the bordome of doing it again.

---

1 Mairet, Philip. British writer and journalist who took over principal editorial control of the *NEW* (22 November 1934) following Orage's death. Nott published Mairet's *The Douglas Manual* in 1934.
2 Newsome, Albert. An editor of the *NEW*.
3 In *Social Credit: An Impact*, EP argues: "Banks differ in their INTENTION. Two kinds of banks stand in history: Banks built for beneficence, for reconstruction; and banks created to prey on the people" (10). EP features the Monte Dei Paschi of Siena as a positive exemplar, and the "Banca S. Giorgio" of Genoa as a negative exemplar. EP praises the Bank of Siena in Canto 44.

I very much want you opinion of the mss/ dont worry about my feelings / send it back with queeries and objections.[4]

The subject is too big for personal vanity and ^{ANY} author's conceit. If you or any INTELLIGENT friend have any suggestions; do lets have 'em. I don't mean I'll take 'em. But I promise to think 'em over and to <u>do some</u>thing as a result /

to try to get whatever you think ought to be there, without sacrificing what I think ought to be there.

/ /

I haven't yet untangles [sic] the complexities[5] of Social Credit organ(or disorgani)ZATION in London. Don't make out who sees or speaks to who(M)...

am all for AT LEAST collusion, even among groups that dislike each other, or who from reasons LOCALLY of HIGH visibility can't openly cooperate
(will do my best to hook up, to cause to colly/borate etc all such lost sheep, fallen women, wild eyed energumen[6] etc.)
/ /
Of course my damn. CANTOS are a store house of ammunition. I dunno when people are going to begin to realize this. I cant

---

4 The manuscript is likely of EP's pamphlet, *Social Credit: An Impact.*
5 EP alludes to what many commentators describe as infighting and the lack of central control within the British Social Credit movement. See Essay 1 and Essay 4.
6 Likely a typo for "energymen."

shout it very much in the text of my own pamphlet , but no reason the jacket blurb shoudn't. WD/ much rather have historians or economists comment of ^{C}antos , esp 31/41[7] than the snoops of bloosmbuggy[8] letteratets.

Orage printed my Seafarer,[9] I think it was 24 years ago, or a quarter of a century / he did Canto 38 , and   41 ^{was} in his last number.[10]

7 *Eleven New Cantos: XXXI–XLI* (1934).
8 The Bloomsbury Group. With his wordplay, EP consistently aligns "Bloomsbury" with "buggery" in the correspondence, jibing at Bloomsbury's respect for the open sexuality of its members. See also letters 14, 26, 28, and 80.
9 EP's translation of "The Seafarer" appeared in the *New Age* (November 1911).
10 Canto 38 was printed in the *NEW* on 28 September 1933, while Canto 41 was printed on 8 November 1934 in the last number edited by Orage. Both cantos address themes and figures central to EP's thought on politics and economics: C.H. Douglas, Mussolini, Jefferson, and Gesell.

P/2   23 Dec/ CONtinuing/[1]

To be any use , I must have the facts/ in answer to various questions sent

to M/B/,[2] Newsome, ^Mairet/ re/ circulation/ subscribers / distribution

of subscribers/ London, Provinces, Empire , U. S. A.

        After all I am older than everyone except Ward/[3] and have
certainly been dans le boutique of more reviews, not always on the
printed list of edtrs/

N/E/W/ bn must be INTERESTING. That means WORK. It dont

necessar [cut off] ly mean the STAR system.

        The stinking wypers[4] that SELL like ballyho [cut
off] are often , Lit/ Digest, Fortune , etc//[5] anonymous/ office rewrite
sys[t]em.
    N/E.W/ has apparently a group of intelligent (up to a point) but
not very distinguished writers.[6]

---

1 Letter 4 appears to be a continuation of Letter 3 (undated).
2 Butchart, Montgomery. Butchart's rank and responsibilities at the *NEW* during this
   time remain unclear.
3 Ward, William. Edited *The National Dividend* (1935), no. 7 in the Pamphlets on the
   New Economics series.
4 EP's shorthand is likely a cross between "vipers" and "wipers."
5 *Literary Digest* (1890–1938) and *Fortune* (1930–), two of the most popular American
   magazines of the time.
6 The *NEW* did not list an editorial staff in its pages until 1942, when the editorial
   committee of Maurice Reckitt, Pamela Travers, T.S. Eliot, Rowland Kenny, and W.T.

I.   WILL the blighters WORK ?

I suggest to you the sottisier , newspaper cuttings/[7]

II.

There seems to be an American wing[8] that can do American notes/
IF someone will correlate the america/ notes , there cd/ be a group
name/

      IF someone IN america sends digest of Econ/ and polit/ news,
and if I send in mine/ it cd/ be welded by a rewrite man in London.

III. Old ^{N}ew Age,[9] had European news sections , signed Verdad.
(S.Verdad)[10] supposed to be A/R/O until Verdad's death was
announced.

      Either S.Verdad , cd/ rise from grave/ or his son cd/ continue, or
his his nephew/ (no need to specify). M. Verdad. or H. Verdad., H.
rather better initial.

I read a collection of papers daily/ I get some American news that
isn't in print.

Symons was announced, with Jessie Orage, Richard Orage, and T.M. Heron joining
shortly thereafter.

7 According to the *Oxford English Dictionary*, a "sottisier" is "A collection of *sottises*; esp.
a list of written stupidities." EP's suggestion, then, is to review other reviews.

8 EP contributed nearly fifty "American Notes" to the *NEW* between 3 January 1935 and
2 April 1936.

9 The *New Age*. Under A.R. Orage, one of the most influential periodicals of its time. See
Appendix 1.

10 "S. Verdad" was a pseudonym under which J.M. Kennedy, "an extraordinary linguist
and member of the Foreign Office," wrote the foreign affairs column for the *New Age*
(Finlay 67).

The tri/party barter scheme , Hungary, Austria , CzekoSlov// ought to be noted.

I think Gesell[11] news ought to be noted , very briefly/ EVERYTHING that goes to demonstarte [sic] the BUST , the diliquescence [sic] and death of old orthodox fake/

Italy's bank measures/ are NOT Doug/ ism, but they show consciousness of reality. I don't think the London press is whooping over 'em.

Can " they " get the fact that I am not howling for front page or more attention to me personally , BUT for a more highly energized paper/

It is the fixed element that keeps a weekly going/ somebody has got[12]

---

11 Gesell, Silvio. German businessman, economist, and monetary reformer.
12 The letter ends abruptly here; the remainder has been torn off.

[AN, EP] *"to S. Nott"*

31 ^Dec. [pencil: "34"]

Dear Nott

Sorry yr/ letter of the eleventh[1] was returned. Porter has orders to send back all advertisements from Eng/ that have ten pence postage due on 'em, but I am supposed to SEE all letters and wd/ certainly have spotted up on yours had I seen it. Am asking Pollinger[?][2] to send you the Jeff/Muss. It follows my A/B/C of Economics[3] (as I think I wrote you)

Am sending you copy of Pagany,[4] which contains the Cocteau Mystere Laic.

.. wd. cost very little to publish...

I have an article on Cocteau[5] in next N. E. Weekly (or the whenever , at any rate it is set up.

---

1 This letter is missing from the correspondence. EP appears to have some arrangement regarding incoming mail that requires postage payment.
2 Pollinger, Laurence Edward (1897–1976). EP's literary agent.
3 EP's *ABC of Economics* (1933). In this longest of EP's pamphlets on economics, developed from a series of lectures EP delivered at the Università Commerciale Luigi Boccioni in Milan in March 1933 and published by Faber and Faber in 1933, EP seeks to "express the fundamentals of economics so simply and clearly that even people of different economic schools and factions will be able to understand each other" (*SP* 233). Writing from his interest in Douglas and Social Credit, EP focuses on the problem of distribution – of money, goods, and work. Here EP marks out conceptual territory that will be developed during the years he corresponds with Nott.
4 *Pagany* (Boston, 1930–33). A quarterly edited by Richard Johns.
5 Cocteau, Jean (1889–1963). French poet, artist, and film director, whom EP met in Paris in the 1920s. EP proposes to include Cocteau's *Le Mystère Laïc* (1928) in the projected Ideogrammic series. EP's article "Jean Cocteau Sociologist" appeared in the 10 January 1935 issue of the *NEW*, in which he praises Cocteau as a "live" writer.

//

All I know about Chinese eggs/[6] is in " Social Credit ", for the last week in Nov. or 1st week in Dec.

//

I shall want the Chippewa Lumber Money , reproduced as frontispiece to the pamphelt,[7] if that is not out of order. It is worth 500 words , in my philosophy.

and proves that there has been an economic background[8] in the family. I find those photos start people thinking a lot quicker than " remarks on the subject ".

//

Only question you haven't answered is: WHEN do you want the mss. ... do the pamphlets announced , get pubd/ in order of names on the list , or are some of the other blokes likely to take six months to start ?

6 This reference points to the letter EP published in the periodical *Social Credit* (14 December 1934), "The Only True Function of the State," in which he attempts to "rectify terminology" used to describe the role of the state in the Social Credit movement in the 14 September issue (*P&P* VI 224).
7 The pamphlet is *Social Credit: An Impact*.
8 In EP's reading, the Chippewa Lumber Money note (see Letter 2, note 12) attests to his economic background, which grants him legitimacy as an economic commentator. See Essay 1.

Speakin' of confirmations: I CONFIRM the terms mentioned in your epistle of eleventh inst/ to apply both to Mr Venison's poems, and my pamphlet, entytled tentatively: Social Credit, THE POETIC ANGLE".

/ /

I am having a lot of fun reading Gesell/[9] I dont know whether Newsome is going to pass my article on G_{es}/[10]

Orage was, I think wrongly, disinclined to mention the subject. I can't conceive its deterring anyone from Douglasism, and it does so neatly wipe off M_{arx} and single tax[11] etc/etc/ and the Money P_{art}, at least is such good reading IF one browses, it dont run straight from start to finish.

9   Although Surette notes that "Pound had to rely on [Irving] Fisher's *Stamp Scrip* for his knowledge of Gesell's economic ideas until he got a copy of Gesell's *Natural Economic Order* early in 1935" (*Purgatory* 179), evidence suggests that EP is referring to the first volume of Silvio Gesell's *Natural Economic Order*, the "Money Part" of the work, which would have been available to him late in 1934. Hugo Fack's Free Economy Publishing Company (San Antonio, Texas) published a two-volume translation of Gesell's *The Natural Economic Order*, the first volume in 1934, the second volume, the "Land Part," in 1936.
10 EP would publish "Leaving Out Economics (Gesell as Reading Matter)" in the *NEW* (31 January 1935) (C1146). EP had earlier published a letter in the *Morning Post* (6 December 1934), "Gesell's 'Natural Economic Order.'" EP's most sustained essay on Gesell would appear in the October 1935 *Criterion*, "The Individual in His Milieu: A Study of Relations and Gesell," in which he suggests that Douglasites and Gesellites need to learn from one another.
11 "Single taxers" are proponents of land value tax as the only method of taxation. The progenitor of the "single tax" movement was Henry George (1839–97), whose *Progress and Poverty* (1879) met with wide acclaim for its economic proposals.

Doug/ did an engineers job/ not concerned with general state of pubk/ stupidity, any more than an engineer worries about the state of mind of his employees. ^{G}esell very much aware of state of circumjacent idiocy...

of course I dont know what the pubk/[12] will BUY. I think you'd enjoy the book yourself as private citizen whatever the tra de aspect.

As to getting money from sale/ I shd think Wade,[13] might function, or possibly Dorothy Sayers[14] might do a ^{v} crime tale (prob. tied up by contract to Gollancz)[15]   social credit

ad interim

and happy New Year

12 EP's professed ignorance of the British public for literature becomes a recurring theme in the correspondence.
13 Perhaps a typo for William Ward.
14 Sayers, Dorothy Leigh (1893–1957). Sayers wrote highly successful detective novels during this period, many of which were published by Gollancz.
15 Gollancz, Sir Victor (1893–1967). Publisher, writer, and socialist, Gollancz helped found the Left Book Club.

[LETTER 6, TL, SN TO EP]
[STANDARD NOTT LETTERHEAD]

Ezra Pound Esq   January
via Marsala   Fourth
Rapallo   1935
Italy

Dear Pound:

Thanks for yours of December 3^rd1 and the copy of Mystere Laic
which I will report on in a few days

I think we shall be able to reproduce the illustration of the Chippewa
Lumber Money.[2] It would be better for us to use your block if you have
one ~~as to illustrate we at least save by having another cut made and by
having the printing done on the pamphlet paper.~~ [Autograph note in left
margin replaces these cancelled lines.]

We will publish the MS[3] as soon as you like to send it. There are no
definite dates for them^ *pamphlets*. We publish them as the MSS come
along, of course the sooner the better. We find that pamphlets are the
things that authors do either in their inspired moments or their odd
moments. Some take a week some 6 months.

A happy New Year to you.

Yours sincerely,

[ASC] *to make a block from your card would rather blur the effect.
Especially as we would have to print on pamphlet paper.*

1 This letter is likely 4 (23 December 1934) or 5 (31 December 1934), the last of which con-
   cluded with EP's "happy New Year"; Nott may have mistyped the date.
2 See letters 2 and 5. As Nott clarifies in the margin, making a block from the card with
   which EP supplies him would further degrade the quality of the image.
3 The manuscript is likely for Pound's *Social Credit: An Impact.*

Jan 11th 35

Dear Pound:

We are putting the Venison poems[1] into work. They are even better than I thought. We've had some good laughs over them. I'm reading your ms[2] which came from Curtis Browne.[3] Its [sic] good stuff. But my first thought is: who in England is interested in Jefferson?[4] However, I've only just begun it. Eliot[5] thinks he may do a pamphlet.

Yours ever,
Stanley Nott.

1 *Alfred Venison's Poems* appeared as no. 9 of the Pamphlets on the New Economics series.
2 This is the manuscript for J/M.
3 Curtis Browne Literary Agency, based in London, handled EP's contracts during this period.
4 Jefferson, Thomas. EP begins J/M by affirming the "fundamental likenesses" (11) between Jefferson and Benito Mussolini.
5 Eliot, T.S. For Eliot's interest in Social Credit theories, see David Bradshaw, "T.S. Eliot and the Major" (1996).

[LETTER 8, TL, CARBON, EP TO SN]

[pencil: "Jan? 35 response to SN, 11 Jan 1935"]

Dear Nott /
      Glad ^Venison savours.[1]

About the Jeff/ Muss.   I am simply held up the whole D/N time by not having it in print.[2]

    It is not a long mss/I dont care how cheaply it is printed. I naturally dont want you to lose on it. AND I think people will slowly HAVE to think about it.

    If the title BOTHERS you, it cd/ be put into sub title. and the ^Jan. Criterion article[3] used to lead it off. with any kind of flach SELL THE GOODS , main title.

    "DUCE to the left ",[4] any damn POINT of interest or lure.

    What is the " Senate ",[5] (magazine has asked contrib/ after seeing my M [orning].Post letters..

---

1 EP acknowledges Nott's good opinion, expressed in Letter 7, of Pound's "Alfred Venison" poems, which Nott will later publish as a pamphlet.

2 The Foreword to Nott's edition of *J/M* attests to the difficulties EP encountered in publishing the manuscript: "The body of this ms. was written and left my hands in February 1933. 40 publishers have refused it." See Introduction.

3 Included in the American Liveright edition of *J/M* is a letter sent to Eliot, the editor of the *Criterion*, entitled "1934 in the Autumn" (C1130), in which EP announces the death of Scarcity Economics in Italy. In the context of the American edition, the letter is retitled "Nothing Is Without Efficient Cause." The letter ultimately did not appear in Nott's edition.

4 EP is willing to change the title to ensure that the book succeeds. "Duce to the Left," as an alternate title, suggests Pound's reading of Mussolini's variety of fascism as leaning more to the political left than to the political right, and it draws attention to Mussolini's socialism during the early days of his political career.

5 *Senate*. EP indicates that this is a magazine interested in his work; no information about it is available. See note 12 below on the *Morning Post* letters.

" Fascism in practice ", fascism close up. A lot of old line guild people are coming "back ", now that the council of guilds ("corporazione)" has been set up .[6]

The cantos 31/41 OUGHT to start a ^{J}eff/ ^{V}anBuren[7] interest.

after all that wiper[8] ^{M}asters come out with a VanBuren poem[9] shortly after ^{C}anto 37[10] was printed in Chicago.

and the whole of the American bank[11] war , 1830/40 will have to come into fashion as converational topic.

How many copies, must you sell to clear printing costs ? also what about the whole series of Morning Post[12] letters , used to load the tail.

They carry a lot soc/ cr/ propaganda. and if the whole cd/ be sold at 3/6/, ought to carry.

---

6   EP proposes catch-phrases as possible lures for *J/M*, which was ultimately subtitled "Fascism as I Have Seen It." As Surette notes (*Purgatory* 84), Odon Por had written two books demonstrating the similarities between Guild Socialism and Mussolini's fascism: *Fascism* and *Guilds and Co-operatives in Italy*. Both appeared in English in 1923. In the early 1930s, Mussolini established the "corporazione," or National Council of Corporations.

7   Thomas Jefferson and Martin Van Buren, eighth president of the United States.

8   EP employs "wiper" here pejoratively, as he does in Letter 4.

9   Masters, Edgar Lee (1868–1950). American poet and dramatist. His poem on Van Buren appeared in his *Poems of People* (1936).

10 In Canto 37, first published in *Poetry*, March 1934, EP presents Van Buren as continuing Andrew Jackson's battle against private banking interests.

11 The "American bank war" refers to Andrew Jackson's refusal to renew the charter of the Second Bank of the United States when it expired in 1836, following a famous dispute with the president of the bank, Nicholas Biddle. EP attributed considerable historical significance to the actions of Jackson and Van Buren during the 1830s and 1840s and believed that they had not been given the attention they deserved (*SP* 179).

12 EP published twenty-five letters in the *Morning Post* between 20 March 1934 and 13 September 1935, nearly all of them addressing economics.

with the ^{C}riterion at 7/6/, mostly full of what people DONT want to read.[13]

I suppose W.E.Woodward[14] dont help for Eng/ ? he wore a damn good letter c recommend for the book.

13 The *Morning Post* letters would not be included in any edition of *J/M*, the special signed edition of which sold for 21s., the unsigned edition for 6s. A yearly subscription to the *Criterion* was 7s. 6d., a "plutocratic price" criticized in a review of the journal in the *NEW* (11 October 1934).
14 Woodward, William E. American historian, biographer, and journalist.

Jan 22 • 35

Dear Pound: The ms for the pamphlet[1] looks very good to me, at first sight. I'm sending it to Newsome today; & I'll write you as soon as I hear from him.

It's refreshing to have passion in economics. So many of the SC's[2] lack passion. Its not good form in England—except at an anti-vivesectionist meeting. Though the Dean[3] of C. has it.

I'll report on the Lac Mystere[4] & your MS shortly

Yrs,
Stanley Nott

1 EP's *Social Credit: An Impact.*
2 "Social Crediters."
3 Johnson, Hewlett. Dean of Canterbury. Nott singles him out, together with EP, as having the passion otherwise lacking in contemporary economics, particularly among Social Crediters in England.
4 EP sent a copy of Jean Cocteau's *Le Mystère Laïc* (1928) to Nott. See Letter 6. The manuscript referred to is likely that of J/M.

23 Jan   [pencil: "1935"]

Dear Mr Nott

I take it you will send me PROOFS of Alf's poEMS[1] before publishing 'em. Always better to see proofs.

/ /

I fell both alf/ and the pamph/[2] better come out SOON, so'z not to miss the general election, if it's coming.[3]

II.

Re/ the Jeff/ Muss.[4] or with changed title

" The Face of Fascism, Close up "

I mean what I wrote. I want to know on what terms you cd/ do it. even if I have to advance part of the printing costs. I dont care about binding. I believe all propaganda etc/ shd/ be ~~printed~~ brought out in paper cove rs/ tho' Brit. book trade mostly geared to make profit on binding only.

I shd/ want fifty copies ANYhow.

I'm hamstrung, having to repeat and repeat in fragments, ALL the time, stuff that I have said in that book.

costs me more to have it unprinted, I mean in time and bother ....

---

1 EP's *Alfred Venison's Poems.*
2 EP's *Social Credit: An Impact.*
3 EP suggests his pamphlets could influence the upcoming general election in Britain, which took place on 14 November 1935 and resulted in a majority for the National Government led by Conservative Stanley Baldwin.
4 EP's *J/M.* This subtitle alters slightly those suggested in Letter 8.

With the Morn/ Post[5] going soft and goofy over Italy, with NO critical measure... mebbe Eng / is ready / esp/ with 'eff removed from the font page.

[ASC]
Once out it can be translated into Italian. though it wont suit 'em here, any better than it does the damn fools in Michigan. Thass' trouble with impartial view. Each sides thinks you are violently prejudiced in favour of the other.

I dont mean Monro's[6] stuff. he's O/K/ and puzzled about England.

Says fascism[7] 17 parts socials and one part Tory/ and

Brit. Tories like it ; whereas the damn fool labourites wont hear it mentioned.

By the way/ is there ANY Brit paper that wd/ keep me info(med as to WHAT if anything in hell , the Labour party is up to/

Lansbury[8] seems to have gone nearly as far as Mussolini, but I spose the rest are stuck in 1892.

---

5 The *Morning Post* was receptive to Italy's actions and sceptical of the League of Nations. R.J. B. Bosworth suggests that the *Morning Post* embodied a conservative ideology sympathetic to the fascist regime that stretched back to Mussolini's initial rise to power (169). This receptivity continued into the 1930s, cracking only briefly over the Abyssinian crisis in August 1935 (see Martin "British Opinion"). The newspaper returns to its receptiveness to Mussolini in Ion Munro's dispatch of September 1935 (see note 6).

6 Munro, Ion Smeaton (dates unknown). Foreign correspondent for the *Morning Post* in Rome, Munro interviewed Mussolini on 16 September 1935. The resulting article is "Mussolini States His Case" (17 September 1935). Munro prompted the Italian leader on Anglo-Italian relations, the Abyssinian crisis, and the League of Nations. Although his article is on the whole impartial, Munro presents Mussolini and Italy as maintaining national integrity in the face of crisis and opposition.

7 On Pound's connections to British Fascism during the 1930s, see Essay 2.

8 Lansbury, George. British politician.

III.

I want answer re/ II. more than anything.

But as a SIDE LINE.

I am starting on Ogden,[9] in N/E/W/[10] .. I don't know whether he will play up or not/ if so Fenollosa's essay[11] on Chinese Written Character , OUGHT to go in the Orthological .. what a pewk term , in the Right=Worders series.[12]

On the other hand Og/ may think it upsets his little apple cart/
in which case someone else will have to reprint it.
(you or faber ??)[13]

IV

Also I keep getting enquiries about my version of the " Ta Hio "[14] the First book of Confucius. 28 pages. I have three copies left , and dont want to lose 'em.

9 Ogden, Charles Kay. Linguist. He invented BASIC (British American Scientific International Commercial) English, a language system that reduced English to 850 common words.

10 EP published "Debabelization and Ogden" in the NEW (28 February 1935). Ogden's *Debabelization* (1931) discussed the theory of a universal language.

11 Fenollosa, Ernest Francisco. American sinologist whose papers were entrusted to EP in 1913; author of *The Chinese Written Character as a Medium for Poetry.*

12 Ogden established an orthological institute at Cambridge. "Orthology" is the branch of grammar that deals with the correct (Greek "orthos" = "correct"), or traditional, use of language, hence the epithet "Right-Worders." EP published four pieces on orthology (C1180, C1215, C1382, C1406). EP is likely referring to the Psyche Miniatures series, as indicated in the Foreword to CWC (5).

13 Faber and Faber. Publishers (London).

14 EP's translation of *Ta Hio: The Great Learning* by Confucius; first published as no. 14 in the University of Washington Chap-Book series (1928); reprinted by Nott as no. 2 in the Ideogrammic series (1936).

You will have seen ref/ to it, in the Jeff/ Muss.

I prefer it to my Cathay,[15] but as it is not PRINTED[16] [line cut off]

It took the buzzards[17] 14 years to discover my " H.S.Mauberley ",[18]

must be getting on toward time for 'em to be ready for the " Written

Character " and the " T_a Hio ".

The two together cd/ start a series of ANTI=OGden pamphs.[19]

if a scrap wd/ be useful.

if my name is any use as editing a series , might run those two and

if they succede , use the Cocteau as the third of the series. after

which , say never more than 32 pages...

    ?? Marx chapter X. on the working day.[20]

    32 pages of Fox[21] introd. to Frobenius.[22]

that wd/ make five things good for the human mind.

15 EP's *Cathay* (1915).
16 EP suggests that the booklet is out of print, hinting to Nott that he might publish it.
17 The target of the derogatory term "buzzards" is unclear from the context, but EP uses the term in several instances in this correspondence to express frustration with conservative forces who hold publishing power, such as Yale University Press.
18 EP's *Hugh Selwyn Mauberley* (1920).
19 EP's edition of Ernest Fenollosa's CWC and *Ta Hio* ultimately appeared as nos. 1 and 2 of Nott's Ideogrammic series, respectively. EP retracts this statement in Letter 12, note 7, calling the pamphlets "post-Ogden" instead.
20 EP proposes Cocteau's *Le Mystère Laïc*, the tenth chapter of Marx's *Das Kapital*, and thirty-two pages of a Douglas Fox introduction to Leo Frobenius's work (see note 21 below) to follow in the series, which is first called "Ideogramic" in Letter 18.
21 Fox, Douglas Claughton. Assistant to Leo Frobenius (see note 22) and dedicated proponent of his work. Fox facilitated a correspondence between EP and Frobenius in the 1930s.
22 Frobenius, Leo. German anthropologist and ethnologist whose work influenced EP.

, and wd/ try to follow with pamphlets of ESSENTIAL
ENLIGHTENMENT by W.C.Williams[23]

E.C.Cummings[24]

T.S.Eliot (if he coud be lured from his own firm... I
think he cd/ for a series).

The Written Character/ NEEDED all Ogden; Richars,[25]
shindy to provide a public that wd/ be in shape to understand its
importance.
With Criterion and N/E/W/to boost ,[26] I think it ought now to
go over.

                    / /
anyhow/ R/S/V/P (I am of a irritbl and impatient nature... but I
am also purrsistent.)

Amsp any stray (and if you wish , confidential) information re/
the 57 varieties of fussing and quibbling, and mutuall biting social
sreditors ; a who ZOO[27] of the fussers ,
                                        .   wd. help me

---

23 Williams, William Carlos (1883–1963). Williams was involved in the American Social
    Credit movement, though by the mid-1930s he grew increasingly discouraged by
    EP's "allegiance to Benito Mussolini and Italian fascism" (*EPE* 305). According to
    Gallup, Williams's *In the American Grain: Seven Essays* was to have been no. 3 of the
    Ideogrammic series, but Nott stopped publishing before the book was printed.
24 Cummings, E.E.
25 Richards, Ivor Armstrong (1893–1979). Rhetorician and literary critic. Richards devel-
    oped BASIC English with C.K. Ogden and collaborated on several key texts, particu-
    larly *The Meaning of Meaning* (1923) and *The Foundations of Aesthetics* (1922), work
    EP believes fostered a public capable of understanding the importance of the *Chinese
    Written Character*. "Shindy" denotes a commotion.
26 EP suggests that the *Criterion* and the *NEW* can be used to advertise the series.
27 "A who's who." EP invites Nott to send him information on the Social Credit
    movement in Britain, which he regards as characterized by "fussing and quibbling."
    See Essay 1.

[part of page cut off]²⁸

Jusr, 's'pose you " tell papa " and I will endeavour to right the matter. Damn it all , the three paper (perhaps they ought to be two papers),²⁹ at any rate each of 'em ought to RECOGNIZE the existence of the others , and divide the work , avoid repetitions or tautology. etc. ^AT LEAST conspire together if they can't openly collaborate.

The question is too serious , to let personal issue cloud it over.

MUST find the points of AGREEMENTS , damn the difference , any ASS can see the DIFFERENCE betwe n (jo/ Ho/ Bo/ and Ko/³⁰

" Swift perception of relations " is wot Harry StoTl³¹ commended.

yrs

28 The bottom portion of the letter is torn off; unclear whether or not a line has been elided.
29 The three papers are likely the *New Age*, the *NEW*, and *Social Credit*. EP indicates that three papers is one too many. See letters 17 and 18 on the proposed merger of the *New Age* and the *NEW*.
30 That is, the differences among rival Social Credit factions are as readily perceptible as are the phonetic and consonantal differences between "jo/Ho/Bo/and Ko."
31 Aristotle. The quotation derives from Aristotle's *Poetics*. EP quotes the phrase in *ABC of Reading*: "Aristotle has something of this sort in mind when he wrote 'apt use of metaphor indicating a swift perception of relations'" (84).

[LETTER 11, TLS, SN TO EP]
[STANDARD NOTT LETTERHEAD]

Ezra Pound   January
Via Marsalla 12-5   Twentyfifth
Rapallo   1935
Italy

Dear Pound:

Yes, all proofs[1] will be sent to you for correction and approval. Both
pamphlet and poems are in the printers hands. But printers are very slow.

Re the Jefferson MS.[2] Had I ample capital I would not hesitate to
publish at once. Things are opening out with the firm in a most hopeful
way. The position is that all of our available capital is in use, but I am
looking forward to certain developments later in the year.

I will get a cast-off done and let you know what it would cost to
print. The difference between a paper cover and a cloth cover is about 3d
per copy. But if we could come up with some arrangement I should be
delighted to publish it. I have tried it on one or two people who like it and
find it very stimulating but get somewhat irritated by being pulled up with
a jerk from time to time; but there is vitality and emotional drive in it and
that's what we need in this country. I used to tell Orage that I enjoyed
your writing and Dyson's,[3] next to his own, more than any I read in the
New English Weekly.

Unfortunately I am not yet in a position to publish all that I
would like.

1   See Letter 10 for EP's request for proofs of *Alfred Venison's Poems* and *Social Credit:*
    An Impact.
2   Nott is responding to EP's query in Letter 10 about *Jefferson and/or Mussolini.*
3   Dyson, William Henry.

I don't know of any paper that will tell you what the Labour Party is up to. You may have to go to America to find out. Personally if I want to get the truth about English affairs I read "Time".[4]

It is interesting that you are starting on Ogden.[5] At one time I used to see a lot of him.

I don't know your "Ta-Hio". Do you want it reprinted?

It would amuse me to publish anti-Ogden[6] pamphlets --- again if I could get my money back on them plus 10%.

I am hoping to publish something of W. C. Williams; I was responsible for getting Orage to publish his articles in the N.E.W.[7]

T.S. Eliot has virtually promised to do a pamphlet for our series:[8] and I am writing to Jeffrey Mark and McNair Wilson.

Confidential.[9] I hate almost all Social Creditors and so far I have kept clear of them. Orage used to say that all his gall was divided into three parts, the largest part went to Social Creditors. They don't want to be united. Now that the movement is growing they want to form as many sects as possible and capitalise their interest in Social Credit. As I said to Orage years ago, when Social Credit in some form is finally put over, the idea will be lifted from under the noses of Social Creditors. A great idea, it seems, needs a noisy, fanatical minority to put it over.

4 In response to EP's request in Letter 10 for a paper that would inform him about the British Labour Party, Nott ironically suggests he turn to America – specifically to *Time* magazine.
5 Odgen, Charles Kay.
6 EP suggests in Letter 10 that his *Ta Hio* and *CWC* could begin a series of "anti-Ogden" pamphlets. In Letter 12, EP revises this to suggest they would be "post-Ogden" pamphlets.
7 Williams wrote two letters printed in the *NEW* (21 July 1932; 10 November 1932); a piece entitled "Social Credit as Anti-Communism" (8 February 1934); two essays, "George Washington" (13 December 1934) and "Jacataqua" (reprint; 3 January 1935); the story "Under the Greenwood Tree" (11 August 1932); and the poem "Our (American) Ragcademicians" (13 July 1933).
8 The series is likely the Ideogrammic.
9 Nott agrees with EP's complaint in Letter 10 about Social Creditors.

Regarding the N. E. W. no sooner was Orage buried than petty jealousies arose so I cut myself right off from it. At the same time I am very friendly with Mairet and Newsome and see them once a week.

However, there is a strong movement here from Read, Muir, Lavrin with Douglas,[10] T. S. Eliot and so on in sympathy to start a monthly magazine[11] with Social Credit as a background. Social Credt from the cultural and philosophic point of view. It should appeal to you and if we can put it over you ought to come in with us. As the N.E.W. lifted Social Credit to a higher plane, this magazine should give it another shove up. I have refused to be drawn into [sic] sect or club connected with Social Credit. I can do much better by remaining outside and keeping in touch with them all.

Yours sincerely,
Stanley Nott [A S]

P. S. I got Muir and Read to meet Jane Heap the other night at our place. Muir and Read never said a word the whole evening while Jane never stopped talking, the result is that they want her to come in on the proposed magazine.[12]   She has become a good Social Creditor.

P.P.S.

Very important Muir and Lavrin would be very glad if you would do an article for the European Quarterly.[13] Something on "Tendencies in Music or Poetry" or whatever you will. A set of the E. Q. is being sent to you.

It is just possible that we may turn the E.Q. into a monthly.[14]

---

10 Read, Sir Herbert; Muir, Edwin; Lavrin, Janko; Douglas, Major C.H.
11 At this time, the *New Age*, the *N E W*, and *Social Credit* were all weekly papers; the suggestion is that a monthly magazine might enable better analysis and access to a different readership.
12 Upon meeting Heap in 1916, Margaret Anderson described her as "the world's best talker," someone who "made ideas" (Pound, *Pound/The Little Review*, xxiii).
13 *European Quarterly*, ed. Muir and Lavrin.
14 The magazine lasted only four issues and did not undergo a change in frequency.

[LETTER 12, TL, CARBON, EP TO SN]

[pencil: response to SN, 25 Jan. 1935
      Jan? 35]

Dear Nott

      Time you saw Hargrave.[1] Man's got a mind. Writes letters 15 pages in long hand , putting in every essential detail. FULL of good sense.

      If Mairet prints my quote from Critica ^{F}ascista,[2] you'll see observer's op/[3]

        i;e; Conservatives will never DO any social credit , till they are SCARED.

      May I cite yr/ " private " pp/[4] without saying who sent it to me.

      I had already thought of quoting (anonymously) yr/ remark on Soc/ Cr/rs lack of passion , with the queery

      HAS this man ever seen the meeting of 2 of 'em of slightly different tints of opinion ?

Yes/ I want the Ta Hio,[5] reprinted. it is BASIC. so clear

---

1 Hargrave, John Gordon. Leader of the Social Credit Party of Great Britain. In the 1930s, Hargrave became the leader of the Green Shirts, a militant wing of the Social Credit movement.

2 *Critica Fascista* (Rome, 1923–43). Periodical founded in 1923 by the fascist Giuseppe Bottai (1895–1959), who also served as minister of corporations and minister of education in Mussolini's government. Preda indicates that, in correspondence with Por and Pellizzi, EP expressed frustration at the "slowness and timidity of journals like *Critica Fascista* or *Ambrosiano*, whose editors often did not dare publish an opinion that was not strictly within the Fascist party line" (Preda, *Ezra Pound's Economic Correspondence*, 50).

3 "observer's opinion."

4 See Letter 11, in which Nott expresses his "<u>Confidential</u>" opinion of Social Crediters.

5 See Letter 11, in which Nott inquires about reprinting *Ta Hio*.

and simple the damn buzzards[6] DON't see it , until the suddenly find they have never really thought anything , and have to START.

I think the way to distribute such stuff is in series.

Will send you Ta Hio/ and the Fenollosa/ Written Character. Not " anti=Ogden " but post=Ogden.[7]   what Oggie didn't know and had orter have known.[8]

I believe by an addition of 50 words , [I] can make Basic into a real language.[9]

For reprint of the Chinese Written Character.

fusion of Fenollosa, or Ch/ Wr/ Char/ with ^{B}asic. and general shake up.[10]

Other possible items for series , indicated in my last.

One shd/ see four items , I think. no need to stick to 'em if something more immediate crops up.[11]

^{L}etter from Og/ this a:m: sounds a bit as if he were STUCK. I mean men[t]ally. (this is provate opinyum .. mebbe coloured by a

---

6 Referent of "buzzards" unclear, but the term may refer to publishers Pound considers obtuse (see Letter 10).
7 Here, EP alters the prefix from "anti-" to "post-" to suggest that his scheme does not oppose Ogden's work but, rather, surpasses it. See letters 10 and 11.
8 "what Ogden didn't know and ought to have known."
9 EP wrote to Ogden that "with fifty more words than Basic at present allowed, he could make it 'into a real licherary and mule-drivin' language…. You watch ole Ez do a basic Canto'" (Carpenter 505).
10 EP suggests that he is interested in combining Fenollosa's work on the Chinese ideogram with Ogden's work on BASIC English, thus further renovating both. See Letter 18.
11 See Letter 10 for EP's suggestions about what might be included in the Ideogrammic series.

personal impression of 4 years ago, when I met him in a Lunnon Club.)[12]

//

I shall need convincing re/ the monthly. IF Mairet will WAKE the literary section of N/E//W, there wd/ be room for all the live thought now being thunk.[13]

The name of Read spreads a dull grey sulphurous fog over all things. Muir seven points better. ᴶane[14] I know from of old. and ᴸavrin dont convince me.

However , dont let me dampen any energies.

SHIT for all writing about " Tendencies "[15] it is   DEAD.

That state of mind , never begot aught but PEWK. Dante didn't write about tendencies. ᴴe said a canzone is a composition of words set to music.

Not chance to slither and Muddily Murry.[16]

---

12 EP exchanged letters with Ogden in the 1930s. Phrases here are "private opinion"; "London Club."
13 In Letter 11, Nott notes a contingent interested in starting a monthly magazine focusing on Social Credit. EP suggests that, instead of undertaking a new monthly review, the literary section of the *NEW* could be used to accommodate the demand for cultural thought on Social Credit.
14 Heap, Jane. EP is referring to his acquaintance with Heap while she co-edited the *Little Review*.
15 In Letter 11, Nott relays to EP a request on behalf of Muir and Lavrin of the *European Quarterly* that he compose a piece on "tendencies" in music and poetry. EP refuses in no uncertain terms.
16 Murry, John Middleton. British critic and editor. EP implies that Murry is caught up with "tendencies." EP uses variations on Murry's name as signifiers for the second-rate (see letters 14 and 15).

There are no tendencies. There is Stra winsky[17] who KNOWS his job. and a lot of blahsters[18] who dont , and never will , cause they are two fkn/ lazy , and conceited. Too lazy to learn , and too conceited to admit anyone else has ever known.

" tendencies " occur when some kike[19] thinks he can SELL an immitation.

In surgery a man either knows his job or don't. Same in writing.

//

I thought Newsome and Mairet were the N/E/W[20] ... have had satisfactory letters from both. Also Mairet has seen Hargrave.

(That dont mean you need to associate overtly ... but we can both work for conspiracy and hidden cooperation). A monthly no use in coming election.[21] and can't think London monthly have ever cut much ice.

IF I saw any liklihood of material being produced that cnd't go into either Criterion or N/ E/W/ I might feel differently.

17 Stravinsky, Igor Fyodorovich (1882–1971). Russian-born composer. EP's translation of Boris de Schloezer's *Igor Stravinsky* was serialized in the *Dial* from October 1928 to July 1929.
18 EP may be playing upon the criticism ("blasting") that he and Wyndham Lewis featured in the avant-garde magazine *Blast* (1914–15), permuting the vowel to suggest the colloquial "blah blah blah."
19 EP's indictment of the current critical climate turns antisemitic with this racial slur.
20 Albert Newsome and Philip Mairet were editors at the *NEW*. EP responds to Nott's assertion in Letter 11 of infighting at the *NEW* following Orage's death.
21 The UK general election of 14 November 1935 (see Letter 10, note 3).

BUT until there are enough LIVE writers to fill ~~have~~ half the pages of N/E/W. ^{I} can't just see the need of arm chair meditations on the relation of soc/ cr/ to the nature of the Athanasian creed or the ^{T}rinity's pancreas.[22]

yrs/ subject to authority etc.

Re/ the ^{F}enollosa and ^{T}aHio/ I understand Eliot has got a Chinaman , saying that I am the cat's pyjamas.[23] in prox/ ^{C}riterion or whenever the sleeper waketh/

that wd/ make the reprints timely.

personally I prefer the Ta Hio/ to my ^{C}athay,[24] but don't expect that idea to spread rapidly.
" Quality of the sage is like water "[25]

nobody is going to TASTE that.
or it won't ~~orru~~ occur to them that they are tasiting anything

22 The Athanasian Creed is a classical statement of Christian Trinitarian doctrine; with "Trinity's pancreas," EP likely criticizes the proposed monthly as too focused on the number of angels on the head of a pin.
23 Nothing appears on EP or Fenollosa and the *Ta Hio* in T.S. Eliot's *Criterion* at this time, though EP might be referring to Hugh Gordon Porteus's *Background to Chinese Art* (Faber, 1935), in the Criterion Miscellany series.
24 EP's *Cathay* (1915).
25 EP quotes this proverb in his *Guide to Kulchur* (1938) in the section on Tradition, which concludes Part 1, noting, "I don't know the source of Allan Upward's quotation" and appending a footnote that suggests the "text is interpreted in various manners" (84).

Jan 31st 1935

Dear Pound:

I met Hargrave about three years ago. He has a good mind and good possibilities. Plenty of emotion too, but adolescent in degree—Kibbo Kift[1] idea is adolescent. But he has drive.

You may quote anything I say, anonymously. I've seen two Social Creditors meet. But I saw irritation & annoyance—not passion. However, your point is a good one. Print it.

Mairet and Newsome <u>are now</u> the NEW. They <u>weren't</u>. My trouble was with Dyson &Mrs. Orage not with M and N. Too long & complicated to explain; it needs a two hours talk. But the situation is clearer now. But how came you to hear about it?

The Ta Hio[2] has just come. It looks very good to me. That is, mentally & emotionally. Physically, how many copies do you think I could sell? and how you would like it printed? 1/- booklet paper covers?

I'm still waiting for the printers answer on Jefferson and/or M.[3] Roughly, I should estimate costs as follows:

Composition	£. 25.00	
Machinery	£. 5.00	£. 30.00
Paper	£. 6.00	for printing 1000 sheets
Binding	£. 12.100	Binding 500
Jacket	£. 3.00	

£ 51.100

---

1 In 1920, out of disillusionment with the ultra-patriotism and militarism of Baden-Powell's Boy Scouts, to which he had belonged, John Hargrave founded the Kindred of the Kibbo Kift, an anti-war movement focused on woodcraft and the revival of folk traditions in England.
2 EP's translation of *Ta Hio* by Confucius.
3 EP's *J/M*.

This is keeping costs low. I'll give you a more exact estimate in a day or so.

Yes! Ogden[4] is stuck mentally. And he will go round in circles now for the rest of his life—unless he can get unstuck emotionally. He got stuck there at the age of 14.

I'm going to publish Saurat's[5] Three Conventions. I think its a very great book. What do you think?

Saurat is a little of Oggy's[6] type—but more developed emotionally. All the Englishmen I can think of at the moment, are stuck. Englishmen are mature & stuck, Americans immature, but with possibilities. My wife[7] is an American (Im English). She has more new ideas about music than any English person I know. Jane Heap is more alive than all Criterion and NEW put together.

I agree with you about tendencies.[8] Please put it down in the N. E. W. It should be there for all to see.

Booklets[9] might be done by the people you mention. T. S. Eliot has practically promised a pamphlet to my series.

Yours ever,
Stanley Nott

---

4 In Letter 12, EP contends that C.K. Ogden is "stuck mentally."
5 Saurat, Denis. Anglo-French writer, contributor to the *New Age*. Nott published two books by Saurat and one that Saurat co-edited with Herbert Read, *Selected Essays and Critical Writings of A.R. Orage* (1935).
6 Ogden, Charles Kay.
7 Nott, Rosemary (1899–1979). Born Rosemary Lillard in Houston, Texas, she met Nott at Gurdjieff's Institute in Fontainebleau in the 1920s. She was a musician.
8 See EP on "tendencies" in Letter 12.
9 See EP's list in Letter 10. On Eliot's promised pamphlet, see letters 11 and 34, note 12. Nott distinguishes between "my series," the Pamphlets on the New Economics series, and the Ideogrammic series to be edited by EP.

"2 Feb"

Dear Nott:

You spoke of printer's being SLOW // do you think it is ON purpose or cause he don't approve yr/ texts ?? There is a helluva lot of conservative stink or inflow/ence in the printin trade.[1]

Re/ the Jeff/ Muss [2] , I am not interested in binding the book. I dont see how I can send up more than a hundred dollars / wd/ that hold the fort, pacify the printer till advance sales (if any) come along. ?

////

I believe ^{H}argrabe boy scouted or K/K's 1[5] years ago.[3] Hiw letters are full of detail, ALL lucid, and COORDINATED. He has written several novels (which I haven't seen). His Hornsey speech[4] seems to me admirably controlled.

//

I dont know the Saurats[5] book. Even I can't give an opinion on work I haven't seen. (I know it smacks of conservatism and Eliot=like prudenceH . But so is it.

---

1 See Letter 11. EP suggests the reasons for delay are political rather than procedural.
2 EP's *J/M*.
3 EP counters Nott's assertion that John Hargrave remains "adolescent" (Letter 13) by stressing that Hargrave started the Kibbo Kift back in 1920 and that he has since matured.
4 Hargrave's speeches, delivered at Social Credit meetings in London and elsewhere, were advertised on the back page of the *NEW* during 1934 and 1935. The speech that Pound refers to took place in Hornsey, a North London district.
5 Saurat, Denis, *The Three Conventions* (see Letter 13).

I didn't know you pubd/ the European Quarterly.[6] Also nothing said about remuneration. I have to have SOME gate receipts. N/E/W/[7] already wants more licherary[8] matter than I in any way want to write. I never DID care about yattering ABOUT aht/ and letters.

One advantage of Nat/ Divs/ wd/ be great diminution in the quantity of printed blah.[9]

Yes/ yes/ America full spurting cocks/ and England never attaining puberty.[10] Thass an established biological etc/etc.

I suspect Hargrave has ripened a good deal // all of us have found a much clearer idiom during the past few years/ AS we have really got the issues more clearly into our own heads/ and the relative importances etc.

"The indifferent have never made history".[11] It aint going to be men of sixty in arm chairs (engineers or whatever) that will put anything into ACTION.

///

As to what I hear of/ people travel/ I ask questions/ people write letters. I allus look fer th nigguh in the wood pile/ old Upwards[12]

6 Nott published the *European Quarterly* 1934–35 (see also Letter 17).
7 The *New English Weekly*.
8 "literary"; "yattering ABOUT art and letters."
9 EP contends that Douglas's National Dividend would also reduce the amount of writing that is of poor quality. EP frequently linked economic conditions to the state of the arts: the best known of his statements on the connection appears in Canto 45, the "Usura" Canto.
10 See Nott's commentary in Letter 13.
11 The phrase, which appears in EP's letter to the *Criterion* (January 1935, C1130) in praise of Mussolini's Italy, is reprinted in the American edition of *J/M* (viii). EP distinguishes between the old guard ("engineers" like Douglas) and the new men of action (Hargrave).
12 Upward, Allen (1863–1926). Writer, lawyer, civil servant, regular contributor to Orage's *New Age*. EP was influenced by Upward's *The New Word* (1910) and *The Divine Mystery* (1913).

chinese ideogram for CAUSE. a man IN a box , or a box with a man inside it.

I never cd/ eat either work or abstract terminology.

What relation between Dyson AND Brenton ?[13] (B/ the forgotten man , who has taken a lot of trouble... which we decorative memebrs of the show git the wreathes for ??? or how come ?)

Dare say N/Age and N/E/W must stay separate ; but shd/ demark their work and colly/borate.[14]

What relation Mairet/ ^Newsome/ ^Brenton ???

///
^Re/ Ta Hio.[15] I know there have been at least 2 edtns/ of I believe 500 copies each.

^Yes/ paper covers at 1/= is what I think it shd/ be. I shd/ ssy print a thousand/ but I am NOT an expert on British receptivity.[16] I shd/ think my own opinion, namely E/P prefers this to his " ^Cathay " ought to push off a few copies. They've got round to the Propertius , I believe.
If you are investing in me and have only 9/8d. in hand , I'd rather the ^Jeff/Muss were done first..

13 Dyson, William Henry; Brenton, Arthur.
14 EP believes the *New Age* and the *NEW* could coordinate their efforts much more effectively, thus keeping both magazines functional in the movement and not in direct competition with one another. For discussion of a merger, see letters 17, 18, 47, and 51. The *New Age* ceased publication on 7 April 1938; the *NEW* changed its title on 5 January 1939 to the *New English Weekly and the New Age*.
15 According to Gallup, until Nott's edition, there had been only one edition of roughly 575 copies of *Ta Hio* printed on 10 April 1928 as no. 14 in the University of Washington Chap-Books series (see Letter 10).
16 EP responds to Nott's Letter 13. Nott would in fact print three thousand copies, according to Gallup. Here EP refers to his *Homage to Sextus Propertius*.

        BUT I beeleev I am reasonable, and [I] sure do NOT want to bust the firm of S/N[17] in its promising egg.

And fer garzake dont listen to ME on british markets and marketability.
        All I know is via Faber/[18] which aint MUCH.
Sales resistence to ME is supposed to be diminishing , but FAR from non=extant.

If the [J]eff/ Muss were sold at 2/6 in paper covers/

300 copies (at 1/8) wd. cover 25 quid printing costs.[19]
                                         on first edtn.
I dont might a <u>small</u> ultimate ~~loo~~ loss . If you can cover your expenses and trouble. I mean if making it 2/6 wd/ MOVE it.

All the other items , I properly and naturally , want a small ultimate profit on.

///
waiting for OG's reaction to my letters/ and coming article .[20]

//
re Jane Heap// when she and Margaret Anderson got to suppressing my stuff because hey they thought it " would do me so much harm in America "/ I passed onward.[21] Whether they EVER distinguish

---

17 Stanley Nott Ltd.
18 Pound likely refers to his contact with T.S. Eliot, who was a literature editor at Faber and Faber at this time.
19 "2s. 6d."; "1s. 8d."
20 Ogden, Charles Kay. EP published "Debabelization and Ogden" in the *NEW* (28 February 1935) (C1158).
21 Heap, Jane and Margaret Carolyn Anderson (1886–1973) edited the *Little Review* between 1914 and 1929. On EP's correspondence with Anderson, see *Pound/The Little Review*.

between Joyce and Elsa von freitag Lorringhoven,[22] I know NOT.

R_e/ " your series " (pamphlets). what I was suggesting was TWO series of pamphlets. YOUR Douglasite series , or strictly econ/ series/[23]

and another series(my name as editor IF you considered it an asset). A cultural series/ general topics.

Whatever Muir and ^Lanvin/ etc/ signify. (I cant believe Read signifies anything but british (well ~~men~~ meaning) DULNESS.[24]

What my part of the Little Review MEANT was an acid test/a dissociation (as in Econ between finance and the rest of the world)// in literature a demaracation between works containing REAL energy , and those merely derivative or boggling.

That also is the drive of my Criticism, and WHY the border line cases and Bloomsbuggars so hate it.

Ultimately they HAVE to accept my ^Criteria/ Joyce IS an author/ etc.

It can't be a policy of quick returns. Cocteau, Cummings, Frobenius , etc/ not immediately popular authors.

No room for the Muddleton Mudshits/[25] etc.

and so FORTH

22 Joyce, James. Freytag-Loringhoven, Elsa, Baroness von (1874–1927) was a German-born avant-gardist, Dadaist, and poet. Many of her poems appeared in the pages of the *Little Review*. EP refers to her in Canto 95.
23 EP responds to Nott's reference to the Pamphlets on the New Economics ("my series") in Letter 13 by distinguishing it from the "cultural series/ general topics" that he believes should be featured in the Ideogrammic series.
24 Muir, Edwin and Lavrin, Janko. Co-editors of the *European Quarterly*. Read, Sir Herbert.
25 Murry, John Middleton.

[LETTER 15, TL, CARBON, EP TO SN]

[AN, EP] *3 Feb* [pencil: 35]

Dear Nott

^{P}rodecin ///[1] wot'z back of this propagoose propaGander in Europ/ Quarterly ??[2] world state , world mess, H.G.Wells,[3] league of infernal bankers , as leg/ of nations or WHAT ?

//

Am not clear re/ what they are (if thye know it) up to .

//

There is

    I.   problem , re/ possibility immediate Social Credit/

        O/K/ if possible.

    II. supposing it takes LONGER , the problem of injecting soc/ cr/ INTO the intelligentzia/

        a/ via N.E.W.

        b/ via some other muggyzeen

Implying/ a program for mental clarity.

    I.   say ? basic english, as per my forthcoming artcl/ in N/E/W/[4]

---

1 "Proceeding."
2 In Letter 11, Nott indicates that he will send issues of the *European Quarterly* to EP. EP clearly puns on the word "propaganda" (goose and gander). EP refers to commentary in the *EQ* on the League of Nations: EP read the League as, at best, ineffectual, at worst, a puppet show of international bank interests.
3 Wells, Herbert George (1866–1946). See note 6 below.
4 EP is referring to "Debabelization and Ogden," which appeared in the *NEW* (28 February 1935). On Basic English, C.K. Ogden, and EP's article, see Letter 10.

II.   Ta Hio,[5] as distinct from all the diarohetic shit of
      Wells/ Shaw/[6] epotch.
                  and all Woodi Wilsons,[7] disguised internat
            banks and beliefe that you cure disease by
            spreading it and making it universal.

MUST be a SPECIFIC perception of LIVE[8] thought, as distinct from
DEAD.

Cant have criteria , or program , until some sort of agreement is
reached bwteen three or 4/ people re/ which is which.

Cant have a literary program , the equivalent of the London School of
Econ/[9] Marx/ and Single Tax.[10]

all right to talk about cultural background to S/CL but it can't be
mere hap hazard.

LIVE ideas must be discussed/ but can't just have dump of ALL

the dead ones, and all the superstitions of blokes who eithr have NO

interest in literature , or have been too lazy to learn anything about

it , apart from what their MAmas told 'em.[11]

//

---

5 EP's translation of *Ta Hio* by Confucius.
6 Shaw, George Bernard (1856–1950). Shaw provided financial support to the *New Age*.
   EP represents Shaw and H.G. Wells derogatorily as pillars of an outdated liberal
   humanism.
7 Wilson, Woodrow (1856–1924). Twenty-eighth president of the United States. His
   internationalist policies led to the creation of the League of Nations. EP attributes to
   him (and rejects) the policy of reducing economic crisis by creating more debt.
8 EP's basic distinction between "live" and "dead" thinking and thinkers, which recalls
   Canto 7, also surfaces in letters 5 and 12.
9 The London School of Economics.
10 On the single tax associated with Henry George, see Letter 5.
11 EP is recalling Nott's magazine proposal in Letter 11.

IF there is ANY clear demarcation/ clear lines of demarcation save those indicated in my ABC of Reading ,[12] lead me to it; and I might discuss it/

BUT until the buggars can put up a <u>schema</u> o f books , you can't discuss it/ it is just MuddletonMudshit blah.[13]
Bastids that never know whether the are writing about literature, reliogion , philosophy, theosophy , or gastronomy in Spain. ///

To change the subject/ ^{H}argrave[14] seems to KNOW WHAT HE WANTS. That to me is a great comfort. I know where I am , but with these bumbling blighters

" non dice di si , non dice di no
dice vai domandar' alla mama "[15]

I do NOT know, and I can't be bothered. IF there is a conscious editorial policy , sic :
to muddle along

then I want that in black and white. The biosophic review[16] means nothing in my young life. etc. Hargrave's speech at Hornsey[17] is something I can get a grip on.

---

12 EP's *ABC of Reading* was first published in London by Routledge, May 1934, and later by Yale University Press, September 1934.
13 On EP's derisive abuse of John Middleton Murry's moniker, see letters 12 and 14.
14 Nott and EP also discuss Hargrave in letters 13 and 14.
15 "they say yes; they say no; they say, I will go and ask my mother."
16 Though EP could be referring to the *NEW*, he is likely critiquing the *European Quarterly* for what he calls its "biosophic" (conveying knowledge about life) quality, which he considers directionless. He might also be drawing upon the title of the *Biosophical Review*, the chief organ of the Biosophical Institute in New York.
17 For Hargrave's Hornsey speech, see also Letter 14.

Have you any views as to "how far the N/E/W" COULD go, toward having a LITERARY policy, one that wd/ carry into UP[18] into respect from the intelligentzia ?

without completely exploding it ?

Any idea, for example; how far they can STAND the

program of my " ABC of Reading "
                    or how low the pubk/[19] is boggit in the muck
of Wells, Squire[20] period ?

        or where the hell, and in what past mud dy era they are
gummed ?

                    all this can take an approx/ answer.

I dont want to worry M_{airet}[21] unnecessarily , or swat him on

the head for not doing the impossible.

                    Any idea WHAT , if anything , he know or

thinks about licherchoor ??[22]

                    ditto Newsome / ditto Brenton /[23] ditto any other

lar ge motor/ tractor " among us " //

---

18 Here, "UP" could be used either directionally (as Nott suggests in Letter 11, a "higher plane") or as a shorthand for "Europe."
19 "public."
20 Squire, Sir John Collings (1884–1958). British writer and editor of the *London Mercury*, 1919–34, Squire was often criticized by contemporaries such as Eliot and the Bloomsbury circle for privileging a clique of Georgian poets and popular writers and critics.
21 EP appears sympathetic to Philip Mairet and the challenges he faces at the *New English Weekly* after Orage's death, but he nonetheless questions Mairet's qualifications for establishing a firm literary policy.
22 "literature."
23 Newsome, Albert and Brenton, Arthur.

Acart from YOUR opinion. 1.
     my opinion 2 x

whose op/ wd/[24] you pay ANY attention to , re a book

    A. econ.
    B. licherchoor or kulchuh .[25]

//

Personally I dont make out WHY etc/etc the opinions of q/x/z/t etc.
COUNT in England , or IF they do count/ or if it is all a matter of
smith and son[26]....

//
about ᴶane Heap/ is there anything shd/ cd/ be put to DO ??

she/ is/ O/K/ , I believe , to see a magazine thru the press , etc.
to arrange the type on the cover etc/ efficient at that. (I suppose

Have ᴸanvin and Muir[27] ANY conscious set of , say, " authors in good

standing "/ live minds, as distinct from dead ones ?

In my ca se; I take it , YOU suggested me, and they said , ah , eh , oh
yes, if you THINK so.

24 "opinion would."
25 "literature or culture."
26 Though the referent of "smith and sons" remains unclear, EP is likely referring to
    W.H. Smith and Sons and the ways in which established, respectable firms hold sway
    whether or not they actually evince discernment.
27 Lavrin, Janko and Muir, Edwin. Co-editors of the *European Quarterly*.

STANLEY NOTT LTD
PUBLISHERS
69 GRAFTON ST., FITZROY SQ., LONDON W.1
Telephone : Museum 3186

Feb 6•1935

I'm writing you about the Jeff/ Muss[1] tomorrow. With your assistance I think we can manage it. Printers[2] are so infernally slow. But will let you [sic] *definitely tomorrow. Also about Ta Hio.[3]*
      Yrs
        SCN

---

1 EP's *J/M*.
2 On printing delays, see letters 11, 14, 15, and 17.
3 EP suggests *Ta Hio*, among others, for the Ideogrammic series, in Letter 15.

[LETTER 17, TLS, SN TO EP]
[STANDARD NOTT LETTERHEAD]

Feb 7th 1935

Dear Pound:

Printers always have been slow - without influence.[1] I'm still

waiting for the estimate.[2] If you will put up 100 dollars I will take on the

Jeff/ Muss MS.[3] Better to put it in boards, the difference is very little.[4] The

idea would be that as soon as we have cleared our costs we are ready to

repay you the £20.from receipts.

We only act as publishers for the E.Q.[5] Agreed to do it for a year.

Personally I dont think very much of it. It has no vitality or purpose.Muir[6]

is getting fed up with it. I want Lavrin to take over Social Credit and put

some sort of life in it *the EQ*.[7] Lavrin can write extremely well,but he's

always got one eye cocked at the principal of Nottingham University,[8] and

that cramps his style.

Are you quite fair to Read?[9] London does drain ones energy and

vitality.And the war.[10] He is at least a man of understanding. But as

---

1 For this thread, see letters 14 and 16.
2 See Nott's estimate of the costs at roughly £52 in Letter 13. See also letters 18–20.
3 See Letter 14, in which EP indicates his willingness to front $100 to cover the initial costs of printing *J/M*. In 1935, the rate of exchange between the American dollar and the British sterling was roughly five to one.
4 Nott suggests binding the book in boards rather than in cheaper paper covers.
5 EP inquires into Nott's involvement with the *European Quarterly* in Letter 14.
6 Muir, Edwin. Nott's indictment echoes EP's criticism in Letter 15.
7 Lavrin, Janko. Co-editor of the *European Quarterly*. Here, as Nott refers to "Social Credit," it is unclear whether he means the actual publication, the journal *Social Credit*, or just this aspect of the *European Quarterly* material. As Nott had no evident ties with the journal, it is most likely the latter.
8 Lavrin was a professor at Nottingham University.
9 EP initially derides Herbert Read in Letter 12.
10 Read served with distinction in the army during the First World War.

A.E.[11] quoted, " one man of action will confound a hundred men of understanding".

Dyson would like to see the N.A. and the NEW fused.[12] But Brenton[13] who towed the ship along for so many years is left paddling his own frail canoe- and prefers to do it: the revivalist who prefers his own little soap box to a share of another man's pulpit. Douglas[14] has no hesitation in dropping anyone when it suits him. The key to D's behaviour lies , I think in two things (I) He is an inverted banker (II) he is lame. He has a twist.

Newsome[15] dislikes Brenton. He suffered under him in the N. A. and Newsome has an idea that Brenton disapproved *of* his (Newsome's) living with his present wife before they were married. Both Mairet[16] and Newsome I think would work with Brenton on the N.E.W. if Brenton contributed a weekly article under the editorship of Mairet.

What are your sales here? 7-800? They ought to be 4000, AE tells me that 4000 is the limit and the usual sale of established writers of his sort here. 4000 out of 40.0000.000![17]

11 Russell, George William ("A.E.," 1867–1935). Irish poet, critic, nationalist, and major figure in the Irish literary Renaissance. Russell wrote the introduction to Odon Por's first book, *Guilds and Co-operatives in Italy*, which outlines the affinities between Guild Socialism and fascism in 1923 (Surette, *Purgatory*, 84).
12 Here the idea for merging the *New Age* and the *NEW* is attributed to Will Dyson. In Letter 14, EP suggests that the papers should remain apart. See also letters 18, 47, and 51.
13 Brenton, Arthur. Editor of the *New Age*.
14 Douglas, Major C.H. According to Finlay, the problems between Brenton and Douglas arise as a result of Brenton's continued independence and criticism of the Social Credit Secretariat. The Secretariat cut off support from the *New Age* as a result and began to issue its own weekly, *Social Credit*, in 1934 (Finlay 139).
15 Newsome, Albert. Editor of the *NEW*. Nott is responding to EP's query in Letter 14.
16 Mairet, Philip. Editor of the *NEW*.
17 Nott is responding to EP's suggestion in Letter 14 that "Sales resistence to ME is supposed to be diminishing, but FAR from non-extant."

We will of course have signed agreements for any books we do of yours.With the pamphlets a letter should be enough.

Jane Heap has matured and mellowed.[18] She dosnt [sic] like England, but she will be here for about a year.I'm trying to induce her to do some sort of literary work again.

The second series[19] of pamphlets,or booklets, would be quite different in format from the New Economic pamphlets.   They might sell at a *1/-n1/6*. You as editor would be O. K. They would have to be short, on a/c[20] of printing costs. However,how would you like to outline a scheme ?[21]

The pamphlets[22] are selling well. I believe Ward's ,a symposium[23] on the Nat Dividend will be a best seller.

The idea of the E.Q. is that Lavrin speaks 16 languages and wants to have a word in each country. It is the expression of intense wish to escape from University College ,Nottingham

For the N.E.W to have a literary policy you have got to have some one person interested in a literary policy.At present it is all haphazard. .The literary blokes here -we round the N.E.W. Muir, Read, Mairet,

---

18 Nott is responding to EP's assessment of Heap in letters 14 and 15.
19 Nott is commenting on EP's suggestion of a "cultural series/ general topics" in Letter 14 for which he would stand as editor. The Ideogrammic series, Nott specifies, would differ from the Pamphlets on the New Economics series not only in cost but also in format. While the pamphlets sold for 6d. each, Nott proposes that the "booklets" for this series be priced between one shilling (1s.) and one-shilling-six-pence (1s. 6d.). According to Gallup, *Ta Hio* and *CWC*, nos. 1 and 2 of the series, sold for 2s. and 5s., respectively. See letters 18 and 20, in which EP and Nott agree on a one-shilling price.
20 "account."
21 EP maps one out in Letter 18.
22 Nott refers to the Pamphlets on the New Economics series.
23 William Ward edited *The National Dividend: The Instrument for the Abolition of Poverty* (1935), published as no. 7 in the Pamphlets on the New Economics series.

Newsome, *etc. etc.*, ~~are~~ all more or less agree on one or two things: A. That no literary policy or new magazine can have any life without the New Economics. B, you can have no new literary policy until the New Economics ~~have~~ are put into practice.

So there it is. Newsome's trouble is that he gets down into the depths but never rises to the heights. Mairet is 'cold fire'. *But he's sympathetic and has one of the clearest minds I know.*

Yours ever
Stanley Nott [A S]

[pencil: "35"][1]

Dear Nott

Right/ letters quite enough for present arrangements. Merely fer friendship sake we better agree on details WHEN there are any , before entering action.[2]

Pamphlets/ simple , letter enough 10% to author.[3]

Jeff/ Muss.[4] , you start repaying my 20 quid when you have cleared. that goes on first edition/ in case of second edtn/ I shd/ get a royalty (say 10%). Thass O/K/ with me. When do you want the chq/

I find my wife[5] has a ballance in London , so can send it in quids , rather than my American chq/ .

When can the blighters[6] get to printing it ? I'll send the chq/ when you say "Go/ " , , I dont want the J/M to delay

---

1 The letter is undated, but appears to reply to Letter 17 (7 February 1935) and to precede Letter 19 (20 February 1935), in which EP indicates that he has not yet received the proofs for *Alfred Venison's Poems*. Key evidence to support this appears in EP's response to Nott's discussion of Brenton, Newsome, and Newsome's spouse.

2 In Letter 17, Nott mentions that signed agreements are needed for book contracts but that letters would be contractual enough for pamphlets.

3 EP clarifies that a 10 percent royalty should go to the author of each pamphlet.

4 EP's *J/M*. EP clarifies that he will be repaid the £20 (or $100) once Nott has cleared costs, thereby foregoing his royalty, and that he will take a standard royalty only when the book enters a second printing.

5 Pound, Dorothy Shakespear (1886–1973).

6 Nott used the Kynoch Press and Western Printing Services Ltd. (Bristol) during this period.

the Venison , or the pamphlet[7] which ought to help ine the elexshun campaign. At least I hope it will.

I'll send chq/ on receipt of Venison's proofs , or when the Jeff/ goes to press. or at once , as you prefer.

/ /

I am by natr/ thank god IMPATIENT , if I hadn't been , I shd/ still be teaching half wits in a desert beanery. at Cra wfurd'sville Indiana , which is lowern hell.[8]

// About Read/[9] I'll grant him all the human virtues , but writing is something else yet again yess. Pore ole Harold Munro ,[10] was also a good guy , and had more juice than read, I suppose ,

I dont this Read is a son of a bitch or anything like that , but I dont know anyone whom I cd/ tell to read him. Let alone doing it myself.

I'll <u>try</u> to peruse his best item , if you send it me .[11]

/ /

---

7 EP does not want J/M to delay the publication of *Alfred Venison's Poems*, and *Social Credit: An Impact*, which he hopes will boost the vote for Social Credit in the upcoming general election (14 November 1935).

8 EP taught at Wabash College, Crawfordsville, Indiana, before leaving the United States for London in 1908.

9 Read, Sir Herbert. EP replies to Nott's defence of Read in Letter 17.

10 Monro, Harold (1879–1932). British poet and owner-operator of London's Poetry Bookshop. Monro also edited *Poetry Review* magazine, *Poetry and Drama*, and several poetry anthologies.

11 Nott published Read's *Essential Communism* (1935) as no. 12 in the Pamphlets on the New Economics series.

Have seen recent New Age/   and think there may be some
sense in their staying separate. N/A/ for convinced and at least
partly educated=in=social=credit.

N/E/W/ to try to spread into literary circles.[12]

/ /

I agree that writers , LICHERARY blokes , shd/ GET social
credit, they shd/ be S/Cr/minded before we let 'em into N/E/W/
and I have already got three young blokes following E.P. into
social credit poetry.[13]

II. BUTT it iz all nuttz , to think ther can't be literary
movement till the buggarn politicians putt thru' soc/ cr/
intelligentzia precedes the politicians. AND I have already putt
over licherary movements.

Also , fer thet matter I (Ez P'O) AM interested
in a licherary policy/

Must say Mairet is slowly tendending more or
less toward the line I suggest. But then there iz these awful
relapses.

(I am not convinced they do any good).

12 Responding to Dyson's suggestion of a merger, EP suggests in Letter 14 that the *New
    Age* and the *NEW* should remain separate, and he here defines the function of each:
    the *New Age* is to reach those already informed about Social Credit and the *NEW* is to
    gain more support from literary circles.
13 EP agrees with Nott's comments in Letter 17 that a grasp on New Economics is crucial
    to any literary policy at the *NEW*. Referents pertaining to the "young blokes" following
    EP into "social credit poetry" remain unclear, though E.E. Cummings, James Laughlin,
    and O. Bird are mentioned below in note 28.

We ought to get ELIOT to WRITE   at least one artcile AT
ONCE. I dunno why there hasn't been any more Bill/ Williams.
and Cumming's can't be expected to go on, if he is shoved in as
Pastiche.[14]

I'm not complaining. Not recriminating/ I just want everyone
who is in favour of going FORWARD , literachoor/ly, to keep up
mild   pressure.

Jane never did actually WRITE much/. Try her on the E/Q/
Lanvin's 16 languages etc/   , le'z have a little manifestation of
her maturity.[15]

Thanks for data/ re/ News/ Mairet/ and Brentn/[16]   I suppose
if I had MET Br/ I shd/ have less sympathy with his position. ,
and WHAT has anybody's wife to do with S/Cr   HELL !
purrsonal , fuss.
/ /
I think the literary pamphs/[17] ought to sell at 1/ , one and six
is an unhandy price. , however , that wd/ be your end of it.

14 EP suggests that more frequently including the work of T.S. Eliot, William Carlos
    Williams, and E.E. Cummings, all of whom have an interest in economics, would
    improve the literary policy at the *NEW*.
15 Heap, Jane. Nott suggests in Letter 17 that Heap has "matured and mellowed."
16 In Letter 17, Nott explains the relationships among Brenton, editor of the *New Age*,
    and Mairet and Newsome, editors of the *NEW*. In Letter 61, EP expresses qualified
    approval of Brenton.
17 "Literary pamphlets" refers to the Ideogrammic series. Nott distinguishes them in
    Letter 17 by format (they are "booklets") and by suggesting that they might command

My poems go into more than one edtn/ both eng/ and U.S/ and
F~aber~ promise a "collected", to follow up the "selected"
which went first in one edtn/ and then into series at 3/6[18]

The series as I see it shd/ stary with Ta Hio[19]

1. Ta Hio.

2. Cocteau[20] Mystere ^L^aic , if there aren't impediments from france.

3. Fenollosa " Chinese Written Character "[21]

4. Eliot , as he probably wdn't get ready for gordknowz how
long.

5. Cumming's new poems (as item 2. perhaps)

> give me number of pages, limit. I will tell him
> how many we can use. He says there are 70 , a lot
> of which are probably unprintable in Eng/

what do we shoot for ? 32 pages, with 24 minimum ?

6. Bill Williams .[22]

Possibilities further

W.H.D.Rouse [23] , new translation of Odyssey , first book or whatever

a higher price than the Pamphlets on the New Economics series. EP, however, believes
1s. to be sufficient, to which Nott agrees in Letter 20.

18 "3s. 6d." EP is responding to Nott's inquiry regarding EP's sales in England in Letter 17.
19 The Ideogrammic series.
20 Cocteau, Jean. The proposed work is a reprint of *Le Mystère Laïc* (1928).
21 *CWC* by Ernest Fenollosa
22 T.S. Eliot, E.E. Cummings (which poems were considered for inclusion remains
   unclear), and William Carlos Williams.
23 Rouse, William Henry Denham. Classicist. Rouse's translation of Homer's *Odyssey*
   appeared in vols. 7–12 of the *NEW*, and his translation of the *Iliad* appeared in vol. 12.

if it comes as good as the sample.

Bunting's[24] Firdusi , IF he makes it more readable than the chunk I have seen.

The Cummings and Eliot cd/ precede everything except the T_a Hio, I think that is a good start. I cd/ use interim to boost the Written Character a bit more.

Did Eliot say he wd/ do ECON/ pamphlet , or just a pamphlet. I mean which series shd/ it be in, IF or When he gets it done ? No harm in having him in both.[25]

Six is enough to contemplate for a start/ There was once a trans/ of Gourmont's[26] Chevaux de Diomede , but I think it wd/ be too long. Cumming's might be persuaded to do a " New Deal "

but the poems are ready/ and a new prose cd/ be used if/when done .[27]

24 Bunting, Basil (1900–1985). British poet who met EP in Paris in 1922 and lived in Rapallo from 1930 to 1933. Pound likely refers to Bunting's translations of the Persian poet Firdusi, c. 940–1020 (also Ferdowsi).

25 EP asks if Eliot's promise (Letter 13) is for the Pamphlets on the New Economics series or the Ideogrammic series. Nott means the Pamphlets on the New Economics series.

26 Gourmont, Remy de (1858–1915). French critic, writer, and Symbolist poet. EP felt Gourmont's influence; however, according to Witemeyer, after 1930 EP "tended to associate the name of Gourmont with pre-1914 aestheticism" (P/W 328). EP translated Gourmont's *The Natural Philosophy of Love.*

27 EP suggests that Cummings might be persuaded to write a prose piece on the New Deal economics in America, but his poems and some prose are already available.

I shd/ also consider your suggestions. But not necessary to include 'em in series unless they fit.

I can see a 32 page anth/ of social credit verse (not Venisonian) from the young , in another year's time.

Cummings, E/P/
Loughlin O.Bird,[28] and others not yet sprouted.

I wd/ add a page to Writ/ Character/ relating it to <u>basic</u> I.E.
jabbing into the subject/

I dunno if OG/ wd/ reply , or if he did, whether he wd/ ant the reply in his own series.[29]

I shd/ be glad to use anything as good as his Idola Fori[30]
(i;e; the essay on Bacon)
in last Psyche , but not the Berkley.
        or prolog/ to
Fox ,[31] summary of FROBENIUS , certainly , only he is now in mid/
Africa.

I thought Butchart's[32] note on Aristotle interesting/ last N/E/W/

28 The "young blokes" mentioned above (note 13), whom EP is leading into Social Credit poetry: James Laughlin and Otto A. Bird.
29 EP's "Foreword" relates the reprinting of the *CWC* to C.K. Ogden's BASIC English and his (and Lockhart's) Psyche Miniatures brochures: "[O]ne of the purposes of this series is not to combat Basic English but to offer, if possible, constructive criticism of it" (5).
30 See *C.K. Ogden and Linguistics*, ed. W.T. Gordon (Routledge, 1994), where "Bacon's 'Idola Fori'" (100), "Berkeley" (110), and "After Berkeley" (111) are grouped together.
31 Fox, Douglas Claughton. Referent to Fox's summary of the work of German anthropologist Leo Frobenius remains unclear (see Letter 10); Fox is apparently in Africa at this time, presumably with Frobenius.
32 Butchart, Montgomery.

but I think all his stuff will go into his new anthology on Money.

I have various historical items re/ econ/ tha might make a literary pamphlet. I mean they are interesting without being soc/ cr/ propaganda.

Stuff I used in Milan Lectures, etc.[33]

however, this is quite enough project for the moment, considerin the normal speed of print=shops.
Once a series is announced, there will be CANDIDATES as showin' up stuff.

As soon as you decide definitely I will write to Cummings and Cocteau / you can choose the order of issuing the pamphlets acc/ yr/ own feelinks re/ the market. The items oughtn't to be announced too far ahead. My name as edtr/ ought to be shock enough.

what about title for series/[34] " Axe and Fagot 5" or Ideogramic series. or whatever.

Might be a bit of Levy/Bruhl,[35] fit to read/ if Og/ came through, and gave one something to hang it on.

ad interim.

33 EP's "Milan lectures," announced as "An Historical Background for Economics," were given at the Università Commericiale Luigi Bocconi, Milan, 21–31 March 1933 (Gallup E1d) and comprised much of EP's *ABC of Economics* (1933).
34 On discussion of the series title, see letters 20, 24, 28, and 29.
35 Lévy-Bruhl, Lucien (1857–1939). French philosopher and anthropologist.

[LETTER 19, ALS, SN TO EP, FOLDER 1580]
[STANDARD NOTT LETTERHEAD]

Feb 20•35

Dear Pound:
   I've been away for a few days. Here are the proofs of the
poems.[1] I think I've got a printer who will do the Jefferson/Muss[2] quite
reasonably. He promises to give me an estimate tomorrow.

   Yours ever
   Stanley Nott

1 EP's *Alfred Venison's Poems.*
2 EP's *J/M.*

Ezra Pound Esq
Rapallo
Via Marsala
Italy

February
Twenty-seventh
1935

Dear Pound:

The more I read Alf Venison's poems[1] the more I like them. The only objection I have to them is that if I am reading them on the bus I go past my stopping place!

You will remember that A.V. offered to dedicate the poems to one who would put up the money for their publication. So I am taking the liberty of dedicating them to S.C.N. I have also made a note on the back of the title page to the effect that they were edited by Orage and appeared in the New English Weekly.[2]

Mairet is delighted with them and thinks it a good literary hoax.

Jefferson And/Or Mussolini

The printer has promised to let me have a proof page today. (This is the third printer I have tried and I think we have got it down to a reasonable cost).

I think the fairest way for both, is for you to send a cheque for £20[3] when you receive the proofs of the MS.

---

1 EP's *Alfred Venison's Poems.*
2 Alfred Venison is Ezra Pound, and the poems are dedicated "To S.C.N." (Stanley Charles Nott).
3 See letters 17 and 18.

The proofs of Social Credit: An Impact, will be sent in a day or two.

I see that Lady Rhondda[4] was complaining in "Time and Tide" that there is no good edition available of Leonardo da Vinci's note books. An edition published by Duckworth, translated by McCurdy[5] is out of print.

What do you think of the possibility of his note books translated by yourself?

1/- for the literary pamphlets is a good price.[6] If they are not too long they could be done for that.

I am still waiting on the printers for another quotation for Ta Hio. Trouble is if printers are busy small things get shelved. The length should be 32 pages or 24 for a minimum.[7]

Elliot said he would try to do a pamphlet in the 6d series.[8] I should like to get him in both.

The series certainly needs a title.[9] I have no idea at all what it should be.

However, next week I will go into the idea of the series thoroughly and write you quite fully about it.

4 Thomas, Margaret Haig (Lady Rhondda, Viscountess, 1883–1958). British writer, editor, and feminist, Lady Rhondda founded the political magazine *Time and Tide* (1920–79) and later assumed the position of editor in 1926.
5 McCurdy, Edward B. (1871–1957). McCurdy produced a number of books on Leonardo da Vinci in English. McCurdy rendered *Leonardo da Vinci's Note-books* into English in 1906.
6 Nott agrees here with EP's suggestion in Letter 18.
7 Nott is responding to EP's question (Letter 18) about the length of each booklet in the series.
8 Nott replies to EP's question from Letter 18.
9 EP suggests titles in Letter 18.

This last two weeks ^{I} have been up to my eyes re-organising and getting in more capital so as to be able to go ahead under full steam in the Summer.

Of course the editor should have a fee.

I am having a contract[10] drawn up for Jefferson/ Mussolini MS.

Yours ever,
Stanley Nott [AS]

---

10   The contract for *J/M* is discussed in Nott's next three letters (21, 23, 24).

{YCAL MSS 43, SERIES 1, BOX 37, FOLDER 1581}
[LETTER 21, TLS, SN TO EP]
[STANDARD NOTT LETTERHEAD]

Ezra Pound Esq   March
Rapallo   Eighth
Itally [sic]   1935

Dear Pound:

    I am sending you a rough draft of the agreement for Jefferson and/or Mussolini.

    If you will pass it with any alterations you think necessary, I will have a fair copy made and stamped and send it to you.

               Yours sincerely,
               Stanley Nott [AS]

SN/ KM[1]

---

1 The initials "SN" are Nott's, and the initials "KM" are likely those of K. Magee, Nott's secretary.

[LETTER 22, TLS, CARBON, EP TO SN, FOLDER 1584]

[pencil: 35][1]

Dear Nott

Answers to questions in yr/ Letter[2] of wha everth inst. are all YES.

R_e/ enclosed , all I want to add is a clause to get me out in case of litigation bankruptcy , etc.[3]

Trus it will be wholly superfluous/ At any rate it can't do you any harm, and might let me step into life boat.

The ten years limit dont matter ,[4] obviously I wont change pubr/ as long as you want to go on with it. It is only I hate to be tied to a firm IF for any reason the personal contact stops. Liveright sold out etc.

I might put it , as long as firm is solve[nt] and S.C.N. is in controll.

All perhaps as remote as Hairs and assignassins. Is that your own heir or a wig sir.?[5]

---

1 The position of this undated letter is confirmed by Nott's reference to the "10 years limit," Letter 23.

2 EP is likely referring to Letter 20.

3 The "enclosed" is likely the "rough draft of the agreement for Jefferson and/or Mussolini" to which Nott refers in letters 20 and 21. Nott confirms EP's request, along with the "10 years limit," in Letter 23.

4 The "ten years limit" would mean that copyright control would automatically revert to EP in ten years. Liveright is an American publisher (see Letter 60, note 1).

5 EP is being humorous about the concepts of heirs (inheritance) and the legal transfer of a right or property.

Itza gentleman's agreement/ and S(oc)C(r) N. is Venison's choice for a dedicatee.[6]

yrz.
EZ P'O

6   EP confirms Stanley Charles Nott as dedicatee of the *Alfred Venison's Poems*. See Letter 20.

Ezra Pound Esq
Rapallo
Via Marsalla
Itally

March
Thirteenth
1935

Dear Pound:

Here are two sets of galleys for Social Credit: An Impact.

Regarding the agreement,[1] of course the bankruptcy clause should have been included, it was omitted by mistake. Also we will put in the 10 years limit.[2]

I will have a fair copy made of the agreement and sent to you. Other alterations can be made in ink.

Yours ever,
Stanley Nott [AS]

SN/KM[3]

---

1 See letters 20 and 21 for details on the agreement.
2 Nott is responding to EP's suggestions in Letter 22.
3 K. Magee.

[TN]
PLEEZ RETURN

TO EZ, the venerabl

vide P/S

Ezra Pound Esq   March
Rapallo   Twenty-sixth
via Marsala   1934[1]
Itally.

Dear Pound:

Your post card[2] received yesterday.

If sheets of Cumming's poems[3] can be bought at a reasonable price
I should like to have some. I take it one would have to take the sheets as
they stand otherwise if some *po*ems are left out it means a special printing
and it would be cheaper to print them here. If you could tell me how they
are going to be published and at what price and how much they want for
the sheets we can go on a little further.

On the other hand it might be better to select 32 pages for the
pamphlet series, and see how they go.

Regarding the series; I should say,

　　　　1. Ta Hio
　　　　2. Cumming's new Poems[4]

1　Though dated "1934," the correct date is certainly 1935, confirmed by Nott's discussion
　of authors' royalties, the Ideogrammic series, and pamphlet length.
2　The postcard is missing from the correspondence.
3　Cummings, E.E.
4　Nott is likely distinguishing between publishing a volume of new poems by Cummings
　not before printed and reprinting hitherto published material. Cummings published
　three poems in the *NEW* (7 February 1935) and three more poems one month later
　(7 March 1935).

3. Eliot[5]
4. Williams Carlos Williams[6]

I should start with the first three and see how they go. Three is enough to publish at one time. If they take on we can carry on with three more.

Author's royalties[7] for the pamphlets should be 10% on the first thousand, 12½ % on the second thousand and 15% thereafter.

I havn't yet worked out the cost so I can't say yet what editor's fee[8] would be. I would suggest a fee for each pamphlet and so much for each thousand sold.

Our only hope of making a little money on this is ^to getting~ an American firm[9] to take up 500 or 1000 sheets.

I can't think of a good title. Axe and Faggot is good but is it too Fascist?[10] Ideogramic is not bad. I'll give another thought to it. What does Axe and Faggot mean?

Yours sincerely

Stanley Nott [AS]

SN/ KM

[cont'd p. 72]

---

5 Eliot, T.S.
6 Williams, William Carlos.
7 See letters 20 and 26 on royalties.
8 EP would act as editor for the Ideogrammic series, selecting and securing the manuscripts from various authors for publication.
9 Florence Codman of Arrow Editions, New York, would purchase 350 sheets of CWC (see letters 65, 77, and 79).
10 "Axe and Faggot" (Letter 18) recalls a concept brought out in EP's rendering of the RENEW ideogram in the "Kung" chapter (XXIX) of J/M. EP presents two ideograms in an ABBA arrangement, explaining as follows: *"The first ideogram (on the right) shows the fascist axe for the clearing away of rubbish (left half) the tree, organic vegetable renewal. The second ideograph is the sun sign, day, 'renovate, day by day renew.' The verb is used in phrases: to put away old habit, the daily increase of plants, improve the state of, restore"* (J/M 113).

Note

If Cummings has enough pornographic poems[11] they might be printed in a private edition.

[AN from EP in large scrawl] *P.S. From Rapallo*[12]

via marsala
12/5

[TN from EP]
Wich comes to sayin' tha   until and/or/either   me an Stan [se]ez

the sheets (an ni shd/ like to see 'um in nanny case) Stan/ can't

tell how ^Hardi he can be.

At any rat he iz zon his way (ist am Zuge)[13]

i shd/ admire to hav the poems in the seereez/ and/or anyhow/   I

THINK the best way to git 'em going wd/ be to do li'l bouk in the seereez/ FIRST and quick n, and then follow it with the big/ galoopus. However , sufficient difference in price , cd/ over come that/ and putt it in reeverse order. them as cant afforkup so much wd/ have to take you in company wiff yr/ elders and dullers.

---

11 Some of Cummings's poems are sexually explicit, which explains why EP suggests in Letter 18 that they are "unprintable in Eng[land]."
12 Included with this letter is a typed fragment that appears to be a portion of an epistle from EP to E.E. Cummings regarding inclusion of his new poems in the Ideogrammic series and, as Nott indicates in his letter, in a "private edition" (the "big/ galoopus").
13 "ist am Zuge" = is on the train – that is, is en route.

Ezra Pound Esq   March
via Marsala   Twenty-seventh
Rapallo   1935
Italy

Dear Pound:

Here is the final draft agreement[1] which I think you will find in order.

Will you please sign it and have it witnessed and return it to us.

I have written to Rouse[2] asking him if he will let me publish his transaltion [sic] of the Od*yssey*.[3] You might perhaps put in a word for me when you write to him again . I have an idea that it might be a steady seller for years.

Yours sincerely,

pp Stanley Nott

K. Magee[4] [A S]
Secretary

SN/KM

---

1 The agreement is a contract for *J/M* (see letters 20, 22, and 23).
2 Rouse, William Henry Denham.
3 Nott never secured Rouse's translation for the firm.
4 K. Magee, Nott's secretary.

[LETTER 26, TL, CARBON, EP TO SN]

April [pencil: "35"]
1   or 2[1]

Dear Nott

Herewith english chq/ for the 20 quid .[2]   I suppose you know you sent me only one copy of contract , not yr/ singed duplicate ?[3] (for my files, memo/ etc.)

Proofs[4] seem pretty clear (but am having 'em read by sharper eyes/ 4 sets , all of whom will miss something.
I dont know that I need page/ proofs/ possibly better..

NOTE / two sheets of front matter, not set by printer are returned with the proofs/
ALSO the chinese characters/ to go on galley 27[5]

where the direction BLOCK TO COME HERE , has been taken as chapter hearding / the block is a little lead block to be made from the chinese characters , described in the i alies / reduce to size of the column.[6]

1 According to Letter 27, the date should be 1 April 1935.
2 See letters 17 and 20 regarding the amount EP must forward to cover printing costs.
3 The contract is for J/M.
4 EP's details indicate that the "proofs" are those of J/M.
5 Unclear what comprises the "two sheets of front matter," but EP added a preface to the front of J/M as well as a postscript. The Chinese characters likely refer to those in the "Kung" chapter (XXIX). See Letter 24.
6 The printer has apparently misinterpreted EP's instructions for the insertion of a block (of Chinese characters) as a new chapter heading.

No attention has been paid to the line spacing of the typescript
but it is probably better as the printer has done it/
at any rate less printer's FAT.[7]
As he has used such small numerals for the chapter headings
and as the flow is fairly constant, and the divisions not very
dramatic/ I don't see any NEED of wasting white paper. I incline to
let the stuff run on, no taking new pages for each roman numberal
or HEADING IN CAPS/

I had forgotten that it was such an advt/ for the FIRST item in the
pamphlet series/

         dare say you can indicate that on the jacket[8]

to our leZope muchoel aadvantdg/[9]

Dare say I better have page proofs ; to be sure about front matter and
the set of the chinese block.

It sure iz one battered mss/ wot nobuddy LuVVd.
And I am very glad to be reminded of the Boss's askin me :[10]
WHY do you wann putt yerr idear in order ?

---

7 The printer likely ignored EP's irregular line-spacing and chapter divisions, regularizing format.
8 Unclear whether J/M will be advertisement for the Ideogrammic series, and thus for CWC, or the Pamphlets on the New Economics series. EP could also be referring to his own first pamphlet in the New Economics series, Social Credit: An Impact.
9 "to our let's hope mutual advantage."
10 The "Boss" is Mussolini. EP interviewed Mussolini on 30 January 1933, and he completed the manuscript for J/M in February 1933. During the interview, Mussolini asks EP: "Perche vuol mettere le sue idee in ordine? (Why do you want to set your ideas in order?)" (GK 182).

T_{ry} that on yer/ pyamy[11] or still better ; try it on the sekkytariYat .[12]

I spose TO SELL it , I had orter have spieled all about that there inchervoo.[13] Wall mebbe I aint so near sighted.

Mebbe date of writing[14] better be emphasized even on title page.

There are two additions/ Preface April 1935 (9 lines)
                    and postscript   April 1935. (5 lines)

as stated on original typescript(where length wasn't stated)

Waa l; naow; there iz some az iz rarin fer to see Mr Venison , an thet IMPAKK.[15]

Pussnly, I shd/ like Alf/ to get reviewed along with 31/ 41[16]

An nespecially I wanna see some of them bloomsbuggy[17]

slickophants that are now tellin' what a great an good writer I am ,

I wanna see them high=hattin' Mr Venison. That I DEW wanna

see. An we WILL see it , save where they don't wear no hats at tall.

---

11 "Pyamy" could suggest a combination of "pappy" and "mammy."
12 The Social Credit Secretariat. Under Major Douglas's control, the Secretariat was the chief office of operations of the Social Credit movement in England during this period, as well as a source of considerable controversy within the movement.
13 EP suggests that publicizing his interview with Mussolini might increase sales of the book.
14 EP stresses the importance of the specific historical moment that informs his work.
15 "Well, now, there [are] some [that are] raring to see [Alfred Venison's Poems], and that [Social Credit: An Impact]."
16 EP's Eleven New Cantos: XXXI–XLI (1934).
17 EP refers to the Bloomsbury Group. In Letter 3, EP indicates that he would prefer "historians or economists" to comment on his Cantos (31–41) rather than the "snoops of bloomsbuggy letteratets." "[H]igh=hattin' Mr Venison" suggests that they would be tipping their hats to his work.

As the Yale[18] University Press, New Haven. Conn. U.S.A. have

written wanting " a book " by E/P/ to go with in the autumn, I

have told 'em they ought to do a MAKE IT NEW ECONOMICS , like

Faber ^Make it New (of literchoor).

/ Wot I suggest is that YOU now write 'em/ laying it as heavy

as possible about your BEELEEF CONviction etc/ and saying you

are doing, Impact , Jeff/ Muss , the pamphlets/ , are shocked at

Amurikurr laging behing CONservative Britain/ that THEY

cd/ do the vollum, of the WHOLE , (including Faber's ABC econ,

which you weren't born in time to print)/ ETC.[19]

YR/ 10% on royalties for that , prob/ worth more than profit on

a few hundurd sheets/[20]

I dont KNOW that they'll do it/ but it wd/ be more

sazisfakkery[21] that having them do fragments. And only way to collect

---

18 EP inquired of Eugene Davidson of Yale University Press (24 February 1935) whether
    Davidson would take sheets of Nott's *J/M* (*Pound/Cummings* 57–8). Faber and Faber
    published EP's *Make It New: Essays* in 1934, which Yale brought out in the United
    States in 1935.
19 EP suggests that a strategic rivalry between America ("Amurikurr") and Britain
    could spur a project to gather his work on economics in one volume, "Make It New
    Economics." Faber and Faber published EP's *ABC of Economics* in 1933, before Nott
    began publishing.
20 According to EP, rather than selling sheets of EP's works on economics outright to
    Yale, Nott would receive a 10 percent royalty on sales of the American edition.
21 EP suggests using a university press to reproduce his recent texts in one volume. EP
    published twenty-two articles and letters in the *Criterion* between January 1923 and
    January 1939. There are nine articles and letters from 1930, up to and including the
    memoriam for A.R. Orage (the "Orage in current issue"), to which EP might be refer-
    ring, several of which Faber and Faber reissued in *Polite Essays* (1937).

the two orcthree Criterion later essays , Orage in current issue , etc. and in general putt Soc. Credit into academic and University circles.

(which point please do NOT make in the letter to them).

Just putt it on grounds on my RISING importance , etc. (if yuh git me). besides they OUGHT to print a decent up to date E/P , not merely what I said 20 years ago about licherchoor which is now perfectly SAFE.

yrz
EZ / P

April
Third
1935

Dear Pound:

Many thanks for the cheque for £20[1] received this morning in your letter dated April 1st. Receipt is enclosed herewith.

We are enclosing also our part of the contract having retained it in case you made alterations on your part,

Please give definite instructions about corrections and additions when you return the proofs of J. & M. The printer thought he had to follow copy with spaces etc. Larger numerals can be substituted for chapter headings if necessary.[2]

We will of course send you page proofs.[3]

Yes, better put date of writing on the title page.[4] If you want to add more you could have an introduction.

Venison's poems and An Impact[5] are promised for this week. Printers have been so busy with Jubilee[6] stuff that our things have been somewhat delayed.

---

1 See letters 17, 20, and 26.
2 EP suggests in Letter 26 that the spacing and chapter breaks need emendation.
3 See Letter 26
4 See Letter 26.
5 EP's *Alfred Venison's Poems* and *Social Credit: An Impact*, nos. 8 and 9, respectively, of the Pamphlets on the New Economics series.
6 Nott indicates that the printers are unusually busy because of preparations for the Silver Jubilee to celebrate the twenty-fifth anniversary of George V's reign.

We are enclosing a copy of each of two pamphlets which we are publishing this week.

I am expecting some fun with Venison.

I will certainly write to Yale University Press.[7] I understand you want them to do a collected edition of your writings dealing with New Economics.

Yours ever,

SN/KM   *Stanley Nott* [A S]

7 See Letter 26.

[LETTER 28, ALS, SN TO EP]
[STANDARD NOTT LETTERHEAD]

April 5th   [pencil: "1935?"]

Dear Pound:

Having thought over Axe & Fagot[1] I've come to the conclusion that it is too much associated in the English mind with execution & the state -. beheading obviously. Ideogrammic[2] is better, but it is going to appeal only to Bloomsbury.[3] Something like "Today & tomorrow" but snappier. Something to do with Pioneers. Axe & Fagot would be all right for America. The idea is "Pioneering". Isn't it? I really can't think of a good title.   Try again.

Butchart says you have authorised him to read revised proofs of Jeff & Impact.[4] You still have Jeff M, I take it.

I saw Porteus[5] yesterday. He's excited about the series. If only we were richer [sic] enough to finance these ideas. Our pamphlets on the N. E.[6] so far have paid. To make the Ideogrammic series (or whatever it may be) pay, we should have to sell 750. We would just get our money back on that. I'll work on it again early next week.

· *Yrs ever*

Stanley Nott

---

1 See Letter 29, in which Nott associates the title with Oswald Mosley, leader of the British Union of Fascists.
2 An "ideogram," usually found in Chinese writing and art, is "a calligraphic notation capable of expressing a multitude of ideas in a very compressed, economical manner" (*EPE* 154). As inspired by Fenollosa's C W C, EP would make the ideogram a mainstay of his thought.
3 See Letter 26, note 17. Because of the linguistic implications and association with C.K. Ogden, Nott worries that "Ideogrammic" might only appeal to the initiated, such as the Bloomsbury Group.
4 E P's *J/M* and *Social Credit: An Impact.*
5 Porteus, Hugh Gordon (1906–93). Author, critic, and sinologist.
6 The Pamphlets on the New Economics series, which Nott indicates has paid for itself through sales.

[LETTER 29, ALS, SN TO EP]
[STANDARD NOTT LETTERHEAD]

April 16/ 35

Dear Pound: I don't mind Ideogrammic.[1] Axe & Fagot is too much associated with Mosley,[2] whom nobody loves. A & F would have been all right just after the war. When I say "nobody" I mean the Communists, Tories, Socialists, Social Creditors – their dislike of Mosley is their only thing in common. His people belong to the late aspidistra age.[3]   Let us leave it at Ideogrammic. All printers are working two and halfs on Jubilee advertising,[4] hence the delay in your MS. I want to get it out soon. I've got good reactions from very different types. Personally, as I said, it is one of the most stimulating things I've ever read. And it belongs to just this age.[5]

I wrote to Yale about ~~your~~ their doing a collected edition of your writings, & am waiting to hear the result.

Yours ever
Stanley Nott

1 See letters 24 and 28.
2 Mosley, Sir Oswald (1896–82). Leader of the British Union of Fascists and one of the more controversial right-wing figures in British politics during the interwar period. See essays 1 and 2.
3 The aspidistra is a plant or flower often taken to represent staid middle-class respect-ability, which Nott connects to Mosley and his supporters. George Orwell published *Keep the Aspidistra Flying* in 1936.
4 See Letter 27.
5 Nott is referring to *J/M*.

[LETTER 30, TL, CARBON EP TO SN]

[pencil: "April? 35"][1]

Dear Stan

coming bak to them timorous buzzards at YALE.[2]

They WANT helltrottem a nice tame book about the middle ages or sumfink innokkerous/

WD/ it be unbusinesslike / or wd/ the econ/ situation , and the groatsworth of good one can do the pore blggared bleedin millions , warrant/

EITHER

your taking sheets of a 300 page "MAKE IT NEW ECONOMICS from them "

or allowing a Faber 12/6 book of that nature to overlap

the Impact/ and Jeff/ Muss ?

NOT that FABER WANT IT / confound it. They also want a nice li'l set of whatnot ornaments , Ez dresden china shepherdesses of yester years et/ BLOODY cetera[3]

---

1 Though not dated, this letter is likely the first of two dated 23 April 1935, to which Nott responds in Letter 33. Letter 31 is the other.
2 EP first mentions Yale's interest in Letter 26.
3 In Letter 26, EP proposes that Nott take sheets and reap a royalty from a collected volume of his writings on economics. The edition never came to pass, though Faber did issue a collection of EP's "whatnot ornaments" as *Polite Essays* (1937).

gheez but it zell ter be pore.[4]

On the other hand I suppose there is limited use in   publishing

books before the god blithering pooplik[5] will buy 'em.

The point being that Neitczhe[6] only printed 45 copies of

Zarathustra/ and that the pooplik does by the real stuff TWENTY

blasted years later/

                    and the gunmen never shoot the folks

that they OUGHT to.

Re/ a backwash of sheets from Yale / confound 'em they GOT

money , but are afraid of losing it/ they are also probably afraid

of the SUBJECT matter .[7]

on the other hand even if I werent such a commendable etc/

indisputable character /   worthy of this that and tother/ to

sooner I get a HHH grand reputation as a kneeconymist , the better

fer the firm of NOTT .[8]

4 "It's hell to be poor." See Letter 33 for a rejoinder.
5 "public"
6 Nietzsche, Friedrich (1844–1900).
7 EP believes Yale University Press suffers both from a fear of losing money and from a
   fear of dealing with potentially controversial subjects.
8 EP suggests that his growing reputation as an economist – which would be better
   established with an anthology of his writings on the New Economics – would ultimately benefit Nott's firm.

ahich aint what we are either of us after; save as means to an end/ but damnd annoying to be held up by its non-existence.

The latest score/ is that the Delphian society[9] (about umpteen millum fadies she female clubs) quarterly, a   condensin my ABC of ECON/

Waal; wot I WANT is a big impressive vol/ of EZ/ on ECON to match Make it New/

I dunno who can evangelize Faber.

I spose the habbits of rhinerorasses/ or Old China in Birmingham under the Regency/ wd/ prob/ be a better trade article.[10]

yrz/ EZ P

<hr/>

9 The *Delphian Quarterly* (Chicago). An organ of the National Delphian Society, a Chicago-based "great books" and "self-education" society for women that has organized chapters across the United States. According to E P, the Society has requested a condensed version of *A B C of Economics*.

10 E P reiterates his desire for an economics-focused counterpart to *Make It New.*

[LETTER 31, TL, CARBON, EP TO SN]

23 April [pencil: "35"]

Dear Nott

You might check this with former list/[1]
all MY stuff and
ALL econ/ pubctns/[2] shd / go to

ODON POR,[3]   Instituto di Politica Internazionale

via del Conservatorio , (Palazzo Ministero Giustizia)

ROMA Italy

and to

Adolfo Salazar,[4] calle Goya 89, Madrid , Spain

All MY stuff (and Vensison[5], where marked A. V.)
shd/ go to.

Lina Caico,[6] 4 via Gargallo, Palermo. Sicily

1 The letter containing this initial list is missing from the correspondence. Nott pairs Letter 31 with Letter 30 ("Your two letters of April 23rd") in his Letter 33 reply. For continuation of this list, see letters 32, 34, and 35.
2 By April 1935, Nott has EP's *J/M*, *Social Credit: An Impact*, and *Alfred Venison's Poems* in some stage of production. Though exactly what constitutes "all econ/ pubctns/" ("all economic publications") is not clear, EP likely implies all issues of Pamphlets on the New Economics series published to date (nos. 1–15 were advertised on the back cover of *Social Credit: An Impact*), and perhaps monographs by Douglas and others that Nott advertised as "The New Economics Library."
3 Por, Odon.
4 Salazar, Adolfo (1890–1958). Spanish-born composer and critic, Salazar interviewed EP and reviewed his *ABC of Reading* in the Madrid publication *El Sol* (27 May 1934), in which he quotes the eight points of EP's Volitionist questionnaire.
5 EP's *Alfred Venison's Poems*.
6 Caico, Lina (1883–1951). Italian translator of EP's works, including an eleven-instalment translation of "A Study of French Poets" for *Il Mare*. Caico reviewed

Fr/ Monotti,[7] Casa del Mutilato, Piazza Adriana , Roma, Italy

Delphian Quarterly,[8] 307 N. Michigan Ave. Chicago.

Bob Brown,[9] Commonwealth College . Mena . Arkansas . U.S.A.

T. C. Wilson,[10] 2557 Bexley Park. Rd. Columbus Ohio; U.S.A.

Ubaldo Degli Uberti,[11] via Cesare Cabella , 11/1 Genova. Italy

(Yale[12] Univ. Press , for other reason).

The IMPACT and the Jeff/Muss[13] shd/ go to Hon.
Senators.

Bronson Cutting[14]

EP's *ABC of Economics* in the Bologna periodical *L'Avvenire d'Italia* (11 May 1935), on which EP later commented (16 July 1935; C1226).

7 Monotti, Francesco (1899–1983). Italian art critic and journalist who wrote regularly for *Il Mare* (Rapallo) and *L'Indice* (Genoa) and translated excerpts from several works by EP for Italian periodicals. Monotti tried to arrange a meeting between EP and Mussolini in 1932.

8 The *Delphian Quarterly* (see Letter 30, note 9).

9 Brown, Robert Carleton (1886–1959). American expatriate who owned and operated the Roving Eye Press, which he established in 1929. *Readies for Bob Brown's Machine* (1931) was a modernist movie of type for his reading machine, including work by Gertrude Stein, William Carlos Williams, Nancy Cunard, and a six-line poem from EP.

10 Wilson, Theodore Carl (1912–50). Poet and critic. EP corresponded with him during this period and, with him and John Drummond, EP co-edited the spring–summer 1935 issue (24.1) of the *Westminster Magazine* (Oglethorpe University, Georgia) (P/Z 224).

11 Uberti, Ubaldo degli (1881–1945). Chief naval press officer in Rome when EP met him in 1934, he later translated some of EP's work. His son later translated EP's *Guide to Kulchur* (1938) into Italian. EP and Uberti corresponded throughout the 1930s.

12 EP wants Yale to produce a cumulative edition of his work on economics (see letters 26, 27, 29, 30, and 34).

13 EP's *Social Credit: An Impact* and *J/M*.

14 Cutting, Bronson Murray (1888–1935). Republican senator (New Mexico, 1927–28, 1929–35) and wealthy newspaper owner, Cutting was part of a progressive bloc in

Wm/ Borah,[15]   all U. S. Senate, Washington D. C.

Huey Long[16]

Hon.   T.A.Goldsborough.[17]   House of Representatives.

Hon/ G.H.Tinckham[18]   Washington D.C.

New Democrasy/[19] 55 Fifth Ave.Noo York

Paul   de Kruif,[20] Wake Robin, rural route 8

        Holland . Michigan U.S.A.

the US Senate towards which EP gravitated. Cutting and EP corresponded exten-
sively during the mid-1930s (see *Ezra Pound and Senator Bronson Cutting: A Political
Correspondence*), and EP published seventeen articles in Cutting's newspaper, the
Sante Fe New Mexican.

15 Borah, William Edgar (1865–1940). Republican senator (Idaho, 1907–40) and unsuc-
cessful candidate for the Republican presidential nomination in 1936. See *The
Correspondence of Ezra Pound and Senator William Borah*, ed. Sarah C. Holmes
(2001).

16 Long, Huey Pierce. Governor of Louisiana (1928–32) and later Democratic senator
(1932–35), Long was a radical populist known as "the Kingfish."

17 Goldsborough, Thomas Alan (1877–1951). Democratic Congressman (Maryland,
1921–39) with whom EP corresponded in 1934–35. EP praised Goldsborough in
his "American Notes" in the *NEW* (2 May 1935). In the House of Representatives,
Goldsborough introduced a Social Credit Bill proposing the National Dividend.

18 Tinkham, George Holden (1870–1956). Republican representative (Massachusetts,
1915–43). Tinkham and EP corresponded during the 1930s and finally met during
EP's visit to the United States in 1939. See *"Dear Uncle George": The Correspondence
between Ezra Pound and Congressman Tinkham of Massachusetts*, ed. Philip J. Burns.

19 *New Democracy*, Social Credit journal based in New York.

20 De Kruif, Paul Henry (1890–1971). Microbiologist and popular author with whom EP
corresponded between 1933 and 1940. De Kruif was well known for published work on
medicine such as *Microbe Hunters* (1926). EP converted him to Social Credit, and de
Kruif acknowledged his indebtedness in the introduction to *Why Keep Them Alive?*
(1936).

J.Crate Larkin[21] 680 Seneca St. Buffalo N/ Y/ U.S.A.

Hon. Sec. H. Wallace.[22] Dept. Agriculture. Washington D.C.

Senator/ J.P.Pope/[23] Senate/

Representative/ S.B.Pettengill[24]

Miss Ethel De C. Duncan,[25] 52 Ave de la Motte Picquet.

　　Paris vii. France.

(thats for Action Francaise/[26] will send justification and names of
papers wherewith these blokes connect , if you insist. otherwise, [I]
certify that they are for legit/ publicity.

21 Larkin, James Crate (1878–1947). American businessman and monetary reformer who
　　published *From Debt to Prosperity*, which discussed Social Credit, through the New
　　Economics Group of New York in 1934. Larkin corresponded with EP in the mid-1930s.
22 Wallace, Henry Agard (1888–1965). Agriculturalist and businessman who served as
　　President Roosevelt's secretary of agriculture (1933–40), his vice-president (1941–45),
　　and his secretary of commerce (1945–46). Wallace and EP corresponded in the late
　　1930s.
23 Pope, James Pinckney (1884–1966). Democratic senator (Idaho, 1933–39) with whom EP
　　corresponded in the mid-1930s. EP objected to Pope's proposal to authorize US entry
　　into the League of Nations.
24 Pettengill, Samuel Barrett (1886–1974). Democratic representative (Indiana, 1931–39)
　　who co-sponsored a bill in 1933 to enable the United States Treasury to issue stamped
　　money. Stamp scrip, to remain valid currency, must be stamped at intervals.
25 Duncan, Ethel M. (dates unknown). Author of *Democracy's Children* (1945) on
　　multicultural education and *Handy Memos* (1940), a collection of aphorisms. EP
　　corresponded with her.
26 *Action Française* (Paris, 1908–44). Newspaper and organ for the influential French
　　right-wing, anti-republican group of the same name.

Jeff/ Muus/ to Gino Saviotti.[27] sestiere Cerisola, Rapallo.

S/E/Galeazzo Ciano/[28] Ministero Stampa , Rome.

send me ten copies, on my account. here.

might also send me packet of Impact , to put on sale here in shop. (shop fairly dumb about importing books , but will pay me in small change.

Alf's Jew/boy/lee pubctn/[29] looks O/K/ I didnt xxxpek to be so protuberant on the cover.

dare say he better not purrzent it to Jarge[30]

shd/ like that shit Kipling[31] to get one/ also try it on the fahrt G/B/Shaw[32]

Impact not yet recd/[33]

---

27 Saviotti, Gino (1891–1980). Italian writer and editor for the journal *L'Indice* (Genoa), for which EP wrote several articles in the early 1930s.
28 Ciano, Galeazzo (1903–1944). Minister of propaganda (1935) and minister of foreign affairs (1936–43), Ciano was also Mussolini's son-in-law.
29 EP's "Jew/boy/lee" refers to the 1935 Jubilee celebration of the reign (1910–36) of George V. Pound's antisemitism clearly informs this witticism. The publication of *Alfred Venison's Poems* was held up because the printers were dealing with a backlog of material (see also letters 27 and 29). EP's "protuberance" on the cover likely refers to the quotation ("Only Social Credit could have produced this poet") attributed to E. POUND, which appears under the title.
30 King George V (1865–1936).
31 Kipling, Rudyard (1865–1936). British author. Along with George Bernard Shaw, Kipling opposed Britain's sanctions against Italy following the invasion of Abyssinia.
32 Shaw, George Bernard.
33 See letters 32 and 34.

//

You might drop line to Wilkie N/[34]

Wilkie N/ Collins, Chinese Legation, London

announcing Ideogramic series/[35] esp/ Ta Hio and Fenollosa/[36]
and ask him if he has any suggestions re/ some chink who wd/
collaborate with me in my nobl (etc/) work of interjuicing Chinese
kulchuh/ honour and glory of celestial empire etc.

better from you than from h me/

tell him to PUT it into ceremonial language when communicating
to Ambassador/ also not Confucian revival in JAPAN, and ask what
China is doing re/ he greatest sage.

valuable connection/ hadnt heard from Col/[37] for years. yr/ letter will
be better than a reply to him from me.

---

34 Collins, Wilkie N. This is not Wilkie Collins, author of the *Moonstone*. The identity of
    this Collins remains unclear.
35 Collins's position at the Chinese Legation, or Embassy, would certainly make him
    amenable to the Ideogrammic series, particularly to EP's two numbers (see letters 33
    and 38).
36 EP's translation of Confucius's *Ta Hio* and Fenollosa's C W C.
37 Perhaps Wilkie N. Collins (see note 34).

[LETTER 32, TLS, CARBON, EP TO SN]

24 April [pencil: "35"]

Dear Stan

     Oversights.[1]

All econ/ pubctns/[2] shd/ go to

Hugo Fack,[3]   309 Madison St. San Antonio, Texas , U. S. A.

and to

E/S/Woodward,[4] fo / Wrigley Printing Co.
       578 Seymour St. Vancouver B/C/

(I recon it means Before Christ as well as Brit. Col.)

the Jeff/ Muss[5] (~~HHHHHHHHH~~ to

~~Donna~~   Gentildonna Margherita Sarfatti[6]

     18 via dei Villini. Roma, Italy

1 EP is emending the list of names given in Letter 31. See also Letter 34.
2 See Letter 31.
3 Fack, Hugo R. Pound corresponded with Fack about uniting Gesellite and Social Credit theory. Fack was an antisemite and supporter of Hitler.
4 Woodward, Eugene Sydney (1880–1970). Canadian monetary reformer and author. Woodward's *Canada Reconstructed* (1933) dealt with economic policy and money in Canada. Woodward's "The Neocratic Manifesto" was printed as an appendix to Fack's translation of Gesell's *The Challenge of Economic Freedom* (1936).
5 EP's *J/M*.
6 Sarfatti, Margherita (1880–1961). Italian journalist, art critic, and socialite who became Mussolini's mistress in 1911. Sarfatti played a prominent role in the rise of fascism in Italy but, because she was Jewish, was discarded as Mussolini's companion when Mussolini turned towards antisemitism.

FRIDAY Mornin [Italic type]

IMPACT[7] *just arruve, and aint that one Jheezus' own bloody fine pamphlet!*

Please sen me another ten/ on account. and I think send rev/[8] *or publicity copies, at any rate send 'em TO*

Robert Hield,[9] *Morning Post 15 Tudor St London E.C.*

Her Excellency, Mrs Franklin D.Roosevelt,[10] *White House, Washington D.C.*

eunited shirts

Ufficio Stampa del Capo del Governo, Roma

In fact that better be IN an enclosed envelope address to

H. E. Benito[11] *Mussolini, Capo del Governo*
S.M.

and the outer envelope to

S. E. Il Conte Galeazzo Ciano
sotto segretario per Stampa e Propaganda.
ROMA

one henvellup hinside the other.[12]

---

7 .EP's *Social Credit: An Impact.*
8 Copies requested "on account" are billed to EP while "rev/" (review) and publicity costs are absorbed by Nott. See letters 31 and 34.
9 Hield, Robert (dates unknown). Assistant editor of the *Morning Post.* On EP's *Morning Post* letters, see Letter 8, notes 12 and 13.
10 Roosevelt, Anna Eleanor (1884–1962). Wife to US president Franklin Delano Roosevelt.
11 Mussolini, Benito.
12 "One envelope inside the other." By diverting Mussolini's copy to Galeazzo Ciano (Letter 31, note 28), EP is likely taking a precautionary measure to ensure it arrives.

what about spending   6 pence[13] on Monty Norman[14] , Home address ?

Oh yesx, can you lend the clich+ of the Wisconsin money to   G. K's
weekly ?[15]

Both Fack and E. S.Woordward are for united action[16]

with the National s/c/ organization in the U.S. , long intelligent an
cordial letters during last few days.[17]

I suppose it ought to go to G.D.H.Cole[18]   and Jeff Mark[19]

and certainly to

Arnold Gingrich,[20] ESQUIRE   919 N. Michigan Ave. Chicago   U.S.A.

and John Hargrave,[21] Wayside , King's Langley , Herts

13   The price of each pamphlet was 6d. (six pence), though EP might also be referring to
      the cost of postage.
14   Norman, Sir Montague Collet (1871–1950). Governor of the Bank of England (1920–44)
      and a central target for EP's criticism of the banking system.
15   *G.K.'s Weekly* (1925–37) was run by Gilbert Keith Chesterton until his death in 1936,
      when the magazine merged with the *Weekly Review* (1938–47). The magazine supported
      Chesterson, Hilaire Belloc, and other followers of Distributism, and it grew increas-
      ingly right-wing in political viewpoint in the 1930s. It is not clear from the context why
      the block is to be lent to the journal, though EP published four pieces there between
      1934 and 1935, the last of which, "A Child's Guide to Economics" (30 May 1935), may be
      the reason for this request.
16   Hugo Fack and E.S. Woodward were both Gesellites and involved in Social Credit
      movements in the United States and Canada, respectively. See notes 3 and 4.
17   EP likely refers to the National Social Credit Association, founded by James Larkin.
18   Cole, George Douglas Howard. British writer, political theorist, and economist.
19   Mark, Jeffrey. British writer on economics and history.
20   Gingrich, Arnold (1903–76). Editor (1933–61) and co-founder with David Smart of
      the Chicago-based *Esquire* magazine (1933–78), in which EP published a number of
      articles on economic reform.
21   Hargrave, John Gordon.

Rev/ copy/ Impact to B.Calvert
    "The Open Road "[22]
       Piegon roo~~st~~ in the~~xx~~oods   woods

     Mountain View/ N/ J/   U.S.A.

also on my acc/

Hon. C.I.White ,[23] *House of Representatives/ Washington .D.C. Usa*

Hon. D.W.Clark[24]   *ditto*
Hon. Merlin Hull[25]   *ditto*
    Senator
Hon. R.M La Follette[26]   */ U.S.Senate*
    Senator
Hon. F.Ryan Duffy,[27] *idem*

              [AS, EP] *EP*

22 Calvert, Bruce T. (1866–1940). Editor of the *Open Road*, a New Jersey-based periodical, and author of *Thirty Years on the Open Road* (Greenberg, 1941). "Piegon roo(st?) in the … woods" remains unclear.
23 White, Compton Ignatius (1877–1956). Democratic representative (Idaho, 1933–47, 1949–51).
24 Clark, David Worth (1902–55). Democratic representative (Idaho, 1935–39) and senator (Idaho, 1939–45).
25 Hull, Merlin (1870–1953). Republican representative (Wisconsin, 1929–31). Hull was again elected as a Progressive and as a Republican to Congress (1935–53).
26 La Follette, Robert Marion, Jr (1895–1953). Senator (Wisconsin, 1925–47). Elected as a Republican and a Progressive.
27 Duffy, Francis Ryan (1888–1979). Democratic senator (Wisconsin, 1933–39).

[LETTER 33, TLS, SN TO EP]
[STANDARD NOTT LETTERHEAD]

April
Twenty-fifth
1935

Dear Ezra:

Your two letters[1] of April 23rd. From your point of view it would be better to get Faber's to let you do a 12/6d book for them. Much better than taking sheets of an American edition. Faber's might induce Yale to take sheets.

If you can persuade Yale to let you do a book we ourselves could take sheets, but it wouldn't be so satisfactory for you.[2]

It may be hell to be poor[3] but its heller to be ahead of the times.

We are glad of the list of addresses[4] and will send copies to all of them. I will also write to Wilkie Collins.[5]

I think we can now go ahead with the ideogramic[6] series. Will you send me your latest words on the subject?

I have had some trouble with the printers over one or two passages in Jeff/Muss.[7] Libel actions have been so plentiful recently that they have got the wind up and object to passages on galleys 9, 17 and 30. I showed them to Mairet who agreed that the printers were right.

1 Letters 30 and 31.
2 On EP's proposed volume on economics, see letters 26, 27, 30, and 34.
3 Nott is responding to EP's comment in Letter 30.
4 EP provides names and addresses to which to send complimentary copies in letters 31 and 32 (see also letters 34–7).
5 Nott is responding to EP's request that he write to Wilkie N. Collins (see letters 31 and 38).
6 EP replies in Letter 34. See his blurb on the series in Letter 37.
7 EP's J/M. Letter 34A contains EP's emendations to the passages mentioned here, for which Letter 34 offers clarification.

Butchart[8] is very keen on the MS, Mairet not quite so keen.

I am enclosing Mairet's letter.[9] If you would re-write these three passages we could go ahead with the page proofs.

Yours ever,
Stanley Nott [A S]

SN/KM

8 In Letter 28, Nott indicates that EP has authorized Butchart as a reader of the manuscripts.
9 Mairet's letter is not included in the correspondence.

[Italics in original typescript]   [pencil: "April? 35"][1]

via Marasala 12/5

RAPALLO

Deer Stan/

LUVV yer enemies.[2]   *Zaharoff*[3] *was asked to leave the country, but I spose thass nothing. Insul*[4] *having been acquitted in in another box. however. I have deleted the offending return proofs sep/ cov/ registered.*[5]

Considering the black idiotic ignorance of Italy in England, I may even by editor Mairet be excused for not looking up the details of local english evils, that are brought in merely to illustrate a point and are not part of the subject matter or of the essential subject matter of the book.[6]

etc/ differences of op/ re/ sales[7] *are extreme, varying from purbrs / to people who think it will outsell anything I have ever done.   oh well, waste to worry about it now.*

1 Though undated, this is likely a response to Letter 33.
2 EP expresses frustration at having to revise three passages "on galleys 9, 17 and 30" (Letter 33) of the *J/M* manuscript. This and Letter 34A constitute EP's reply.
3 Zaharoff, Sir Basil (1849–1936). Born Basileios Zacharias, Zaharoff was a notorious arms dealer and financier who was said to fuel conflict in order to profit from both sides. Zaharoff appears in the *Cantos* as Sir Zenos Metevsky. The passage(s) EP deletes likely addressed Zaharoff, though no evidence of this remains.
4 Insull, Samuel. A utilities magnate (see Letter 34A).
5 EP discusses the proofs for *J/M* in detail in Letter 26, but here he refers to the "offending" passages Nott forwarded in Letter 33, which EP revises.
6 According to Nott in Letter 33, Mairet backed the printer's objection and was "not quite so keen" on the manuscript as a whole. The context here indicates that EP is responding to criticisms in Mairet's letter (not included in this correspondence).
7 EP refers to differences of opinion regarding the potential sales of *J/M*.

Of course M/ dont LIKE it.   What is present sale of N/E. W ?
and how fast is it rising   ? The best resistence was the little yid in
Detroit who had imbibed contrary opinion from American Mercury.[8]
Is there an Englishman with guts enough to disinfect
Northumberla land , or has it been done   ?   Bunting wd/ if asked   ,
I suppose.[9]

                              /// /
Waaal; naow fer progruss and konskructn/[10]
IDEOGRAMIC SERIES.
First item is the Ta Hio , which you have on hand.[11]

Eliot not sent in mss/   Cumings idem ?[12] *do we wait fer these blokes or*
go ahead with whats on hand/

CHINESE WRITTEN CHARACTER , I dont think you have the mss
of that, and I must do a new one page introd. connecting it with
orthology.[13]

8   EP is likely striking out at Mairet's criticism by questioning the circulation and influ-
    ence of the *NEW*. EP's antisemitic comment involving the *American Mercury* remains
    unclear.
9   Bunting, Basil. A Northumbrian poet.
10 "progress and construction." What follows is EP's clearest vision of the Ideogrammic
    series to date.
11 EP's translation of Confucius's *Ta Hio*.
12 Precisely what material T.S. Eliot and E.E. Cummings were to submit to the
    Ideogrammic series remains unknown. On Eliot's "promised" contribution to the
    Pamphlets on the New Economics series, see letters 7, 11, 13, 18, and 20; on Eliot's con-
    tribution to the Ideogrammic series, see letters 10, 18, 20, and 24.
13 See Letter 10, notes 9–12, on EP's interest in orthology.

The Cocteau[14] you have ?   Mystere Laic HH

I must write to him about it as soon as , but not before , I am
sure it is be done.

Bill Williams[15] says some aGent is on way to London. We will have
to CHOOSE something of Bills, we cant just take the most unsellable
chunk of his profundity.

        //
About the Make it New ECON/[16]

Do you want to Tell Yale you cd/ take sheets/ ?

or do you care to print it and sell them sheets , if

Faber will cede the rights to ABC econ/[17]   seems hugue job
for what I spoose to be yr/ resources, and Yale are tight fisted re/
sheets.

You might discuss it by phone with F. V. Morley[18] of Fabers . They
pretty much hate my doing econ/ but still if you showed you
wanted to , they might git contrary and go ahead.

All this is most UNbusiness like on our parts. Prob/ the most
efficient action wd be an enquiry from you to Yale as to what they
wd/ let you have sheets for IF they do an E/P/ big vol all his econ/
stuff.

That wd/ be ABC
        Jeff/M

---

14 Cocteau, Jean. The work is *Le Mystère Laïc* (1928).

15 Williams, William Carlos. EP specifies they should choose something that fits the
    series. See Letter 40 on Williams's agent, Mavis MacIntosh.

16 EP proposes a volume on economics to Yale University Press, but the project never
    comes to fruition. See letters 26 and 30.

17 EP's *ABC of Economics*.

18 Morley, Frank Vigor (1899–1980). A founding director of Faber and Faber, Morley com-
    missioned EP to prepare an anthology of contemporary poetry, published as *Active
    Anthology* in 1933.

Impact/

  *Orage from Criterion , and divers essays and notes , plus
the new currency book. that shd/ work out about size of ABC.*[19]

I spose I'll   have to wait ten years...   but the pore bdy pubk[20] *wd/
EAT sooner   if I cd/ crash thru NOW .*

   //
re addresses , I keep fergittin 'em. please send rev/ cops[21]
  of me , and I shd. think it worth while other stuff to

H.R.L.Cohrssen[22] *, 313   East 17 th St. New York.*

   (Fisher's assistant)
an damnit   there was another very important/ I cant remember.

I like appearance of Vensison and Impact/ but if Ideo/ is s to

  *sell at shilling/ I spose the cheapest difference wd/ be a stiff cover like
present Ta Hio , with paper folded over.*[23]   *Anyhow, thats yr/ dept.   I
havent any suggestion save that same amt/ ofc printed matter at
twice the price , must have some difference in appearnce to elude
the pubk/*

19 The proposed volume on economics would include EP's *ABC of Economics* (1933), *J/M*,
    Social Credit: An Impact, and "In the Wounds (Memoriam A.R. Orage)" from the
    Criterion (Letter 26). EP also mentions "diverse essays and notes" and "the new cur-
    rency book," his *What Is Money For?* (1939).
20 "poor bloody public." On this topic, see also Letter 30.
21 EP requests another set of review copies of his works along with "other stuff" (likely
    the other issues in the Pamphlets on the New Economics series) to H.R.L. Cohrssen
    (see note 22; see also letters 31 and 32).
22 Cohrssen, Hans R.L. (1905–97). German economic commentator closely associated
    with the American economist and Gesellite Irving Fisher, collaborating with him
    during the 1930s and early 1940s. Cohrssen assisted Fisher on *Stamp Scrip* (1933),
    which EP reviewed in the *NEW* (26 October 1933), and *Stable Money: A History of the
    Movement* (1934).
23 *Alfred Venison's Poems* and *Social Credit: An Impact* both had paper covers, consistent
    in design with the rest of the issues in the Pamphlets on the New Economics series. As
    Gallup reports, *Ta Hio*, in contrast, was bound in paper boards and cost 2s.

Odyssey[24]

Rouse[25] *better be pub/ entire not in pamph. I think.*
  for your sake

Series as now projected.[26]
  TA HIO

CUMMINGS   az as soon as stuff ariives

CHINESE WRITTEN CHARACTER

ELIOT   if he ever rises again from the grave

COCTEAU

WILLIAMS 2   if suitable

ROUSE has found a pre Elizabethan trans/ of ~~*Iliad*~~ *ILIAD*
              I think we shd/ do either a book of it
              or selections, with one page introd by Rouse.[27]
it is in Golding's[28] *metre. evidently no author's name on it.*

*You can announce that we are " projecting " or in communication with
the above authors/*
  or you can wait till I write to Cocteau/ but AS ~~*the*~~ *Pagany*[29] *never
paid HIM and sent me a rubber chq/ I dont want to bother him*

24 W.H.D. Rouse translated Homer's epic as *The Odyssey: The Story of Odysseus* (1937). See
    letters 18 and 25.
25 EP suggests that Rouse's edition of the *Odyssey* will be better published as a complete
    volume than abridged in the pamphlet series. See also Letter 41.
26 On projections for the series, see also letters 18 and 24.
27 EP suggests a pre-Elizabethan translation of the *Iliad* as a pamphlet, with an introduc-
    tion by Rouse.
28 Golding, Arthur (1536–1606). British poet and translator.
29 *Pagany*. A quarterly edited by Richard Johns.

till I know we are going to do it on receipt of permission.[30]   That
I take it ? depends on whether   A.   he comes into the first   three or
B.   whether the pubk/ rises to   the   first 3.

If we aint libeled on Alf/ and IMPACT , I shd/ think we
  are safe...

Why   not git Hargrave[31] for the Econ/ pamphs/   he writes better
than the highbrows   ANY how, and W ANYwhere.

  Rouse shd/ let you have the Odyssey/   as I put him up to   doing it.[32]
  At any rate I am writing him   re/   that, as you asked.

---

30 Unclear what is meant by "receipt of permission," but Pound tries to ensure that
    Cocteau will be paid.
31 Hargrave, John Gordon.
32 EP assisted Rouse with his translations of portions of the *Odyssey*, which were later
    printed in the *NEW*.

[LETTER 34A, TYPESCRIPT, EP TO SN]
[Italics in original typescript]

[pencil: "Nott re: SC: Impact?"]

Galley 9 read[1]

Hatrys ,[2] *Kreugers*[3] *and and other unconviceted financiers whose tropisms conform*[4]   .

galley 17

Some of the follies and cruelties of great English owners wd/ not now be permitted in Italy. Certain kinds of domestic enemies would be shipped to the coni f confino[5]

---

1 Nott mentions three offending passages "on galleys 9, 17 and 30" in Letter 33 that caused a problem with printers working on *J/M*. These appear to be EP's emendations.

2 Hatry, Clarence Charles (1888–1965). British businessman sentenced to prison in 1930 for issuing false securities to finance his companies. Hatry is considered a major contributor to the stock market crash in 1929.

3 Kreuger, Ivar (1880–1932). Swedish financier and industrialist known as the "Match King" because of his monopoly on matches (Kreuger's companies would give loans to European governments, thereby guaranteeing his monopoly). Kreuger forged bonds in a vain attempt to protect his failing investments in the early 1930s.

4 The sentence as it appears in *J/M* reads: "It is probable that a reader in 2133 looking over the record of nineteenth-century villainy will feel a revulsion from 'irresponsibility,' growing more acute as he comes down into the debauch of Hatrys, Kreugers and other unconvicted financiers whose tropisms conform" (38). EP recalls the two figures again a little later: "Not only do frontiers need watching but man in a mechanical age, you me'n'the'other fellow, need help against Kreugers and Hatrys" (45).

5 The paragraph as it appears in *J/M* reads: "Get it into your head that Italy was, even in 1900, immeasurably ahead of England in so far as land laws and the rights of the man who works on the soil are concerned. Some of the follies and cruelties of great British owners would not now be permitted in Italy. Certain kinds of domestic enemy would be shipped to the *confino*" (70).

galley 30

     merely omit any more than Insuls[6] etc.

letter sep/cov/

---

6 Insull, Samuel (1859–1938). Anglo-American utilities magnate. Insull's empire collapsed in 1932 when he was indicted on securities fraud. No evidence of this passage remains in *J/M*, and, thus, this is likely an instruction to "omit." See Letter 34, in which EP indicates "I have deleted the of fending return proofs sep/ cov/ registered."

[LETTER 35, TL, CARBON, EP TO SN]
[Italics in original typescript]

[AN, EP] 28 AP [pencil: "35"]

Dear Stan:

               smallest
    Wots the number of pamphlets that can be regarded as
" greater *quantity* " ?
        TO the orther ?[1]

I keep remembering names/[2]

ON MY ACCOUNT , postal charges , hole/sale rates etc.[3] *please send
impact*[4] *to*

Lady Cunard[5]   (*look up address , it was C avendish Sq.*
         and I think she now calls herself
      Emerald Lady Cunard   (*tho her mama*
                       christened her Maud)
Lady Ottoline Morrel[6]   (*also consult phone book.*)

and to
Th
Princess Jane di San Faustino[7]
      via Maria Adelaida   8
           Rome, Italy
(*must try to get the ideas into XXXalted circles, and under political
noses*)

1 "author." EP is likely replying to a letter missing from the correspondence.
2 In Letter 34, EP keeps forgetting addresses.
3 Review and publicity copies requested by EP "on my account" (see letters 31–4, 36).
4 EP's *Social Credit: An Impact.*
5 Cunard, Lady Maud Emerald (1872–1948). London literary hostess and mother of
   Nancy Cunard.
6 Morrell, Lady Ottoline (1873–1938). Patron of arts often closely associated with
   Bloomsbury.
7 Campbell, Jane Allen (1865–1938). When she married Don Carlo Bourbon del Monte,
   the Prince di San Faustino, in 1897, Jane became Princess di San Faustino.

/
rev/ cops/ shd ALSO go to
Poetry,[8] *232 East Erie St. Chicago*

and I shd/ say the following wd/count as rev/cops[9]

Jeffry Mark[10]
　　　　5 Cadogan Rd/ Surbiton Surrey
　McNair Wilson[11]
　　　　40 a Frognal Lane , N/W/3

　　?? Belloc[12]
　　　Rebecca West[13]

?? Violet Hunt,[14] *South Lodge , Campden Hill. W.8*
　　　　　　(send it anyhow, and chg/ it to me, if you
wish)
　　　　it means TALK if not a review.
　　　send her ALF.[15] *also. don send him to the others on this list/*
I am picking the mentalities suited to WHICH and what.

I dare say God Dam Hell COLE[16] *ought to get" Impact".*

does Colburne[17] *get all the pamphs ?*

8　*Poetry: A Magazine of Verse* (Chicago, 1912–). Founded by Harriet Monroe in 1912, the magazine became a crucial venue for modern poetry. EP served as foreign correspondent and advisor from 1912 to 1921.
9　"review copies." See Letter 31.
10　Mark, Jeffrey.
11　Wilson, Robert McNair.
12　Belloc, Hilaire (1870–1953). Prolific writer on topics such as history, politics, economics, and religion. With G.K. Chesterton, Belloc is responsible for the school of thought that became known as Distributism (see Essay 1). This theory was debated in the pages of the *New Age* with H.G. Wells and G.B. Shaw.
13　West, Rebecca (1892–1983). Anglo-Irish writer, journalist, and critic.
14　Hunt, Isabel Violet (1862–1942). British writer and suffragist.
15　EP's *Alfred Venison's Poems.*
16　Cole, George Douglas Howard.
17　Colbourne, Maurice Dale.

you might even send it to
C.Cockburn,[18] The Week, 34 Victoria St.   S.W.I.

   and to the peeled ONION[19] of Democratic Controll, same office
building.
   mebbe to the sekkertary of that semi=fake institution.

What about the Chandos[20] group ??

Will Reckett,[21] and Hammond,[22] and old F.J.Gould[23] see it, or ought it
to be sent to them ?

   Have you any leverage on MacDonald,[24] edtr/ of G/K's. I think he does
what he can. Old G/K/[25] himself is nearly as worse as Eliot[26]
about answering ANYthing.
                         ?? too old ?

18 Cockburn, Francis Claud (1904–81). British journalist and novelist known for his
    Stalinist-communist sympathies; a cousin of novelist Evelyn Waugh.
19 EP is poking fun at the Union for Democratic Control (UDC), a political organiza-
    tion formed in 1914 by Charles Trevelyan, Ramsay MacDonald, Normal Angell, and
    E.D. Morel to oppose the First World War. By 1915, the group was the leading anti-war
    organization in Britain. In the 1930s, the UDC took up the fight against fascism in
    Germany and Italy and supported Indian independence.
20 The Chandos Group.
21 Reckitt, Maurice Benington.
22 Hammond, Featherstone (dates unknown). Hammond authored the pamphlets
    Economics in the Middle Ages (1933) and *Financial Armageddon* (1936). EP wrote a
    letter to *G.K.'s Weekly* congratulating it on printing Hammond's articles on economics
    (C1088).
23 Gould, Frederick James (1855–1938). Founder of the Leicester Positivist Society and
    lecturer for the Moral Education League. According to Finlay, Gould's positivist phi-
    losophy found a bridge to Social Credit in A.R. Orage and the Chandos Group (183).
24 Identity of "MacDonald" remains unclear. According to EP, he was an editor at *G.K.'s
    Weekly* (Letter 32, note 15).
25 Chesterton, Gilbert Keith.
26 T.S. Eliot.

*I got a nidea fer cover of Ideogramic series/what about the
RENEW character/*[27] *not the four, but a bigger and better sample
of the verb, the fancy one at both ends of the block used in J/M/*[28]
or on the Faber M/I/N[29] *title page.*

       I will try to get it done better.

  *I had a "Rays" on the cover of the fist edtn. Cathay, and on
MacMillan Noh.*[30]

   But the RENEW , is what we want here.

   Rev/ cop/ IMPACT
Theodora Bosanquet,[31] *38 Cheyne Walk, S.W.3 , ought to do it for
Time and Tide.*

   ? Ernest Rhys,[32] *co/ Dent and Co., good heart , ought to be mobilized
for S/C*

*he wd/ be a reader for ALF. also, but dont send 'em both at same
time. He knows my EARLY work.*
better send him ALF/ now. and Ipact in a few weeks time.
                  Impact
rev/ copy IMPACT
to Bob Brown/[33] *commonwealth college , Mena. Arkansas. U.S.A.*

     (local paper fer kummynists)[34]

27 EP proposes the Chinese character "renew" for the cover, the same character used
in the "Kung" chapter of J/M. EP specifies using only the verb of the block, the two
characters at either end of the ideogram showing "the fascist axe for the clearing away
of rubbish" (J/M 113) and the two characters in the middle representing the "sun sign,
day," so that the ideogram reads, "renovate, day by day renew" (ibid.). See Letter 24.

28 EP's J/M.

29 EP's *Make It New.*

30 EP also mentions the character "rays" from the cover of the first edition of *Cathay*
(1915) and on the Macmillan publication of *Noh* (1916).

31 Bosanquet, Theodora (1880–1961). Secretary to Henry James (1907–16), Bosanquet
was a feminist who published *Henry James at Work* (1924) and *Paul Valery* (1933). She
served as literary editor (1935–53) at *Time and Tide.*

32 Rhys, Ernest (1859–1946). British poet and editor.

33 Brown, Bob. American-born writer and owner of Roving Eye Press.

34 Reference unclear.

authors copy[35] *of ALL MY stuff, as it appears to*

e:e CUMMINGS

> *4 Patchin Place*
> *New York U.S/A.*

    cummings poems just recd/[36] *I spose he has sent you a copy.*
only 70 pages.
        I leave it to you, seems to me waste to use
em in pamph/ series IF you can print 'em. or mebbe you can
import hundred sheets as they stand/ and use the re/feend ones
in pamph..
        any how; I leave it to you.
    mebbe 32 pages is all hengland will STAND   ??

35 Courtesy copies given by the publisher to the author for personal distribution and use.
36 On the possibility of Cummings's contributing to the series, see letters 24, 34, 36–38,
    40, and 41. The "poems just recd/" likely refers to Cummings's *No Thanks* (1935).

{YCAL MSS 43, SERIES I, BOX 37, FOLDER 1582}
[LETTER 36, TL, EP TO SN]
[Italics in original typescript]

> *3 May*
>> *XIII*   [pencil: "35"]

Dear Stan

> *vide enc/   re   cumminhs   prublum.*[1]

Sante Fe New Mexican[2] *, shd/ receive rev/ copy of IMPACT*

>> *and of all my stuff. prob. / of all yr*
>> *econ. pubctns.*

Not sure they aint promotin me to status of columnist or sumfink similar.

Those TYourapeein 1/4 ly boys[3] *ought to get next to* <u>*Books*</u>

<u>*Abroad/*</u>[4] *I have sent a copy to Selver/*[5] *they ought to innoculate*

it with ECON/ it is pubd/ University of Oklahoma. U.S.A.

1   EP has enclosed something regarding E.E. Cummings to which he directs Nott's attention, but the enclosure is missing from the correspondence. Generally, the "problem" is how to proceed with Cummings's work, but the specifics remain unclear. See also letters 35, 37, 38, 40.

2   *Santa Fe New Mexican* (Santa Fe, NM, 1898–1951). English and Spanish daily newspaper owned by Republican senator Bronson Cutting (Letter 31), with whom EP engaged in correspondence during the mid-1930s before Cutting's untimely death. EP contributed articles to the paper under "Ez Sez" in 1935.

3   The *European Quarterly* "boys" in question are the magazine's two editors, Edwin Muir and Janko Lavrin.

4   *Books Abroad* (1927–76). Quarterly magazine, based at the University of Oklahoma, that reviewed books and periodicals.

5   Selver, Percy Paul (1888–1970). Polish translator in the *European Quarterly* and author of *Orage and the New Age Circle* (1959). Selver's booklet of poems, *A Baker's Dozen of Tin Trumpets*, was published by Nott in 1936.

Can you get Dobrée[6] to liven up N/E/W/.[7]   He ought to be

made to help somehow.

[Line drawn to <u>Books Abroad</u>; remaining words AN, EP.]
Impact[8] & to

> *Costigan[9]*
> *Bone[10]*
> *Black[11]*
> *Weeler[12]*
> *Wagner[13]*
> *Lafollette[14]*

6   Dobrée, Bonamy (1891–1974). British academic and critic. Nott published *An Open Letter to a Professional Man* (1935) as no. 14 in the Pamphlets on New Economics series.

7   The *New English Weekly*.

8   EP's *Social Credit: An Impact*.

9   Costigan, Edward Prentiss (1874–1939). Democratic senator (Colorado, 1930–36).

10 Bone, Homer Truett (1883–1970). Democratic senator (Washington, 1933–44).

11 Black, Hugo LaFayette (1886–1971). Democratic senator (Alabama, 1927–37). EP supported his plan for a thirty-hour week in the *NEW* (9 May 1935).

12 Wheeler, Burton Kendall (1882–1975). Democratic senator (Montana, 1923–47) with whom EP corresponded in the late 1930s.

13 Wagner, Robert Ferdinand (1877–1953). Democratic senator (New York, 1927–49).

14 La Follette, Jr, Robert Marion (see Letter 32, note 26).

[LETTER 37, TL, CARBON EP TO SN]
[Italics in original typescript]

[pencil: "May? 35"]

Dear Stan

Herewith blurb or announcement for Ideog/[1] *series.*
G not T is the terminal of that abbreviation. in contrast to
IdeOGDONic.[2]

3 *copies*

POlease send Impact[3] *, my account to*

HARVE POUND[4] *567 , 18 avenue*
Longview
Washington. U.S.A.

Dad says Harve is the only other man who will know what the
D/ on the frontispiece means ,[5] *" an how he did hate him "*

Dush Delano, cashier (see under uncl/ Albert's signature)

Drummond[6] *seems to think cummings will have to be used in*
pamph/
if so , I cd/ do half page introd.

1 The Ideogrammic series.
2 EP distinguishes between "ideog" and "IdeOGDONic" to emphasize how the series is distinct from C.K. Ogden's work (see letters 10–14, 18).
3 EP's *Social Credit: An Impact* (see also Letter 32).
4 Pound, Harve, relative of EP (Terrell 722).
5 EP is referring to the "Chippewa Falls" Wisconsin Lumber Money block that appears as the frontispiece to *Social Credit: An Impact* (see letters 2, 5, 6, 32, and 107).
6 Drummond, John. British friend of EP who lived in Rapallo in the 1930s. Surette (*Purgatory* 246) suggests that Drummond influenced EP's increasing antisemitism (see essays 1 and 2; Appendix 1).

anyhow, I wrote all that yester.[7]   *it ZUPP   to   you.*

Review copy   Impact ^ *3 copies to*
P
Sir   Montagu   Webb,[8] *" Better   Money " , Daily   Gazette Building*
                        KARACHI , India

   He has just printed   a   good   col/ of mine in hiz   wyper.

[New page – pencil, AN: "see letter May? 1935 to Nott"]

IDEOGRAMIC SERIES

This   series   is   not   run   in   opposition   to   C.K.Ogden . It   is   not   a comment   on   his   Psyche   series[9] *, but   it   is   definitely   offered   in CONTRAST. A   ni number   of   the   pamphlets   are   basic   in   a   sense older   than   the   special   one   associated   with   Ogden's   simplified vocabulary . If   the   intellectu li   lively   reader   use   one   set Ogden's   tool   as   lever   he   may   here   find   a   useable   fulcrum.   The whols   whole series   is   for* ^ *drives toward ORTHOLOGY*[10]

7 EP is likely referring to Letter 36 ("enc/ re cumminhs prublum") – which would place this letter on or around 4 May 1935 – but the letter could be missing from the correspondence.
8 Webb, Sir Montagu de Pomeroy (1869–1938). British businessman, publisher, and chairman of the Daily Gazette Press (Karachi, India). Webb published the periodical *Better Money* and wrote several works on economic conditions and money in India (e.g., *India's Plight* [1934]).
9 See letters 10 and 18.
10 "Orthology": branch of grammar that deals with correct or traditional uses of language (see Letter 10, note 12).

Ezra Pound   Esq   May
Rapallo   Fourth
                                                        1935

Dear Ezra:

    I have heard from Wilkie Collins[1] who has promised to search for a collaborator.

    Did I tell you that I had heard from Yale? I have wtitten [sic] to them again . I will get in touch with Faber's next week.[2]

    The sale of the N.E.W. is just what it was two years ago, 2000 copies per week.[3] When I was working with Orage I tried ~~tried~~ every possible means to push the sales. Since I left them I have tried all the same means but I don't think it's made a difference of half a dozen copies.

    I have had Cummings book[4] and have written about taking 100 sheets. Frankly I don't understand these typographical curiosities. Perhaps you can tell me what he is after. However the book is amusing, particularly one or two of the poems. Ruth Pitter[5] has it at the moment.

---

1 Wilkie N. Collins, of the Chinese Legation in London.
2 For discussion of Yale University Press and Faber and Faber regarding an edition of EP's writing on economics, see letters 26, 27, 29, 30, 31, 33, and 34.
3 EP inquires about the recent performance of the *NEW* in Letter 34.
4 EP notes receiving Cummings's book in Letter 35. It remains unclear exactly which book they are discussing, though it might be *No Thanks* (1935).
5 Pitter, Ruth (1897–1992). British poet. She contributed regularly to the *NEW*.

I have a new manager[6] coming in next week who will also be the town traveller. I will discuss the "Ta Hio" series[7] with him and write to you again next week.

Yours sincerely

SCN [A S]

SN/KM[8]

---

6 Identity of "new manager" remains unclear; Kenneth Gee is still with the firm as of Letter 93.
7 Nott is referring to the Ideogrammic series.
8 Stanley Nott and K. Magee, Nott's secretary.

[LETTER 39, APCS, SN TO EP]
[NOTT POSTCARD LETTERHEAD]

May 11 [pencil: ["1935"]]

I've <u>never</u> seen a copy of Attack;[1] they've never sent us a copy. I'll write to Hargraves[2] & send him review copies.

N.E.W.[3] is going to do an article on the pamphlets. They will always advertise if we <u>pay</u> them. We are very friendly--whatever that may mean.

I suppose you've seen T & T ?[4]

> *Yrs.*
> *SCN*

---

1 *Attack!* (dates unknown). Periodical for John Hargrave's Green Shirts, later the Social Credit Party of Great Britain.
2 Hargrave, John Gordon.
3 The *New English Weekly.*
4 Nott refers to the current issue of *Time and Tide,* which published EP's vituperative "Letter to Sir Norman Angell" (see Letter 42).

[LETTER 40, TLS, SN TO EP]
[STANDARD NOTT LETTERHEAD]

Ezra Pound Esq   May
Rapallo   Thirteenth
Italy   1935

Dear Ezra:

G.K's have the block of the lumber note.[1]   I spoke to McDonald[2] about it and he seemed to be pleased to have it.

Pamphlets have been sent to all the addresses you have given us so far.[3] We will charge you 3d each for all pamphlets that you buy from us.

Ideogram^*mic*[4]

I should like the first three to be:
   1. Ta Hio
   2. Either Eliot or Rouse
   2. [sic] Chinese Written Characters

Let's start with those three. My idea is to have each booklet in a different fount of type. Price to be [ASC] *about* 1/- . They will be quite different from the pamphlet series. In fact they are in a quite different category. [ASC] *We can't fix price until* [illegibile word] *we have cost worked out.*[5]

I think the "Renew" idea is a very good one . Let us have it as a sort of imprint for the series. We will get a speciman [sic] page done and send it to you.[6]

---

1 In Letter 32, EP requests the block of the Chippewa Lumber note be sent to *G.K.'s Weekly*, presumably as an illustration. See letters 2, 5, 6, 32, and 37.
2 McDonald, an editor at *G.K.'s Weekly*, appears as "MacDonald" in Letter 35.
3 For this thread, see letters 31, 32, and 34–7. EP will be charged half the list price for each pamphlet.
4 Nott alters slightly the order EP suggests in Letter 34: *Ta Hio*, T.S. Eliot, W.H.D. Rouse, and *CWC*. Nott adds more below.
5 The issues of the Pamphlets on the New Economics series sold for 6d. The Ideogrammic booklets are proposed here for twice that price – one shilling or more, depending on cost. See letters 17, 18, 20, and 34.
6 The imprint (or colophon) registers those responsible for the production of a text. Nott's suggestion modifies EP's notion in Letter 35 to have it on the cover of each number.

Enclosed is a letter from Yale. Please return it.[7]

We must try to keep the series down to 64 pages, this makes it so much cheaper to print. [ASC] *Though we might go 96 in some cases.*[8]

I have written to America saying that we would consider taking some sheets of Cumming's [sic] poems but I think it would be much better to include them in the series, so I will cancel the letter.[9]

Yours sincerely

Stanley Nott [AS]

[remainder of letter ASC]

Cummings poems for No 4
W C.W   No 5[10]

Since writing I have had an idea. The series should be typographically interesting as well as intellectually. <u>Each booklet will be done in a different face of type.</u> We want to make them a well-printed series.

I've just received from Mavis Mackintosh,[11] *W.C.W's lit agent 4 MSS. I suggest Spring & All, as being the shortest, & most suitable in length.*[12]

---

7 The letter from Yale is not included in the correspondence (see letters 41–3).
8 See Letter 35. Nott wishes to limit items in the series to 32 or 64 pages. *Ta Hio* is 32 pages and *Chinese Written Character* is 52 pages.
9 Presumably, Nott is writing to Cummings's publisher in America (which would be Golden Eagle Press in the case of *No Thanks*). See letters 38 and 41.
10 According to Gallup, William Carlos Williams's *In the American Grain* was to appear as no. 3 in the Ideogrammic series. See Letter 18.
11 MacIntosh, Mavis (dates unknown). Williams's literary agent.
12 It remains unknown what four manuscripts Nott perused aside from *Spring and All* (1923). Williams's *Collected Poems 1921–1931* (1934), *An Early Martyr and Other Poems* (1935), *Adam and Eve and the City* (1936), and *The Complete Collected Poems of William Carlos Williams, 1906–1938* (1938) were all being produced around this time.

[LETTER 41, TL, CARBON, EP TO SN]
[Italics in original typescript]

[pencil: "May? 35"][1]

Dear Stan

immaterial

The "enclosed letter from Yale"/[2] *evidently* ^ *mmaterial as no trace of it is tangible in yr/ last. Look round th orfice floor an mebbe you'll find the gross earthly substance.*

(In plain woids , yeh fergot to enclose it.)

How soon do you want text of Chinese Written Character

(singular not plural)[3]
also re/ blurbs/[4]
you have that for the series

Rouse[5] *? you mean the Elizabethan Iliad ?? not his present trans/ of Odyssey, which shd/ be published entire ???*

or not ?

Will Eliot DO[6] *anything for the series ? I mean withing the say three lifetimes , or that of the youngest inhabitant ? Better go on with the 100 cumming's sheets*[7] *in the interim ?*

---

1   This letter is undated but replies directly to Letter 40.
2   Nott fails to enclose the "letter from Yale" (Letter 40), which likely refers to EP's proposed volume on economics. Nott includes it in Letter 42.
3   Nott types the plural "Characters" in Letter 40, which EP corrects here.
4   EP provides the blurb for the Ideogrammic series in Letter 37.
5   In Letter 40, Nott proposes "Eliot or Rouse" for the second number in the series. In Letter 34, EP argues that W.H.D. Rouse's translation of the *Odyssey* should be printed separately, not as part of the series, suggesting instead the "pre Elizabethan trans/ of ILIAD" Rouse has uncovered.
6   On T.S. Eliot's involvement with the series, see letters 10, 11, 13, 14, 18, 20, 24, and 40.
7   Cummings, E.E. See also letters 38 and 40.

(waal, that up to you/ also the selection from Willyum the Walrusss C Williams.[8]

write yr/ own ticket, as to wot you think the barmy Britons will stand.

All right let the orther's choose their fonts/[9] I like Caslon/ I like

monotype whatever they call it, old style. There is good Plantin, but rare and hard to come by.[10]

Kumminkz[11] ought to be photostatted from the American edtn/ to save nervous collapses of English printers.

so ought the OLD Iliad.

However. Your printin' has allus been good. HHHHHHH so write yer own ticket. The booblik[12] loves uninformity.

But with the zumminks and the old Iliad, there couldn't be[13]

8 Williams, William Carlos.
9 See Letter 40, in which Nott suggests producing each booklet "in a different face of type," and Letter 42, for his negative response to EP's suggestion here.
10 Caslon, a typeface originally designed by William Caslon (1692–1766), is considered one of the most reliable typefaces. Plantin typeface, inspired by sixteenth-century Dutch printer Christophe Plantin, influenced Times Roman.
11 EP suggests that, in order to save British printers from dealing with Cummings's "typographical curiosities" (Letter 38), the text should be photostatted (slower and more expensive than photocopying because of its ability to replicate with high resolution) directly from the American edition. See letters 35–8.
12 "Your printing has always been good." EP is also punning on "uniformity" and "uninformed" here.
13 Remainder of letter cut off here.

[LETTER 42, TLS, SN TO EP]
[STANDARD NOTT LETTERHEAD]

May 17th 1935

Dear Ezra:

I had a talk with Morley[1] today, and I'm going to see Pollinger.[2] Morley is agreeable toanything [sic] which will help you and them.They have n made a good job of Make it New.[3]How different from the Yale edition! Why on earth didnt Yale take sheets and make a good looking book of it? What do you think of Time and Tide[4] publishing your letter? Angell[5] of course died years ago – if he ever lived.

I am enclosing the letter form [sic]Yale.[6] What exactly do you want them to do? I also am agreeable to anything that will help you.

Newsome and Mairet tell [sic] that your letter in answer to Chandos questionnaire[7] is a master-piece.

I'll send them J and m[8] when it is ready.

You can send text of Written Character[9] as soon as you like. Will you write to Eliot and ask him to do something? He will probably want to see what the series is like first.

1 Morley, Frank. A director of Faber and Faber.
2 Pollinger, Laurence Edward (1897–1976). EP's literary agent.
3 Faber and Faber published *Make It New* in 1934, while Yale published an offset American edition in 1935.
4 Dated "13 April anno XIII," EP's letter is printed in facsimile by *Time and Tide* (11 May 1935; C1191). Norman Angell (see note 5), who sent the letter to the paper, explains in an accompanying note how it is addressed to him at the Bank of England, which he claims never to have entered. The letter is a direct attack on Angell's character.
5 Angell, Sir Norman (1872–1967). British economist and writer who was knighted in 1931 and won the Nobel Prize for Peace in 1933.
6 See letters 40 and 41.
7 Newsome, Albert and Mairet, Philip. Editors at the *NEW*. The nature of the questionnaire and EP's response to it remain unclear, but it is clearly associated with the Chandos Group.
8 EP's *J/M*.
9 *CWC*.

It seems to me that Spring and All[10] should be published entire; but that would send up the cost a bit.   Let us produce three booklets[11] and then decide on the price.Perhaps we can average them out.

I dont think the authors should choose thier [sic] own type, except yourself.[12] We have a range of 12 types to work from with the printer who will do the series- all the accepted faces. The booklets will be uniform as to size and appearance.[13]

Yours ever
Stanley Nott [A S]

10 Williams, William Carlos. Williams's *Spring and All* (Letter 40) was originally published in 1923 and comprises 93 pages, much longer than Nott's preferred lengths of 32 or 64 pages.
11 Nott offers his first three selections for the Ideogrammic series in Letter 40.
12 Nott refers to his exchange with EP about typeface in letters 40 and 41.
13 With twelve different typefaces from which to choose, Nott suggests the booklets will vary while remaining uniform in size and appearance.

[LETTER 43, TL, CARBON, EP TO SN]
[Italics in original typescript]

[AN, EP, scrawl] 19 May
[pencil: "35"]

Dear Stan

What the Yale BUZZARDS <u>want</u> is 300 pages of Eliot or something innocuous with my NAME on it.

The questions is what can we make 'em take.

I am suggesting "Essays on Time in Action".[1]
The essentials being Jeff/Muss[2] , the Treatise on Harmony[3] (varying the rest of the Musical stuff. using things notv in the Antheil[4] Volume) Ta Hio.[5]

and whatever else is necessary to OIL the pill.

What they want is 300 pages/

There is new stuff. there are som Criterion Essays/[6]

---

1 EP originally proposed a "Make It New Economics" (Letter 26) volume with Yale but has altered the proposal to include his work on subjects other than economics. EP did publish *Polite Essays* (1937) with Faber and Faber, though the selection varies considerably from that given here.
2 EP's *J/M*.
3 Three Mountains Press published EP's *Antheil and the Treatise on Harmony* (1924).
4 Antheil, George (1900–59). American avant-garde composer.
5 EP's translation of Confucius's *Ta Hio*.
6 Essays from the *Criterion*.

There are N.E.W. items.[7]   Orthology/[8] Private Worlds.[9]

the Orage[10] cd/ be put over with the Housman ,[11] Monro;[12] Binyon.[13]

On the hole I think my 1930 writing IS more readable that stuff done 20 years ago.
                                   but that may only   mean   more
readable BY   ME.

    I do not understand the boild potato in the   public head.

    HHHH   Question of who is set it up. Cert/ better in Eng/

I suggest you write to Yale/ saying I have told you they prefer a BOOK ,

well you can offer 'em.   300 pages of E.P. selected by S/N
                (at my suggestion etc.)[14]

        IF Jeff/ Muss type not already
        distributed, you might keep it standing
        till   negotions procede.   ought to
        save on comp/ of my bif IF ever vol.[15]

7 The New English Weekly.
8 EP is likely referring to "Towards Orthology," published in the NEW (11 April 1935; C1180). On orthology, the correct use of words, see Letter 10, note 12.
9 EP refers to "Private Worlds," published in the NEW (2 May 1935).
10 Orage, A.R.. EP is likely referring to "In the Wounds (Memoriam A.R. Orage)" published in the Criterion (April 1935), though he could be referring to several pieces published on Orage at this time (see also C1118, C1125, C1127).
11 Housman, Alfred Edward (1859–1936). British scholar and poet.
12 Monro, Harold (1879–1932). British poet.
13 Binyon, Robert Laurence (1869–1943). British scholar and poet.
14 Though EP suggests that England, and thus Faber and Faber, might be better suited to set up his volume on economics, he encourages Nott to pursue further negotiations with Yale by offering them three hundred pages of EP's work on economics as selected by Nott.
15 "ought to save on composition of my book if ever [there is a] volume."

also as THEY aren't geared to sell pamphlets.

POINT OUT TO THEM that you can supply the sheets of

THE best econ/ symposium of the time/ and that yr/ series of

6 D econ? pamphlets , beeyewteefully printed , wd/ form a very

tempting BOOK.[16]

No reason for it to be offered to America in 6 d. fascicules.

The Ward/ is already a symposium.[17]

Orage[20]

At any rate the Colbourne/[18] *Doug /*[19] *Tank/*[21] *Tav/*[22] *E/ P/*[23]
The Dean.[24]

16 While Yale is not "geared to sell pamphlets," EP suggests, it could collect the issues
    of the Pamphlets on the New Economics series into a single volume. Though EP here
    indicates nos. 1 through 9 and 11 of the series, Nott would publish ten pamphlets in
    one volume in October 1935 as *The Social Credit Pamphleteer* (nos. 1, 4–6, 8, 11–14,
    and 17). EP seems unaware that Nott already distributes the pamphlets in the United
    States.
17 Ward, William. *The National Dividend: The Instrument for the Abolition of Poverty*,
    a symposium edited by Ward, was published in 1935 as no. 7 in the Pamphlets on the
    New Economics series.
18 Colbourne, Maurice Dale. *The Sanity of Social Credit* was published in June 1935 as no.
    11 in the Pamphlets on the New Economics series.
19 Douglas, Major C.H. *The Use of Money* and *The Nature of Democracy* were published
    in 1934 as nos. 1 and 2 in the Pamphlets on the New Economics series.
20 A.R. Orage's *The BBC Speech and the Fear of Leisure* was published posthumously in
    1935 as no. 5 in the Pamphlets on the New Economics series.
21 Bennet, Charles Augustus Ker (no dates available). The Eighth Earl of Tankerville.
    His *Poverty amidst Plenty* was published in 1934 as no. 4 in the Pamphlets on the New
    Economics series.
22 Russell, Hastings William Sackville (1888–1953). Twelfth Duke of Bedford and Marquis
    of Tavistock, Russell was a wealthy pacifist and chairman of the pro-German British
    People's Party in 1939. Kazu Ishiguro, in *Remains of the Day*, loosely based Lord
    Darlington on him. Tavistock's *Short Papers on Money* was published in 1934 as no. 3
    in the Pamphlets on the New Economics series.
23 EP's *Social Credit: An Impact* and *Alfred Venison's Poems* were published in 1935 as
    nos. 8 and 9 of the Pamphlets on the New Economics series.
24 Johnson, Hewlett. "Red" Dean of Canterbury. *Social Credit and the War on Poverty*
    was published in 1935 as no. 6 in the Pamphlets on the New Economics series.

that list of names OUGHT to sell as a BOOK in the U.S.A.

, with let us say a preface by John Dewey,[25] for the American edtn.

or by Larkin[26] or DeKruif[27] as they see fit. WOULD sell

They hate Fisher/[28] so a different brand of Econ/ wd/ suit 'em, i;e; wd/ annoy 'em less.

With title A SYMPOSIUM of the New Economics.

writings by ..... etc. with pref/ to Am/edtn/ by .....

That wdn't of necessity blok an E/ P/ vol.

Yale governed by ther accounts dept/ but still.

They may as well take the whole series/ or not/ dont mat ter

---

25 Dewey, John (1859–1952). Modern American philosopher.
26 Larkin, James Crate. Monetary reformer.
27 De Kruif, Paul. Mircrobiologist whom EP converted to Social Credit. See Letter 31, note 20.
28 Fisher, Irving. American mathematician and economist.

[LETTER 44, TLS, SN TO EP]
[STANDARD NOTT LETTERHEAD]

Ezra Pound Esq
Italy

May
Twentieth
1935

Dear Ezra:

I am enclosing you a page from "Time & Tide"[1] The general idea is that Norman Angell[2] is a dirty dog.

Yours sincerely
Stanley Nott [AS]

---

1 *Time and Tide*. See Appendix 1.
2 Angell, Sir Norman. British economist and writer (see Letter 42). The page contains a brief note from Angell to the editor of *Time and Tide*, followed by a short note from the editor confirming the authenticity of the letter and EP's letter reproduced in facsimile. *Time and Tide* printed it 11 May 1935, and it was also reproduced in *After All: The Autobiography of Norman Angell* (1951). See Letter 44A for Pound's letter (C1191) and Angell's note.

[LETTER 44A]

LETTERS TO THE EDITOR

Sir,—As the writer of the enclosed letter—whom I have never seen or communicated with in any way—would presumably like his views to have a wide publicity, I send the enclosed to you for publication if you deem it of any interest. It is addressed to me at the Bank of England (which I have never entered) in "Thread and needle street." I am, etc.,

NORMAN ANGELL.

[*We do indeed deem that the communication sent to us by Sir Norman Angell is of considerable interest, literary and psychological, and we feel that only facsimile reproduction can do it justice. –Editor,* TIME AND TIDE.]

[The facsimile letter appears here]

[ASC, EP]
13 April
anno XIII

Norman Angel*l*

Sir / a s a man who has exploited pacifism, who has made money and a career bleating about pacifism but contributed nothing to the knowledge of the economic causes of war. You merit not only contempt but loathing when you bleat publicly of things you and your accomplices have been too lazy to s tudy.

I regret that you are too cowardly to moet me, and that dueling in prohibited in yr/ enslaved country.

However as a banker's pipm, please consider yourself slapped.

And may hell rot your bones.

I am glad to inform you that Nic Butler has been called a traitor in the American House of Representatives. The lot of you fakers will be known in due time.

And now go lick someones' boots

yrs
EZRA POUND [A S]

[LETTER 45, TL, CARBON, EP TO SN]
[Italics in original typescript]

22   May [pencil: "35"]

Dear Stan

The   T   and   T/[1]   affair   seems   to   have   been   pleasing   to
everyone   except M_{airet}.[2]

At   any   rate   whoever   did   it, has   served   to   get   Nic Butler's[3]   foul
name   where   it   ought   to.   There   was   a   very   good   review   of   Cantos
31/41   in   the   same   issue.[4]

and   the   edt/   note   is   ambiguous.[5]

Use   yr/   own   judgement   whether   the   enclosed[6]   shd/   be   forwarded
to   T   and   T/   or   not .
            Let   the Chandos   group[7]   sett   on   it.

Shd/   ole   EZ   preserve   a   diggyfied   silence,   or   let   'er   zip.

1   EP's "Letter to Sir Norman Angell" was published in *Time and Tide*. See letters 42, 44,
    and 44A.
2   Mairet, Philip.
3   Butler, Nicholas Murray (1862–1947). President of Columbia University (1901–45),
    Murray also served as president of the American Academy of Arts and Letters
    (1928–41), won the Nobel Peace Prize in 1931, and held the presidency of the Carnegie
    Endowment for International Peace (1925–45). EP considers Butler, Norman Angell
    (Letter 42), and others hypocritical in "The Causes of War: 'Why Do Pacifists Evade
    Them?'" which was printed 12 July 1935 in the *Morning Post*.
4   EP's *Eleven New Cantos: XXXI–XLI* was reviewed by D.G. Bridson in *Time and Tide*
    (11 May 1935).
5   See Letter 44A.
6   Remains unclear, though likely the enclosed is a second letter to *Time and Tide* upon
    which EP wishes to receive Nott's (and the Chandos Group's) opinion. Nott replies to
    this effect in Letter 46.
7   The Chandos Group. See Appendix 1.

Sense of HUMOUR in Angell[8] can't be vurry developed ,o r the addressing him at   Bank of Eng/   wd/ have perforated his obtosity.

I   have done the new (and I think lively foreword (2 pages typesc script)   for Chi/ Writ/ Char/[9]   Am sending the ORIGINAL ideograms , for new and better blocks than those in Instigations. there will be no letter with the mes/ (I;e; the pages from Instig/ the ideograms , and the new preface.
                              so keep this memo.

// the Seraph/[10] and HOT damn if I can remember what slobbery slither of his it was that caused me to notice his oblique existence . . .

all good men true shd/ rejoice that the LID has been pried off nic Butler.
                    I wonder if pipm[11]
is libelous
        , prob/ just as well I didn't correct it.

8   EP had addressed his letter to Angell to the Bank of England, upon which Angell comments in his note.
9   CWC. EP has written a new foreword (Letter 34) and is sending along the original blocks of the Ideograms (Letter 35) used in EP's *Instigations* (1920). See letters 40 and 42.
10 A "Seraph" is a high-order angel; EP is likely employing the word in reference to Sir Norman Angell.
11 EP refers to Angell as a "banker's pipm [pimp]" in the letter in *Time and Tide*. See Letter 44A.

Neville Chamberlain[12] *has NOW got the brit/ all empire record for bootlicking.*

T/ andT/ have taken only way to get TWO facts into print.

Though I doubt whether their motives were 100% or cent pour cent. Their note is pleasantly ambiguous. Angell wont send 'em my second letter[13] *(which wuzza model of suavity in the dialect employed by the Times and Morn/ Post .)*[14]

BUT which did offer N/A/[15] *to his own impartial contemplation.*

I wrote out another letter^ to T and T[16] *last night , when I finally found my carbon of the orig/ to N/ A/, but decided it was too good for 'em.*

^H*ad forgotten I sent the letter to Angell's spiritual home.*[17]

By the way , what IS good English custom re/ letters recd ?

I had some from Bernie Shaw[18] *years ago , and was strongly tempted to print 'em, but then felt it indecent to expose the old ewe's fatuity.*

---

12 Chamberlain, Arthur Neville (1869–1940). British prime minister (1937–40). Chamberlain was chancellor of the exchequer (1931–37) in the National Government under Ramsay MacDonald.
13 Apparently EP sent a second letter to Angell (see note 6).
14 The *Times* (London) and the *Morning Post*.
15 Angell, Norman.
16 *Time and Tide*.
17 The Bank of England.
18 Shaw, George Bernard. Nott replies to this query in Letter 46.

I don't pretend to unnerstan Englishmen, but outside the tea party area, wdn't the stern COMMON MAN rather approve my remarks to N Angell ?

I'm askin', I never pretend to unnerstan that cold boiled potato that fills so MANY cervical and cerebral cavatives in yr/ Island.

The boot; the hunting for the boot/ Neville C/ hunting for Monty Norman's[19] boot; in order to perform the scared rite and exercise the inaleinable privilege of the free bot born briton to LICK BOOTS, ANY boot, so long as it is shoe leather and in reach of the british tongue .

SOMEone, ANYone to say: The emperor is NOT wearing clothes, the emperor has on nothing at all.

will send you the other draft ,[20] if you want to see it.
BUT think TIME is perhaps the best agent. Let 'em stew a bit in their own juice.
several letter has been sent to T and T/ at least two good one's from total strangers who then sent me copies.[21]

The complacency complex of ALL that god damn milieu...

which is alas ALSO the milieu whereinto social credit mostly started to penetrate....

19 Chamberlain, Neville and Norman, Montague, then governor of the Bank of England.
20 Likely the second letter mentioned above, which EP chooses not to send to *Time and Tide*.
21 EP indicates that readers have responded to the affair, but the letters have not been printed.

baint thar no MEN on the Clyde , or some sort of yeoman England that is thinking of action ?[22]

Nuthr/ matter

My wife , long a Eng/ reader of W/C/Williams, is rereading all available works of his , to see if any suggestions re alternative.[23]
                I trust you will see her when she gets to England
        at any rate she will know more about English receptivity than I do. tho' 21 years of cohabitation with afurriner like me, do disqualify her as specimen Briton.

        At any rate she'll be able to tell you which parts of Bill[24] she has found most   interestin' .

Oh, yes. I dug up two clever sketches by Paaason Eliot. Eldrop and Appleplex[25] , pubd/ in Little Review 1917. That wd/ make 12 pages. IF he cant squeeze out another drop of lubricant/ we cd/ do 'em at 6 pence. and NO WORK required from the retardative and cunctative T.S.E.

---

22 The SS *River Clyde* was a steamship involved in the Battle of Gallipoli (1915) in the First World War. Several soldiers aboard the SS *River Clyde* displayed extraordinary valour and were rewarded with Victoria crosses; accordingly, EP seems to point to men of courage.
23 Pound, Dorothy. EP's wife. Since William Carlos Williams's *Spring and All* (1923) would be set up for over ninety pages, and thus considerably more expensive than the thirty-two- and sixty-four-page booklets, Nott and EP are considering "alternative" works by Williams to publish in the Ideogrammic series.
24 Williams, William Carlos.
25 T.S. Eliot's short story "Eeldrop and Appleplex" was published in two parts in the May and September issues of the *Little Review* in 1917.

[LETTER 46, TLS, SN TO EP]
[STANDARD NOTT LETTERHEAD]

May 31st 1935

Dear Ezra:

I had along [sic] talk with Hargrave[1] yesterday. He certainly is a live wire;and he doesnt spend his time interfering with other people,like the Secretariat do.[2] He gets on with his job. I have made an arrangement with them to take our literature.[3]

You mat [sic] be interested to know that Simpkin Marshall[4] have sold 100 of Impact[5] and have ordered 50 more. The first edition of Venison[6] is out of print (500). Of course a good many have been sent out for publicity. I have a feeling that J/M[7] is going to make a little stir.We will get the printers[8] to get a move on again.

I am still waiting for a word from Mairet and Co abot [sic] the letter to TT.[9] Havent seen them for a few days.

We shall be sending you a specimen page for Ta Hio[10] next week.

I had lunch with Beevers of TT.[11] He's all for you. He says,and for the moment I agree with him,that you should come over here for a spell. Why dont youcome over and get a acquainted. Many people would like to see you. I do hope your wife will call on me or let me know shes here. The

---

1 Hargrave, John Gordon. On EP's and Nott's mutual admiration for Hargrave, see letters 12–15, and 34.
2 Nott distinguishes Hargrave's energetic dedication to Social Credit from the quarrelling often associated with the Social Credit Secretariat. See also letters 17 and 26.
3 By "them," Nott likely means Hargrave's Green Shirts (the Green Shirt Movement for Social Credit became the Social Credit Party of Great Britain just before the general election in 1935), to whom EP dedicated Social Credit: An Impact.
4 Simpkin, Marshall, and Co. British publisher and bookseller.
5 EP's Social Credit: An Impact. According to Gallup, four thousand copies were printed.
6 EP's Alfred Venison's Poems. According to Gallup, two impressions of two thousand copies each were printed.
7 EP's J/M.
8 On the printers, see letters 11, 16, 17, 20, 27, 29, and 31.
9 Mairet, Philip. The "Co" here likely refers to the Chandos Group.
10 EP's translation of Confucius's Ta Hio.
11 Beevers, John Leonard (1911–75). A regular contributor to the NEW, at this time affiliated with Time and Tide.

English over here,99 9/10ths % are as dead a [sic] mutton – but mutton is not quite dead,it makes good food.[12]

With regard to letters ,the idea is that they are the writers personal property and cant be published without his consent. Shaw[13] at one time threatened to sue someone in America who published a batch of his letters. Ask his permission and let us publish them. But the old chap is terrribly out of date. Only spinsters go to his meetings now.

Can you find another 12 pp.of Eliot[14] and a few over so that we can make a 32pp booklet of it?

A Social Creditor writes today:"Of the pamphlets you send me, I dont like Nos 9and 8. Vulgarity will not help us at all. I return these two and keep the rest."[15]

Yours ever
Stanley Nott [A S]

12 Nott is responding to E P's claims regarding the British reading public in Letter 45.
13 Shaw, George Bernard. Nott replies to E P's inquiry regarding the publication of letters in Letter 45.
14 In Letter 45, E P recommends T.S. Eliot's "Eeldrop and Appleplex" for inclusion, though it would only comprise twelve pages of the booklet.
15 Nos. 8 and 9 in the Pamphlets on the New Economics series are both written by E P (*Social Credit: An Impact* and *Alfred Venison's Poems*, respectively).

{YCAL MSS 43, SERIES 1, BOX 37, FOLDER 1583}
[LETTER 47, TL, CARBON EP TO SN]
[Italics in original typescript]

[ASC, EP, red crayon] *3 June with copy of*
l. to Dyson
[pencil: 35]

Dear Stan
Enc/ copy of letter to Dyson/[1]
which read, and then proceed with this
piece.
Gibson[2] *thru here/ damn fine chap, but his heart has*
flopped on him, so he is at least temporarily out of action.

ConNIzance tookn of yr/ nooz; banzai !! Now what IS cloggin the
merger ?[3]
And IF Mairet[4] *can't organize a review service*[5] *lets*
US do it for him.
I dunno if you cd/ SEIZE both papers or if it
would be worth your while to pub the MERGED one ?[6]

1 The enclosed copy of the letter to Will Dyson is missing from the correspondence.
2 Gibson, Arthur Leslie (dates unknown). Gibson served on the advisory council of the
   Social Credit Secretariat and authored *What Is This Social Credit?* (1935) as no. 17 in
   the Pamphlets on the New Economics series. EP and Gibson corresponded between
   1934 and 1940. In a letter to John Hargrave (June 1935), EP writes: "'Nott is capable
   of more quiet enthusiasm than you think. Both he and Gibson are J/H/ men/ Gib
   very nice chap. Too bad he is out of action with heart=smash'" (Preda, *Ezra Pound's
   Economic Correspondence*, 154).
3 Though EP could be responding to the news of recent sales of his works, he is more
   likely referring to the proposed merger between the *New Age* and *NEW*, news that
   apparently comes through Gibson and Dyson. See letters 14, 17, and 18. Nott responds
   in Letter 51.
4 Mairet, Philip.
5 EP insists that a "review service" be a necessary feature of the merger.
6 Nott published the *European Quarterly* during its brief run (1934–35), so EP may
   be thinking his interest would lie in publishing a merged *New Age* and *New English
   Weekly*. See Letter 51.

BUT wedge must have an edge. Long time pubr/ needs orgum.[7] Place where blokes can try out their material, do rough drafts/ etc.

Colbourne[8] is O. K. ; he ought to meet Hargrave[9] // both got idea of DOING a job , that others aren't doing.

Butchart[10] is I understand , diligent. You used to read Dyson.

(I don't profess to know WHY... but I am NOT here to wean , to separate , to impose my personal limitations on the MOVEMENT.
     If Dyson, as Gib/[11] said, was deelighted with the idea of the merger AS a FLEET ST coup. that's enough. He SEES the point.

Colbourne and Coussens[12] are both out of London. Ricketts[13] is on both papers , handwriting bad, but one can read it.

IDEOGRAMIC[14] series , following my ABC of Reading[15] (which follows 25 years WORK) does offer schema of general kulchoor[16] IN HARMONY , and organicly coherent with soc/ credit.

A paper ought to have a policy.

G/K's policy[17] is to maintain CONTACT with his readers.

---

7 "organ."
8 Colbourne, Maurice Dale.
9 Hargrave, John Gordon.
10 Butchart, Montgomery.
11 A.L. Gibson (see note 2, above).
12 Cousens, Hilderic Edwin. Social Credit commentator from the *New Age* and *NEW*.
13 Reckitt, Maurice Benington. Nott suggests in Letter 51 that Reckitt, who came from wealth, provides money to "keep [the *NEW*] going."
14 The Ideogrammic series.
15 EP's *ABC of Reading* (1934).
16 "Kulchoor" and "kulchuh" are two of EP's variants on "culture."
17 *G.K.'s Weekly* (see letters 32 and 40). Editorial policy was leaning to the right during the mid-1930s.

That is GOOD, a necessary ELEMENT in a policy of action.

G.K.[18] said he had no objection to MY economics.

He cert/knows a damn sight more about the NATURE of the english than I ever shall.

18 Chesterton, Gilbert Keith.

June 4th [pencil: "1935?"]

Dear Ezra:

I'm sending your letter to T & T.[1] *If they won't publish it N. E. W.*[2] *will, though it won't have the same effect. Fenollosa*[3] *arrived today. Very good stuff. Enclosed is a specimen of Ta Hio.*[4]

Yrs

SCN

---

1 Nott refers to EP's second letter responding to the "Angell affair" (see Letter 45). EP's initial "Letter to Sir Norman Angell," which sparked the controversy, appeared in *Time and Tide* (11 May 1935). See also letters 42, 44, and 46.

2 The *New English Weekly.*

3 Fenollosa, Ernest Francisco. Nott refers to the manuscript of *CWC*, which EP promises to send in Letter 45. For this thread on the *CWC*, see letters 34, 41, and 42.

4 EP's translation of Confucius's *Ta Hio*. See Letter 46, in which Nott promises to send a sample page.

[LETTER 49, TL, CARBON, EP TO SN]
[Italics in original typescript]

5 June [pencil: 35][1]

Dear Stan

We shd/ get onto PELMAN[2] and the Polytechnics.[3]

especially BOTH. I forget the name of Polytechnic secretary, prob/

promoted by now anyhow. But one of my first jobs in London was lecturing
ir. The Regent St. polytechnic.

IF they WONT look at Impact ,[4] might be almost worthwhile
to rent a bulletin board 2 ft. 6 by ' ft. and keep a steady LEARN

ECONOMICS with Nott and s:c: publ cations listed. Board naer as poss to

Polytechnic entrance.[5]

The Pelman STUDENTS are the next large class we ought
to get.

Leese[6] has a grand issue of the FASCIST.[7] He ought to get yr/ econ/ pubctn

for review.

---

1 A carbon copy of letter written by EP to A.S. Leese (see note 6) is included and carries the same date. See Letter 49B.
2 "Pelmanism" is a form of popular self-help psychology that developed a card game known as "memory," or "pairs," to aid in the training of the faculties of the mind and concentration. The original Pelman Institute is in London and offers courses in Pelmanism and self-realization.
3 EP lectured at the Regent Street Polytechnic during his early years in London.
4 EP's *Social Credit: An Impact.*
5 "social Credit publications"; "near as possible."
6 Leese, Arnold Spencer. British Fascist. See Essay 2.
7 Page 4 of the 5 June 1935 issue of the *Fascist: The Organ of Racial Fascism*, official organ of Leese's Imperial Fascist League, contains an antisemitic list of the Jewish aristocracy of Britain entitled "Our Exotic Nobility!" In Letter 49B to Leese, EP applauds this issue and promotes the Pamphlets on the New Economics series to Leese.

I have got him pointed more to sane econ/

tho of course most of the paper is kike chasing OF the best possible variety

as such, and great fun.

A.S. Leese   30 Craven St. Strand W. C. 2

/Can you make any NONEY on Wyndham Lewis?[8] *Digging up Eliot's
scraps in Little Review.*[9]

   am reminded that some of Blast might be reissued.[10]
   It dont strict adhere to Ideogramic aim, but still for old sakes sake.
   IF it is good business for Stan, the idea can be entertained.
   *W.L. difficult to handle. But we may as well keep in mind them there
resources which can be available.*

Dont mention it to anyone else, until/ if you are ready.

8   Lewis, Percy Wyndham (1882–1957). British artist and writer.
9   See Letter 45, in which EP offers T.S. Eliot's "Eeldrop and Appleplex" for the
    Ideogrammic series. In Letter 46, Nott asks for more material to make a full thirty-
    two-page pamphlet.
10 *BLAST* (London, 1914–15). Avant-garde periodical and official voice of the Vorticist
    movement during the war, *BLAST* was edited by Wyndham Lewis and published only
    two issues.

[LETTER 49A, TL, CARBON, EP TO SN][1]

[pencil: 5 June 1935]

Just to keep the Ideogram idea[2] fluid in mind, I recapitulate

TA Hio[3]

Eliot ,[4] if

Chinese Writ/ Character[5]

Cummings[6]

W.C.Williams (my wife is bringing over another vol/ with her pickings , so you can talk it over between you.[7]

Fox(on Frobenius)[8]

Cocteau[9]

Elizabethan trans/ of Iliad , edited by Rouse

Odyssey ?? entire, and allied to series. that wd/ be best might even be issued three or four books at a time in fascicules, pur chaseable united. or listed as

---

1 EP continues Letter 49 on the reverse of a carbon copy of a letter written to A.S. Leese (see Letter 49B).
2 The Ideogrammic series. EP last addressed it in Letter 40.
3 EP's translation of Confucius's *Ta Hio*.
4 Eliot, T.S. The "if" suggests the uncertainty surrounding Eliot's appearance in the series.
5 *CWC*.
6 Cummings, E.E.
7 Williams, William Carlos. On Dorothy Pound, EP's wife, see letters 18 and 45.
8 Fox, Douglas Claughton. American assistant to Leo Frobenius, German anthropologist and ethnologist.
9 Cocteau, Jean.

One Vol/ containing numbers 7/11 of series.[10]

W.Lewis ?[11]

E/P/ perhaps , something or other.[12]

?? by that time an ~~aiho~~ anthol of poetry by men AWARE of the econ factor.

Angold,[13] *Bunting,*[14] *Jex Martin,*[15] *Loughlin,*[16]

Sylander.[17]

whatever has cropped up.

[AN, EP] *leese verso*[18]

---

10 Rouse, William Henry Denham. The "Elizabethan translation" of the *Iliad* is likely Arthur Hall's edition of 1581 (see Letter 34). EP remains firm that Rouse's translation of the *Odyssey* should be published independently of the series, though not without a marketable link to it.

11 Lewis, Percy Wyndham. See Letter 49, note 8.

12 EP's intentions remain unclear.

13 Angold, John Penrose (1909–43). British poet and advocate for Social Credit, killed during the Second World War. EP corresponded with Angold during the 1930s.

14 Bunting, Basil.

15 Martin, John Jex (dates unknown). Admirer of Father Coughlin who corresponded with EP in the 1930s.

16 Laughlin, James.

17 Likely Gordon Sylander, who wrote a review of Kenneth Rexroth's *In What Hour* (1940) in the *Partisan Review*.

18 EP indicates that a copy of his letter to A.S. Leese (Letter 49B), founder of the Imperial Fascist League and editor of the *Fascist*, is included on the verso (back) side.

[LETTER 49B, TL, EP TO A.S. LEESE]

[pencil: "copy made, filed"]

5 June[1]

Dear Leese

Damn good number.[2] Has Nott sent you Impact[3] , if not; tell him you want his Econ/ Pamphlets for review.

If that don't strike his fancy, tell him the author said you were to have an author's copy of Impact.

Please send June Fascist to

Hon. Geo.H Tinkham,[4] House of Representatives , Washington. D.C. U. S. A.

He has already called that shit Nic Butler,[5] a traitor in the House debate. and he has written me he intends to call for an investigation. of Endowments (Carnegie and the whole damn caboodle).

---

1 A carbon of Letter 49 continues on the recto of a copy of EP's letter to A.S. Leese (see Letter 49A).
2 EP is referring to the June 1935 issue of Leese's the *Fascist*, organ of Leese's Imperial Fascist League, which printed a list entitled "Our Exotic Nobility: More about the Jewish Aristocracy of Britain" and which included members of the aristocracy whom the newspaper, in an antisemitic campaign, identified as Jewish. The piece is billed as the fruits of research into the "contamination and destruction of the Aryan aristocracy of this Kingdom" (4). See Letter 49, note 7. See also Essay 2.
3 EP's *Social Credit: An Impact.*
4 Tinkham, George Holden. Republican representative for Massachusetts from 1915 to 1943 (see Letter 31). EP corresponded with Tinkham during the 1930s, and the two finally met during EP's visit to the United States in 1939.
5 Butler, Nicholas Murray. See Letter 45.

Please MARK second pp/ in col 4. Page one.[6]

Tinkham is ~~th~~ said to be the richest man in congress

(aryan)

//

Re/ yr/ glorious list.[7] *I dont believe Becky Franks*[8] *has had much influence of Hal Johnson's*[9] *mentality. (solid hickory I sh shd/ think. with a wife like a deacon.*

re/ Ellerman,[10] *you mean the young kid has married a kike ? The old man was 100 yitt, I had always supposed , and the most venemous variety.*

> *Though his (finally wife) was british victim,*[11]

---

6 EP indicates a section (second paragraph of the fourth column on page 1) of the *Fascist* that he would like Leese to mark off for Congressman Tinkham. It begins: "A common present-day Jewish practice is to finance side-tracking societies, whose object is ostensibly patriotic and decent, but which are so directed and governed that they accomplish nothing and keep many people out of the fight who would be useful in a genuine Aryan-led movement. Another effect of these side-tracking societies is to disgust keen people and wear them out so that they will no longer try to do anything against the powers of destruction" (June 1935, no. 73, p. 1).

7 Leese lists members of the British aristocracy (peers, baronets, knights) "who are of Jewish blood" or who have "married Jewish women" (4). The list follows one printed in the March 1935 issue.

8 The list on page 4 of the *Fascist* for 5 June 1935 mentions a woman named "Rebecca Franks" as the great grandmother of Sir H.A.W. Johnson, baronet.

9 Johnson, Sir H.A.W. Baronet. Johnson is listed among the "Jewish Aristocracy of Britain."

10 The reference is likely to Sir John Reeves Ellerman (1909?–73), second baronet, son of Sir John Reeves Ellerman (1862–1933), first baronet, shipping magnate and financier, heir to his father's fortunes. John Ellerman had a sister, Annie Winifred Ellerman, who published under the pen-name Bryher.

11 This remains unclear, but in an antisemitic vein, EP suggests that Ellerman's wife was not Jewish.

Howeffer   itza   peech   ova   list   ~~Hoff~~   uff   deh   kunitehoot.[12]

//

Has brit/ press   noted   order   to   expulse   Masons   from   Turkey ?[13]

12 "However, it's a peach of a list of the ["knighthood"?]."
13 Due to the infiltration of Nazi propaganda into Turkey, some Masonic lodges were
    closed in 1935 by the minister of the interior.

June 5 [pencil: 1935]

Will answer your letter, rec'd yesterday, on Thursday.[1] *Page proofs*[2] *of Jeff/Muss arrived today. They look very well.*

I've seen T T.[3] *They will I think, publish your letter. M*[4] *& I agree that it should be published.*

SCN

---

1 Nott would reply to EP's Letter 47 (3 June 1935) in Letter 51 (8 June 1935).
2 EP's *J/M*. See Letter 34.
3 As he mentions in Letter 48, Nott gave John Beevers of *Time and Tide* EP's second letter written in response to the Angell affair. See Letter 42 on Norman Angell as well as letters 44 and 52.
4 Mairet, Philip.

June 8th 1935
8L Rosslyn Street NW 3

Dear Ezra:

    It being Whitsun[1] I'm writing you in answer to your letter of June 3rd from my home address.
    Thanks for letter to Dyson.[2] I agree with almost all (perhaps all) you say. The difficulty is this: When Orage[3] was alive everyone turned to him. He was the key man. A constant stream of people from every S.C. sect (and others) went to his office every day. He was <u>the</u> key man. When he died each stone of the arch went off on its little own. Practically no one goes to the office now (of the N. E. W.)[4] Though Mrs. O[5] owns the paper, Reckitt[6] supplies the money to keep it going. Douglas Secretariat[7] seem chiefly to be concerned with establishing a dictatorship. They are even going to the trouble of trying to start an opposition London Social Credit Club.

2

Dyson is dynamic – but his force goes in cartoons & occasional writing. He is not a leader. Dyson lacks a certain understanding, and he's shy, & tries to cover his shyness by a rather facetious downrightness.
    This is the first I've heard of the merger.[8] Its [sic] a good idea. NEW reviewing is unorganized and carries little weight.[9] But they have some good people round them. If the merger comes off the NEW should be reorganized typographically. It doesn't look important enough – too

---

1   Whitsun is a Christian festival held on the seventh Sunday after Easter.
2   In Letter 47, EP encloses a carbon of a letter (missing from the correspondence) to Will Dyson.
3   Orage, A.R.
4   The *New English Weekly*.
5   Jessie Orage, who remained intensely involved with the *NEW* following her husband's death in November 1934 (see Letter 13).
6   Reckitt, Maurice Benington. Funded the *NEW* with family money.
7   Douglas, Major C.H. On the Social Credit Secretariat, see Letter 26, note 12.
8   Nott initially attributes the idea of a merger between the *New Age* and *NEW* to Dyson in Letter 17 (see also letters 14 and 18). EP responds to news of this merger in Letter 47, to which Nott replies here.
9   Nott seconds EP's criticism in Letter 47 of the review section of the *NEW*.

feminine. But criticisms from me are not taken kindly by Mrs. O &
Dyson. We all know each other too well perhaps.   *So I stick to my*
lair – publishing.

3

Time may throw up a key man or rather 'leader' in the S. C.[10]
movement.

We are selling from £25 –£40 of S. C. literature per week from our few
books and pamphlets. But our Autumn list will contain mostly general
literature. It's not good to publish only S. C. We are going slowly, but
always open to ideas or MSS.

Ta Hio[11] *page will be changed somewhat. Anyhow it will look much*
better set up.

I'll write you again on Tuesday about ideogrammic.[12]
     Yrs
     Stanley Nott

---

10   "Social Credit."
11   EP's translation of Confucius's *Ta Hio*. See also letters 48, 52, and 56.
12   Recent discussion of the Ideogrammic series appears in letters 45–49A.

June 14 · 35

Dear Ezra,

We have decided to re-plan the whole of the Ideogramic series typographically. We want it to look more important than we had first planned. We feel that it will be a really important series from a literary point of view. Also it may not be possible to sell them all at the same price. We can't sell 20 pp. for the same price as 96. Next week I'll send you a dummy. We shall scrap the specimen of Ta Hio & do another. They will have to look like books, not pamphlets.[1]

Time and Tide have returned your letter. I sent it to Beevers who is on holiday, & he sent it to the T & T office.[2]

Yours ever

Stanley Nott

1 Discussion of the design and price of the Ideogrammic series appears in letters 17, 40, and 42. See letters 46, 48, and 51 on recent mention of *Ta Hio*.
2 Nott attaches the letter from *Time and Tide*, which he had originally sent to John Beevers (Letter 46), an editor. On EP's second letter on the affair regarding Norman Angell (Letter 42), see letters 45, 48, and 50.

Ezra Pound Esq
Italy

June
Seventeenth
1935

Dear Ezra:

I wonder if you will agree to my publishing 25 copies of Jeff and/or Muss, on special paper numbered and signed by yourself? I do feel that it is an important book, and I think at least twenty people would be willing to pay 21/- for signed copy. You yourself might like to give away a few of them.[1]

I have heard from your wife[2] this morning and we are going to meet in the next few days.

Enclosed is a revise of the title page.[3] I shall not send the final one to you as with the few alterations it is ready for press.

Yours ever.

Stanley Nott [AS]

SN/KM

[AN] *P.S. Will you send us as soon as possible an idea for a blurb (a) Jeff Muss. & (b) Ideogramic.*

---

1 EP's *J/M*. Gallup explains that Nott would publish thirty copies at 21s. of a special edition signed by EP, twenty-five of which would be for sale. Each edition had the signature page tipped in, which EP numbered and signed. Nott sends EP the cancel pages to sign and number in Letter 55. In Letter 64, however, Nott indicates that he has refused to publish the edition, only setting aside ten copies of the ordinary edition (which sold at 6s.) with EP's signature pages tipped in. The outcome of the special edition remains unclear. According to Gallup, the special edition was published in July 1935 and the ordinary edition in August 1935.

2 Dorothy Pound arranged to meet Nott to discuss the selection of William Carlos Williams's material for the Ideogrammic series and to settle outstanding accounts (see letters 45, 46, 55, and 56).

3 EP approves the design in Letter 54 and the entire book in Letter 56.

20 June [pencil: /35]

Dear Stan

The Jeff/ Muss[1] title page is O.K.

thass arl rite/[2]

The Ideogramic blurb[3] you already HAVE. I dare say your files are as easy to search as mine.

As for the Jeff/[4] you can include. E/P's parralel between two creators of government with reference to a third.

E/P/ has refused time and again to write memoirs ; but this vol/ contains a very considerable amount of them in the form of direct observation.

Readers of Impact[5] will here find E/P on the fundamentals of state organization/ Confucius,[6] Jefferson, and his analysis of why modern Italy is fact and not merely a theory.

---

1 Nott encloses the revised title page for J/M in Letter 53.
2 "That's all right."
3 EP provides a "blurb" for the Ideogrammic series in Letter 37.
4 The blurb would appear on the front left flap of the dust-jacket of J/M, beginning with "Ezra Pound's parallel between two creators of government" and concluding with "why Mussolini has DONE something and the others have merely talked."
5 EP's Social Credit: An Impact.
6 Pound refers to Confucius in J/M.

Or to put in another way , why Mussolini has DONE something and the others have merely talked.

I dunno that the book lives up to all that , but blurb is usually discounted. ANYhow.

E/P's parralel between two

If this wont go/ quote the preface or zummat[7]

creators of government
with reference to a third

I shd/ putt I/T on yr/ title pages. don't bother about it in this[8]

---

7 "something."
8 The remainder of this letter is cut off.

July 5th 1935

Dear Ezra:

Herewith cancel pages for signing. Will you fill in numbers and sign each one please.[1]

My wife[2] and I had tea with your wife[3] last Saturday and a very pleasant talk.

Ideogramic is being re-designed.[4] You will get a specimen page in a few days.

Ive made three appointments to see Morley,[5] then when he at last fixed it I was unable to go. Im very run down and must get away for a few days. Shall be back at the end of next week. July 13th.

Yours ever.

Stanley Nott [A S]

---

1 In Letter 53 Nott proposes the printing of thirty copies of a special edition of *J/M* that would bear EP's signature. A "cancel" page in printing signifies any page or portion of a book that is substituted for the original, most often to correct a mistake or omission in the original publication.
2 Nott, Rosemary.
3 Dorothy Pound was visiting London at this time (see letters 45, 46, 53, and 56).
4 Nott decides in Letter 52 to redesign the items of the Ideogrammic series so that they will "look like books, not pamphlets." The discussion of design and cost continues in letters 56 and 57.
5 Morley, Frank. A director of Faber and Faber publishers (see Letter 34, note 18). It remains unclear whether Nott is still pursuing a volume of EP's economic writing with Faber and Faber or whether he is pursuing another matter.

29 Luglio[1] [pencil: 35]

Dear Stan

ItZa damn fine lookin' book[2]

an' I appreciate the care and discrimination spent on producin it.

Hope the Boss[3] gets his copy for his birthday , wich iz tomorrow.

Naow , about that thaar INVOICE.[4] I trust D.P. has settled re. Impact. ,[5] if not , she will.

re. Jeff/M,[6] I haven't my lists , but some of the copies are pure REVIEW copies , and all but a very few are certainly sent out for the sake of the book , publicity copies aiming at help of sales.

And I think I ought to get 'em for COST[7]

---

1 29 July 1935.
2 EP refers to *J/M*. In Letter 53, Nott suggests the book is ready for press.
3 The "Boss" is Mussolini. In Letter 32, EP requests a copy for him.
4 "Now, about that there invoice."
5 Dorothy Pound is currently visiting London (see letters 45, 46, 53, and 55). EP's *Social Credit: An Impact*.
6 EP's *J/M*.
7 On EP's requests for publicity copies and copies "on account," see letters 31–37.

Dont think my mother in=laws flat indicates my scae of gate receipts.[8]

　　　　　If you are ham strung for the "ready " I'll try to fork 　something.

Am alarmed at Prices for Ta Hio, and Writ. Char.

have been looking to pamphlets for years. BUT it is your affair.

IF in the ruddy sunset of the gombeen era them books has

got to be bewteeful to feed me ,[9]

At any rate one will like the look of one's own copy.

and the royalties will be higher.

　　　　　I leave it to you.

I note theJ/M follows what I HATE in Eng. printing.

nameky INNER margin tooo god damn narrow.

Minor detail. I shd. like a bit more , at least 1/4 th inch. in

the other books. The pamphlets have wider innner marg.

　　　You will have to fight ANY and every brit. printed with

an AXE over this , at least once , probably six times , but the CAN

be druv to it.[10]

8　Shakespear, Olivia (1864–1938). EP's mother-in-law. EP suggests that her wealth is no indication of his own. By "scae" EP could mean his "share."

9　·EP is likely referring to the cost of each booklet on the above-mentioned invoice. The sale price for *Ta Hio* was 2s.; for *CWC*, 5s. See Letter 40 for discussion of potential costs and Letter 57 for Nott's reply. By "gombeen era," EP is referring to usurers.

10　EP is dissatisfied with the width of the inner margins of *J/M*, which he reads as endemic to British printing. The actual width of the inner margin measures 1¼ inches;

Was the chinese putt there special , or simple slip.[11]

on Kung chapter ? .

It is O. K. chinese front way.

The book is b eautifully done. dont lose any seleep over these two points. one of which can pass for a refinement. and the other IS the accepted printer's custum in Eng. correct from certain pt. of v. if not over done.

Whaterver you decide re/ RATE. please send yet one more copy Jeff/M.

to Hon. Bennett Clark[12]
U.S.Senate. Washington D.C.

(buzzard is said to be writing a bk/ on Jeff. and we ebtter guide him.

---

the outer margin approximately 1½ inches. Nott used the Western Printing Services Ltd. (Bristol) for *Social Credit: An Impact*, *Alfred Venison's Poems*, and *J/M*, and he used the Kynoch Press for *Ta Hio* and *CWC*.

11 The nature of EP's quibble remains unclear, though the recto side of the leaf (page 111) is blank, perhaps indicating a late alteration to the text. In Letter 57, Nott expresses confusion about EP's comments. In letters 26 and 35, EP discusses the ideograms in *J/M*.

12 Clark, Joel Bennett (1890–1954) better known as Bennett "Champ" Clark. Democratic senator in Missouri from 1933 to 1945. According to EP, Clark was writing a book on Jefferson during this time, though no record exists of its publication. The Champ and Bennett Champ Clark Papers at the University of Missouri include biographical material on Thomas Jefferson.

[LETTER 57, TLS, SN TO EP]
[STANDARD NOTT LETTERHEAD]

August 1st 1935

Dear Ezra:

Thanks for your letter of July 29th.[1] We are charging you 3/- for the copies.That is 2/6 each copy and 6d. postage on each copy. They were charged up at 4/- so I am sending a credit note. The cost is high on account of our reckoning on a sale of 500. If we sell a thousand the cost will be considerable [sic] less. So that if the book goes well we could make you a further reduction.[2]

We cant tell yet what the cost of Written Character[3] will be.We have to reckon on a sale of 500.There will be a good many blocks.If we can do it cheaper we will. A book like this will go much better if ~~done~~ produced well than if done in pamphlet form. The cost of setting ,printing, blocks is the same for a pamphlet as for an expensive book.Paper is almost the same.

The margins of J/M[4] are not what they should be. The printer blames the binder ,the binder the printer.I kicked up a row about them.   I dont understand your point about the Kung chapter.[5] As far as we can trace it we followed your instructions.Will you   explain more fully. In the other books we will send you an imposition sheet[6] so that youcan check the margins.

                    Yours
                    SCN [AS]

[AN] ps: Your wife settled the bill.[7]

1 See Letter 56.
2 Nott clarifies that an accounting error has resulted in EP's being overcharged for the copies of J/M he has taken on account. See letters 31–37.
3 CWC.
4 Nott replies to EP's complaint about the narrow margins of J/M in Letter 56.
5 Nott replies to EP's complaint about Chinese characters in the chapter on Confucius (see Letter 56).
6 An "imposition sheet" provides pages arranged in the right sequence, or the arranging of pages of type in the forme, which would enable EP to judge the book's physical design.
7 EP notes in Letter 18 that Dorothy banks in London and is thus able to pay Nott with British currency rather than with a cheque from EP drawn on an American bank.

{YCAL MSS 43, SERIES I, BOX 37, FOLDER 1584}
[LETTER 58, ALS, SN TO EP]
[STANDARD NOTT LETTERHEAD]

[across top, A S C, above letterhead]
    Have a letter from Odon Por.[1] *Am writing him*

Sept 3rd 1935

Dear Ezra:

    I'm just back from my holidays. Have you seen the reviews[2] *in New Statesman and New Verse? Who is the yelping puppy in New Verse who signs himself a. m ?*[3]

    Anthology[4] *is now in press. Your idea for a collection of Brenton's stuff is not bad.*[5] *I'll work on it.*

    I shall now get down to Ideogrammic,[6] *which is very much on my mind.*

---

1 Por, Odon. Hungarian-born Italian journalist and economist.

2 The *New Statesman* (1913–) became the *New Statesman and Nation* in 1931, though it retained its original socialist leanings. During the 1930s the weekly attracted a host of famous writers and solidified its socialist reputation with Kingsley Martin at the helm (1930–63). A. Desmond Hawkins's luke-warm review of *J/M* in the weekly (31 August 1935) appreciated some of EP's stylistic flourishes and "vivid" perceptions but read his style as interfering with argument.

3 *New Verse* (1933–39) was edited by Geoffrey Grigson and regularly published W.H. Auden, Louis MacNeice, C. Day Lewis, and Stephen Spender. The review of *J/M*, along with *Alfred Venison's Poems* and Herbert Read's *Essential Communism*, appears in no. 16 (August–September 1935) and is signed "A.M." The identity of the reviewer remains unclear. The review examines the attraction of Social Credit for "middle-aged intellectuals" and treats EP scathingly ("Having parted from reason Ezra needs no facts and no arguments. His bawl is the same in prose or verse" [19]). As an announcement indicates in no. 23, Stanley Nott took over distribution of *New Verse* until nos. 26–27 (November 1937), the Auden double number, when Lindsay Drummond took over.

4 Nott is likely referring to Montgomery Butchart's anthology *Money* (1935), which he is in the process of publishing and which EP lauds in Letter 59.

5 EP likely proposed a collection of material by *New Age* editor Arthur Brenton in a previous letter that is missing from the correspondence. See Letter 61.

6 The Ideogrammic series.

Business is moving very well, but I'm in handcuffs for want of capital. I'm on the look-out for someone with £2000.00 with that we could move along and branch out. I have one or two things up my sleeve on which money could be made – text books for schools – two are in preparation. I have to keep my family out of this small but growing business: so its [sic] *hard going for the moment.*[7]

Yrs

Stanley Nott

7 EP presses the marketing angle on textbooks more fully in Letter 59.

[LETTER 59, TL, EP TO SN, FOLDER 1583]

[pencil: July? 35][1]

310 San Gregorio. Venice[2]

Dear N/ Butch's book[3] magnificent. You can blurb   it (tho   as my name occurs so early,   I dont know about using my name on the blubr. // do   as you   like.[4]

MONEY, by M.B.[5]

Not a dull page in over **** 300 . It ought to be required reading   in   every   high=school. Non=doctrinarian , the fruits of over 150 of the best minds of the n/ race , recorded in   a   period of three   centuries. "

An essential book for every economist or student of economics.[6] ///

mebbe you better   use my name. but do as you   think   tactful.

───────

1 The letter is undated, but likely 9 September 1935 as Nott refers to it in Letter 62 ("yours of 9th").
2 EP often met Olga Rudge (see Letter 72A, note 10) and their daughter, Mary, in Venice during this period.
3 Montgomery Butchart's *Money: Selected Passages Presenting the Concepts of Money in the English Tradition, 1640–1935*, published by Nott in 1935. See Letter 58.
4 EP's name appears early in the Preface to *Money*, where Butchart thanks him for arousing "my interest in economics" and credits him with "suggestions" that "have been a constant provocation to clarity" (5).
5 Butchart, Montgomery.
6 Remains unclear whether EP's blurb was used on the book jacket. On the back cover of S.G. Hobson's *Functional Socialism* (1936), Butchart's book is advertised as "An anthology from Aristotle to the present day on what men have said about money: what it is and how it works."

As N. Dem.[7] and all the rest, ^New Age[8] " Library "etc. seem to prefer doctrinaire, sectarian and often UNREADABLE books ,

Hargrave[9] or someone might start to blurd " Library of Eco Economics "[10]

Munson[11] has now got some organization to subscribe en bloc to N.Dem.

SOME ORGANIZATION ought to support Nott.'s econ. publications, or at least the BASIC ECON.[12]

confer with Butch and Hragrave. Harg/ WANTS money but people might invest where they wont or fear to SPEND.

Green Shirts, shd. be furnished with the READABLE books. readability in ECON. Comes from GOOD WRITING, it comes from ORTHOLOGY. (in my sense , as ameliorated from Ogden.)[13]
hush.

The Chandos inellect shd. be clarified for Harg's use. Butch is the liason officer.[14]

---

7 *New Democracy* (New York, 1933–39).
8 EP could be referring to the "Credit Research Library" of the *New Age*.
9 Hargrave, John Gordon. Leader of the "Green Shirts" and the Social Credit Party of Great Britain.
10 EP is likely referring to Nott's "The New Economics Library," the banner under which Nott advertised six books by E.S. Holter, A. Newsome, and C.H. Douglas.
11 Munson, Gorham B. Editor of *New Democracy* and founder of the American Social Credit movement.
12 EP suggests that an organization such as Hargrave's Green Shirt movement, which took EP's *Social Credit: An Impact* as a textbook, should subscribe to Nott's publications.
13 The Green Shirts were Hargrave's wing of the British Social Credit movement. EP stresses the "readability" of Nott's publications, which EP connects with his own brand of "orthology" (Letter 37), an improvement upon C.K. Ogden's.
14 EP suggests Butchart as a potential bridge between Hargrave's more action-oriented approach and the intellectual approach of the Chandos Group.

This book MONEY, ought to be "money" I mean it is basic enough to support you and Butch for the rest of your lives IF you puch it properly.

BUTCH, has some short time ACTION jobs to do. But as

personal career , he ought next to do a similar book on BANKING.[15]

These shd. aim at PERMANENT place in high school and university curricula. There is a fortune or at least a solid livlihood in TEXT BOOK (I have known a man to LIVE , and travel in Europe on ONE measly high school reader see/luksHuns of authors)

Page 234 , line 9 MISPRINT. shd read x TO, not or be delivered.[16]

Young Swabey seems willing. possibly diffident. Send him post card. Henry Swabey.[17]

Yew Hedge, Forrest Row. Sussex.

invite him to call. and then put him on to ASSIST Butch and run errands.

Better write Munson, that YOU are pub/ing READABLE econ. with that carries a PUNCH , and that you want his support.[18]

---

15 Butchart's next editorial enterprise, *To-Morrow's Money, by Seven of Today's Leading Monetary Heretics*, was published by Nott in 1936.
16 Butchart's *Money* includes five pages from *Social Credit: An Impact*, *ABC of Economics*, and *J/M* (230–4).
17 Swabey, Reverend Henry S.
18 Munson, Gorham B. See note 11.

Heaven knows I aint layed DOWN on him.   This orthodox
stuff, the Nieland idea of controll.[19]

(keep   that for Munson's benefit)

not the BEST line. Any how the Butch book. FUNDAMENTAL,
basic. and beyond ARGUMENT.
                    all the profs. got to take it.

Munson's loyalty to Orage,[20]   who also saw the NEED of such a bk/
before we cd. get on with the work .
            and the NON_Doctrinarian element to be starred.

Is Buchan (now Lord Tweedsmuir)[21] still viceroy ? and is title
inherited ?

            someone ought to make contact there.

Murdock[22] ought to get copy of the MONEY.

so shd/ Geo. Tinkham,[23] congressman, Huey,[24] and Coughlin.[25]

all this you can talk with Butch. and save , my writing more letters.

19 Likely refers to Nyland, W.A. (1890–1975). Dutch-born chemist and Gurdjieffeian.
    Nyland met Gurdjieff and later Orage in New York in 1924 and became closely involved
    with Gurdjieffian teachings for the rest of his life. EP corresponded briefly with Nyland
    in the mid-1930s.
20 Orage, A.R. Munson was moved to publish *New Democracy*, a Social Credit paper
    based in New York, as a result of Orage's lectures.
21 Buchan, John (1875–1940; Lord Tweedsmuir). Diplomat, journalist, historian, writer.
    Buchan is best known for his spy thrillers, such as *The Thirty-Nine Steps* (1915), but he
    also served as governor general of Canada. EP reviewed Buchan's *Oliver Cromwell* in
    the *NEW* (6 June 1935).
22 Murdoch, Kenneth Ballard (1895–1975). Professor of English at Harvard.
23 Tinkham, George. Republican representative from Massachusetts (see letters 31 and
    49B).
24 Long, Huey Pierce. Governor of Louisiana and Democratic senator (see Letter 31).
25 Coughlin, Father Charles Edward. Roman Catholic "radio priest" who preached eco-
    nomic reform over the airwaves in the 1930s.

Possibly USURY w. be a better subject than Banking.[26] but the tradition is so enormour , before English existed .. that I dunno about Butch doing it.

limit it to usury in Eng. tradition. with foreword by E. P. might get over that.

---

26 The book, *To-Morrow's Money,* would be a collection of essays on money written by "leading heretics."

Sept 10 · 35

Dear Ezra:

A letter from Liveright[1] asking for price of 500 sheets of Jeff/Muss. I've cabled 1/9 per sheet. It is a low price but if they take the book it will be a help to you and will go a long way towards expense of publishing.[2]

Yours ever
S.C.N.

1 Liveright, Horace Brisbin (1884–1933). An American publisher. According to Gallup, Liveright Publishing Corp. would publish the American edition of *J/M* on 24 January 1936, though the number of copies of this edition remains unknown. The Liveright edition also included EP's letter to the *Criterion* (January 1935) at the beginning.
2 Nott suggests a price of 1s. 9d. per sheet. EP approves of the Liveright interest in Letter 61.

[LETTER 61, TL, CARBON, EP TO SN, FOLDER 1583]

[pencil:
July?
Aug? 35][1]

Dear Nott

I Though Angold's review[2] very good. I suppose Mairet's[3] freudian complexes responsible for omission of publishers name and price. probably unconscious. " defense "

HAVE you any means of communication with Brenton.[4] If not try to get it. The idea of selected writings[5] OUGHT to open him up.

You shd. as they say here " accarezarlo ".[6] He is a good man, and knows it. I think he still despises me as an amateur.

Thatnk GOD someone else in England does NOT like amateurs.

He shd. see advance copy of Butch MONEY.[7] He shd. also get a ++++ J/M telling his sto skip everything up to p. 116, and

---

1 The letter is undated, but EP's discussion of Angold's review, a Brenton collection, Liveright interest, and Routledge places it circa 13–15 September.
2 J.P. Angold (Letter 49A) reviewed *J/M* in the *NEW* (12 September 1935).
3 Mairet, Philip. Editor of the *NEW*. Angold's review omits standard information on the publisher's name and book price, which EP attributes to Mairet's dislike of *J/M*.
4 Brenton, Arthur. Editor of the *New Age*.
5 EP likely proposed a collection of Brenton's writings in a previous letter that is missing from the correspondence, to which Nott responds favourably in Letter 59.
6 EP uses the Italian verb *accarezzare*, which means to caress or stroke gently.
7 Nott is in the process of publishing Montgomery Butchart's anthology, *Money* (1935).

suggest he quote some of the summary of Jeff.[8]

Butch. book shd. be sent to
 His Eccellency
    O.K.Allen[9]
        Governor of Louisiana
            Baton Rouge
            La.   U.S.A.

we MUST go all out for Huey's flock.[10]

Send a copy to YALE press. I have already written to them.
Right Oh re/ Liveright *& J/M*. sfar as I'm concerned.[11]

You have tried YALE or not ? they OUGHT to take it. or at
least make an offer.   no harm in having two strings[12]

Re/ my book on BUTCH compendium[13] etc. would it be better

publicity if I tried to shoot it into Routlege.[14]
that wd. buttress Butch. and reach different market

8 EP suggests that Brenton skip everything to page 116 (the middle of Chapter 30) of
    J/M, where EP summarizes "Jefferson's doctrines" (114).
9 Allen, Oscar Kelly (1882–1936). Democratic governor of Louisana from 1932 to 1936. He
    was a close associate of Huey Long, whom he succeeded as governor of Louisiana.
10 Long, Huey Pierce. In Letter 59, Pound instructs Nott to send him a copy of Butchart's
    Money.
11 Liveright was an American publisher (see Letter 60).
12 In Letter 62, Nott indicates that he has sent a copy to Yale.
13 EP is likely referring to his *What Is Money For?*, which was published by the British
    Union of Fascists' Greater Britain Publications in 1939.
14 Routledge and Kegan Paul Ltd. British publisher. Nott replies to this suggestion in
    Letter 62.

Spet [sic] 16th 1935

Dear Ezra:

Glad that you like the Money book.[1] And hope it will go as well as we expect.

Sales of Jeff[2] slow so far. Have not heard from T.R.Smith[3] yet. I'll send a copy to Yale at once.[4]

I see Brenton[5] ocassionally [sic]. Had thought of ge tting him to do a book and a pamphlet.

Write to Chas.T.Hallinan[6],11 Belsize Sq,London N.W.3 . I have no newspaper connections in America But Hallinan has a great many. He's a very nice Irishman extremely pro-English and an old friend of mine. I'll send him a copy of the book,Jeff/ Muss[7].If you start corresponding with him ,you may find him useful. He's with the associated Press here(or is it the United Press?)[8]

If you are thinking of doing a compendium it would certainly help things if Routledge would take it.[9]

1 Nott published *Money* by Montgomery Butchart in 1935. See letters 59 and 61.
2 EP's *J/M*. See Letter 63, in which Nott is more positive about sales.
3 T.R. Smith is the editor at Liveright who was handling the publisher's interest in *J/M*. See Letter 65.
4 See Letter 61.
5 Brenton, Arthur. Brenton ultimately did not publish with Nott's firm.
6 Hallinan, Charles T. (dates unknown). Little information is available on Hallinan. He wrote the introduction to Robert Liefmann's *International Cartels, Combines and Trusts* (1927), published *American Investments in Europe* (1927) as part of the same Europa series, and is listed as a co-debator in the pamphlet *Universal Military Training* (1919).
7 EP's *J/M*.
8 The Associated Press, a publisher's collective formed in 1848, and the United Press, a privately owned conglomerate formed in 1907, were competing media outlets.
9 Nott is likely referring to EP's *What Is Money For?* (1939), published by the British Union of Fascists' Greater Britain Publications. See Letter 61.

Referring to yours of 9th. I have hadthe idea in mind of doing an Econ Ref library myself.Have you any ideas on it?[10]

Yes: I am going in for text books.[11] We have three or four on the stocks.[12] But they need time and a hell of a lot of money. Thats why so many publishers go in for fiction. S.P.Q.R. I look for better profits and slow returns.

We shall have published 43 books and pamphlets by the end of next month - in about 19 months.

Yours

SCN [A S]

---

10 EP suggests in Letter 59 that more should be done to obtain subscriptions from a large Social Credit organization, such as John Hargrave's Green Shirts of Britain, to boost sales of Nott's pamphlets and other publications. The proposed "Economics Reference Library" would presumably differ from "The New Economics Library" (Letter 59, note 10), though no further discussion arises on the subject.

11 On textbooks, see letters 58 and 59.

12 The Latin phrase for which this is an abbreviation, *Senatus Populusque Romanus*, means "the Senate and the People of Rome," a motto used in ancient Rome to refer to Rome as a civilized republic that belonged to both the Senate and the people. Nott suggests that those publishers who "go in for fiction" imply that fiction belongs to the people only – but Nott believes otherwise; he will make unpopular decisions. Mussolini had S.P.Q.R. inscribed on civic buildings and manhole covers in Rome as propaganda for his regime, and public monuments and artefacts in Rome still often bear this acronym.

September 26th 1935

Dear Ezra:

J/M is going better than I expected.[1] We have sold about 200 copies including the ones sent to you. And about 50 presentation and review copies have gone out.

I cabled Liveright[2] but no news from him yet. Have written also.

Sent a copy of J/M to the secretary Italian Embassy here . They should buy copies for distribution. The book is the one stem against the flood of anti-Italian sentiment here. Feeling is strong against Mussolini.[3] People have to vent their resentment against life on someone - it has turned from Germany to Italy. And though I myself think that Italy's excuses are an insult to any half intelligent person,and that the invasion is [sic] belongs to gone and dead 19th century Imperialism, one must not go altogether with the tide. For that reason I am interested in pushing J/M. And it is a very good book.[4]

About finances.[5] By the end of October we shall have published 43 books and pamphlets in a period of 19 months. Five books - 2 economics,1 religious,2 cookery - which have been refused by several well established publishers, have been sold by us to the U.S.A. and have paid us well.
I am waiting until our Autumn list is out,and our printed catalogue, and then I am going to look round for more capital . We are more than solvent. But the total capital is only a little over £1300,and I have to try to keep my family out of the business.

1 EP's *J/M*. In Letter 62, Nott expresses concerns over slow sales.
2 See letters 60–62.
3 See Essay 2.
4 Mussolini ordered the invasion of Abyssinia on 3 October 1935, though the build-up to the invasion was evident long before this.
5 See letters 58 and 62.

However I shall not hold up Ideogrammi c[6] on that a/c,but I must get out the Autumn books within the next three weeks. Afterthat I shall go ahead with the early Spring ones.

I should like to get an American in^{to} the business of the type of Felix Morley.[7] I think I may put an ad in the N.Y. Publisher's weekly.[8] There are plenty of saps here Public School ninnies with money. The man with me[9] is that type. Faithful retriever type. Still, that is better than the plausible scoundrel.

I must say that the business is going very well; and it is intensely interesting. But this building up takes all of one's time. None left for S.C. politics.[10] Yours

     SCN [A S]

6 See Letter 58, in which Nott is eager to resume production on the Ideogrammic series.
7 Morley, Felix Muskett (1894–1982). A Pulitzer Prize-winning journalist and author. He was also editor of the *Washington Post* (1933–40) and the brother of Frank Morley (see Letter 34, note 18) of Faber and Faber.
8 The *Publisher's Weekly* (New York, 1873–). American trade magazine for publishers, booksellers, literary agents, and librarians on matters related to publishing.
9 Nott is likely referring to Kenneth Gee.
10 "Social Credit."

[LETTER 64, TLS, SN TO EP]
[STANDARD NOTT LETTERHEAD]

September 30th 1935

Dear Ezra:

Liveright thinks I quoted him too high on the sheets of Jeff/Muss.[1]
I priced them at 1/9. So I have written him again offering them at 11d
persheet,as he says that he will pay you the royalty. I hope he will
accept this offer. For one thing it will help us.In the second place if he
manufactures it himself he will have it photo-lithoed,and make a sorry
looking job of it,same as Yale did of "Make it New ".[2]   In any case we will
pay you a xxxxxx royalty on the sheets and since weare pricing them so
low they will pay you a royalty,I suggest 20% if they take 1000 sheets and
10% if they take 500.

The signed edition[3] came out so badly that I refuse d to publish it.But
I have had 10 copies of the ordinary edition put on one side and have had
the leaf tipped in. So if you want copies of the signed edition for your
friends you cann have them.

They may ahve [sic] a collectors valuee in time.

Yours ever
SCN [AS]

1 Nott reduces his price for sheets of *J/M* by nearly half, from 1s. 9d. to 11d.; however, in
  Letter 65, according to Nott, Liveright would opt instead to set up the book on its own.
2 Nott notes the faulty Yale edition of *Make It New* (1935) that followed the original
  Faber and Faber (1934). See letters 26 and 42.
3 Nott's refusal to publish here reads as at odds with Gallup's evidence for thirty copies
  of the signed edition, sold at 21s. The half-title-leaf tipped in reads: "Of this edition
  there are XXX copies numbered and signed by the author of which XXV are for sale."
  See letters 53 and 55 on the signed edition.

Have just received Muirs[4] MS for his pamphlet.Its very good. What
do you think of the NEW[5] these days, I think it is almost unreadable,
aprt [sic] from one or two odd articles ,yours,[6] TSE,[7] and the notes of the
week I had a talk with Mairet[8] and told him so. Mrs. O[9] looks after the
reviews I understand. They are pretty awful. If you will stop the war I
may come and see you next year.[10]

4 Muir, Edwin. Wrote *Social Credit and the Labour Party* (1935), no. 15 in the Pamphlets
   on the New Economics series.
5 The *New English Weekly*.
6 EP wrote fifty-nine "American Notes" columns for the weekly between 3 January 1935
   and 2 April 1936, in addition to many other articles and letters.
7 Eliot, T.S.
8 Mairet, Philip.
9 Jessie Orage was Orage's widow. On reviews, see also letters 47 and 51.
10 Italy would not invade Abyssinia until 3 October 1935, but tensions had been building
    for weeks, and at this point war in Africa seemed inevitable.

October 7th 1935

Dear Ezra :

Yours of the 1st.[1] I have written to Liveright[2] saying that they had better set up the book in the U S A . Much more satisfactory to you of course. I didnt know that they had written to you. I did say that I was willing to make any arrangement which would be in your interest, so I take it that T.R.Smith[3] will go ahead and manufacture. I have written them again since I heard from them offering them sheets at alower [sic] price. But I will withdraw the offer.

Have heard again from Arrow Editions[4] N. Y. They are interested in the rest of the series but not so much in WCW.[5] In a few days I will go into the matter and write to them. I hope we can fix up something with them.

Yours ever
SCN [A S]

1 This letter is missing from the correspondence.
2 For more on American publishing firm Liveright's interest in *J/M*, see letters 60–64. Despite Nott's efforts to sell sheets of his edition, in the final arrangement, Liveright set up another edition entirely in the United States.
3 Smith, T.R. Editor at Liveright. See Letter 62, note 3.
4 Arrow Editions would reprint *CWC* in 1936.
5 Nott indicates that Arrow Editions is also interested in the rest of the Ideogrammic series, though not as much in the work of William Carlos Williams.

[LETTER 66, TLS, SN TO EP]
[STANDARD NOTT LETTERHEAD]

Ezra Pound Esq   November 4th 1935
Hotel Italia
Via Quattro Fontane
Rome

Dear Ezra,
        It has just occurred to me that the long quotation which you
have taken from the American edition of the Chinese Character[1] may be
copyright. Will you let me know whether this is so or if you have obtained
permission from the American publishers.

                              Yours ever,
                              SCN [AS]

---

1 Gallup indicates that the Nott edition of *CWC* is reprinted from *Instigations* (1920)
   "with a few minor changes and the addition of a 'Foreword,' pp. 5–6, a brief 'Terminal
   Note,' p. 37, and an appendix 'With Some Notes [on *Chinese Written Characters*] by a
   Very Ignorant Man,' pp. [39]–52." The "long quotation" is likely the explanatory note in
   italics (signed "E.P. 1918") on page 7.

[LETTER 67, APCS, SN TO EP]
[NOTT POSTCARD LETTERHEAD]

Dear Ezra:

Nov 18[1] [pencil: "= 35"]

One copy of ∧*of J/M on* invoice Oct 26[2] *was sent to Sir L. Money.*[3]
2 copies sent to you. Three were charged. Does this explain it?
    Did you see review of Impact[4] *in Programme?*[5]
    Have heard again from Odon Por.[6]   *Hope we may be able to do*
something with him later.

Yrs
SCN

---

1   Given the nature of Nott's response, it is likely that EP had questioned the method of billing in a letter missing from the correspondence.
2   The invoice is for *J/M*.
3   Money, Sir Leo George Chiozza. British politician and writer.
4   EP's *Social Credit: An Impact*.
5   The *Programme* (Oxford, 1935–36) was a periodical of the Oxford University English Club, edited by A. Hodge, which had a short run of twenty-three numbers.
6   Por, Odon. In Letter 58, Nott mentions a letter from Por.

[LETTER 68, TLS, EP TO SN – HRHRC]

400 Corso Umberto

ROMA[1]
20 Nov [pencil: "35"]

Dear Stan [pencil: Nott]

The point of a Por pamphlet[2] is that is is practically certain to have large sale here. It can't be subsidized ; but it is practically certain to be bought. Save the trouble of having an official publication translated[3]

I suggested starting with pamphlet , because I though the experience wd/ lead you to idea that same result cd. be profitably attained with a book.

[ASC]
Pamphlet cd. be immediate.[4]   *AT ONCE*

Por is well known in England , from back in 1920. Sid. Webb[5] and THAT biological level , also he has an article due

1 For this address, see letters 66 and 71.
2 Nott mentions his correspondence with Odon Por in letters 58 and 67.
3 Por had "official" connections with the Italian government. EP notes this again in Letter 69.
4 Por published a series of articles on the New Economics in *Civiltà Fascista*, a monthly review brought out by the Fascist National Institute of Culture in Rome.
5 Webb, Sidney (1859–1947). Orthodox Labour economist, active member of the Labour Party, and long-time member of the Fabian Society along with G.B. Shaw. Webb, together with the Labour committee set up to evaluate it, found the Social Credit scheme "theoretically unsound and unworkable in practice" (qtd. Surette, *Purgatory*, 123).

in <u>Contemporary review</u>/[6] *proofs done* outside ^ the Social Credit pamphlet audience , in fact putting him in series might carry the rest of the series into new territory.[7]

      yrz

        EZ P   *E P* [AS]

6 *Contemporary Review* (1866–). Por's article, "The Italian Corporations at Work," which appeared in the December 1935 issue, praises the current economic system and government in Italy.
7 EP suggests that Por's popularity could attract a wider audience for the pamphlet series beyond the community already interested in Social Credit.

[LETTER 69, TLS, EP TO SN – HRHRC][1]

Church of Eng.   Have you seen Swabey's[2] stuff on
                              [ASC] *ME*?

        WOULD a VATICAN pamphlet be addition to New Econ.
series? might be GRAND stunt and seller.[3]

[following paragraph cancelled with a penstroke]
~~Nott shd write that letter to Por/ for sake of circumjacent effect on officialdom.~~[4]

        BUT he can write me one, NOT an order but an enquiry that I
can send ON and UP, It wd. at least stimulate INTEREST in social credit
in quarters where the interest wd. proliferate.
                    I want FORMAL letter to Mr Pound
not to Ez. in terms: "Wd. the Vatican authorities, or some catholic
authority be INTERESTED in collaborating or producing 15,000 ^*words*
on position of Church in 1936 on usury and the New Economics?

        At least might lead to collection of what I have writ and can write
on ethics of econ.[5] WITH archipiscopal benediction and license,thus
spreading the sales into new territory.

---

1 Part of Letter 69 is missing and it is undated, but content suggests it falls between letters 68 and 70.
2 Swabey, Reverend Henry S. Anglican minister and editor of the Social Credit paper *Voice*. Swabey's article, "The English Church and Money" does not appear until 1937 in the *Criterion*. EP's unpublished "Money and Morals" is edited by Swabey. "The Church of England and Usury" appears under Swabey's name in the Ezra Pound Collection at the Harry Ransom Humanities Research Center, the University of Texas at Austin.
3 EP claims below that the Vatican's views on usury are akin to those of Social Credit because both are against usury. EP would publish "The Church of Rome" (20 March 1936) in the periodical *Social Credit*. Surette notes EP's turn to the Roman Catholic Church 1936–42 (*Purgatory* 270–6).
4 Por had connections with the Italian government. See letters 67 and 68.
5 EP wrote several short pieces on usury and the church in various magazines during this period, including the *Morning Post*, the *NEW*, *Social Credit* , and the *British-Italian Bulletin*. His work on the ethics of economics is likely the unpublished "Money and Morals" book, collected and edited by Henry Swabey (see note 2).

I dunno if Mark[6] has anti=church PRINCIPLES. this second half page might worry him. Hell, we need a MAJORITY.

we need ALL the dynamics we can muster, and THEN

some. The Churrrrch is RIGHT about usury.

Ez

P [A S]

---

6 Mark, Jeffrey. Mark's *The Modern Idolatry* (1934) deals with usury and the pathology of debt.

Ezra Pound Esq   December 16th 1935
Hotel Italia
via Quattro Fontane
Rome

Dear Ezra,

      I hope the enclosed letter[1] is what you you [sic] want. I think
the idea of a book with the title 'THE CHURCH OF USURY- 1936'[2] or a
similar title is a very good one . But I should like to say, that if you are
going to do it, you could somewhat alter your style.

      You have been knocking them over the head with a big stick for
a long time now and I think they have become used to those sort of blows.
While retaining your force, which you must do in any case, you could
drop your large caps and write the book in another tone of voice. You
would make a great impression on your old public as well as on a new one.
It would be a most interesting experiment and I am sure would startle a
good many people.

      Anyhow let me know what you think of the idea.

        Yours ever,
         SCN [A S]

1 Nott is likely referring to the letter to Vatican authorities EP requests in Letter 69,
    which was designed to encourage the Church to take an official position on the New
    Economics. No evidence of the letter remains.
2 A typescript entitled "The Church of England and Usury" (302 pp.) appears under
    Henry Swabey's name in the Ezra Pound Collection at the Harry Ransom Humanities
    Research Center, the University of Texas at Austin. See Letter 69.

[LETTER 71, APC (NOT STANLEY NOTT) TO EP]
[NOTT POSTCARD LETTERHEAD]

21.12.35

*The proofs of "Chinese Written Character" were sent registered post
December 16th to you at Hotel Italia*
    via Quattro Fontane
    Rome.[1]

Perhaps you would kindly let us know when they reach you.

---

1 This autograph note is in a hand other than Nott's; perhaps that of associate
Kenneth Gee.

{YCAL MSS 43, SERIES I, BOX 37, FOLDER 1585}
[LETTER 72, TL, CARBON, EP TO SN]

[pencil: "Jan 36"][1]

Dear Stan

The proofs with the block proofs pasted into place; went off registered this a/m:[2]

I reckon yr/ title page was O.K.

it looked bad WITHOUT the ideogram/[3] but is , I think O.K. with it IN.

I had intended that occidentalized design to be reprod/ the same size as the ink drawing/ for use on jacket etc.

The cubistic effect was aimed at larger block/ however it goes very well/ and no need further expense.

The BIG " RAYS"[4] sign as used by Macmillan might be rescued if they still have the DIE/ it was stamped into cover of the Fenollosa vol.

---

1 Letter 72 is undated, though likely 17 January 1936 since EP marks its composition with the proofs being sent "registered this a/m": thus, EP wrote Letter 72A (16 January 1936) first, but sent it together with this one.
2 The proofs and blocks (of ideograms) are for *CWC*, which Nott would publish in March. The proofs were sent to EP along with Letter 71 (16 December 1935). EP likely aligned and pasted the blocks into place to show the printers where and how the ideograms should be positioned.
3 The ideogram appears below EP's name and above the imprint of Nott's firm (see Letter 72A). See EP's assessment of the title page of *J/M* in Letter 54.
4 The ideogram "Rays" is noted by EP as "bright + feathers / flying" (41). EP suggests that the die cast used by Macmillan for *"Noh" or Accomplishment: A Study of the Classical Stage of Japan* (1916) may still be recovered. See letters 35, 40, and 45.

Must be a brass die/ if they havent scrapped it
they wd. sell it to you cheap as it cant be any use to them.

(Mathews[5] had so common line block of it, used on Cathay
cover.)

THAT cd/ be used on jackets/ etc. and the" RENEW "[6]
on title pages.

/ / however I started to write about something else.
vide Enclosure.[7]

Elias Lowe ,[8] good guy/ putt me wise to Manuldruk.[9] Has a
comfy job doing HARMLESS paleography. great authority etc.

He broke into the close university racket/

has no capital/ BUT he wd. SYMPATHIZE
with the aim of the Ideogramic series/

You wd/ have to handle him. He is no bull
moose/

---

5 Mathews, Charles Elkin (1851–1921). British publisher and bookseller who printed
   many of EP's first publications, such as *Personae* (1909), *Cathay* (1915), and *Lustra*
   (1916). He used the "RAYS" ideogram on the cover of *Cathay* (1915).
6 The ideogram "Renew" (see letters 24, 35, and 40).
7 Letter 72A is likely the "Enclosure" and thus written prior to Letter 72 (see note 1).
8 Lowe, Elias Avery (1879–1969). A paleographer and correspondent of Pound.
9 Manuldruck (Dutch) is a type of flat surface reproduction (planographic) invented by
   Max Ulmann (1865–1941) in which a film or glassplate with a chromate layer is laid
   down on the page to be copied. Under the right illumination this film-plate becomes
   a negative, which is transferred to an offsetplate. According to Richard Sieburth,
   EP used the process when collecting Cavalcanti manuscripts in Italy. See "EP/LZ:
   Corresponding Cavalcantis," paper delivered at the Louis Zukofsky Centennial
   Conference, Columbia University and Barnard College, 17 September 2004.

Best type of semite   . INTERESTED.

He might put you in the WAY of touching something.

Of course HE is INSIDE now , in the Oxford press to

which however , I take it he brings american foundation money.

But no reason why YOU by noble aims shouldn't arrive at

that fountain.

even the you aint Oxfoot or the Fatty can city.[10]

anyhow, it is a long chance.

If you are in Oxford , drop in on him.   6 Oriel St.

I have just writ him this morning[11] apropos of other matters and

not naming YOU.

One never knows ENOUGH people.

we cd/ both do with a subsidy for SCHOLARLY publications.

verb. sap.[12]

yrz. EZ

---

10 Lowe's relationship with Oxford remains unclear, but he published a number of works
    through Oxford University Press and Clarendon Press. EP seems to think there is a
    chance of advancing Nott's interests through Lowe. The "Oxfoot or the Fatty can city"
    remark is likely a reference to Oxford or Vatican City.
11 EP corresponded with Lowe during the mid-1930s.
12 *Verbum sapienti*, or "a word to the wise."

[LETTER 72A, TL, EP TO SN]

16   Jan [pencil: "36"][1]

Dear Stan

The ideogram[2] will have to stay on TITLE page as it is the only thing that holds the page together.

It couldn't have been larger for that position.

The RAYS is CHINESE. Japs. use the ideogram. It is the second character on page 10.

but Fenollosa had a BIG one by itself

I used it also on cover of Cathay.[3]

P. 19 the ideogram must have its TOP pulled to the right. side lines shd/ be perpendicular not leaned backward.

P.42, Ideograms LINE 1, No. 2. etc. Not column 1.[4]

Will try to collect strength enough to shove off the proofs tomorrow morning.[5]

---

1 The year is not given but is certainly 1936. The letter is included with Letter 72, though it was composed one day prior.
2 See Letter 72.
3 EP is likely responding to a particular question raised in the set of proofs or in a separate letter now missing from the correspondence. On *Cathay* (1915) and the ideograms, see letters 35 and 72.
4 EP is providing instructions for the proper setting of the ideograms.
5 See Letter 72.

Lowe[6] is in Spain at the moment. however, write to him ANYhow. May
be back any time.

   can not / I my preference
be ware / emphasizes original meaning.
I dont mind what you do   re/ italica[7]

The american spelling can stand as Felollosa's and the new notes

as mine. I have no great urge one way or the other.[8]

but so far as I am concerned I see no use

paying printer to make alterations that dont affect the SENSE

  There are no more blocks, and no more needed at various

p points queeried.

   The brackets etc/ dont matter TO ME. and please settle

any such trifles at your end. I will be content with whatever

you do. But I dont NEED any alterations. seems waste of time

and printing charges.[9]

---

6 Lowe, Elias Avery. See Letter 72.
7 EP is likely responding to some general questions regarding consistent use of italics,
   spelling, brackets, and so on and is giving his preference for "can not" (over "cannot")
   and "be ware" (over "beware"). He believes that this idiosyncratic spacing conveys his
   precise meaning. In contrast, he has no distinct preference regarding the use of italics.
8 Nott likely pointed to a discrepancy in British and American spelling since CWC was
   first printed as an essay in *Instigations* (1920). For the Nott edition, EP supplied more
   material. See also Letter 66.
9 EP closes the typography discussion by questioning the value of alterations that do not
   "affect the sense."

The proofs sent by O/R/[10] have
evidently been lost. are are held up somewhere. Anyhow not needed. I
MEANT them to be sent to YOU , without coming out here.

10 Rudge, Olga (1895–1996). An American violinist and music scholar. Rudge met EP in
Paris in 1923, and the two remained lovers and companions until his death.

[LETTER 73, APCS, SN TO EP]
[NOTT POSTCARD LETTERHEAD]

Jan 27ᵗʰ · 36

A parcel of books is being sent to you. Tomorrows Money and Orage Polite Essays from Butchart. The rest from me.[1]
Ive been ill nearly two months – am off to Paris for a change. I hear from Gill[2] *that you seem still to be interested in Social Credit. If there is anyone in Paris whom you think I might see, will you send a p.c. to me c/o Shakespeare & Co.*
            Yours
                Stanley Nott

1 The books from Montgomery Butchart are *To-Morrow's Money, by Seven of Today's Leading Monetary Heretics* (1936) and *Political and Economic Writings of A.R. Orage* (1936), both edited by Butchart and published by Nott. The books Nott sent remain unclear.
2 Likely Eric Gill (1882–1940), a British sculptor, engraver, and typographer. Gill published *Money and Morals* (1934) on the tenuous balance between material wealth and moral life.

Ezra Pound Esq   February 7th 1936
Via Marsala 12/5
Rapallo
Italy

Dear Ezra,

Herewith page proofs of Ta Hio which I think will be a worthy successor of Ideogramic No. 1.[1]

There should be very few corrections but I should like to get it back with your O. K.

Personally I am very pleased with it and now we can get on with the W.C.W.[2]

Yours ever

Stanley Nott [AS]

1   EP's translation of Confucius's *Ta Hio*, which Nott would publish in May 1936 as no. 2 in the Ideogrammic series.
2   William Carlos Williams's *In the American Grain* was the next projected booklet in the series. See Letter 75.

Feb 18th 1936

Dear Ezra:

Attached is a list of the Seven Essays of WCW which we propose to make the 2nd Vol[1]   Will you do a short blurb showing the connection between "In the American Grain" and Ideogrammic? I don't see the connection myself.[2] ~~What do you~~ And I think we ought to have a note on the scope & purpose of Ideogrammic. Also what do you propose to make the next three titles?[3]

Final proof of jacket enclosed.[4] I'm very pleased with it.

Yrs ever
Stanley Nott

I'm writing to Jane Soames.[5]

---

1 Here Nott slates *In the American Grain: Seven Essays* by William Carlos Williams as no. 2 in the Ideogrammic series.
2 There is no evidence of either the "blurb" or a reply to this letter.
3 For this thread, see letters 10, 14, 24, 34, 40, and 49A.
4 CWC, which Gallup notes is in "[b]lack cloth boards, with imitation vellum back stamped in red with rule on each side and lettered in red down the spine; end-papers; top edges stained black. Cream dust-jacket printed in red and black." See also letters 72 and 72A.
5 Soames, Jane (1900–88). Author and, in the 1930s, assistant to Hilaire Belloc (see Letter 35, note 12). She is responsible for the authorized translation of Benito Mussolini's *The Political and Social Doctrine of Fascism* for the Hogarth Press in 1932. Soames was also on the staff of the *Times* in Paris. It is unclear why Nott is writing to her. Nott would publish Soames's *The English Press: Newspapers and News* later in 1936.

ANNO XIV   VIA MARSALA 12-5

1936   {Gaudier-Brzeska head of EP}

E. POUND   **RAPALLO**

[ASC, EP, upper
RH corner:]
Routledge
19 Feb[1]   *won't advertise*
re Butchart.
Dear Stan   *CON found it.]*[2]

I enc/ another copy Corriere rev/[3]

Armed with this, you might (or even if it hadn't occurred) you might

combine virtue with profit. They are well disposed to me at <u>15 Greek</u>

<u>Street</u>.

Fascio di Londra.[4]

^*I* have done a bit for their British Italian Bulletin.[5] If you called IN

PERSON you cd. graciously give 'em permission to QUITE the Jeff/ Muus[6]

---

1 EP uses the Gaudier-Brzeska letterhead and dates the letter by the fascist calendar,
   notable markers of this period of his writing.
2 Routledge is a British publishing firm. See letters 61 and 62. Montgomery Butchart
   published *Money* (1935) and *To-Morrow's Money* (1936) with Stanley Nott Ltd.
3 *Corriere della Sera* (1876–1945), an influential Milan-based daily newspaper. According
   to Preda, Camillo Pellizzi's review of *J/M* in *Corriere della Sera* (14 February 1936) was
   written at Odon Por's request.
4 Camillo Pellizzi (see note 12), a professor of Italian at University College London, organized Italian Fascists in London in the 1920s and 1930s. The relation of the "Fascio di
   Londra" to other British Fascist organizations remains unclear. See also Letter 79.
5 *British-Italian Bulletin* (dates unknown). A propaganda organ edited in England by
   Carlo Camagna for the Italian government. Redman notes that it was a supplement
   to *Italia Nostra*, an Italian newspaper published in Great Britain (*Ezra Pound and
   Italian Fascism* 168). EP published twenty-nine pieces there between 27 December
   1935 and 24 October 1936. In a letter to Odon Por (4 March 1936), EP suggests that his
   own articles in the magazine "convert the converted" (Preda, *Ezra Pound's Economic
   Correspondence*, 185).
6 EP's *J/M*.

(carry a copy with you) and GET
IT INTO their heads that it is REALLY the most important
piece of Italian propaganda yet printed in English or in
England.[8]

[In R margin,
ASC, EP:]
*They ought to
review it in
either Ital or
Eng. section*[7]

Dont say I said so/

take S/N the virtuous pubr/ (damn it all you had

the GUTS to print it when it was NOT favoured by the Keynses[9] and shits/
It dont need the SAME blurb as in Corriere. but

it is full of ammunition for <u>them</u>. and of the kind that shd/ heal a lot of

idiocy/ and clean up the Genevas.[10]
yrs. EZ

Camanga[11] may not have felt free or may not have felt it as timely to lay on
Soc Credit as thick as Pellizi[12] has, but with the Corriere behind him he cd
face whatever financial current there may be.

EP [AS]

7 The *British-Italian Bulletin* published both Italian and English sections.
8 EP strokes two heavy lines beside this paragraph to emphasize its importance.
9 Keynes, John Maynard (1883–1946). A British economist and professor at Cambridge.
   He is considered by many to be the father of modern macroeconomics, whose proposals for a planned economy and theory of full employment as set out in the *General
   Theory of Employment, Interest, and Money* (1936) revolutionized the field. Keynes
   was critical of Social Credit, and particularly of Douglas's A + B Theorem, though he
   admitted the value of both Douglas's and Silvio Gesell's work. See Essay 1.
10 EP is convinced of the positive reception and impact his book will have with the
   London-based fascists and believes his work to be an antidote to the Geneva-based
   League of Nations. The League of Nations had condemned Italy's aggression in
   Abyssinia and imposed economic sanctions in November 1935.
11 Camagna, Carlo (dates unknown). Editor of the *British-Italian Bulletin* (see note 5).
12 Pellizzi, Camillo. Friend of EP and professor of Italian at University College, London.
   Pellizzi was president of the National Institute of Fascist Culture.

Ezra Pound Esq   March 16th 1936
via Marsala 12/5
Rapallo
Italy

Dear Ezra,

　　　　Miss Codman of Arrow Editions[1] of New York tells me that another publisher in the United States is anxious to procure and publish the 'CHINESE WRITTEN CHARACTER' in a specisl edition.[2]

　　　　I have informed her that all rights belong to you and as she is taking an American edition from us this will establish copyright for her. Please let me know by return if this is correct. The fact that she is taking 350 sheets from us makes it possible to pay the printers bill.

Yours ever,
SCN [AS]

[AN] *I went to see Fascisti Londra and left a copy of the book.[3] This was over a week ago. No news yet.*

1　Codman, Florence (dates unknown). Owner of Arrow Editions (see Letter 65) in New York. She purchased 350 sheets of CWC, which appeared through Arrow Editions in November 1936.
2　Unclear who the "other publisher" is, but Nott attempts to clarify that, while EP retains the rights, Codman and Arrow Editions own the copyright in the United States. No special edition appeared.
3　EP's *J/M*, which, in Letter 76, EP requested Nott deliver a copy of to the Fascio di Londra.

[LETTER 78, TLS, EP TO SN – HRHRC]
[EP, GAUDIER-BRZESKA LETTERHEAD, ANNO XIV, 1936]

[pencil: March ? 36]

18 March[1]

Dear Stan

The sale to Codman STANDS.[2] I told the other nibbler[3] that you were arranging it.

If the " other pubr " is ^ or wants to be any use he can print something ELSE.

E. P
[AS]

Was about to send the enc/ on Frobenius[4] to Butch[5] to pass on to you. Will you, pass it on to him/ at r/ convenience.

---

1 The copy of this letter in the Harry Ransom Humanities Research Center is dated 18 March, although Pound scrawls on the carbon copy "About 20."

2 EP is replying to Nott's request in Letter 77 for confirmation of the sale to Florence Codman and Arrow Editions. See also letters 79 and 91.

3 An unnamed publisher, perhaps Charles Reznikoff, is discussed in Letter 77. See also Letter 91.

4 The enclosed piece is on Leo Frobenius, the German anthropologist whose work EP admired. In Letter 79, Nott thanks EP for an "article on Frobenius."

5 Butchart, Montgomery.

Ezra Pound Esq   March 23rd 1936
Via Marsala 12 – 5
Rapallo
Italy.

Dear Ezra,

The sheets have gone off to Codman and I have allayed her anxiety about the other publisher.[1] Codman does not want to take Ta Hio.[2]   Do you know of any other publisher who would take it? It seems to me there should be someone in America who could sell 350 copies of a well printed book like this. What about the Limited Editions Club?[3] I will send them a copy.

Thanks for the article on Frobenius.[4] Has the book been translated into English?

No word from your friends the Londera Facisti. I lent them a copy of Jeff: together with the article, over three weeks ago.[5]

A note from Mr Soames this morning saying he has sent his sister's Ms.[6]

1   The sheets have been sent to Florence Codman (see Letter 77) of Arrow Editions to produce the American edition of CWC. See also Letter 78.
2   EP's translation of Confucius's Ta Hio.
3   The Limited Editions Club (New York) was founded in 1929 by George Macy and focused on producing highly specialized editions for subscribers, often of literary classics, in limited numbers. An illustrated edition of EP's Cathay: Poems After Li Po by Francesco Clemente was published by Limited Editions in 1992.
4   Frobenius, Leo. German anthropologist.
5   Fascio di Londra. See Letters 76 and 77.
6   The manuscript is likely for Jane Soames's The English Press: Newspapers and News, which Nott would publish later that year. See letters 75 and 81.

We shall have to wait a little before we publish William Carlos Williams.[7]

Have you seen our full page advertisement in the New English Weekly?[8]

As to publishing more non-sellable good stuff - the position is that we have been going now for two and a half years on a very small capital. We can last another two months. If something does not turn up by then we shall have to close up or sell the business. The business is a very good going concern. I am in touch with a few people who may be interested and I hope by that time we shall be able to reorganise.[9]

Yours ever,
Stanley Nott [AS]

---

7 Here, Nott alters his ambitious schedule for the Ideogrammic series slightly from that noted in letters 74 and 75.
8 Nott often advertised his books and pamphlets in the *NEW*.
9 In Letter 76, EP praises Nott as a virtuous publisher because of his non-profit motive, but Nott's comments here indicate considerable financial challenges as a result.

VIA MARSALA 12-5

E. POUND

RAPALLO

26 March[1]

Sorry/ capitalists always HAVE shunned me.[2] I dont know whether
Hughes[3] still has copies of Ta Hio/ or whether he had electros made. I
shd/ think he probably had electros; and wd. u use 'em rather than import
sheets/ unless he is dead or gone out of business. NO/ of course Frobenius
isn't translated. Fox is preparing a pamphlet. 32 pages/[4] BUT   if you are
stuck, I spose that goes goes WEST. ... heaven knows the catalogs of other
pubrs/ do NOT reflect any glory on England or indicate literacy or even
human etc/ etc/[5]

Ed Wallace[6] THE voice of the nation and absolootly the HIGHEST they
can stand. Not without merit/ and preferable to Bloomsburry.

Yrs. E. P.

1 The postmark is not entirely legible, but EP's date and the content of the postcard
   suggest that it replies to Letter 79.
2 EP is responding to Nott's want of capital, which is made clear in Letter 79.
3 Hughes, Glenn (Arthur) (1894–1964). An American writer and editor who published EP's translation of Confucius's Ta Hio in 1928 as no. 14 in the University of
   Washington Chap-Book series. EP also responds to Nott's inquiry about an American
   publisher willing to take on the booklet, suggesting that Hughes might be interested in
   reissuing it. "Electros" are electro-static copies, which means that Hughes would not
   need sheets.
4 Frobenius, Leo. German anthropologist. Frobenius's assistant was Douglas Fox. In
   Letter 83, Nott comments on the recommended number of pages of Fox's piece.
5 In Letter 79, Nott notes the financial trouble facing the firm.
6 Wallace, (Richard Horatio) Edgar (1875–1932). Writer, playwright, and journalist whose
   mysteries and thrillers were popular during the first half of the twentieth century. EP
   invokes him as the pinnacle of British popularity (on EP on Bloomsbury, see letters 3,
   14, 26, and 28).

Ezra Pound Esq   March 27th 1936
Via Marsala 12 – 5
Rapallo
Italy

Dear Ezra,

We have given Jane Soames manuscript "The English Press"[1] a
hasty glance through and we are very interested in it. We are going to give
it a thorough reading before finally deciding.

In the meantime perhaps you could tell me something about Jane
Soames.[2] My first impression is that it is quite a brilliant piece of work.

I take it she is no longer with the 'Times'.

Higham[3] has just sent in your book on 'Money'.[4] I thought the idea
was for some other publisher to do the book and I still think it is the best
idea. However I shall be interested to read the Ms., but I don't think we
ought to publish it.[5]

Yours ever,
Stanley Nott [AS]

---

1 Nott would publish Jane Soames's *The English Press: Newspapers and News* in 1936.
2 See EP's reply, Letter 82.
3 David Higham Associates is a UK literary agency that was established in 1935.
4 Likely *What Is Money For?*, which the publishing wing of the British Union of Fascists,
   Greater Britain Publications, issued in April 1939.
5 The initial idea for "some other publisher" was Routledge (see Letter 61), which EP
   confirms in Letter 82.

[A SC, EP]
30
March[1]

Dear Stan

" The idea ~~WASH~~ WAS "[2]

dont mix your tenses. May ideas have
Was'd.

Warburg[3] who was interested has left Routlege. Faber is
F_{aber}/ I spoose I shd/ write for the nurshing mirror.[4]
WAAAAL/

If you aint got any KAPITALLLLLLL , tha'zat. You can read
it to increase yr/ culchurl heritage.[5]

I suggest you see Bardsley[6]   AFTER you get
THOROUGHLY enthused over the high quality and general
indespiensib=ility of the work (E. P. on ~~MONEY~~%)   and see wot
can be did about it.

---

1 The letter responds directly to Letter 81 (27 March 1936).
2 Referring to EP's *What Is Money For?*, Nott writes in Letter 81: "I thought the idea was for some other publisher to do the book."
3 Warburg, Frederic John (1898–1981). Publisher and co-owner of the Secker and Warburg firm.
4 Faber and Faber publishers. The *Nursing Mirror* was a weekly magazine owned by Sir Maurice and Lady Gwyer, who merged with Geoffrey Faber in 1925. The magazine was sold in 1929, and they parted ways, leaving behind the successful Faber and Faber.
5 See Letter 58 for Nott's "want of capital."
6 Bardsley, William L. (dates unknown). Editor of *Social Credit* ("the official organ of the Social Credit Secretariat Limited") and secretary of the Social Credit Secretariat.

Bardsley is IMPROVED. He thinks YOU are tinged with Chandosi⌐Sm or Cursitor St. etc.[7]

Damn it all SOMEONE has got to do some sales talk.

Butchart's *"Money"* ought to (as I am telling 'em) ^ *be* ON their list of required reading.[8]

If NOBODY every talks to anyone else / if every segment of S/cr movement limits its activity to chiseling thaZATT. Tell the Secretariat you want to COLLABORATE.[9]

My ~~ar/~~ series on Douglas ,[10] which Mairet[11] says he is starting to print OUGHT to bring closer relation between the two offices.

I dont know what they are publishing apart from Soc/ CR[12]

2d   weekly
^ let 'em SERIALIZE the" Money "[13] if they like. or get into a pow wow as to how much is essential/

---

7 "Chandoism" refers to the Chandos Group, and 38 Cursitor Street is the address of the *NEW*.
8 Montgomery Butchart's *Money* was published by Nott in 1935.
9 EP voices his frustration over the failure of Social Credit factions to work together, and he suggests that Nott should attempt to bring them together. On the Social Credit Secretariat, see Letter 26.
10 Douglas, Major C.H. EP published four articles on Douglas's *Economic Democracy* in the *NEW* in April and May 1936 that he believed would help bridge the gap between the Secretariat and other Social Credit factions.
11 Mairet, Philip. Editor of the *NEW*.
12 The rest of the sentence is cut off at the bottom of the page.
13 Unclear whether EP means his own (note 2) or Butchart's book on money (note 8), and whether he is suggesting it be serialized in *Social Credit*, the *Fig Tree* (another periodical under the auspices of the Social Credit Secretariat), or another publication altogether. However, as Pound scrawls "weekly" at the top of page 2 of this letter, he might be referring to *Social Credit*, which was a weekly, rather than the *Fig Tree*, which was a quarterly. Pound did contribute "The Language of Money: Extracts from an Unpublished Manuscript by Ezra Pound" to the *Fig Tree* (no. 2, September 1936).

There is an ad/ of the Ta Hio in British Ital Bulletin.[14]
al*l* premature if you can un=hock it from the squinters.

/ /

Soames gal/[15] all I know IZ she had a good article in English
Review[16] and I wrote to her to GIT ON with it, whereto she
sez " IMA workin goil , and I am a ritin to livv. " Bully sez I ,
I wish I could do both or either.

I sez most pubrs/ iz skunks but mebbe Stanny[17] wd. print it.

*H*ence yr/ unrivaled opporchoonity IF you can get the
spondes oligos[18] or however you spells it , the small tribute az
the dirty greeks called it. /the ooliks.

Why aint ^*you* got a WAY wiff olde ladies. Damn it all I cant
do everything. sweetness an light[19] sez EZ/

E P   [A S]

---

14 E P refers to an ad in the *British-Italian Bulletin* (see Letter 76) for *Ta Hio*. E P was
    publishing frequently in the *British-Italian Bulletin* at this time, and he indicates
    that the ad might be "premature" because the booklet is held up at the printers
    ("squinters"). See Letter 84.
15 E P is replying to Nott's request in Letter 81 for information on Jane Soames (see Letter
    75).
16 The *English Review* (1908–37) was a literary magazine edited by Ford Madox Ford.
17 Stanley Nott.
18 The phrase roughly translates as "little promise," or "little tribute."
19 The phrase is Matthew Arnold's from *Culture and Anarchy* (1869).

Ezra Pound Esq   March 30th 1936
Via Marsala 12 – 5
Rapallo
Italy

Dear Ezra,

     Thank you for your card of March 26th.[1] Is Fox doing a
Frobenius pamphlet[2] for us? If so it certainly ought to be more than 32
pages. We can't get more than 1/- for a pamphlet but we can get 2/- and
sell just as many for a 62 page booklet.[3]

     What shall we do about your Money book?[4]

     Yours ever,
       Stanley Nott [A S]

1 See Letter 80, a postcard.
2 Fox, Douglas Claughton. Assistant of German anthropologist Leo Frobenius.
3 In Letter 40, Nott draws a distinction between a "pamphlet" and a "booklet."
4 In Letter 81, Nott notes that David Higham Associates sent him the manuscript of
   What Is Money For? Nott chose not to publish the book, which was later printed by the
   British Union of Fascists' Greater Britain Publications in 1939.

[ASC, EP]
1 Ap[1]

Dear Stan

If you are absolootly blocked and frozen and the Ta Hio[2] still held by avid printers, I dunno as it is much use discussin the length of FOX's tale.[3]

/ /

The POR you <u>could realize</u> on, as a number of copies would certainly be bought for distribution by parties having more than passive interest in the matter.[4]

Do you want me to put that more plainly. BUT every day of delay weakens their specific interest.

Wait for the final collapse of Eden[5] and those god drivveling idiots / by the time the Shitish Empire is completely off the map etc/

---

1 The letter replies to Letter 83.
2 *Ta Hio* appears to be held up at printers for want of capital to guarantee the bill.
3 Fox, Douglas Claughton.
4 Por, Odon. The work in question remains unclear, and no evidence exists of a Por publication through Stanley Nott Ltd. See also letters 67 and 68. Considering EP's comments below "about Italy, and the Corporate state," the book in question may be a collection of Por's articles published in *Civilta Fascista* under the heading "Chronicles of the 'New Economics.'"
5 Eden, (Sir Robert) Anthony (1897–1977). A British politician and prime minister (1955–57). He was Britain's minister to the League of Nations in 1934. Whether EP is referring obliquely to Eden here or, more generally, to England as a nation that is soon to lapse from an Edenic state of ignorance remains unclear.

and the Impact of a book

on Italy wd. NOT interest people on this side of the frontier.

You can't get an order until the book is at least in printers hands.

I dont know what a " great many "[6] means, it ought to cover
the printing bill.

[ASC]: *To*
^Not accelerate support , write at once t*o* Por/
  1. That book has gone to printers.
  2. that it will be pubd/ in the U.S.A. or at least that you are
making ever effort to that end.

THREE/ N.B. that IF the book sells well, you will [page cut off
here, but likely continues as below]
[...]

would like to go on with FURTHER publication of his writings
about Italy, and the Corporate state , such as his

article on *B*ankers in N.E.W. for March 26.

Such a letter ought to go to him at once. Sticking to facts

I suppose Butch[7] has delivered the mss/ If not GET IT AT ONCE
and write to Por that you have recd. it.

E. P.   [AS]

---

6 EP's quotation marks indicate that he likely responds to a letter missing from the
   correspondence.
7 Butchart, Montgomery.

6 Maggio[1]

[AN, EP]: *TA HIO* <u>*recd*</u>[2]

Dear Stan

Gorr noze[3] whether you've got any business sense/O Hara Cosgrove[4] says you haven't but you are a damn good publisher and constructor of format.[5]

I spose you'll git yr/ reward in heaven ... and an honourable slab in some crematorium.

Howz the innellexshul life in the fog=Bound ? ~~Woe~~ do you meet anyone who can answer letters or discus problems of current interest?

N/quirinly yrn *E. P.* [AS]

---

1 The date is 6 May 1936, as indicated by the postmark.
2 EP indicates here that he has finally received the copy of *Ta Hio*. See letters 82 and 84.
3 "God knows."
4 Cosgrave, John O'Hara (dates unknown). Literary editor of the *New York World* and editor of *Everybody's Magazine*. In his memoirs, Nott mentions him as a member of Gurdjieffian circles (*Teachings of Gurdjieff* 88). Cosgrave contributed to the NEW in 1933 and 1934.
5 In letters 56 and 76, EP also praises Nott's sense of design.

May 13[1] [pencil: "36"]

Dear Ezra:

I should consider myself a bad business man if I published Jack Cosgrave's books.[2] *About the only persons who have anything to say these days are Jane Heap & T. S. Eliot.   Jane Heap & I are proposing to start a magazine. Quarterly review of the various sides of life. Art & lit & all that.*

I'm trying hard to get more capital. In two weeks I'll either have it or have no business.

One of these days I'm going to send out a questionnaire to Cosgrave etc. : "What is a business man"?

When C. H. Douglas says to me, "Well, I'm a business man," it means that if he I can pay a higher royalty than any one else he'll give me his book. I'm in touch with a group of "business men" who make mistakes that no second-rate poet would make. I hate the "business man" in quotation marks. What one looks for is commonsense in business.

SCN

1 The date of this letter is likely 13 May 1936.
2 Cosgrave, John O'Hara. See Letter 85. Nott seems to use Cosgrave to exemplify business-minded publishers and editors who go in for popularity and moneymaking rather than principled ideas. As editor for *Everybody's Magazine*, unlike Nott, Cosgrave aimed to reach wide audiences and to make money. Critics of *Everybody's Magazine* derided it as sensationalist.

[ASC, EP] *20 May*[1]

Hope this arrives as CONGratutations and not as a lily to putt in th' 'and of the firm.[2]

Did you sell Chi/wr/Charac sheets to some gal in the U.S.A.? and did she pay? and if so, how long is decent before answering requests fer an american edition?[3]

HereZZ to Jane/[4] an of course a maggerzeen that cd/ PAy contributors wd/ be manna and blessing// and one that wd. specialize in printing stuff fit to read wd/ be antistorico as far as England is concerned but here's to it.[5]

E. P. [AS]

1 The date on the postcard is handwritten, and the postmark confirms it to be 20 May 1936.

2 EP is responding to Nott's dire predictions for the firm in Letter 86. See also letters 93 and 94.

3 EP is likely referring to Florence Codman (see Letter 77) of Arrow Editions and the purchase of 350 sheets of *CWC* for reprint in America. It remains unclear who is making the request. EP also indicates in Letter 91 that "rez," likely Charles Reznikoff of the Objectivist Press, may also have inquired.

4 In Letter 86, Nott notes that he and Jane Heap propose to begin a quarterly magazine.

5 EP notes the importance of magazines that can pay contributors and print "fit" matter, two specialties EP considers "antistorico" (against the grain of history) but supports. In the "Letter" introducing the Liveright edition of *J/M*, EP notes: "One element of the Duce's gamut is the continual gentle diatribe against all that is 'anti-storico,' all that is against historic process" (v).

May 22[1] [pencil: "36"]

Dear Ezra:

I brought T. S. Eliot and Jane Heap together the other day at lunch. They got on fine - & we had a very good talk. T. S. thinks your [sic] the greatest living critic. Did your ears burn last Tuesday? Jane and I are thinking of starting a new quarterly[2] New Age, Little Review. I'll tell you more about it in a few days. Could you get a translation by a young Italian writer who has something to say – prose or poetry? If anyone has anything to say there. <u>Not</u> straight New Economics. Also something from you – not straight SC to begin with.

Yrs ever

Stanley Nott

I think Eliot is right about you. Since Orage,[3] theres no one but yourself who <u>can</u> criticize. But you seem to have made it impossible for many people to read you – they refuse to read you or they can't abide you.

---

1 The year is not given, but the content clearly follows that of Letter 87 (20 May 1936).
2 On the possibility of a new magazine, see also letters 86, 87, 89, and 92–4.
3 Orage, A.R.

[LETTER 89, TLS, EP TO SN – HRHRC]
[EP, GAUDIER-BRZESKA LETTERHEAD, ANNO XIV, 1936]

24 Maggio[1]

Dear Stan :   and " jh"[2]

Granting all   that you say

1. What is the USE of a magazine unless it is to feed the
greatest livin' etc.   ??

2. Why the bleeding HELL shd. I write ANYTHING for
bug^gars who are too snotten DUMB to be interested in
economics ?

Econ/ AS motivation

Econ/ as conditioning circumstance.

????[3]

If the Criterion[4] can't pay for Cantos, I dont suppose Jane can.
Also WHAT program is there ?
There has been ONE really vital influence in Eng/ criticism and
Eliot don't recognize him at all.

1 The letter replies to Letter 88.
2 Heap, Jane.
3 EP reiterates his steadfast investment in economics, likely a response to Nott's request
   in Letter 88 for other than straight economics.
4 EP is referring to the *Criterion* (1922–39), a periodical edited by T.S. Eliot, and to
   his own *Cantos*. EP restates his belief that a magazine must pay its contributors and
   maintain a clearly defined program or policy.

Or say that there was   ONE man who was RIGHT in 1908

and that none of the highbrows can abide <u>him</u>.

I mean F.M.Ford[5]
                    who has tal^ked and written a lot of fluff
but was right about WRITING

Eliot came to Versona and we made a program for the Criterion

which   was   never published, and   then   not   USED

I am not going to collaborate in the program of the FABER[6] anthology

(Mike Roberts[7])

I see NO use in a mag/ that can not pay at least as much

as the Little Review did.

Unless I can ha^ve 150 quid[8] a year for myself and the people

I choose to ask. I am damned if I see how or why.

5 Replying to Nott's and T.S. Eliot's praise of him as the only living critic (see Letter 88),
   EP offers Ford Madox Ford (1873–1939) instead.
6 The significance of EP's refusal to "collaborate in the program" of editor Michael
   Roberts's *The Faber Book of Modern Verse* (1936) is ambiguous. A selection of EP's
   poetry does appear in the anthology but, as Janet Adam Smith recounts in the 1983
   reprint from Faber and Faber, not without issue. When first approached by Roberts
   about inclusion, according to Roberts in a letter to T.S. Eliot (28 March 1935), with
   whom he negotiated the book, EP "roared" and was "difficult" (qtd. in Smith, xvi). By
   May, Roberts had reworked his selection of EP to Eliot's approval and suggested he
   could offer EP £20 of the £150 he had at his disposal for the entire project. EP seems to
   have relented.
7 Roberts, Michael (1902–48). British poet and critic who edited *The Faber Book of
   Modern Verse* as well as *New Signatures* (1932) and *New Country* (1933) for the Hogarth
   Press.
8 The *Little Review* did not pay contributors until EP joined the staff in 1917, securing
   £150, or $750, from New York lawyer and patron John Quinn (see note 12) over a two-
   year period.

You note jane says " N.Age , Little Review ".[9]

WELL, Orage[10] paid me a guine^a a week. (NOT during the years Beatrice[11] writes of , but later when she had departed.) And I had 750. dollars per year for two years from Quin n.[12] who wanted me to take it myself/ but which I used as *foreign* edt. salary and payment for contributions.

UNLESS one can spend at least that amount , you can NOT make a mag/ /

And I see no reason of my trying to carry a lot of duds.

Until a milieu will support me to that extent/ a mag is mere throwing away printing expenses.

And as for chasing sprouters/ and playing office boy and agent and fussing over translations/ and then the translator not getting PAID.

                    [ASC]   *??!*

9 Nott and Heap wish to model their new quarterly magazine on the *New Age* and the *Little Review.*
10 Orage, A.R.
11 Hastings, Beatrice (1879–1943). Partner of A.R. Orage during the early years of the *New Age*, she contributed Paris letters under the name Alice Morning. EP may refer to *The Old "New Age" – Orage and Others* booklet (1935), no. 16 in the Blue Moon Press series.
12 Quinn, John (1870–1924). American lawyer and patron of the arts. He was also a wealthy collector who supported many individual writers and artists during the

Also/ there wd. be a minimum of authors whom I can read.

HALF the mag/ wd. as with Littl Rev/[13] have to be used for THEM. The other half can go gay or accommodate itself to the milieu.

Whether England is ready for jane, I leave to you.

A magazine is made with FOUR writers. Less than that means paucity.

" The Lesser Review or Twenty Years After "

???

Not with Ez as house boy and kitchen maid.

YES. I am all for a GOOD magazine devoted to LIFE, and not to Criterion=archeology.[14]

I had request from Cincinnati on Friday/ and the VOU club of Tpkyo[15] is sending me theirs.

formative years of Anglo-American modernism, including James Joyce, William Butler Yeats, T.S. Eliot, and EP.

13 The *Little Review.*

14 EP suggests the magazine would not be equal to the *Little Review* and would come twenty years after the halcyon days of the *New Age.* EP published in the *Criterion* in October 1935 and April 1937 but regarded the magazine as dealing only in ideas of the past.

15 *Vou* (Tokyo) was edited by Katue Kitasono (see note 17 below). This avant-garde magazine was the chief organ of a group of Japanese poets admired by EP who formed the VOU Club in Tokyo in 1935. *Vou* (pronounced "vow") published early poems and essays by EP between 1936 and 1951, translated by Kitasono (*EPE* 302). EP wrote "Vou Club [Introduction]" for the *Townsman* (1938).

AND there is no reason for m y not writing prose in Italian UNLESS the decaying sag/ saxons and Nordics WANT it.[16]

and the WANT needs proof. I'll SAY it needs PROOF.
Besides, as *Mr Katue*[17] reminds me ,I began life as a poet. and once we git Stamp scrip in Alberta,[18] and open up ole Douggie's[19] mind, etc.
why should I go on writen PO/etry ?[20]

This aint crabbin' the project. This is just to keep you and jane from slumberin at the switch.

[ASC, EP] *The Fig Tree dont bar econ.*[21]

Yrz Ez [AS]

[ASC, EP] *Be yew tew seee –ree- yus?*[22]

16 EP defends his prose in Italian by suggesting that there is no demand for his insights outside Italy.

17 Kitasono, Katue (1902–78). Japanese poet and editor of *Vou*. He provided EP with an audience in Japan and corresponded with him between the late 1930s and late 1950s.

18 *Schwundgeld* or *Freigeld*, vanishing or free money, was the brainchild of Silvio Gesell and was instituted for a brief period (1932–33) in Wörgl, a small Austrian town.

19 Douglas, Major C.H.

20 EP's comment remains unclear. He might mean "shouldn't" rather than "should."

21 The *Fig Tree* (1936–39, London [New Series: 1954–55, 4 issues, Liverpool]), edited by C.H. Douglas, subtitled "A Douglas Social Credit Quarterly Review." The magazine's first issue, under the auspices of the Social Credit Secretariat in London, appeared in June 1936. EP's pointed comment that the magazine does not "bar econ[omics]" recalls his objection to Nott's solicitation for a new monthly (see Letter 88).

22 "Be you two serious?"

[Verso, AN, EP]:
            N. B.
            it za good
            IDEA
            to have
            a
            maggerzeen[23]

            ================

23   "It is a good idea to have a magazine."

Ezra Pound Esq   May 27th 1936
Via Marsala 12 / 5
Rapallo
Italy

Dear Ezra,

Many thanks for your letter of May 24th. I'll be writing you again in a day or two.

Do you know anything about the book that Por is doing?[1] I am waiting to see a set of proofs. I believe it is a sort of propaganda book.

We've sold the Chinese Written Character to Arrow Editions,[2] 444 Madison Avenue, New York. They don't say when its going to be published but they have promised to send us a copy as soon as its bound up.

I will get the office to go into your various accounts shortly and see how we stand. We ought to be owing you a little money by now.

Can you tell me more about F.N. Ford?[3]

Yours ever,
SCN [AS]

1 Por, Odon. The book in question remains unclear. For this thread, see letters 84, 91, and 94.
2 CWC was issued by Arrow Editions in 1936.
3 Ford Madox Ford. See Letter 89.

[ASC, EP] 29 *Maggio*[1]

Por "PROOFS"^? Por writes articles all over the place. I supposed
Butchart and spouse[2] had the material and that she was translating what
you wanted to use... obviously it wont be printed in ENGLISH here.
whatch^*a* mean PROOFS?[3]

      Butch[4] ought to have mss/
re/ Arrow edtn/[5] what I want to know is WHEN am I decently free to
arrange anything FURTHER?

      [ASC] *how many did rez[6] buy . ?*

F.M.Ford,[7] address care Duckworth.[8] Last address I had was in S. France
and letter retu returned saying gone without leaving address.

1 The date is handwritten and the postmark illegible, but the postcard replies directly to
Letter 90 and thus is surely 29 May ("Maggio") 1936.
2 Butchart, Montgomery. Little information is available about Butchart's wife, but she
had some involvement with the *NEW* and the *British Union Quarterly* (where she
reportedly translated EP's *Rassegna Monetaria* [see Letter 106]), and EP suggests she is
translating Por's latest book.
3 Buchart, Montgomery.
4 Por, Odon. EP strikes a tone of exasperation because Nott appears confused over the
state and destination of Por's book, which is at the manuscript stage and portions of
which are supposed to be translated for Nott's use. In Letter 94, Nott explains the
confusion.
5 Arrow Editions, owned and operated by Florence Codman (see Letter 77), issued *CWC*
in 1936. EP replies to Nott's confirmation in Letter 90.
6 Likely Charles Reznikoff (1894–1976), an American poet who became associated with
"objectivist" poetry and who later operated the Objectivist Press with Louis Zukofsky
and George Oppen. A short piece in the *NEW* (8 March 1934) on Reznikoff's *Testimony*
indicates that the Objectivist Press regarded itself as "an organisation of writers who
are publishing their own work and that of other writers whose work they think ought
to be read." Whether Reznikoff purchased copies remains unclear, but he is likely the
other "publisher" or "nibbler" EP mentions in Letter 78.
7 Ford Madox Ford. See Letter 89.
8 Gerald Duckworth was Ford's publisher.

whacha mean MORE?   ref/ British mus. catlog F. Madox Ford
(Hueffer).[9]

And I HOPE pp/ 4. *of yr. letter* is true. The OUGHT is beautifully
moral, and wd. give the ONLY known reason for present social system
being [typewritten on side] allowed to continue another 15 or 20 minutes.
Por's bk/ shd/ be sane econ/ not propaganda save in the sense that all
science is[10]

[postcard verso]

propaganda for better life. Whether ole Webfoot[11] has stangle hold on all
Ford's brit/ rights I dunno.

But   *E* [A S]

---

9   EP, exasperated with Nott's expressed ignorance of Ford's career (see Letter 90),
    directs him to the British Library.
10 EP replies to Nott's suggestion in Letter 90 that Por's book is "propaganda."
11 Duckworth (see note 8).

[LETTER 92, TPCS, EP TO SN – HRHRC]
[EP, POSTCARD LETTERHEAD]

How far wd. you/and jane[1] go in combining yr/ magazine urge[2] with an extant paper ?? pubd. in Noo Yok ?

               A.
I mean what are the minimum demands of yr/ program ?
            B. maximum intentions ??

C. (nacherly ; resources if any ???)

E

13 June[3] [ASC]

---

1 Heap, Jane.
2 In Letter 86, Nott inaugurates discussion of a quarterly magazine (to be run with Jane Heap). Unclear what New York–based "extant paper" EP has in mind, but perhaps Gorham Munson's *New Democracy*.
3 The postcard is dated 13 June (in ink) and postmarked 14 June 1936.

June 22[1] [pencil: [1936?]]

Dear Ezra:

At the moment I'm in despair. I've got some really good books in preparation for the Autumn – about 12 or 14 – good from the point of view of making money & good ideas.[2] We have no money left. I need about £1000 to make this into a good publishing firm (good money, good ideas). I've tried no less than 73 people in the last 15 months. I'm seeing a publisher tomorrow to offer the business to him – on terms. If I can't get <u>terms</u> *I'll give it to him.[3] Unfortunately I depend on it for a living. At present we stand something like this:*

Debts	*£850*
accounts owing	*£450*
Value of stock	*£1200*
Capital pay	*£1500*

In two & half years our losses show about £500 & we are just at the point when we could ^ begin to make money. I'll let you know what happens later on this week. Its a great mistake for a man with a family & no private income to be interested in half an idea. I raised about £2000 for ARO on the N.E.W.[4] but Im damned if I can raise money for a publishing business, yet in this last 3 years I've seen thousands put into doubtful publishing concerns. Desmond Harmsworth,[5] I understand went through £10,000 in 3 years.

---

1 The year is not given, but the letter replies to Letter 92 (thus the date would be 22 June 1936).
2 Stanley Nott Ltd. published twenty-five books in 1936, roughly half of which Nott indicates made up the "Autumn list." See Letter 63 and Essay 4.
3 The publisher whom Nott intends to see remains unclear: Bailey Bros. (Letter 100) would ultimately take over the firm's stock; Fairbairn, Wingfield, and Wykes (Letter 102) would serve as liquidators; Nott suggests that Allen and Unwin (Letter 102) is taking over some contracts. According to Gallup, Faber and Faber would take over CWC.
4 Orage, A.R., at the *New English Weekly*.
5 Harmsworth, Desmond (dates unknown). Poet, painter, and publisher. He published EP's *How to Read* in 1931.

Jane[6] *has gone back to France & is* <u>not</u> *interested in* <u>running</u> *a magazine but wants to help out with advice etc. I am still interested in the idea & may go ahead with it. And I would be interest* [sic] *in cooperation with an American magazine.*

      A. yes.   <u>*B. not formulated*</u> *as yet. C. none, so far*[7]
Social Credit is pretty dead here for the time being. It may wake up in the Autumn. Alberta has given it a nasty smack.[8] *All lit on the subject has stopped selling. The accounts are kept by Mr Gee .*[9] *a very nice public schoolboy, absolutely honest-but who ought to have had a government job & wrote poetry in his spare time. I'll tell him to send you your a/c.*

              Yrs.
              SCN

6 Heap, Jane.
7 Nott indicates his interest in EP's proposal to collaborate with an "extant paper" (see Letter 92) in New York. In addressing EP's questions, Nott appears to have misread Question A from Letter 92: "yes" is not a complete answer.
8 The Alberta situation refers to the failings of William Aberhart's Social Credit government in the Province of Alberta, Canada, to implement promised Social Credit reforms and a national dividend. Aberhart's Social Credit Party had been elected in August 1935, but things soured by the end of the year because the provincial government of Alberta did not have the constitutional authority to issue its own currency. See also Essay 1 and Bob Hesketh, *Major Douglas and Alberta Social Credit*.
9 Kenneth Gee was Nott's manager and business partner.

July 9th 36

Dear Ezra:

*The situation[1] is easing a little. I've had a promise of some money &
I'm interviewing another promise tomorrow. I am convinced that if we hold
on till Xmas we shall be on our feet. And we shall be put there by one book
viz: "Creative Art in England" by William Johnstone.[2] It's the most exciting
book I've seen for years [2 words illegible – perhaps 8vo 4to for "octavo
quarto"] & 200 illustrations. By the way he wants to reproduce "Boy with
Coney" from your G-B book.[3] Will you give us permission.*

*C. Written Character[4] is just beginning to sell. The enclosed p-c is
from a man which goes to prove that all teachers in public schools are not
dead.[5] Will you write to him? I've answer acknowledged the p.c.*

*The great racket now is surrealisme. 17,500 people attended the show.[6]
A Sur group is being founded & will shortly publish a manifesto. We are
thinking of doing one or two books (1) Hebdomeros (but we can't get any
word from Chirico[7] or his publisher. (2) Voyage to Africa[8] (3) a collection of
E. C. Large's.[9]*

---

1 See Letter 93.
2 Johnstone, William (1897–1981). Scottish painter. Nott published his *Creative Art in
England* in 1936.
3 "Boy with a Coney" from EP's *Gaudier-Brzeska* (1916).
4 CWC.
5 F. McEachran, MA, a teacher at the Shrewsbury School, wrote Nott a short note (8 July
1936), in which he complimented CWC and inquired after an English transliteration
of the three characters (page 12): "I am teaching from this book and my boys are
interested to know."
6 The International Surrealist Exhibition was held in London from 11 June to 4 July 1936;
it included lectures by André Breton, Herbert Read, and Salvador Dali, among others.
7 Chirico, Giorgio de (1888–1978). Influential pre-Surrealist Greek-Italian painter and
the founder of the *scuola metafisica* art movement. Chirico's *Hebdomeros* is considered a landmark of Surrealist fiction.
8 The reference to "Voyage to Africa" remains unclear, although it may refer to John
McLeod's book of this title from 1820.
9 Large, Ernest Charles (dates unknown). Contributor of short articles and stories to the
NEW. He wrote several fictional and scientific books in the 1930s and 1940s.

I also hope, if I can get the money, to go ahead with more Ideogramic.[10]

I didn't connect "Ford" with F.M.F.[11]

Re Por:[12] *Just before the ab. was finished. He wrote to me about a book his people were doing & wanted us to handle the English Edition. A proof of the book was 'on the way'. The war stopped suddenly & the proof "got lost in the post'!*

We sold 350 sheets of CWC to Arrow Editions New York.[13] *I believe it is out now. Have just received 2 copies from her of which I am sending you one. She has paid. We sold them at 1/4 per sheet. I'll get a statement of things sent out to you soon.*

Jane[14] *has gone back to Paris and is now out of the picture for a mag. But I'm still interested and would be willing to cooperate with an American mag. But Money!!!*

Yrs ever

SCN

---

10   The Ideogrammic series has been absent from discussion since letters 74 and 75.

11   Ford Madox Ford. See Letters 89, 90, and 91.

12   Por, Odon. Nott responds directly to Letter 91. The context for Nott's statement is unclear, but he is likely referring to the lifting of sanctions against Italy on 4 July 1936 by the League of Nations. (Italy officially annexed Ethiopia on 7 May 1936, creating Italian East Africa on 1 June 1936.)

13   Florence Codman's Arrow Editions purchased 350 sheets of CWC.

14   Heap, Jane. Nott reiterates information conveyed in Letter 93.

{YCAL MSS 43, SERIES I, BOX 37, FOLDER 1586}
[LETTER 95, TLS, SN TO EP]
[STANDARD NOTT LETTERHEAD]

October 7th 1936[1]

Dear Ezra,

I asked Mr. Gee[2] to send you your royalty statement. Perhaps you will have had it by now. We have about 100 copies or so left of Jefferson and/or Mussolini[3] and I am wondering if you can suggest what we could do with them. We haven't sold a copy now for months and I think the sale, as far as England is concerned, is finished.

Would you be interested in our selling them to you at a very low figure. I think its [sic] a pity that something shouldn't be done about them, *though* the public apparently doesn't like the book.

We are in the throes of our Autumn List and have a few books which possibly may sell. In any case I think you will be interested in Creative Art In England".[4]

Now that the lira has [ASC] ^ *been* devalued[5] perhaps I shall be able to come to see you one of these days.

Yours ever,
Stanley Nott   [AS]

---

1 A three-month break since Letter 94 (9 July 1936) likely indicates that several letters are missing.
2 Kenneth Gee, Nott's assistant manager and business partner.
3 EP's *J/M*. According to Gallup, the number of copies printed is unknown. In Letter 99, Nott gives 126 as the number of bound copies left over.
4 See Letter 93. Nott published William Johnstone's *Creative Art in England* in 1936.
5 Italy's strong lira policy came to an end on 5 October 1936; the lira was devalued by nearly 41 percent. The move followed the lifting of sanctions against Italy in July.

[LETTER 96, TLS, SN TO EP]
[STANDARD NOTT LETTERHEAD]

4th December 1936

Dear Ezra,

Thanks for your postcard.[1] I will send Ta Hio and The Chinese Written Character to Japan.[2]

Mairet[3] has no type standing for Frobenius but we could easily reset it.[4] In any case I will write to you again shortly.

Yours ever

Stanley Nott [A S]

SCN/AC[5]

---

1 EP's postcard is missing from the correspondence.
2 Nott is likely sending *Ta Hio* and C W C to Katue Kitasono, founder and editor of *Vou* (see Letter 89).
3 Mairet, Philip. Co-editor of the *N E W*.
4 This remains unclear, but context suggests that the *N E W* printed an article by or about Leo Frobenius, a German anthropologist. The article could be the one discussed in letters 78 and 79, in all likelihood authored by Douglas Fox, Frobenius's assistant. See also Letter 97, in which Nott indicates that Frobenius may follow William Carlos Williams in the Ideogrammic series.
5 The identity of "AC" remains unclear.

[LETTER 97, TLS, SN TO EP]
[STANDARD NOTT LETTERHEAD]

9th December 1936

Dear Ezra,

That was a very good review in the Aryan Path.[1]   I suppose you did not see the one in the Adelaide Advertiser, South Australia.[2] It is just the sort of thing one would expect from a barbarous country.

After Christmas I will let you know definitely about William Carlos Williams and Frobenius.[3]   I am hoping that we shall be able to do them both.

Have you seen Creative Art in England?[4] And would you like a copy at half price.

Things move very slowly but they seem to be a little less hopeless than hitherto.

I am expecting developments at Christmas or the New Year and will write to you again then.

What do you think of Axis[5] ?

Yours ever

Stanley Nott [A S]

SCN/AC[6]

---

1 The *Aryan Path* (Bombay, India) was edited by Sophia Wadia and printed in English. The paper was published by the Bombay Theosophy Company and was sponsored by the Indian Institute of World Culture. EP published two pieces there in August 1937 and October 1939, both on religion.
2 The *Advertiser* (Adelaide, Australia: 1889–31, 1931–). Though it has experienced a title change, the *Advertiser* continues its long run in print to this day.
3 Williams, Carlos William. Williams was the next intended instalment in the Ideogrammic series. According to Nott, work on or by the German anthropologist Leo Frobenius was to follow Williams.
4 Nott published William Johnstone's *Creative Art in England* in 1936.
5 *Axis* (New York, Arno Press, 1935–37) was a quarterly review of contemporary abstract painting and sculpture. It was edited by Myfanwy Evans and ran for eight issues.
6 Stanley Charles Nott; the identity of "AC" remains unclear.

A tax is not a share

A nation need not and
should not pay rent for
its own credit.

1937
anno
XV

EZRA POUND
Via Marsala 12-5
RAPALLO

[ASC, EP] *15 May*[1]

Dear Stan:

General report that Brit/ Soc/ Credit is in doldrums/ or
at least economic publication is.[2]

Question have you the funds to print another pamphlet IN that
series[3]

/ /

Have you read my stuff in British Union Quarterly.[4] ?

Bother having it tied up at 2/6   / or 7/6 for anyone who
wants the three articles.

/ /

---

1 The date indicates another lengthy break in the correspondence, though EP is
   responding to Nott's discussion of Williams in letters 94 and 97.
2 The context for these comments is unclear, but Nott has suffered financially from the
   outgoing tide on Social Credit reading material.
3 EP likely means the Pamphlets on the New Economics series. Nos. 1–17 came out in
   1934–35, and nos. 18–19 came out in 1936. Nothing more would be published in 1937.
4 In the *British Union Quarterly*, EP published "Demarcations" (January/April 1937),
   "Intellectual Money" (April/June 1937), and "Towards an Economic Orthology"
   (October/December 1937; translated from *Rassegna Monetaria*), as well as a translation (with notes) of Odon Por's "Systems of Compensation" (July/September 1937).

You may have heard of split in the B.U.F.[5]   ??

Whether the N.S.League[6] wd. publish with you I dont know, or how you feel about them.

Both lots have "accepted Douglas analysis".[7]
  [ASC, EP]: *B. U. F. & N. S. L.*
/ /
The Alberta 1937 Soc/ Credit Bill[8] looks rather good. ' (repealing earlier and erroneous %.

Also U.S. congress active/ /

Also Hitler on " jeder kontrahenten des Sozialprozess "[9]
    acc/ to some equals Doglas dividend.

Have you tried to get a pamphlet from Chris Hollis ?[10] His stuff sells. You cd/ ask him for one on MONEY , its nature.

That wd/ wake up the series/ also McNair Wilson[11] sells.

5 The British Union of Fascists (1932–40) was the most popular and well known organization of fascist supporters in Britain, led by Sir Oswald Mosley. See Essay 2. The "split" refers to the dismissal of William Joyce, John Beckett, and John Angus McNab in March 1937 – allegedly prompted by Mosley's preference for Benito Mussolini over Adolf Hitler as inspiration for the movement. Together with Count Potocki, Joyce, Beckett, and Angus formed the National Socialist League (1937–39).
6 National Socialist League.
7 Douglas, Major C.H. According to EP, the two fascist factions have adopted a version of Social Credit. See Essay 2.
8 The Alberta Social Credit Bill of 1937 concerned the implementation of stamp scrip in the province – Alberta Prosperity Certificates – which sought to tax, or require the endorsement of, the money with affixable stamps.
9 Hitler, Adolph (1889–1945). This phrase means "Everyone is a contracting party of the social process" ("Kontrahent," a contracting party, implies being entitled to something by social contract). EP thereby suggests that, according to some, one of Hitler's ideas approximates Douglas's National Dividend.
10 Hollis, Christopher (1902–77). A British political writer. He was the author of *Two Nations* (1935) and *The Breakdown of Money* (1937).
11 Wilson, Robert McNair. British writer of history and economics.

Butch[12] got a good bit *of stuff* from Soddy ,[13] but rest of the seven
          heretics not so lively. Still Soddy ought to be good for a
pamph that wd/ sell.

          In any case , IF you are still broke,[14] let me know
          on what conditions pamphlets CAN be got out.

          Cantos XLII/51[15] thru page proofs/ and another bk/
contracted for with Faber/ on KULCHUR. oh KUL/chur ...[16]

forechoonately Arry Stotl[17] iz kulchur. and he econ's.

RE/ pamphs/ say 32 pages.[18]

There iz ME
          Hollis
          Soddy
          Mc N/Wilson[19]

also might be four brief HISTORICAL essays/
          Young Laughlin[20] is active , and seems to run some
sort of printing show/
          not bad business to INTEREST him.

12 Butchart, Montgomery.
13 Soddy, Frederick (1877–1956). Professor of chemistry at Oxford University who later
    turned to economics. The "seven heretics" refer to those writers collected in Butchart's
    second book on money, *To-Morrow's Money* (1936): J. Stuart Barr (Silvio Gessell),
    Arthur Kitson, Frederick Soddy, McNair Wilson, C.H. Douglas, G.D.H. Cole, and
    Jeffrey Mark.
14 EP forwarded Nott money for the publication of *J/M*.
15 Faber and Faber published *The Fifth Decad of Cantos* in June 1937.
16 Faber and Faber published *Guide to Kulchur* in July 1938. By repeating "Oh KUL/
    chur," EP is treating ironically a term that was weighty in the 1930s.
17 Aristotle. In *Guide to Kulchur*, EP is fascinated with Aristotle and the *Nicomachean
    Ethics*.
18 Most of the issues of the Pamphlets of the New Economics series consist of thirty-two
    pages.
19 This list refers to Ezra Pound, Christopher Hollis, Frederick Soddy, and McNair
    Wilson.
20 Laughlin, James. Founded the press New Directions Books in 1936. Laughlin's article
    on Roman banking remains unclear.

[ASC, EP]
4 items

[ASC, EP: brackets around the following 5 lines]

A good pamph/ cd/ be made of his little essay on

    Roman banking

Swabey ,[21] on Church of Eng/ mints/

    note by me on Cairoli's[22]   Just price in Middle ages/

    and ?? Butch[23] on someone. on ??

[ASC, EP]
or pamph

/./

Just how MUCH is holding up Williams Americ/ Grain.[24]   ??

Laughlin is PRINTING the White Mule , and looking for someone to take sheets in England/ /[25]

Mebbe you cd/ exchange some of yr/ unmoved stock with N.Directions (Laughlin) for sheets of that if Faber don't buy 'em...

Also mebbe that wd. interest L/[26] in hoisting forrard the Americ Grain..

√ *Ez P* [AS]

21 Swabey, Reverend Henry S.
22 Cairoli, Luigi Pasquale (dates unknown). Italian writer on economics and the church and state.
23 Butchart, Montgomery.
24 EP returns to the question of blockage, this time considering what is preventing Nott from publishing William Carlos Williams's *In the American Grain*, intended as no. 3 in the Ideogrammic series.
25 James Laughlin published Williams's *White Mule: A Novel* (1937). EP attempts to bring the two publishers together. See note 20 and Essay 4.
26 Laughlin, James.

May 25th 1937

Dear Ezra:

We have 126 copies of Jeff/Muss bound.[1] The liquidator[2] thinks we ought to ask 1/3 per copy for them.I think you should be able to dispose of them atthis [sic] price. However,you will know.

No one so far as I know yet is taking over the entire business,i.e. name and stock. I imagine that the stock will be disposed of in various lots to various publishers.

Yours ever
Stanley Nott [A S]

1 EP's *J/M*. See also Letter 95.
2 Fairbairn, Wingfield, and Wykes (see letters 102 and 108). It remains unclear whether the copies are to be let go at one-third the cover price or at 1s. 3d., which is consider-ably below the sale price of 6s. See Letter 101 for EP's instructions on handling leftover stock.

June 8th 1937

Dear Ezra:

Here are the royalty accounts. The one for Jeff/m was in such a mess.I have tried to straighten it out. It looked as though you owed us about £6. However,I thought the best way was to cancel it,and pay you royalties on all copies over 200. We have not charged for sales so I think you come out best. I hope you will accept these as final accounts.

I have finised [sic] with the business now,but you can write to me c/o Bailey Bros 32 Ludgate Hill E.C.,who are handling the stock and will send your books off.

After the last two years of strain and worry it is an enormous relief to be free of trying to run a publishing business without money. Another £2000 would have put us on our feet - with reorganisation. To run a biz without money is bad enough ,to run it with inexperienced partners and inefficient ones at that (however nice they may be) is not worth the candle. However I feel Ive done my bit for S.C. Other people will make money out of my ideas.

I dont know what I'm going to do . Nothing for a time. I do know Eliot and Morley.[1] If you can put in a word somewhere it might help. Though I do not want a routine job until the Fall. At first it all seemed very disappointing.But now I'm indifferent.

Send me a line sometime. I dont want to drop out of the literary life entirely. But for the time, Ive completely lost interest in S.C.and Monetary reform. I'm interested in money only to the extent of getting enough to keep my family for the next few months. At present I do not possess one cent,nor a penny of insurance. But then I am not a business man.

We owed only about £1500 when we stopped.

Yours ever

SCN [AS]

---

1 T.S. Eliot and F.V. Morley were both employed at the publishing house Faber and Faber.

10 June[1]

[ASC, likely SN: *Ta Hio*
CWC for Allen Unwin]

Dear Stan

Morely[2] is well disposed toward you (very much so) but hasn't a job open at the moment.

I can't make out ANYTHING much from yr/ letter. Nacherly I don't want money from you, especially as you have none.

I want as MANY copies of the books as you can save from the wreckage. And shd/ be prepared to put in as big a bill as possible to keep 'em from less worthy creditors.[3]

ANYTHING I can do to get you started again in any way , I shall be glad to do. You turned out some good books, and printed 'em extremely well. You deserve well both of the public in general, and of the reformers ; who (as I see it) have been damn'd snotty.

---

1 EP is replying directly to Letter 100.
2 F.V. Morley, a founding director of Faber and Faber. EP responds two days after Nott's request for a recommendation to Morley and Eliot (see Letter 100).
3 EP's exchange with the liquidators is housed at the Beinecke Library.

At any rate you got Butch's " Money "[4] into print. and you have not lived in vain. Very *h*igh % of real stuff printed, and no trype printed intentionally (at least that is the way I see it.)

I have NO idea which letters ^ *of mine* your letter is intended to answer.[5]

I want a <u>few</u> copies ~~of~~ of my various ooks sent here.

I want the bulk of the Jeff/ Muss held in London.

I want to know WHERE the remaineders go when the do go/[7]

I dunno what you mean "by contra"/ ?? contract ??[8]

or there being no royalties on first 500 Chi/ Wr/ Char/

I am not even sure I ever saw a contract.

If by "contra" you mean copies that I had/ thass O. K.

ANYhow, I am not going to add to yr/ troubles. That is clear.

[ASC, EP]
as per list +
add 5 Chinese
Character to it[6]

4 Nott published Montgomery Butchart's *Money* in 1935 and *To-Morrow's Money* in 1936.
5 EP's last letter is dated 15 May 1937 (Letter 98), another indication of the likelihood of several missing letters from this stage in the correspondence.
6 A missing letter likely contains a list of books and the number of requested copies EP wishes sent to him in Rapallo, to which he here adds five copies of *CWC*.
7 A "remainder" is a book sold at a reduced price after sales have slowed, though EP also means any and all copies that remain.
8 In Letter 102, Nott clarifies that "contra means copies that you had." There appears to be confusion over royalties for *CWC*, for which EP claims he never saw a contract.

For the rest, get me as many copies of the books as is possible.

And I am willing to pay up a spot of cash for the remain*der* of the *Jeff*/[9]

The Chi/ Writ/ Char WOULD have brought me in something on 530 copies, had Faber done it.
        BUT they <u>didn't</u> , and I am damn glad to have it DONE.

        One don't live by and for cash alone.

        You have been worth meeting, and you have
        done several good bits work, and I shan't forget it.

I think you MUST by a business man ,[10] or you NEVER wd/ have been ABLE to owe £ 1500 quid.

        I forget how long you have pd/ office RENT etc/

and think on the BOOKS themselves, or at least on those I think worth having done, you may have come out even or a bit on the right rise.

        All of which is human interest.
not business.

A few blokes in Rome have sense enough to see what I mean

re/ ORTHOLOGY or decent terminology in econ//

---

9 EP wishes to gain control over as much of the stock as possible and specifies his willingness to pay for the remaining *J/M*.
10 See letters 85 and 86, in which "business sense" is addressed.

I dare say I shall find it better to be an Italian economist than an eng/ one .[11] at any rate here's hope/ and a pleasant summer.

Re/ delivery of Jeff/ Muss, please await instructions as to where and to have someone IN THE FLAT to open the dorr and receive 'em when delivered.

cordially yrs.

E P [AS]

---

11 Unclear who the "blokes in Rome" might be, but EP prefers his prospects as a writer on economics in Italy over those in England. On orthology, the branch of grammar that deals with the correct or traditional use of language, see Letter 10, note 12.

[LETTER 102, TLS, SN TO EP, FOLDER 1586]
[STANDARD NOTT LETTERHEAD, MODIFIED][1]

32 Ludgate Hill
E.C.4

June 15th 1937

Dear Ezra

Your letter[2] to hand today. The liquidators[3] have asked me to write to you about Chinese Written Character. Allen and Unwin[4] are interested in it. They want to know if you would be willing for them to take it over on the terms as we published it. I would suggest that you write to them and say that they can have it on a flat 10% royalty. You should write to Messers Fairbairn Wingfield and Wykes, 67 Watling St.E.C.4. Also if you will send them the cheque for £5.5 [?].0. for Jeff/Muss they will hold them for you. There are about 126 copies. They want cash in advance these liquidators for everything they sell. There are 10 copies of Jeff waiting to be sent off to you.

Contra means copies that you had.[5]

I amvery [sic] glad to have been able to publish your books and pamphlets. We have not yet paid the cost of any of them. BUT we should have done so in a very short time. We had almost paid for them.

I'm glad Morley[6] is well disposed. One of these days I'll go and see him. I'm still clearing up but hope to finsih [sic] this week.

---

1 Nott uses his standard letterhead but replaces the address with that of Bailey Bros., the firm handling the leftover stock. See Letter 100.
2 See Letter 101.
3 Fairbairn, Wingfield, and Wykes.
4 Allen and Unwin is a British publishing house. Nott suggests it will take over *CWC*. Faber and Faber would, however, eventually take over the remaining copies as well as those for *Ta Hio*.
5 See Letter 101.
6 F.V. Morley was a founding director of Faber and Faber. See letters 34, 100, 101, and 104.

I think I've been trying to do in publishing what Orage[7] did in Journalism - without public support. By the way.Jane Soames book did very well considering.[8] We sold about 1500 copies.and it is being taken over by another publisher. And Allen and Unwin are taking over all S.C.books and Butcharts MONEY.[9] If I had had a £1000 when the firm went broke I could have bought up all the stock and started again free of debt,and,I think ,made money. It certainly does rile me to think that other publishers are going to reap where I sowed.

I'm just beginning to realise that I have been through a rather bad time: A long spell of illness, then the business going,then breaking up the home.My wife had to go out and earn her livingand [sic] the children had to go to friends.and now we meet only at week ends. However, when things are at their worst they begin to get a little better. The worst is over I think.

Ever yours
Stanley Nott [AS]

7 Orage, A.R.
8 Nott published Jane Soames's *The English Press: Newspapers and News* in 1936.
9 It remains unclear whether Allen and Unwin took over Nott's Social Credit books and Butchart's *Money* (1935).

32 *Ludgate Hill*
E. C. 4

June 16/37

Dear Ezra:

Would you be prepared to make an offer for "Ta Hio." At present there are 550 sheets unbound & 100 bound copies; all at the binders. If you should take them I would suggest having the rest of the copies (when the hundred are finished) bound in paper covers.[2]
You might get some American bookshop to take some stock. Apparently there is not enough in it for the publishers here. I believe Allen and Unwin are going to take C. W. C.[3]

Yrs
Stanley Nott

1 Nott uses his standard letterhead but replaces the address with that of Bailey Bros., the firm handling the leftover stock; see Letters 100 and 102.
2 EP's translation of Confucius's *Ta Hio*. According to Gallup, a total of three thousand sets of sheets were printed, of which 196 were taken by New Directions and issued as no. 4 in the New Directions Pamphlet Series in November 1938. Another 648 were taken over by Faber and Faber in October 1937.
3 Nott indicates in Letter 102 that Allen and Unwin would likely take the remaining Social Credit books, and here he includes C W C. According to Gallup, however, Faber and Faber took over the remaining stock of C W C in September 1937.

7 Dec[1]

Dear Stan

Morley[2] was I think genuinely sorry that Faber cdn't take on ANYONE more, anywhere, and appreciative of yr/ work.

My wife also too occasion to rub it IN to him and Eliot,[3] when she was in London /
Eliot , I understand , giving way to protective frivolity/
re Faber printing
however .. exegencies of conversation etc/ and E's loyalty to the firm's team.
HOWEVER// thazzat.

The FUTURE is with microphoto/ and photostat[4] combinations at any rate for music and all oriental studies.

WHEN these processes will PAY , gorr knoze BUT it is worth while watching them.

A shame to put a *?* good typographic eye onto them/
or perhaps NOT.

Whether you cd/ push Fa Faber or anyone else into putting you in charge of a NEW dept/ for this kind of work I dont know.
It needs doing.

---

1 The year is 1937, considering Nott's reply in Letter 105.
2 F.V. Morley, a founding director of Faber and Faber.
3 Eliot, T.S. In Letter 105, Nott notes being snubbed by Eliot.
4 EP contends that the future of publishing, at least in the more complicated formats for music and oriental publications, is in microphoto and photostat, technologies of projection reproduction that create a negative print from which positive prints are made.

O/R/[5] has short note in Townsman[6] IF Butch/[7] and Dunc/[8] EVER get that off off the press.

You better see Butch/ and discuss the whole subject.

I shall probably waste a few shekels in turning out samples/

wherefrom Gollanck[9] or some other bleeder will in TIME reap/ /

BUT ... cant spoil the ship fer a ha p orth[10]

cordially yrs.

r;s;v;p; if only to talk about dickybirds.[11]   *y E. P.* [AS]

5 Rudge, Olga.
6 The *Townsman* (Cornwall, 1938–44; became the *Scythe* 1944–46) was edited by Ronald Duncan (see note 8) and associate editor Montgomery Butchart. EP contributed frequently on economics, music, and religion, particularly in the first few years. Other contributions included music by Olga Rudge (see note 5), poems by E.E. Cummings, and visual work by William Johnstone.
7 Butchart, Montgomery.
8 Duncan, Ronald Frederick Henry (1914–82). British poet, playwright, and editor of the *Townsman*. In his autobiography, *All Men Are Islands* (1964), Duncan recalls how, upon meeting EP in 1937, "Ezra taught me more in one day than I had learned in a year at Cambridge" (158). The correspondence between Duncan and EP is considerable, spanning over thirty years.
9 Gollancz, Victor. During the 1930s and 1940s, Gollancz was a successful publisher with leftist sympathies.
10 "hapennyworth."
11 In other words, please respond even if only to talk about the weather or "shoot the breeze."

58 Gondar Gardens N W 6[1]

21/12/37

Dear Ezra:

It has done me good to hear from you.[2] *Mairet*[3] *and Butchart*[4] *excepted, from not one of all the S.C, N.E.W. gang have I heard a sound. I wrote to Eliot*[5] *& many others. Not one of the bastards replied. And why should they? Life is becoming more and more strenuous and exacting here. I retired into the country to recover – & out of sight, out of mind. Had it not been for two American friends of ours, Dole & Morss, educational publishers, things could have been very bad with self & family. My wife, until a few weeks ago, practically kept the family since March.   In November I was offered the job, at £3.0.0 a week of re-organising a hat factory owned by some relations of mine. At first, the idea was nauseating; but after a week or so I got interested. And then, to my surprise was offered through a friend of mine a job at Cassells which a year or so ago, would have been beyond my dreams.*[6] *They wanted a liason officer between the various departments at about £400 a year. I considered it very seriously. Disadvantage was, it was fixed routine job. fixed hours & days. and I came*

1 Nott uses a different letterhead; the address is in West Hampstead, London.
2 Nott is replying to Letter 104.
3 Mairet, Philip.
4 Butchart, Montgomery.
5 Eliot, T.S. See also letters 100 and 104.
6 Likely Cassell and Company, British publishers.

to the conclusion that I was not now the type for that. So I gave it up for the hat factory. I get about £5. a week with the prospect that if it succeeds I become a director with full liberty. I think if I work at it for a year I may have a small measure of financial independence. Then I can go back into the publishing world – but as a free lance. Perhaps take up your idea, microphoto.[7] I should like to know more about it.   Never did I think I should ever give up a good job in the publishing world for a job in a hat factory! This particular thing is one of the few where the machine – apart from a sewing machine or two, does not enter in at all.   So that's that.

I'm beginning to understand Orage's attitude to the Social Creditors.[8] He used to say he hated them. The way they hung on his doorstep, praised him up – and never did a hands [worth?] for the paper – none of 'em. It used to rile him that the paper was kept going by Americans.[9]   I am now, I think, almost completely disillusioned about myself, about people, about 'causes'; I feel much better for it.   As for S.C. I see my prophecy to Orage little by little coming true. "Social Credit will come but not as we know it; not one of those ^now working for it will have any reward. I see that Unwin has announced his 8th Impression of Mathematics for the Million as "No 1 of the Age of Plenty Series"[10] and Unwin was very very

7 EP raises the reproduction process in Letter 104.
8 Orage, A.R.
9 It remains unclear which Americans sustained the paper, but Will Dyson's appeal to readers of the NEW (22 November 1934) following Orage's "The Future of the 'New English Weekly'" indicates that the paper was running on the generous support of an "American Friend."
10 Professor Lancelot Hogben (1895–1975) wrote popularizing books on language, science, and mathematics, and he published Mathematics for the Million: A Popular Self-Educator with Allen and Unwin in September 1936.

By the way, a friend of mine, Miss Lucy Phillimore[?] is going to Rapallo for 3 mos in January. I've asked her to call on you. She helped start my business. Will you be nice to her?

nervous about taking the book. Anyone could have had it.

Ever yours,

Stanley Nott

[ASC, EP]   2 *Ap*[1]

Dear Stan

How much time have you to COordinate anything ?
We NEED a/publisher. I have just writ to *Brenton*/[2] Holmes /[3]
Swabey.[4] . Have you a personal list of people you cd/ organize.
Laidlaw[5] can be useful on ONE line/ if he puts a few quid into
art pocket, and gets estabd/ that is all he can do.

ANYhow a propa ganda or unpop/ econ/ pubr/   ought not to
be a noose round someone' else's neck. Whether it wd/ be safe
even | for him to give you desk/room, I dont know. BUT a house
like the EGOIST[6] as wuz dont NEED office overhead.

Swabey has collected a vol :of my econ/ essays.[7] no pubr/
Brenton OUGHT to be combed out/ I mean his best stuff,
MUST be a/vol. of his worth collecting and printing.[8]

---

1 2 April 1939. Nott replies in Letter 108.
2 Brenton, Arthur. Editor of the *New Age* (1922–38).
3 Referent remains unclear.
4 Swabey, Reverend Henry S.
5 Likely from the publisher Laidlaw and Laidlaw, which reissued *Gaudier-Brzeska* in February 1939.
6 EP emphasizes that the success of the *Egoist* (1914–19) did not depend upon office space. See also Letter 101 for EP's comment about the costs of office space.
7 EP's "Money and Morals," edited by Henry Swabey, was never published.
8 The idea for a collection of Arthur Brenton's writings is proposed by EP in letters 61 and 62.

I can get you a few subscriptions of 5 quid each/ God knows where you wd/ find more than TEN .

What about Lymington[9] ? Certain things cdn't be pubd. by British Union/[10] and their imprint wd/ prevent sales in some
quarters/
B. U.

There is a Labour ~~bol~~ bloke that is going to find it HARD to git a pubr/ for a general symposium. whether he cd/ stake you to any extent I dont know.

McN.Wilson[11] is doing a news letter/ I wonder how many of my friends you know or cd/ contact.

Angold /[12] ∧ O/K. Mark,[13] not very collaborative ,   Duncan[14] active and has courage. We NEED a forum for ideas. B.U.Quarterly[15]

9   Wallop, Gerard Vernon (Viscount Lymington). Politician, environmentalist, writer, and key figure in several right-leaning movements in Britain.
10 The British Union of Fascists (BUF). See Letter 98. EP notes the ideological differences between Lymington (note 9) and the BUF as well as the limited reach of Greater Britain Publications, which published EP's *What Is Money For?* (1939), during this period.
11 Wilson, Robert McNair. British writer of history and economics.
12 Angold, J.P. British poet and artist who was killed in the Second World War.
13 Mark, Jeffrey.
14 Duncan, Ronald. British poet, playwright, and editor of the *Townsman*.
15 The *British Union Quarterly* (1937–40, formerly known as the *Fascist Quarterly*, 1935–36) was the official organ of the British Union of Fascists, in which EP published ten items (see Letter 98, note 4). See letters 98 and 106.

cant hold all the necessary mental/activity. Criterion[16] didn't try to. whether ole Miss Weaver[17] (Egoist) still/is cooptable I don't know.

Ten times 5 quid is 50! waal You said Five thousand[18] ? I think. My Kulch[19] has sold 462 copies in Eng/ plus American sales not recorded at moment.

I see various sporadic pamphlets/ news letters etc.

Unwin never liked me/ never wd print anything.

You DID I believe sell yr/ pamphlet series/ and make small turn over ?

I wish you wd/ meet Swabey(address Theological College , Chichester.[20]

possibly look thru his collection of my econ/ essays.

and WEED it out ; or suggest amelioration).

Have just come on " Progres Civique";[21] Sept. 10. 1921. two full pages *from Ecrits Nouveaux* quoting an articl/ in french of mine on Douglas .

16 The *Criterion* (1922–39) ceased publication in January 1939.
17 Weaver, Harriet Shaw (1876–1961). Founder of the Egoist Press and a wealthy patron of James Joyce. She was also the principal shareholder of the *New Freewoman*, edited by Dora Marsden.
18 The "five thousand" is unclear, although likely EP is misremembering how much Nott indicated as necessary to get his firm back on its feet.
19 EP's *Guide to Kulchur* was published in England by Faber and Faber in the summer of 1938 and in the United States by New Directions in the fall of 1938.
20 Chichester, Sussex.
21 *Progrès civique* (Paris). Gallup indicates that excerpts from (C624) EP's "Le major C.-H. Douglas et la situation en Angleterre" in *Les Écrits Nouveaux* (August/September 1921), were printed in *Progrès civique* (10 September 1921) under the title: "La réforme du credit est la clef de toutes les autres."

and DO they really think Pontifex stutterings more useful than my mental processes? If so WHO are they.   *E. P.* [A S]

TH*AT* ought to prove my continuity. ought to be reprinted possibly as foreword to the econ/ essays.

Pollinger[22] merely told Swab/[23] NO HOPE of finding pubr.

So far/as I know NO notice taken of my Rasegna Monetaria[24] essays/ apart from the first one/ transd/ by/Mrs Butch and printed in B.U.Q.

Do YOU(personally)realize need of DEFINING a few WORDS/ money credit etc/[25] some/of you MUST work on that. vide the ass in N.E.W. re/ measure of value.. what/the/ HELL do they expect to TEACH and HOW if they none of 'em know what they mean by the most frequently used words/ interest/usury/ partaggio/[26] MONEY/ debt ...

22 Pollinger, Laurence. EP's literary agent.
23 Swabey, Reverend Henry S.
24 *Rassegna Monetaria* (Rome): See Gallup C1406, C1410, C1416, and C1542. EP's "Verso un'economia ortologica" in *Rassegna Monetaria* (May/June 1937) was, according to Gallup, "translated by Editorial" (in Letter 91, EP suggests Butchart's wife did the translation) into English and printed under the title "Towards an Economic Orthology" in the *British Union Quarterly* (October/December 1937).
25 On orthology, or the correct use of words, see Letter 10, note 12.
26 "Partaggio" (Italian) derives from medieval parlance, which EP clarifies elsewhere as "a true and just dividend" (*SP* 351).

7 Ap

Dear Stan

IS it possible to get hold of the block of my/grandfather's[1]
timber *lumber* money,[2] that was used as frontispiece of *I*mpact.[3]

Raven Thomson ;[4] Sanctuary Buildings (British Union)
      Great Smith St   S. W. I

is bringing out my paph pamphlet on MONEY. have just heard that their
war chest wont run to illustrations/

Illustrations HELP

I am leaving for trip[5] and can't do more than send you this S.O.S.

    IF the block is available do get it too him as soon as possib*l*e and

oblige.

booklet is in press/ may be printed off by time you get this, but unlikely.

E. P. [AS]

---

1 Pound, Thaddeus Coleman.
2 The block of the paper money issued by Thaddeus's Chippewa Falls Union Lumber
   Company was used as the frontispiece of *Social Credit: An Impact*.
3 EP's *Social Credit: An Impact*.
4 Thomson, Alexander Raven. Director of Policy of the British Union of Fascists.
5 According to Carpenter, EP set sail for America on 13 April 1939 and docked in New
   York on 21 April.

THE COTTAGE · THREE CHERRY TREE FARM · HEMEL HEMPSTEAD · TEL: BOXMOOR 419

April 16th 1939[1]

Dear Ezra:

About the block. Everything connected with the company went to Fairbairn Wingfield and Wykes the liquidators,[2] just two years ago! It would take some weeks of research to get it now. It would cost only a few shillings to get one reproduced.

With regard to your letter on co-ordination.[3] I was saying to Mairet[4] the other day that the time is now ripe for another series of pamphlets. With 50pounds [sic] and a good series the money would come back easily.

Seven years ago last Thursday Orage[5] and I brought out the first number of the N.E.W.[6] and two years later I began publishing books on the New Economics. I am convinced now,as I was then,that the time has come, Or will shortly come, when another effort of that sort will have to be made.

At present I am like a beetle on its back,I cant move. And unless someone comes along and turns me over I dont quite know what I shall do. My wife and I are seriously thinking about going to America.[7]
W
A New Economics Publishing Co (or something like that)is needed . For five pounds a week I would run it;and it c^Ould make money. It might be run in conecton [sic] with the Economic Reform Club.[8] If you

---

1 Hemel Hempstead is a town northwest of London.
2 Fairbairn, Wingfield, and Wykes. See Letter 102.
3 The "letter on co-ordination" is Letter 106.
4 Mairet, Philip.
5 Orage, A.R.
6 The *New English Weekly* published its first issue on 21 April 1932.
7 Stanley Nott sailed to the United States in 1940, his family having preceded him by several months.
8 The Economic Reform Club and Institute.

could put me in the way of doing soething like this you would go far to lifting me out of a three years fit of acute depression. There ought not to be much difficulty with all the names connected with the Ec Ref Club. But perhaps you are not interested in it. I have never been there. It carries weight.

Your Text Book[9] looks interesting. I shall geta [sic] copy.

About the rest I will see what can be done. But I am sweating in another factory[10] just now ,in Luton.

Yours ever

Stanley Nott [AS]

9   The *Introductory Text Book E. P.* (Rapallo, 1939) was, according to Gallup, printed by Bonner and Company for private distribution. The work, three pages in length, consisted of quotations from John Adams, Thomas Jefferson, Abraham Lincoln, and the US Constitution, as well as a note by EP. The work was reprinted in several periodicals, including the *Townsman* (April 1939).

10   The city of Luton is located north of both London and Hemel Hempstead.

[LETTER 109, TL, CARBON, EP TO SN]

30 June[1] [pencil: "39"]

Dear Stan

The copies of my Gold/ War article[2] seem to have arrived. but nowt else. Drummond[3] has seen only that. Praps you lost my list of exchanges or thought it not worth the postage.

Is the enclosed ∧ article[4] any use to you . I enc. two bucks to cover postage on any issues of Cap Dail since May 9th that you think I ought to see.

What do you do in the summer ? suspend ?[5] might be an economy or to appear weekly or in two page format when Congress not sitting(depends on yr/ contracts with scruffscribers.

Did Ph Johnson[6] turn up ? any use ? What about Wythe Williams ?[7] did you git my Greenwich Time interview ???[8]

---

1 EP is still in the United States at this time. According to Carpenter, EP received his honourary doctorate there on 12 July 1939.
2 EP published "Ezra Pound on Gold, War, and National Money" in the *Capitol Daily*, Washington, DC (9 May 1939).
3 Drummond, John. EP's friend in Rapallo. Drummond's role here is unclear, but he translated several of Pound's essays in Italian and helped Pound with proofreading and indexing *Guide to Kulchur* (Preda, *Ezra Pound's Economic Correspondence*, 265).
4 The enclosed article remains unclear.
5 The reference here remains unclear. Nott's autobiography suggests that he was working for his father's hat factory at this time, then for a government organization that assisted Czech refugees from Hitler's Germany (*Further Teachings* 114, 120).
6 This may well be architect Philip Johnson, who, like EP, was interested in figures linked to American fascism in the 1930s, including Huey Long and Father Coughlin. See Arthur Schlesinger, *The Politics of Upheaval 1935–6* (2003), 72.
7 Williams, Wythe (1881–1956). Author and correspondent for the *New York Times*.
8 "The Cabinet of a Dream, and Congress Should Go on the Air" was published in *Greenwich Time* (13 July 1939).

Give me luvv to th Missus/ you sure did right to pick thqt
gal.

   / /

Praps I might hit ONE economic idiocy per article in a series
of two or three   more artcls   ??

                                                yrz

and greet the staff.

ESSAYS

ESSAY I
EZRA POUND AND SOCIAL CREDIT

Italy's bank measures/ are NOT Doug/ism
—Pound to Nott on Italy and the Social Credit
theories of C.H. Douglas (Letter 4)

In 1918, Ezra Pound met Major C.H. Douglas, founder of the Social Credit movement. He was introduced to Douglas by his friend A.R. Orage, influential editor of the *New Age*, the "weekly review of politics, literature and art" for which Pound had written since 1911; Pound's and Douglas's initial meeting, in fact, took place in the journal's offices. Thus was inaugurated the connection to Social Credit that would later consume Pound's attention and command his devotion. Pound would afterwards characterize the meeting as a conversion experience that catalyzed his serious commitment to the study of economics in general and to Social Credit in particular.[1] More than ten years would elapse before his later immersion in economic thought in the early 1930s; however, in retrospective accounts, he would feature that 1918 encounter as the moment of origin for his work in the domain of "econ." Not surprisingly, given Pound's bent for hyperbolic self-mythologization, this narrative distorts somewhat: David Kadlec notes that Pound's interest in economics clearly predated his convergence with Douglas by a number of years.[2] But it was the impact of Douglas's ideas that ushered Pound into a new phase of focused thought about economics, laying the foundation for his more committed economic engagement of the 1930s.

As Alec Marsh notes, the Social Credit movement has often been "maligned" as "crack-pot, reactionary, antisemitic, and even proto-Fascist" (5). Accordingly, much commentary in Pound scholarship has read Pound's attraction to Social Credit as resulting from pathology, an uncritical absorption of ideology, and/or antisemitism.[3] But even if these factors contributed to Pound's adherence to Social Credit, his commitment to the movement also grew from a series of logical choices stimulated by signals in his cultural environment: many activists and intellectuals in Pound's orbits during the 1920s and 1930s were likewise persuaded by the movement's ideas.[4]

As Tim Redman notes, "In our decidedly post-Keynesian age, Pound's writings on economics seem at times, even to the untutored among us, quaint, naïve, or a bit obvious ... [But] much of what Pound was advocating was quite radical for the thirties" (*Italian Fascism* 124). John Finlay, a major historian of the development of Social Credit in Britain, acknowledges that Social Credit always remained a bit "shadowy" – in Keynes's term, part of an economic "underworld" (1–2). But it was recognized as a significant oppositional effort of its time, part of the realm of what might today be termed "alternative economics."[5] It opposed orthodox economic theory, and specifically equilibrium theory, an opposition that John Kenneth Galbraith suggests is generally the factor used to distinguish "reputable" economists from "crackpots" (qtd. Surette, *Purgatory*, 35). But many efforts at economic reform of this time were likewise contesting classical economic theory, and, as the counter-hegemonic sphere of economic reform became robust, such dissenting positions carried authority.[6]

Accordingly, Pound's involvement in the movement placed him among a sizeable and internally diverse group of economic reformers of the interwar years. Moreover, while Social Credit unquestionably involved antisemitic patterns of thought (the movement's signature demonization of usury, international finance, and the banking system often fostered antisemitic assumptions and claims), and while the conceptual habits that Pound had absorbed from the movement indeed contributed to the escalation of his own antisemitism, it was not antisemitism that initially drew Pound to Social Credit.

POUND'S RECEPTIVITY TO SOCIAL CREDIT

At first, other factors contributed to Pound's receptivity to Social Credit. In 1918, Pound was primed to be galvanized by Douglas's arguments. Initially, Pound was influenced towards Douglas's ideas by the good opinion of A.R. Orage, whose judgment Pound had respected for a number of years. Douglas was a somewhat mysterious figure about whom biographical information is still scarce: he was a retired engineer and military man, formerly associated with the Royal Flying Corps, born in England (rather than Scotland, as was widely surmised from his name), and, in the late 1910s, was new to the field of economics.[7] He had begun developing his economic theories through conversations with Orage about a year before the end of the First

World War (Hughes 38), forging them during meetings with Orage and A.J. Penty in an ABC Restaurant in London (Mairet 74–5). These initial collaborative sessions were so important to the formation of Social Credit, and Orage's role, in particular, was so crucial, that Orage is sometimes read not only as a major advocate of Social Credit but also as its co-founder (Hutchinson and Burkitt 7).

Orage's journal the *New Age* first touted Douglas's ideas in the 12 December 1918 issue, which praised him for an "ingenious and convincing article" in the *English Review*, and it first published his work in January 1919. Douglas's prose then began appearing regularly in the magazine in June, July, and August 1919. These discussions were later consolidated and published in 1920 in *Economic Democracy* (Surette, Purgatory, 32). Another of Douglas's books, *Credit Power and Democracy* (presented as co-authored by Douglas and Orage), appeared the same year, likewise gathering into book form writing that had been serialized in the *New Age* during 1920. Pound reviewed both books.[8]

The primary objective of Douglas's new Social Credit program was increased purchasing power for consumers. As a result, as Finlay and Surette note, Social Credit forms part of a lineage of significant underconsumptionist theory in economic thought, arising in the nineteenth century among commentators such as John Ruskin and Pierre Proudhon, who challenged the economic orthodoxy of Adam Smith and, in particular, Say's law of supply and demand (Surette, *Purgatory*, 8). Countering the sanguine assurances of classical equilibrium theory – that the forces of supply and demand would yield a self-correcting, self-regulating system – underconsumptionist economic thinkers maintained that, given the conditions of contemporary capitalism, there was often "poverty in the midst of plenty" (as the Social Credit slogan had it): a state of affairs in which many consumers did not have the credit to buy all they needed, or all that was produced, within an economic system. In Douglas's reading, this lack of purchasing power led to poverty, surplus unused product, and thus the need for nations such as Britain to conduct aggressive searches for foreign markets to purchase the products that their domestic populace could not: and this competition for foreign markets, in turn, paved the way for war.

According to Douglas, the principal cause for this shortfall in purchasing power was the workings (and often the corrupt machinations) of finance: private banks that controlled the right to extend credit, exact interest on loans, and turn a profit. While the solutions Douglas proposed to this problem were not always clear, they usually involved the idea of a national credit association that, assuming the role ordinarily played by banks, would issue credit to consumers in the form of a "National Dividend."

During this time, Orage exerted significant sway over Pound, as he did over many others. For Orage's detractors, his charisma was bound up in a dilettantish bent for successive short-term enthusiasms;[9] for his admirers, it was an outgrowth of a powerful mind, wide cultural awareness, and a capacity for cultural leadership, all of which lent authority to his judgments. By this point, Orage had anointed Douglas as an innovator and spokesperson for an important new program in postwar economic reform. Between 1918 and 1922, Orage was actively promoting Social Credit; as of 1919, he made Social Credit the primary cause of the *New Age*.

As Redman notes, Pound had received an important early apprenticeship in economic thought through writing regularly for Orage's journal between 1911 and 1921 (*Italian Fascism* chap. 1). During this avant-guerre period, Pound's engagement with economics was also fostered by his reading the work of economist Arthur Kitson in the pages of the *New Freewoman* and his correspondence about economics with Dora Marsden, the *New Freewoman*'s editor (Kadlec chap. 2).[10] During the period of Pound's economic education, the *New Age* was known for featuring a wide range of economic and political positions and programs. Through association with the journal, Pound thus intersected with a diverse group of economic reformers whose variety of positions reflected Orage's signature openness to reform-minded thinkers of many stripes.[11]

Redman characterizes the *New Age* as "socialist" (*Italian Fascism* 17), but this implies that the journal's leading political line was more consistently leftist than it actually was: while Orage presented himself as socialist in orientation, he supported Guild Socialism, a hybrid of syndicalist and socialist thought; and he was conspicuously sympathetic to the views of politically right-leaning figures such as T.E. Hulme.[12] After the *New Age*'s initial years of eclecticism, it was indeed Guild Socialism that the journal featured most prominently between 1911 and 1919 (Corrin 81). But even using Guild Socialism to encompass the journal's program, as does Ann Ardis, tends to feature Orage's consistent view after 1911 (which was promulgated by the journal during the window framing the Great War) at the expense of recognizing the evolution of Orage's politics over time as well as the political heterogeneity of the journal's contributors.[13] Economic reformers affiliated with the *New Age* significantly included both leftists such as G.B. Shaw and H.G. Wells and rightists such as G.K. Chesterton, Hilaire Belloc, and A.J. Penty (Surette, *Purgatory*, 21).[14] Working at the *New Age*, Pound thus had exposure to a notably varied array of political and economic viewpoints.

What members of this heterogeneous group shared was an interest in unorthodox economic thought that took issue with laissez-faire capitalism and the classical economic theory that informed it, along with a distrust of statist socialism. Accordingly, from 1911 onward, Pound was steeped in a heady brew of debates among participants in *New Age* circles – including Fabian Socialists such as Shaw and Wells, Distributists such as G.K. Chesterton, and Guild Socialists such as G.D.H. Cole and Orage. While commentators such as Kadlec and Surette differ on how much of this radical political discourse Pound was actually absorbing into his own intellectual bloodstream, it is safe to say that, by the time he crossed paths with Douglas, Pound had long been accustomed to commentators in his environment proposing sweeping challenges to the current capitalist system. By the late 1910s, Douglas's heterodox proposals, initially read by many as "original" and even "alarming" (Mairet 74),[15] constituted no departure from Pound's comfort zone.

Another important contribution to Pound's receptivity to Douglas's ideas was the war death in 1915 of Pound's comrade, the French sculptor Henri Gaudier-Brzeska, whom Pound commemorated in *Gaudier-Brzeska* (1916). Not only did Pound's grief sting him into outrage at the war (as Pound would note in his 1920 poem, *Hugh Selwyn Mauberley*, there had been "wastage as never before") but it also engendered in him the fierce resolve to investigate "the causes of war ... to oppose same" (*Selected Poems* 1949, viii).[16] Pound's quest to counter war was increasingly channelled into his commitment to Social Credit. In Pound's view, his opposition to war was well served through Social Credit, which discerned the dominant motives for the First World War in the conditions of contemporary laissez-faire capitalism – in the view of Social Crediters, dominated by the machinations of international finance. Pound underscored this anti-war emphasis of Social Credit in his early review of Douglas's *Economic Democracy* (1921): here, he applauded in Douglas's work "a new and definite force in economic thought ... directed to the prevention of new wars, wars blown up out of economic villainies at the whim and instigation of small bodies of irresponsible individuals" (*P&P* IV, 39). Also indicating that the carnage of war was on Pound's mind as he wrote this review is that, as in the passage from *Hugh Selwyn Mauberley* quoted above, he employs the word "wastage": Douglas's book succeeds in part, Pound notes, because of its "underflow of protest against the wastage of human beings" (*P&P* IV, 38). In his 1921 review of Douglas's *Credit Power and Democracy* in *Contact*, Pound likewise notes that, if Douglas's ideas became known, they would act as a "deterrent" to "war making" (*P&P* IV, 156).

Thus after the war, Pound sought a cause to which he might attach himself so as to transmute his personal grief at Gaudier-Brzeska's death into a broader and more objective societal project to wage peace,[17] and to do so in the style to which, as an aggressive impresario of "movements" in the arts, he had become accustomed and for which his polemical muscles were trained. Given his path to artistic maturity, Pound's "feel for the game," in Bourdieuian terms, required a focused movement, a set of principles susceptible to being articulated in plainspoken language, and a typical avant-garde stance oppositional to mainstream trends.[18]

Social Credit, then, was what Pound was equipped for, what he easily accepted, and what met his needs in the late 1910s. Given the influences of his context, it is no wonder that he was persuaded of it so rapidly. But that a significant constellation of factors in Pound's environment and background fostered his receptivity to Social Credit does not mean that specific substantive points of Douglas's work did not also influence his commitment to the movement. As his review of *Economic Democracy* indicates, Pound favoured what he read as Social Credit's effort to stand up for the individual, whose agency could be eroded by forms of centralized control – either under the conditions of laissez-faire capitalism (under which Social Crediters believed that finance reigned supreme and that power was concentrated in the hands of those few who controlled the supply of credit) or under the domination of statist socialism. In *Economic Democracy*, Douglas resisted the "demand to subordinate individuality to the need of some external organisation" (12). Pound also favoured Douglas's plainspoken style (which, in his review, he referred to as "rugged" and "unpolished," "but hard-hitting" – and, likely for Pound the rhetorical cowboy, capable of hitting hard *because* "unpolished") because of the distance it marked between Douglas and the suave economists of the university set. For Pound, this positioned Douglas on the side of the angels. Moreover, given his emergence from the *New Age* ecosystem, Pound read underconsumptionist reforms like those Douglas proposed as being conducive to a culture hospitable to the arts. As Surette notes, *New Age* circles tended to interpret underconsumptionist theory in general as stemming from the work of John Ruskin and thus as advocating climates in which the arts would be funded and would flourish. Social Credit also proposed as a telos a society in which everyone would have sufficient purchasing power and would be able to choose to work or not as they wished. As Pound phrases this concept in Canto 8, "So that he can work as he likes,/ Or waste his time as he likes/ … never lacking provision" (*C* 29). Individuals in such a "Leisure State" would be free to express their creativity – and this clearly made for an artist's utopia.[19]

SOCIAL CREDIT IN THE CONTEXT OF EARLY
TWENTIETH-CENTURY ECONOMIC RADICALISM

During the interwar years, Social Credit drew noteworthy support in England, Scotland, Australia, the United States, and especially in Canada, where it rose to political office in the province of Alberta. Fuelling its rise was a postwar wave of economic dissidence stemming from pervasive disillusionment with liberal democracy and the laissez-faire form of capitalism with which it was closely associated. This disenchantment intensified during the Great Depression, as did interest in Social Credit. In particular Social Credit appealed to those simultaneously distrustful of both laissez-faire capitalism and socialism (whose emphasis on a centralized state raised for many, as it were, a red flag) and suspicious of the power of big finance and big business. Social Credit sought to preserve the freedom of the individual within a modified capitalist system that would guarantee sufficient income and resources for all. And again, in its focus on demand-side economics, it formed part of a significant underconsumptionist tradition in economic thought, associated with predecessors such as Ruskin and Proudhon, which looked to increases in purchasing power as the best way of addressing interrelated economic and social ills. Far from anomalous in its cultural milieu, then, Social Credit existed in close accord with larger efforts of economic reform of its day and with underconsumptionist reform in particular, which, at the time, commanded assent in many quarters. Even John Maynard Keynes would acknowledge Douglas's ideas in his watershed 1936 *General Theory of Employment, Interest, and Money* (370–71), where Keynes would position himself as an underconsumptionist (Surette, *Purgatory*, 53). Keynes credited Douglas with having important insight into the economic problems of the day and suggested that the economic establishment had no adequate reply to his critiques; but because of flaws in Douglas's thought, Keynes relegated him to the rank of a "private" rather than a "major" within "the brave army" of economic "heretics" (371).[20]

Although the Social Credit movement emerged from England, it was in Canada, in the western province of Alberta, that it ascended to greatest official prominence.[21] The Social Credit movement in Alberta was spearheaded by William Aberhart, an evangelical preacher and schoolteacher who, in the 1930s, turned politician out of a conviction that he had a duty to respond to the dire economic conditions on the Canadian Prairies. Social Credit was welcomed in Alberta as a heroic program that could lead the province, struggling during the Depression, out of poverty. Aberhart's Social Credit platform was voted into provincial office in 1935, and Aberhart became provincial premier. At the time, supporters viewed Social Credit as the means by which Alberta could pull itself out of economic crisis, achieve self-sufficiency as a province, and take its stand against a federal government that had ignored its pleas. As Pound's comments in the Pound/Nott correspondence indicate ("The 1937 Alberta Soc/ Cred Bill" looked good, he remarked), he was interested in what Douglas termed "The Alberta Experiment"; and, while ignorant of western Canada, expressed a willingness to travel to Alberta to facilitate the implementation of Social Credit policies in the province. The movement in Alberta would ultimately founder because of Aberhart's difficulty in developing a plan of action, the challenges of achieving provincial support for his proposed measures, and the fierce resistance of the federal government. According to Ottawa, Alberta's Social Credit policies clashed with constitutional regulations and accordingly were declared ultra vires.[22] Internecine factionalism also hobbled the Canadian movement throughout the late 1930s and early 1940s, and it would eventually decline into ineffectuality. Under Ernest Manning, the disciple of Aberhart's who became premier upon Aberhart's death in 1943, Social Credit as it had been conceived in the 1930s would permute into a more conventional conservative program – with the result that, although the Social Credit name was maintained until the 1970s, Socred policies afterward retained few of Douglas's original principles.

For a time, however, Social Credit was a giant on the scene. Bob Hesketh traces the powerful appeal that the movement held for many Albertans: the majority of its followers were small-scale independent farmers and small business owners.[23] One major attraction of Social Credit stemmed from the way that its program resonated with Prairie populism, promising Alberta the chance to fulfill a long-standing desire to assert its independence from the federal government. Also compelling was Social Credit's refusal of economics-as-usual and its battles against both big finance and big government, as well as its planned economic reforms, which could distribute greater purchasing power to all. And its lure resided in an overriding commitment to economic justice – rather than the rapacities of laissez-faire capitalism – and to creating conditions that would enable individuals to fulfill their creative potential by their own lights.

In these respects, Social Credit was kindred to British economic reform programs of the early twentieth century such as Guild Socialism and Distributism, both of which, like Social Credit, issued from a two-pronged disillusionment with both economic liberalism and statist socialism.[24] These two movements provide useful coordinates with which to understand Social Credit. Distributism, whose leading theorists were G.K. Chesterton and Hilaire Belloc, advocated the creation of professional guilds; worker control of commerce, agriculture, and industry; and equitable distribution of property to small landowners. Animated by an agrarian vision and ideals drawn from medieval England, insisting on property ownership as fundamental to liberty, Distributists sought to cultivate not only an economic program but also, more generally, a way of life that could combat the atomization of modern society through responsible stewardship of the land and the values this entailed. Vigorously anti-statist, Distributists promoted an approach informed by Christian – in the case of most adherents, Roman Catholic – values.[25] Guild Socialists, meanwhile, whose ideas were initially formulated by S.G. Hobson, then supported and promulgated by G.D.H. Cole and Orage, likewise supported the creation of guilds that would control production and advanced a critique of the wage system (Finlay 79). Where syndicalists sought to abolish the state, the Guild Socialist blend of syndicalism and socialism sought to forge, as Orage put it in the *New Age* in 1912, a "partnership" between guilds and the state, which would oversee the guilds (Finlay 75). Members of both reformers' groups moved in *New Age* circles and, sharing a wellspring of disenchantment with laissez-faire capitalism, big government, and state socialism, enjoyed significant propinquity. But although both Distributists and Guild Socialists advocated the formation of guilds, the latter sought to establish guilds within the framework of the existing factory system, while the former, more radical in their objections to industrial society, sought to use guilds to abolish it (Corrin 85). The two groups also differed on the role of the state: Distributists sought to reduce its role as much as possible, while Guild Socialists, although also anti-statist, were more receptive to the prospect of a benevolent managerial state, albeit divided on the question of how large and active a role the state should play.[26]

The two movements of Distributism and Guild Socialism not only overlapped with each other but overlapped significantly, in both values and membership, with Social Credit. Like these other schools of thought, Social Credit advocated neither socialism-as-usual nor capitalism-as-usual but, rather, a "third way." Also like Guild Socialism and Distributism, Social Credit sought to remove control from the hands of powerful elites in business and finance and distribute more to the people, thus demonstrating a similar Sherwood Forest idealism.[27] One crucial difference between Social Credit and these other programs, however, was that, whereas Guild Socialists were chiefly interested in control of production and Distributists in the cultural benefits of private property, Social Crediters concentrated on consumer purchasing power and control of credit.[28]

Another context important to understanding Social Credit involves the idealistic reform efforts of its era – those associated with what James Webb terms the "illuminated viewpoint."[29] Social Credit took root in the same postwar British soil that produced many reform-minded Utopian movements, many of which involved beliefs in unseen realities that could improve the spiritual health of the British people. Webb convincingly places Social Credit within this 1920s and 1930s climate, thereby revealing that Social Credit, contrary to what might usually be assumed of an economic reform program, was anti-materialist: it was chiefly concerned with people's spiritual well-being and with economic justice, to which redress of objectionable material conditions was merely an avenue. Social Credit's vision of justice was expressed in its effort to wrest credit from the hands of the few, while its commitment to the improvement of spiritual life appeared in its assertion that it was not only a program for economic reform but also a philosophy of life – which that program served. As Douglas remarks in *The Approach to Reality*: "as I conceive it, Social Credit … comprehends a great deal more than the money problem … Social Credit fundamentally involves a conception of the relationships among individuals and their associations in countries and nations, between individuals and their associations in groups" (6).

This idealism helps to account for Social Credit's attraction for many members who were committed to spiritual viewpoints and religious creeds. Many were explicitly Christian, such as the Dean of Canterbury; some, such as Maurice Reckitt and John Hargrave, had been raised as Quakers. Still others were animated by non-Christian but spiritually illuminated viewpoints: Nott and Jane Heap, for instance, followed the mysticism of G.I. Gurdjieff (see Essay 4). In part, this attests to the influence of A.R. Orage, who was famously interested in both Social Credit and mysticism and who encouraged acolytes to adopt the two separate enthusiasms he had himself taken up. Accordingly, as Surette points out, the circles Pound encountered early in his career at the *New Age* – those who were interested in mysticism (at that juncture, usually Theosophy) and those who "shaped his interest in economics" – were "not two sets, but a single set" (*Purgatory* 48). However, the frequent proximity between mystical circles and Social Credit circles, and the overlap in their membership, also stemmed from their kindred structural positions as cultural fringe movements as well as by their attendant openness to non-mainstream views. More substantively, occultists and the Social Crediters shared ideals: a desire to better the spiritual welfare of the community, a passion for justice, and a wish to advance a state of affairs within which everyone, regardless of background or fortunes, could attain self-actualization and the full expression of their creative potential.

ANTISEMITISM AND THE DEMONIZATION OF FINANCE

In Douglas's view, the principal cause for the shortfall in purchasing power endemic to contemporary capitalist society was the fact that the banks controlled the right to extend credit and to profit from interest on loans. One of Douglas's chief tenets was the "A + B Theorem," widely disseminated by his followers and derided by his detractors as simplistic. For Pound, the theorem's simplicity showed up the unnecessary complexities of orthodox economists. It suggests that if, within an economic system (which Douglas represented synecdochically as a factory), the producer was obliged to set prices according to the need to (1) pay workers in salaries, wages, and dividends; (2) cover costs of production; (3) pay overhead costs; (4) repay, with interest, banks that had extended credit to the business; and if (5) the worker was only receiving the sum of money in category 1, then prices for the products of the economy would necessarily always exceed the worker's ability to pay them. "A" stands for the payment to workers in the form of wages, salaries, and dividends; "B" stands for all costs incurred by the producer. Hence, if the price had to equal "A + B," and "A + B" was always necessarily greater than "A," then the consumer would perforce suffer from a lack of purchasing power.[30] Pound summarized this theorem in Canto 38, first published in Orage's journal, the *New English Weekly*, in September 1933. As Orage had founded the journal to promulgate Social Credit thought, it offered the theorem a hospitable audience.[31]

Social Crediters maintained that it was the banks that were primarily responsible for the discrepancy between "A" (wages, dividends, etc.) and "A + B" (outlay from producers). It was the banks that had initially provided the capital to the producer with which to produce, and therefore it was the banks that ran the show. In Douglas's view, what was amiss was not only that the structural role of the banks left them in an advantaged position and contributed to consumers' lack of purchasing power but also that finance actively sought to exploit the ordinary consumer. As years passed, Douglas would increasingly demonize finance as a sinister international conspiracy.

And this tendency, in turn, was significantly bound up in Douglas's antisemitism. Bob Hesketh argues persuasively that too little attention has been paid to how, in the development of his paranoid ideas, Douglas was deeply influenced by the *Protocols of the Learned Elders of Zion*: this was the notorious document claimed to be a record of a vast international conspiracy, led by a group of powerful Jewish Zionists, who sought, at the expense of poor and powerless Jews, to subvert Christianity and to gain world control. The text had purportedly been wrested from the fin-de-siècle group of Zionists whose malign sentiments it registered. It became available in English in 1917 (Surette, *Purgatory*, 260), just at the time that Douglas was formulating his ideas for Social Credit; and it was famously publicized in *The International Jew* (1920), a volume of articles from Michigan's *Dearborn Independent*, a newspaper owned by antisemitic American industrialist Henry Ford. Although the *Protocols* was revealed as a forgery in 1921 in the *Times of London* (Stingel 17; Thurlow, *Fascism in Britain*, 57), Douglas, like many others, maintained his belief in its basic tenets. Even if the *Protocols* was not authentic, Douglas suggested, the ominous international conspiracy it exposed was real.[32] Epitomizing this sentiment is a statement by Social Crediter L.D. Byrne in the December 1936 issue of the Social Credit periodical the *Fig Tree*, edited by Douglas:

> No review of such matters under consideration can be complete without reference to that remarkable document, "The Protocols of the Learned Elders of Zion," which, unfortunately, has not received the serious attention it demands because of its association with irresponsible and mischievous anti-Jewish propaganda ... It has been asserted repeatedly that the Protocols are a forgery, and at least one law case has been fought out to establish this. Whether they are a forgery or not seems immaterial. The important fact is that the pattern of the world today conforms with extraordinary accuracy to the plans laid down in this document many years before the actual occurrence of the events, and alleged to be those of a self-appointed hierarchy which has been scheming the enslavement of mankind for many centuries. (224)[33]

As Hesketh observes, Douglas's efforts to reform the existing economic system so as to reduce the stranglehold of the banks need to be understood in the context of his conspiratorial view of history, which was fuelled by the *Protocols*. In Douglas's reading, the trouble lay not with a structural flaw in the existing system but rather with the banks, which, for him, became a metonym for an actively malevolent "hidden hand" steering Europe towards ruin. And as became more and more evident in his prose as years passed, that "hidden hand" was identified with the Jews. The conceptual linkages that the *Protocols* drew among the banks, the Jews, and world conspiracy not only reinforced existing cultural antisemitism but also, as Thomas Linehan suggests, ushered in a wave of antisemitism of a new variety (47) – one that read each of these terms as implying the others. Douglas's ideas both drew upon and perpetuated this new kind of antisemitism.

As John Finlay notes, antisemitism in the form of the identification of corrupt finance with Jews was certainly not uncommon for this time and place, and it was less malignant than the more virulent forms of antisemitism that later appeared during the 1930s under the Nazis. Janine Stingel also points out that Social Credit's antisemitism was strictly rhetorical and ideological: "At no time was the movement antisemitic in the Third Reichian sense of officially adopting and transforming that ideology into a policy of discrimination" (4). But this neither warrants downplaying the importance of antisemitism to Social Credit nor exculpating those who participated in it. If Social Credit's antisemitism was not programmatic in the Nazi sense, it was nevertheless woven into the fabric of Social Credit and intimately interlinked with the vilification of international finance that lay at the heart of the movement.

Social Credit's integral conceptual habit of blaming international finance for the world's ills and associating it with a cabal of Jews conspiring towards world domination left the door wide open to antisemitism. Although certainly not all Social Crediters were actively antisemitic, the movement's characteristic conspiracy-minded thought with regard to Jews was eminently receptive to antisemitic thought. The strain of antisemitism displayed by Social Credit became widespread in Britain in the 1920s and 1930s as the country was regrouping defensively, often spreading in a way that entailed paranoiac and xenophobic responses to a host of perceived threats to the strength of British society. And this variety of antisemitism found hospitality in, and contributed to the rise of, many proto-fascist and fascist groups in interwar Britain.[34]

When Social Credit began to take hold in Alberta, these antisemitic patterns followed. As Hesketh and Stingel note, both of the two prominent Canadian leaders associated with Social Credit, William Aberhart and Ernest Manning, repeatedly denounced antisemitism and publicly denied that their movement was antisemitic. Manning, who became premier of Alberta in 1943, even sought to rid the movement of antisemites.[35] But their efforts demonstrate how much of a problem this had become: Social Credit discourse, as fashioned by Douglas and as absorbed by Alberta's Social

Crediters, necessarily conjured, even demanded, the spectre of international finance; and along with this came a strong temptation to link this spectre to the Jews. In an era riven by economic privation and thus susceptible to the hunger for scapegoats, this temptation was often too strong to resist. Whatever its overt gestures to the contrary, Social Credit displayed an antisemitic ideological unconscious.[36]

POUND'S ANTISEMITISM

To suggest that Ezra Pound "caught" antisemitism from Douglas or Social Credit, however, is to oversimplify. As Redman notes, Pound had been absorbing a suspicion of bankers and other antisemitic patterns for years, starting at least with his involvement in the *New Age*, which tended to disseminate such patterns (Redman, *Italian Fascism*, 49–50), and likely beginning even earlier, with the populist ideas on monetary reform that circulated in his environment during his youth.[37] But the entrance of Douglas and his thought into Pound's purview unquestionably enhanced the likelihood that Pound's antisemitic inclination would grow from seedling to rampant vine.

This said, I would resist the claim that Pound was drawn to Social Credit primarily because of its antisemitism. Like many of those attracted by Social Credit in the 1920s and 1930s, Pound was given to the populist reflex of demonizing big money. This tendency is what made the moves of Social Credit fit so comfortably and easily the mental gait of so many, including Pound, during this period. Moreover, Pound was clearly prone to the conceptual habit of finding one reigning enemy, in Manichean dualistic fashion, to oppose to the forces of life and vitality. Early in his career, inspired by his immersion in the work of Dante, he had placed in that enemy camp "usura," or usurious practice. Pound's apprenticeship with the polemical *New Age* circle reinforced these conceptual habits. Thus by the time Pound encountered Douglas, the infrastructure of his imagination was well paved to allow for the easy travel of antisemitic prejudices. He did not begin to move forcefully towards antisemitism until the 1930s, however: like Surette, I would place the turn in 1934. The significant volta that occurred at this point was enabled by the company Pound was keeping at this time, both in person and through his correspondence. The Pound/Nott correspondence invokes many of the figures composing that company – figures often acquired through Pound's desire to disseminate both Douglas's ideas and what he read as Mussolini's magnificent example.

Pound's antisemitism begins to appear in his responses to a 1934 article by William Pelley, which held that "Jewish Conspiracy" was responsible for the American Civil War,[38] as well as in his replies during this year to correspondent Hugo Fack, an economic radical in Texas who shared Pound's interest in the economic work of Silvio Gesell and the possibility of joining Gesellite with Social Credit thought (Preda, *Ezra Pound's Economic Correspondence*, 267). Surette also suggests that, by this time, Pound's own cast of thought had been swayed in an antisemitic direction by exchanges with economic reformer Arthur Kitson, which began in 1933 (*Purgatory* 215).

Also likely contributing to the rise of Pound's antisemitism at this time was his relationship with John Drummond, a poet and editor whom he met in the early 1930s. Drummond spent a significant amount of time with Pound in Rapallo from 1934 onward, and Pound enlisted him during this period as a research assistant on the "Jewish question" (Surette, *Purgatory*, 247), though whether this was at Pound's behest or in response to Drummond's initiative is not clear. Among Pound's books at the Harry Ransom Center at the University of Texas at Austin is a copy of *Are These Things So?*, credited to the "World Alliance against Jewish Aggressiveness." According to the inscription on the flyleaf, the book originally belonged to Drummond. The edition dates from 1934. While there are no annotations from Pound, there are ample marginalia from Drummond, whose notes suggest that he has been persuaded by many of the book's arguments and its faith in the authenticity and claims of the *Protocols*, thirteen years after the latter had been exposed as a forgery. In the book's index, in a note next to the name of Nesta Webster, an antisemitic conspiracy theorist notorious for promulgating claims about an ominous worldwide Jewish plot, Drummond notes, laconically, "must get some of her stuff."[39] While the degree to which Drummond supported either the assertions of this antisemitic book or the claims of Webster is impossible to determine with certainty, at the very least, he appears to have tolerated them.[40]

Another crucial factor in the escalation of Pound's antisemitism – one that the Pound/Nott correspondence highlights – is Pound's exchanges with Arnold Leese, leader of the Imperial Fascist League. This was one of the smaller groups of fascists in Britain during the 1930s, known for its extreme antisemitism and racist invective. As Essay 2 details, Pound's correspondence with Leese during 1934 and 1935 was prompted by Leese's sending him a copy of the official newspaper of the Imperial Fascist League, the *Fascist*, as well as a desire to persuade Leese and his organization of the benefits of Social Credit. Although Pound's letters at times chide Leese for overt antisemitism, they also echo, often in a chillingly jocular vein, the spirit and logic of many of Leese's most virulently antisemitic remarks. The correspondence with Leese reveals Pound's antisemitic conceptual patterns at this time and may well have brought these to the surface of his thought.

POUND'S HETERODOX AMALGAMATIONS

Leon Surette poses the provocative question, "Was Pound really a Social Crediter?" (*Purgatory* 4). Indeed Pound was never an "orthodox" Social Crediter; even within this heterodox domain of endeavour, Pound typically avoided the orthodox position. Although just after his "conversion" experience of 1918, Pound was clearly reading Douglas as his man, characteristically, he soon sought to augment the ideas of Social Credit with his own eclectic mixture of "finds." Surette reads this proclivity charitably as showing Pound to be less "hidebound" than his economic mentors, Orage and Douglas. What I would underscore here is the continuity between this and Pound's general bent for introducing his own discoveries: he sought to leave his distinctive mark on Social Credit and find a way to create a show that he could manage, much as he had the Imagist movement and other avant-garde endeavours he had led in the past.

Letters of the 1930s indicate that Pound's correspondents at this point, Nott included, were likewise interested in removing themselves from strict Douglasism. Hugo Fack, for instance, supported Pound's effort to inform Social Credit with Gesellite ideas. Similarly, members of the British Union of Fascists indicated that they would be hospitable to the ideas of Social Credit if Pound could move away from strict Douglasism and offer an alternative line of economic reform through a fusion of Douglas's arguments and those from other schools of thought such as Gesell's. On this basis, Pound found common cause with correspondents and political incentive to imagine his hybrid economic program.[41]

The two significant additions Pound sought to contribute to the Social Credit program were (1) advocacy of the economic theories of German economic reformer Silvio Gesell, which he discovered in 1932, and (2) support of Social Crediter John Hargrave. As Tim Redman notes, Pound encountered Gesell's ideas through the work of the one establishment economist he would favour, Irving Fisher, a professor of economics at Yale. Pound reviewed Fisher's *Stamp Scrip* in 1933. Fisher was an admirer of Gesell's ideas, as was John Maynard Keynes (though, given Pound's scorn for Keynes, the approbation of the latter would likely have dissuaded rather than encouraged him in his support of Gesell). What attracted Pound to Gesell was an economic scheme, pursued in the Austrian town of Wörgl, enlisting Gesell's principles: the village implemented "stamp scrip," or Schwundgeld, which was designed to encourage the circulation of money through the local economy.[42] If residents did not spend currency within a certain window of time, they would have to pay for stamps to maintain a note's original purchasing power: the longer they held on to it without reintroducing it into the economy, the more they would have to pay to maintain its original value. This scheme appealed to Pound in part because, as Preda notes (*Pound's Economic Correspondence* 207), it provided a corrective for the inflationary tendency of Douglas's Social Credit measures, what Surette calls the "Achilles heel of Social Credit monetary theory."[43] It also attracted Pound because Social Credit had emphasized the importance of the circulation of money through a system. In general, Pound gravitated towards procedures that were conducive to swift circulation.[44] As Pound observed in *Rassegna Monetaria* through an anatomical analogy typical of his thought: "Gesell concentrated on the concept of *circulation*, and planned the means in order that they wouldn't stagnate. Blood circulates in the veins."[45]

During the early 1930s, Pound corresponded with two proponents of Gesellite thought, Hugo Fack in Texas and E.S. Woodward in British Columbia, both of whom appear in the Pound/Nott correspondence as potential recipients of Pound's work on the New Economics. However, Pound's intervention into Social Credit with his Gesellite contributions was not well received by his original Social Credit mentors: both Douglas and Orage remained sceptical of the ability to combine Gesellite and Social Credit ideas (Surette, *Purgatory*, 176; Redman, *Italian Fascism*, 128). But whether or not Gesell's approaches could be effectively grafted onto Social Credit measures, what this reveals, significantly, is a general feature of Pound's intellectual work: his bent for making and promoting a "find." This was a habitual manoeuvre born both of his disposition and his work within avant-garde propaganda projects of the 1910s. Pound characteristically used such a contribution to reshape a program he had encountered: to implicitly critique the original and to attempt to supersede it with his own insightful improvement. This pattern displays Pound's distinctive version of the anxiety of influence. It also demonstrates his characteristic insistent effort to synthesize — as he put it, to "correlate" (Redman, *Italian Fascism*, 186) — disparate interests.

Accordingly, by the early 1930s, Pound found himself considerably at odds with the economic allies whose thought had shaped his. Surette suggests that, during the 1930s, Pound "clung" to Douglas despite his awareness that Douglas's theories were "ragged" and his leadership "incompetent" (*Purgatory* 34, 196); British economist Meghnad Desai contends, likewise, that Pound "just stuck by Douglas" (95). I would suggest instead that, although Pound remained loyal to the nostrum of the A + B Theorem, he became increasingly aloof from Douglas during these years, and the close relationship with Nott, which corroborated his disenchantment with Douglas, spurred and reinforced his removal from the latter. In fact, this was one of several important bases of camaraderie between Pound and Nott, who both expressed disaffection with many Social Crediters. (Nott observes in Letter 11, with uncharacteristic emphasis: "I hate almost all Social Creditors.") Nott and Pound portrayed themselves as committed to the creation of a purer form of Social Credit, far from the internecine wrangling of various warring groups. Rather than form another faction of Social Credit, they saw themselves as transcending and seeking to correct the errors of all. Devoted to continuing in the name of Orage, Nott sought to accomplish this by remaining apart from all parties while "keeping in touch with them all" (Letter 11). This shows his *imitatio* not only of Orage's ideas but also of his style: Orage had likewise seen himself as above the melée, building strength from detachment.[46]

Pound also sought to offer an original permutation of Social Credit through his support of John Hargrave. Hargrave was a maverick figure who had been a Social Crediter since 1924, when he made Social Credit policies an official plank in the program of his group, the Kibbo Kift. A quixotic eccentric, he built a movement that, in caricature, reads as a quest to create a Boy Scouts for adults – although it was initially founded out of a quarrel with the militaristic tendencies of Baden-Powell's Scouts. His group pressed for regeneration of British society through the creation of a disciplined elite dedicated to ideals of honour, service, physical strength and fitness, as well as contact with nature. Members committed themselves to a mystical belief in the virtues of folk culture and often drew their models of conduct, as well as their lavish rituals and pageantry, from medieval England. When, in an effort to jump start his movement after a lull, Hargrave decided to adopt Social Credit ideas in the early 1920s, orthodox Social Crediters generally did not receive him seriously, often responding to his ideas with amusement (Finlay 160). While Hargrave was initially recognized by Douglas, by the late 1930s, Douglas had ceased to support him. Hargrave, in fact, tried to participate in the effort to implement Social Credit in Alberta, seeing an opportunity to carry out his ideals in a territory not blocked by political opponents. In so doing, however, he ended up crossing Douglas, and his efforts in Canada ultimately came to little.

Given these vicissitudes, Hargrave was well positioned for the approval of Pound, who sought a fellow rebel against extant power centres. Beyond this structural affinity, what also clearly impressed Pound about Hargrave was his vigorous energy. Like the heroic figures Pound revered, Hargrave was unmistakably a "man of action." Hargrave had been taken under the wing of the *New Age* group in the mid-1920s precisely because he had impressed them with his dynamism and charisma. Nott mentions to Pound that, in his reading, most Social Crediters lack vitality and force: accordingly, he is receptive to Pound's suggestion that Social Credit might be rescued from its internal conflicts by an electric force like Hargrave. As he notes to Pound on 31 May 1935, "I had a long talk with Hargrave yesterday. He certainly is a live wire" (Letter 46). Nott's and Pound's shared attraction to Hargrave, specifically to his energy, indicates the problem with Social Credit that both sought to ameliorate: its lack of dynamism.

What this brings into view is the fact that, although both Pound and Nott were dedicated Social Crediters, what brought them together was an effort to help Social Credit to develop in healthier, less internally riven, directions. The Social Credit in which they believed was notably not the orthodox Social Credit of the Social Credit Secretariat: both Pound and Nott carved out a heterodox version of an economic movement already positioned as heterodox. In tandem, they committed to distancing themselves from Douglasism. Thus when Pound says to Nott in December 1934 that "Italy's bank measures/ are NOT Doug/ ism" (Letter 4), he initially indicates a measure of disappointment. However, by the latter part of their correspondence, Pound's stance on Douglas has shifted so that such a statement no longer indicates dismay: by 1937, Pound would not wish Italy to be showing strict "Doug/ism." As Essay 2 addresses, even if Italy were not adopting Douglasism per se, Pound certainly did believe it to be open to, and even tending towards, another variety of Social Credit – which, for him, fortunately, was not "Doug/ism."

As a term in our contemporary cultural lexicon, "fascism" remains compellingly mysterious – widely, although usually imprecisely, used. But as Michael Levenson notes of the term "modernism," "Vague terms still signify": like "modernism," "fascism" is "at once vague and unavoidable" (vii) as well as powerfully influential. In common parlance, "fascism" connotes totalitarian government, draconian measures, and brutal force born of a purist will to order. Benito Mussolini coined the term "fascismo" for the movement that enabled his rise to command in Italy in 1922. Initially, "fascism" merely indicated the notion of "grouping" or "bundle" (Surette, *Purgatory*, 16).[1] During the interwar years, as "fascism" became a spectre haunting European contexts, the category came to be associated with authoritarianism and violence, with both Mussolini and Hitler, Dollfuss in Austria, Franco in Spain, and Salazar in Portugal. By the postwar moment, in "Politics and the English Language" (1946), George Orwell suggested how pervasive and imprecise the term had become: "The word *Fascism* now has no meaning except insofar as it signifies 'something not desirable.'" In the 1970s, Foucault echoed this sentiment when he suggested that "fascism" had become a "floating signifier whose function is essentially that of denunciation" (139). The ambiguity remains today: we still seem to need the term to signal semantic realms of tyranny and atrocity, and this need fosters ambiguous usage.

This edition of the Pound/Nott correspondence aims to recover the "fascism" with which Ezra Pound became infatuated in the 1920s and 1930s – that is, what fascism came to signify for Pound in his context, the implications the term bore for him at the time of his encounters with it, as well as the cultural phenomena with which it was then linked. In addressing the nexus between Pound and fascism, I engage only glancingly with the definitional debates in which fascist studies has been involved over the past fifty years. Noted commentators on the rise of fascism include Zeev Sternhell, whose argument about fascism as a reaction against Enlightenment thought and as a revision of Marxism remains among the most influential, as well as Eugen Weber, Stanley Payne, George Mosse, Robert Paxton, and Roger Griffin.[2]

In focusing on Pound, however, I am not dealing with a case in which an individual, after intensive study of the ideas associated with a school of thought, elected to become an adherent. Guarding against a widespread view of fascism as doctrinally incoherent,[3] Michael Mann suggests that we need to recognize that fascists "were not people ... with a 'rag bag' of half-understood dogmas and slogans flitting through their heads (or no more so than the rest of us)" (3).[4] Mann's general point notwithstanding, I would suggest that Pound's particular variety of allegiance to Italian Fascism did indeed emerge from such a "rag bag" (a term that Pound famously used early in his career to indicate the form that the *Cantos* would have to assume in order to encompass modernity) and that, much of the time, it did consist of such "half-understood dogmas and slogans."

POUND'S ALLEGIANCE TO ITALIAN FASCISM

As Richard Thurlow notes, in order sensitively and robustly to assess the genesis of the phenomenon of fascism, one often needs to look not so much to the lines of thought associated with the movement as at the "historical, sociological, and political factors" that made it take hold in particular instances and contexts (Thurlow, *Fascism in Britain*, x). In Pound's imagination, fascism came to be established through a collection of cathexes, chance encounters, wishful thinking, paltry data, quixotic campaigns, misreadings, reinforcements from external cues, and partial, even scant, understandings. To quote Lawrence Rainey, most important and relevant for understanding Pound's commitments are the "homely contexts" (*Monument* 3), sociohistorical and psychological, out of whose conditions Pound's interest in Italian Fascism was fostered; and the caprices, delusions, and forms of intransigence that governed his investments.[5] Accordingly, this essay traces aspects of those "homely" conditions that fostered the growth of Pound's allegiance – especially the cues in his environment that reinforced his tendencies to pursue his work with fascism and his economic work with Social Credit. Such an approach is crucial when taking up Surette's challenge to understand how ordinary men and women, neither monsters nor diabolical killers, could have been compelled by the ideals and achievements of fascism.

In modernist studies, Michael North has encouraged work that considers contemporaneous isomorphic developments in different cultural arenas: this kind of work underscores the fact that Mussolini's March on Rome, in October 1922, occurred during the same *annus mirabilis* that witnessed the consolidation of the modernist movement in literature – in whose rise Pound, of course, played a central role. At this time there was also a significant strengthening of modernism's purchase on cultural legitimacy.[6] This was the year of the first publication in book form of Joyce's *Ulysses* and, in the same month as the March on Rome, Eliot's *The Waste Land*. Thus, as the fascist "bundle" rose to power in Italy, players in the game of cultural production such as Ezra Pound sought the bundling of modernist work around a set of central commitments, within the pages of a group of avant-garde little magazines, and under the aegis of publishers hospitable to experimental work. However, more to the purpose of this study is what significance this coincidence likely bore for Pound. In 1922, Pound was vividly aware of his role as builder of a movement: he had just emerged from the intensive collaboration with T.S. Eliot on revisions to *The Waste Land*, and he was scouring Italian archives in search of material for the *Cantos* that would kindle the "long poem" with which he hoped to make his major contribution to, as he put it in 1922, "the 'movement,' ... our modern experiment, since 1900" (*L* 180). That his first encounters with Italian Fascism occurred at this juncture in 1922 steered him towards discerning significant linkages between the two cultural projects of Italian Fascism and modernism. I have said more on this point elsewhere (*Geometry* 109); here I will only say that encountering fascism when he was hard at work uniting various artists under the banner of modernism disposed Pound to believe that he could rightfully participate in Italian Fascism, interpret its significance with insight and authority, and assimilate its projects to his own.

Pound's sustained residence in Italy began in 1925, and by the time he wrote *Jefferson and/or Mussolini* eight years later, he was in the throes of what Fredric Jameson has called "manifestly hero-worshipping celebrations" of Mussolini (120). As demonstrated by the prevalence in his poetry of portraits of historical figures such as the troubadour Bertran de Born from medieval France, the Spanish El Cid, and, as of the early 1920s, the Renaissance Italian condottiere Sigismondo Malatesta, Pound was eminently susceptible to such hero worship and was easily swayed by figures who displayed a combination of the qualities he most admired: fierce strength, artistry, ingenuity, passion, guts, and generosity of spirit. These were figures who showed the Dantescan *directio voluntatis*, the forceful will that pointed definitely in one direction and that was characteristic of those who not only inhabited history but also actively shaped it.[7]

As of the early 1920s, after a struggle with the composition of the *Cantos'* opening poems, Pound had decided to feature such a heroic personality in his poem – that of Malatesta – and had pursued extensive archival research to recuperate from the *oubliette* of history the feats of this impressively canny mercenary soldier who was also a superb patron of the arts. Pound's focus on Malatesta in Cantos 8–11 resolved his uncertainties about the direction and shape of the poem; this block of Cantos crystallized the poem's design and reigning ideas (Rainey, *Monument*, 4). Pound had been hungering for a contemporary figure who embodied the qualities he celebrated in his imaginative gallery: in his reading, Mussolini fit the profile.

In *Jefferson and/or Mussolini* (1935), Pound exalted Mussolini for vigour, decisiveness, and the insightful "opportunism" he shared with the American founding father, Thomas Jefferson, likewise sanctified by Pound (17). Pound also praised Mussolini for his incisive "EDITORIAL eye and ear" (*J/M* 74) – his ability to cut to the heart of matters, to "pick out the element of immediate and major importance to any tangle" (*J/M* 66) – and his talents as a "Debunker" (35, 74). Moreover, Pound constructed Mussolini as an artist figure – imaginative, lavish, adroit, capable of rich creation: "Treat him as *artifex* and all the details fall into place. Take him as anything save the artist and you will get muddled with contradictions" (34).

Pound's commentary on Mussolini often comes across as the wishful projections of a smitten schoolboy. Having lived in Italy since 1925, however, Pound also knew something of the policies of Mussolini's government: in *J/M*, Pound admires the policies of *"grano, bonifica, restauri"* (73) – Mussolini's bold and successful projects to drain the swamps in order to reclaim land for cultivation and to undertake restoration of many of Italy's treasured buildings. Under Mussolini's regime Pound had also witnessed a program for the renewal of the Italian language and an improvement in the books displayed in bookshop windows – which, for him, indicated an "AWKENED INTELLIGENCE in the nation" (73). He also approved of the "de facto" (43) freedom of conditions in Italy, where, he said, contrary to what readers might assume, he felt at greater liberty than in London or Paris to say what he thought and to publish what he liked (74).

But Pound's approbation of Mussolini, overdetermined by many other desires in play in his imagination, far overshot what any of the leader's accomplishments invited. Wanting the Italian leader to embody the noble and powerful qualities he sought, Pound credited Mussolini with abilities, values, and plans for which evidence was either scarce or absent. That he constructed Mussolini as an artist is a giveaway that he was often fashioning him according to his ideal as well as assuaging a psychological need to identify with him. Like Antonio Beltramelli, who published the first biography of Mussolini in 1923,[8] Pound likened Mussolini to Malatesta, imagining the two as avatars of the same essential spirit.[9] This comparison indicates Pound's search for a leader who would not only show a capacity for artistry but who would also create a society as receptive to the work of artists as had been that of the Italian Renaissance. And proceeding from the assumption that it takes an artist to know one, he believed that he himself possessed the qualifications for assessing Il Duce's accomplishments.

Pound had only one opportunity to meet Mussolini – in January 1933. The way he recalled the meeting indicates both the grand scale of his infatuation and the great extent to which he was ruled by it afterward. In the months preceding the encounter, Pound had attended the exposition of the Fascist Decennio, whose narrative of fascism's ascent and accomplishments had greatly impressed him (Hickman, *Geometry*, 104–12). Seeking involvement in the government, in 1932 he agreed to collaborate with film director F. Ferruccio Cerio on a documentary chronicling the achievements of Mussolini's regime. After submitting a copy of the documentary script to Mussolini's office in December of 1932 as part of a petition for an interview with Mussolini, he was permitted to meet with Il Duce in January of 1933 (Carpenter 490). Pound planned to spend the meeting relaying ideas and counsel to the Italian leader.

The interview finally granted was brief, perfunctory, and superficial. Mussolini had a copy of Pound's *Cantos* open before him and said simply, in response to Pound's entrance, "Ma qvesto ... è divertente" ("but this ... is amusing"). Pound recorded this rejoinder in Canto 41, using Mussolini's Romagnola dialect to link him implicitly to Malatesta, who likewise hailed from the Italian province of Romagna. Rather than accept this as the polite and brief remark of a busy and important man hastily humouring a famous guest, Pound read it as signalling Mussolini's genius for conciseness and insight: as he noted in Canto 41, in his view, Mussolini caught the "point" of the *Cantos* "before the aesthetes had got/ there" (C 202). He believed that Mussolini had been able to cut through superfluities to a succinct, sincere expression of appreciation of what Pound had sought to accomplish. And, for Pound, given his modernist tendency to equate the laconic with the deeply felt, the sincerity was evidenced *by* Mussolini's conciseness. In years afterward, Pound would insistently praise the quick intelligence that Mussolini had displayed in producing such a vigorous and decisive remark, which in his reading achieved understanding according to the epistemological strategy Pound increasingly favoured – a visionary flash. The enthusiasm of Pound's response juxtaposed with the paucity of data from the interview indicates a cluster of temperamental habits of Pound's that grew more pronounced over time: an inability to hear what he did not want to hear, detachment from what was actually happening in his external environment, and susceptibility to an egoistic insulation that prevented his registering what did not suit his wishful visions.

Both Redman and Surette read Pound's intense interest in Mussolini as surfacing at approximately this juncture, as a new development coinciding with Pound's more general turn to "econ/and politics" (Kadlec 58) after the onset of the Depression. In this reading, admiration for Mussolini and commitment to Social Credit formed twin prongs of Pound's campaign in the early 1930s to make contact with what he conceived of as the realm of the "real"[10] (again, by this point in Pound's career, a sphere composed of the bordering and interrelated domains of economics and politics) and to assume his public responsibilities. Lawrence Rainey's recent scholarship, however, has uncovered a persuasive alternative narrative of the origins of Pound's cathexis. He dates Pound's investment in Mussolini from much earlier, from even before Pound's move to Italy. Rainey contends that Mussolini first caught Pound's attention in 1923, when Pound was travelling through Italy to research his Malatesta sequence: Pound had in fact first encountered fascism when travelling through Italy the year before, but 1923 brought his first major engagement with it.

In part, Pound was favourably impressed by the fascists because of an experience that befell him in 1923 in Rimini. At that point, he had just seen for the first time the magnificent "Tempio" at Rimini, the impressive structure built against the odds by Malatesta, which Pound would enshrine in the *Cantos* as an epitome of heroic artistic achievement. Pound now turned to the library in Rimini for archival records about Malatesta's life, only to find that the custodian was ill and the librarian was away, that it was impossible to enter, and that his visit would be wasted. At this point, the fascist official who happened to be his hotelkeeper was able to overcome the resistance of the local librarian and grant Pound access: it was the official's capacity to slice through the tangle of Italy's bureaucratic structures to assist a poet's work that struck Pound as splendid. This seduced him into both a durable enthusiasm for fascist efficacy and a conviction that the fascists were on the side of the artists. Pound pays tribute to this episode in *Jefferson and/or Mussolini*: "My hotel-keeper was also Commandante della Piazza, we had got better acquainted by reason of his sense of responsibility, or his interest in what I was doing." Through a deft "or" here, Pound equates "interest in what I was doing" with a "sense of responsibility." He continues: "The local librarian had shut up the library, and the Comandante had damn well decided that if I had taken the trouble to come to Romagna to look at a manuscript, the library would cut the red tape" (27). At this point, Pound was also in touch with American sculptor Nancy Cox-McCormack, an ardent admirer of Mussolini well placed in Italian circles to gain access to the dictator. During the early 1920s, as Pound developed the Malatesta Cantos, Cox-McCormack was communicating with Pound frequently about Mussolini. She was caught by Mussolini's charisma and found him highly receptive to the plight of artists. Kindled by her news and praise, disposed towards the idea that the fascists had an "interest" in art, Pound began to read Mussolini as a figure who might be approached to continue in present-day Italy the achievements of Malatesta. At this point, Pound sought to collaborate with Cox-McCormack to present to Mussolini a program of cultural patronage that could transform Italy into an international cultural centre of the kind that it had been during the Italian Renaissance (Rainey, *Institutions of Modernism*, 140–1).

Rainey thus advances a strong case for Pound's interest in Mussolini taking hold nearly ten years before the point that Surette and Redman locate, and three years before Surette places the first adulatory remarks from Pound about the Italian leader (Surette, *Purgatory*, 70). Also convincing is his reading of Pound's experience of constructing the Malatesta Cantos as crucial to shaping Pound's responses and receptivity to Mussolini (*Institutions of Modernism*, 142). Moreover, whereas Surette maintains that Pound's relocation to Italy had nothing to do with his ties to Mussolini (*Purgatory* 70), Rainey's account suggests that it was the work with Malatesta that led Pound to Italy, enabled him to witness fascism in action, and primed him for his responsiveness to Mussolini – to the point where his hopes that Mussolini could build the new Italy into a society harking back to the Italian Renaissance guided his decision to move to Rapallo. And as Rainey's account also suggests, initially, Pound's fascination with Mussolini, born out of his work with Italian history and powerful figures from history, had nothing to do with his economic convictions – and nothing to do with his postwar shift of attention, through the impact of Douglas, to economics and politics. This leads to a founding tenet of this edition of the Pound/Nott correspondence: Pound's two efforts of the interwar period – his campaign to combat war via economic reform and his endeavour to gain proximity to Mussolini in order to foster a renascence of the Italian Renaissance generosity to artists – originally emerged from two conspicuously distinct sites in Pound's thought. As this essay indicates, it was only later that his interest in Social Credit and fascism would intertwine.

What needs to be emphasized is that Pound certainly was not alone in his reverence for Il Duce at the time. Between 1918 and 1935, admiration for Mussolini ran high and wide in many quarters, not only in Italy but also throughout Britain, Continental Europe, and the United States. Even naming specific supporters, such as T.S. Eliot, W.B. Yeats, and Winston Churchill, does not adequately capture the pervasive respect that the Italian leader enjoyed at this juncture, when, in many contexts, he was read as laudably anti-communist, strongly nationalist, and severe on crime, as well as a saviour of capitalism, and an adversary of anti-clericalism.[11] Although he increasingly admired Il Duce's effectiveness as a leader, Pound's reasons for supporting him were not so specific: Pound initially revered Mussolini out of a habit of veneration for charismatic figures; out of a belief that Mussolini was the contemporary manifestation of a heroic spirit that, throughout history, manifested itself repeatedly through extraordinary personalities; out of a conviction that Mussolini governed like an artist; and out of a strategy of reading Mussolini's success through the prism not only of Renaissance Italy but also of eighteenth-century America.[12]

THE ROLE OF POUND'S ECONOMIC COMMITMENTS

Pound's allegiance to Italian Fascism, however, did not stem only from his reverence for Mussolini. Surette importantly underscores that Pound's political sympathies – which inclined him at this point against liberalism, democracy, laissez-faire capitalism, big government, big finance, and socialism – accorded with those of fascists of the time.[13] And both Surette and Redman also address the role played by Pound's economic commitments in his later investment in fascism, beginning in the 1930s. Thus although at first Mussolini's force as a "leader" exercised the greatest influence over Pound's infatuation, what contributed significantly to the intensification of his interest in Italian Fascism was his increasing conviction in the 1930s that Mussolini's government would soon implement the Social Credit reforms that he advocated.

Pound's belief that Mussolini's government was on the verge of adopting economic policies like those of which he approved was significantly fostered through his correspondence with Odon Por, a Hungarian-born Italian journalist and economist (Surette, *Purgatory*, 84; Redman, *Italian Fascism*, 123). Por struck up an acquaintanceship with Pound in April 1934, a few months before A.R. Orage's death and Stanley Nott's first contact with Pound (see Introduction). At that point, Por identified himself as someone who had written for the *New Age* in the 1910s, who was still sympathetic to schools of thought dominant during the early *New Age* years such as syndicalism and Guild Socialism (see Essay 1), and who was seeking to promulgate Social Credit in Italy (Redman, *Italian Fascism*, 160). Pound responded enthusiastically; Por and Pound would correspond extensively during the 1930s. While an admirer of Mussolini who had marked his rise to command in Italy with a book explicating and supporting fascism, Por insisted to Pound that he was not a "fascist" per se; nonetheless, he held a minor post within the Italian government, serving as director of the Rome office of the Milan-based Institute for the Study of International Politics, and was therefore able to exercise influence within the Italian government and to supply Pound with apparently credible insider information about behind-the-scenes governmental decisions.[14] By March 1935, Por was writing to Pound that he believed "the corporate system" that Mussolini was establishing was "heading straight towards S. C. or something like it" (Redman, *Italian Fascism*, 161). Pound, desiring a place of importance in Italy, as well as driven by his typical desire for the amalgamation of various lines of thought he supported, wanted to believe in the likelihood both that Mussolini would take up Social Credit and that he, Pound, could be of crucial assistance in its integration into the new Italy. As Redman suggests, it is little wonder that, given both Pound's own wishes and Por's evident credibility, Pound was swayed by Por's eager assertions about the probability of Social Credit's being put into effect under Mussolini. Pound came to see himself as engaged in a joint effort with Por to ensure the adoption of Social Credit in Italy and thus, concomitantly, to "capture Italian fascism for Social Credit" (Surette, *Purgatory*, 84). While Social Credit did not lead Pound to Italian Fascism, then, his increasing belief in the 1930s that the implementation of Social Credit in Italy was imminent made him drink more deeply of it.

There was another factor, however, contributing to Pound's conviction that Italy would soon adopt Social Credit policies – a factor that has yet to be thoroughly addressed in Pound scholarship. The Pound/Nott correspondence signals the significant role likely played by British Fascist circles of the 1930s both in strengthening Pound's resolve to support Mussolini's fascism and in bolstering his belief that economic reforms of the kind he supported, those associated with Social Credit and otherwise, would likely be undertaken in Italy.

POUND AND BRITISH FASCISM

As the Pound/Nott correspondence indicates, during the 1930s, Pound maintained regular contact with members of British Fascist circles. In 1934, as he and Nott began to correspond, Pound was also beginning to write to Oswald Mosley, leader of the British Union of Fascists (BUF), the dominant British fascist group in England, which, after its formation in 1932, largely eclipsed other fascist and proto-fascist groups on the British scene during the interwar years. When Nott at one point observed to Pound that "nobody love[d]" Oswald Mosley (Letter 29, 16 April 1935), Pound was already in epistolary contact with the latter, with whom he continued to correspond occasionally between 1934 and 1940. What prompted Nott's remark was Pound's suggestion that they call a series they were planning together "Axe and Faggot," a tip-off that Pound had the fascist insignia on his mind.[15]

Despite what Nott's comments imply, the circle with which Nott was affiliated through the *New English Weekly* (*NEW*) was not only sometimes paying attention to Mosley but also sometimes even favouring him. Members of the BUF were writing for the *NEW*: Leigh Vaughan-Henry, of the BUF's policy department, published, in instalments, a favourable piece on Germany in early 1934;[16] and, in September of that year, Alexander Raven Thomson, Director of Policy for the BUF and known as the organization's leading intellectual,[17] contributed an essay entitled the "Economics of Fascism."[18] Although the tenor of a letter to the editor by Raven Thomson from earlier that year (29 March 1934) suggests that the BUF's position was just one among many others in the pages of the *NEW*, and often athwart the views of the magazine's leading editorials, that British Fascists were appearing in the *NEW*'s pages at all is itself significant. In a 1933 article, Gorham Munson notes that the "Mosley Fascists" were acknowledged at this time as part of a cluster of groups "seeking to influence public opinion in favour of a particular economic change" (551);[19] their appearance in the *NEW* both indicated and facilitated their status as participants in a coalition of economic radicals seeking to redress economic conditions through innovative measures.

At this time, Pound was striking up correspondences not only with "Mosley Fascists" but also with a cluster of other British Fascists, seeking to educate them about the benefits of Social Credit. What appears to have prompted the first contact with members of the BUF and other fascists, however, was not Pound's association with the *NEW* per se but, rather, a letter to the editor that Pound wrote to the *Morning Post* in March of 1934, in which he expressed dismay that he had experienced such difficulty getting his supportive arguments about Mussolini's Italy into print in England:

Although the English boycott against my writings has been recently raised in so far that I seem to be able to publish books or articles on

almost any subject within the frontiers of Britain, yet whenever I
venture a plain, unvarnished account of the constructive nature of
Fascism IN ITALY, it is extremely difficult, if not impossible, for me
to get as far as a printing press.

I would give a good deal to know whether this implies a British
belief that the false idea of conditions in a foreign country can
possibly help any other country *as a whole*, or whether certain people,
for private and anti-social ends, see an advantage in peddling a
caricature or distortion of Italian conditions? (*P&P* VI: 143; *Morning
Post*, 20 March 1934)[20]

Spurred by his comments, members of British Fascist circles reached out
to Pound. A BUF official, G.A. Pfister, wrote Pound in a direct follow up,
essentially shaking his hand in epistolary form and replying with explana-
tions about the British "blackout" on Mussolini as well as asking Pound
how many British people he knew in Rapallo who might be interested in the
BUF.[21] Also in response to this letter, Pound was sent a copy of the newspaper the *Fascist* by Arnold Leese, director-general of the Imperial Fascist
League (IFL): this newspaper was the organ of the IFL, one of the British
Fascist organizations of this time distinct from and opposed to Mosley's
BUF. Given the proximity, even in some cases the overlap, between *NEW*
and fascist circles, Pfister and Leese were likely also familiar with Pound's
work from the pages of the *NEW*.

This initial contact, in turn, seems to have inspired Pound to write not
only to these British Fascists but also to figures in British Fascist orbits
more widely, including Alexander Raven Thomson. Pound's motives here
apparently included a desire to ensure that British Fascists knew about
Social Credit as well as the hope that he might be instrumental in bringing Social Credit to a position of political power in Britain through a fascist channel kindred to the one he admired in Italy. Prompted in part by
the contact British Fascists made with him in response to his letter in the
Morning Post, Pound assumed he had a sympathetic ear among them because he supported Mussolini, and he sought to use this to forward the
Social Credit cause. What the replies to Pound suggest is that he had not
thoroughly reviewed the economic principles and policies that the British
Fascists espoused: often his respondents protest that he wrongly accuses
them of negligence of issues to which they have already paid close attention. One of the letters from Leigh Vaughan-Henry also suggests that, if
Pound could move away from strict Douglasite policy (and Pound was cer-

tainly inclined to do so, seeking to craft his own hybrid of Douglasite and Gesellite ideas – see Essay 1), he would all but guarantee a receptive audience within the BUF for the Social Credit ideas Pound proposed.[22]

Whether fielding responses of this nature, or more indignant ones from correspondents who found him regrettably ignorant of their views, Pound received from such British Fascist groups active and engaged feedback of a kind that encouraged him. What his correspondents objected to was his lack of awareness of what they were doing, not the spirit of what he was advocating. Some even seemed to relish the typically Poundian combative scolding they received as part of the sport. After giving Pound an energetic dressing down for his naïveté about BUF practices, one of his spikier recipients from the BUF noted, "I am enjoying this correspondence." And Arnold Leese, responding in indignant capital letters to claims of Pound's that suggested he mistakenly equated the IFL's point of view with the BUF's, followed this, playfully, with: "Now I feel better."[23]

POUND AND ARNOLD LEESE

Leese, in fact, was one of Pound's most extreme fascist correspondents. His IFL was one of the most radical non-Mosleyite fascist groups of the interwar period, one of those most closely linked to the Nazis in Germany.[24] Stone terms Leese an "ultraextremist";[25] Linehan describes him as "one of the period's most fanatical, uncompromising, and idiosyncratic of fascists" (71).[26] Leese's organization was one of the most baldly and viciously antisemitic of the British Fascist groups, known for its violence. The IFL emphasized "race" as the major factor in its campaign to cleanse and strengthen England. Basing its claims on pseudoscientific research, it sought to remove from Britain what Leese called the "Armenoids" – or "Hither Asiatic" peoples. Both Leese's letters to Pound and the material in the official organ of the IFL, the *Fascist*, indicate the organization's belief in Aryan superiority and its support of the Nazi program.[27]

Startlingly, in June 1935, Pound observes in a letter to Nott that Arnold Leese has a "grand issue of the FASCIST," the IFL's virulently antisemitic newspaper, of which Leese sent Pound a copy in 1934. Letters between Pound and Leese during 1934 and 1935 suggest that, as of October 1934, Pound was signed up for a year's subscription of the *Fascist*, though it remains unclear who prompted the subscription.[28]

Most striking here is Pound's readiness not only to correspond with the comparatively mainstream BUF but also with Leese, one of the most antisemitic and pro-Nazi fascists in Britain. Pound is comfortable enough with the interchange that, in his letters, he even jokes with Leese in an antisemitic vein (see Letter 49B). By this juncture in 1935, as Surette points out, Pound had been significantly swayed towards his most virulent antisemitic stage by an article by William Pelley, leader of the American fascist group known as the Silvershirt Legion, suggesting that the Civil War and Lincoln's assassination were "fomented by a Jewish Conspiracy" (241–2).[29] At this point, Pound was also in regular correspondence with antisemitic Gesellite Hugo Fack, whose influence began to tell on Pound's attitudes. For a few months before this, he had been enlisting the assistance of John Drummond (see Essay 1) in research into what he calls the "jew prob" (246). Also, since November 1933, Pound had been maintaining correspondence with antisemitic economic radical Arthur Kitson. As Leese was a close comrade of Kitson's, it is likely that the Kitson connection facilitated his openness to Leese.[30]

That Pound casually mentions Leese to Nott in a letter indicates his lack of compunction about reaching out to an antisemitic fascist steeped in pseudoscientific theories about the racial inferiority of Jews. Richard Thurlow argues that, though Leese has often been dismissed as part of a lunatic fringe, and while his group was extremely small,[31] his IFL was able to perpetrate considerable harassment of Jews in London during the 1930s, creating a climate of fear and violence.[32] Thurlow further suggests that it was the pseudo-scientific thought of Leese and his group that exerted the greatest impact on the British Fascist tradition as it developed after the Second World War.[33] Startlingly, Pound seems to take no offence at Leese's newspaper the *Fascist*, characterizing it to Nott as "grand" – even though the issue he praises is filled with swastikas and articles that unmistakably evince an obsessive, paranoiac, and ruthless hatred of Jews.

Pound's responses to Leese indicate that his antisemitism had progressed in a more racially based direction by June 1935 than accounts such as Surette's have maintained. That Pound would comfortably direct praise towards such a newspaper as the *Fascist* indicates more tolerance for racism than even Robert Casillo has attributed to Pound's condition of mind in the mid-1930s. Admittedly, nothing can signal definitively that Pound agreed with everything he found in the issue of the *Fascist* that he praised to Nott. Moreover, Pound's letters to Leese do at times take issue with Leese's antisemitism. For instance, after noting sympathy with Leese's economic positions, Pound observes that he could never tolerate Leese's racism – his tendency to include Jews among "Armenoid" peoples. Further taking issue with Leese's racism and paranoia, he suggests that his generation was raised to believe that not being prejudiced against individuals because of their race was a "sacred principle":

I dont think you will get men of my generation or older to do an about face of what we were brought up to think a sacred principle/ I. E. no prejudice against a man because of race, creed or colour ... Japs, ... nigguhs and red injuns aren't conspiring against all humanity, and one can't shift a basic principle (at least it seems needless) just to cover Judea.[34]

He encourages Leese to redirect his attention to economic matters, which Pound considers more important than the issues of race that are paramount to Leese.[35] And, in a later letter, he chides Leese for his tendency to fly off the handle through his antisemitism, although he does not condemn the antisemitism per se; rather, he suggests that it leads Leese into irrelevancies.

However, that Pound says in 1934 that he could "never" tolerate Leese's racism (he knows Leese's term "Armenoid") implies that he has been paying attention to him for some time. Furthermore, throughout his letters to Leese, Pound gives in to the tendency Leese shows in spades – to identify Jewishness in specific individuals – and he appeases, or appears to try to bond with, Leese by calling those he despises "semites." Thus, while Pound reproaches Leese for extremism, he evinces a current of sympathy for Leese's racist viewpoint, articulates his own antisemitism, and displays a tendency to use invective that he knows will find a ready ear in Leese. At best, Pound's willingness to joust with Leese reads as the product of a disturbing readiness to engage in rhetorical appeasement in order to gain Leese's sympathy for Social Credit – a kind of passive complicity. At worst, this indicates an underlying racist tendency that found a hospitable reception, and thus an opportunity for expression, in Pound's exchanges with Leese.

On an overt level, then, Pound's epistolary gestures to Leese remain jovial and even, at times, resistant to Leese's most extreme views. On another level, however, Pound's racist impulses are simultaneously given an outlet through the conditions created by the correspondence. Also significant is Pound's receptivity towards a man who, by this point, was more interested in German National Socialism than in Mussolini, which Pound acknowledges in a letter to Leese of early November 1934: "the first real account I had of I. F. L. was from one of the World Service people, last week. He said you were hot Hitler, anti/ Muss."[36] Leese had turned away from fascist Italy by 1935, dissatisfied with what he took to be Mussolini's "soft" stand on Jews (Linehan 74).[37] Surprising as well is Pound's unhesitating decision to share his praise of Leese with Nott. As there is no indication of any antisemitism from Nott (while Nott usually replies conscientiously to most of Pound's major issues in a letter, he conspicuously refrains from replying to Pound's comment on Leese), Pound's comradely willingness to relay details of his enthusiasm for Leese to Nott suggests that, by this point, his impervious confidence verges on obliviousness: he has lost the ability to judge how those around him will react.

By late in the correspondence with Nott (Letter 98), Pound is also indicating that his work has just been published by the official organ of the BUF, the *British Union Quarterly*, through which Pound published fairly regularly (Preda, *Ezra Pound's Economic Correspondence*, 283). By 1939, Pound will also note that his *What Is Money For* is being published through the firm of Alexander Raven Thomson, the publishing outlet for the BUF. However, during these late letters in the correspondence, he also suggests that Nott consider publishing the material of a group that has "split" from the official BUF, the National Socialist League (NSL), which included infamous British Nazis John Beckett and "Lord Haw-Haw" William Joyce.[38] Like the IFL, the NSL housed some of the most virulent of the British Fascists and was recognized for violence, ruthless antisemitism, and sympathy for Hitler rather than for Mussolini. Although this letter to Nott does not provide sufficient evidence to maintain Pound's strong support for the NSL – and Pound acknowledges that he doesn't know how Nott will feel about publishing them – significantly, Pound's offhand remark does not criticize the group.

Moreover, when brainstorming in 1939 about ways to help Nott out of the doldrums – by this time Nott is out of the publishing business, working in a hat factory, and seeking professional prospects – Pound unflinchingly mentions "Lymington," or Gerald Wallop, Viscount Lymington, another member of the non-Mosleyite British right, first a member of a fascist group known as the "English Mistery" and then leader of the "Array," a pro-Nazi, anti-BUF fascist group formed out of a schism within the Mistery in 1936.[39] Although it is not surprising that Pound would have been aware of Lymington through *NEW* circles, what is striking is that he does not seem disturbed by Lymington's pro-Nazi sympathies. He acknowledges that Lymington is anti-BUF, and that publishing through him might reach audiences that the BUF cannot, but the political implications of this seem not to unsettle him.[40]

What all this suggests is that Pound at this time had considerable connections not only to Italian Fascism but, significantly, to British Fascism as well – specifically to British Fascism of a non-BUF, racist, often pro-Nazi variety. If we are to reckon with Pound's relationship to fascism, we thus need to accommodate not only the Italian example, and Pound's interest in Hitler (which intensifies during this period),[41] but also the British strains of fascism that inform Pound's interest and the exchanges with British Fascists that shape both his understanding of and commitment to fascism.

BRITISH FASCISM AND SOCIAL CREDIT

Pound's involvement in economics clearly played a role in the growth of his engagement with British Fascism, as did his ties to the NEW and his beliefs about Mussolini's Italy. I would argue that this engagement – given the nature of the replies he received from British Fascists interested in, if not always in agreement with, his ideas – suggested to him that Social Credit principles and fascist perspectives were compatible, which then heightened his conviction that, if the economic reforms he desired were likely to be accepted by British Fascists, they would soon be accepted by Italian Fascists as well.[42] And this, in turn, reinforced his investment in Italian Fascism.

One might initially assume that Pound's interest in Mussolini facilitated his ability to establish connections with fascist groups in Britain, and, to some extent, this was true. Pound did write for the *British-Italian Bulletin*, the British supplement to *Italia Nostra* (Redman, *Italian Fascism*, 168). The opportunity to write for this bulletin had been arranged by his contact Carlo Pellizi, a professor of Italian at the University of London (193), and he had been invited to write for it by a journalist, Carlo Camagna. The periodical was run by an organization in London called the "Fascio di Londra" (see letters 76, 77, 79). But this group appears to have been anomalous in Pound's dealings with fascists in Britain, and, moreover, his work for it did not begin until December 1935.[43]

Indeed, it was Pound's willingness to go public with his strong support for Mussolini – specifically, his letter to the *Morning Post* in which he stood up for Fascist Italy and insisted on Britain's need for more accurate information about Italy's achievements – that initially attracted British Fascists to him. It is not surprising that the British Fascists would have responded favourably to Pound's support of Italy: British Fascist groups initially formed out of admiration for Mussolini's government in the 1920s, and they were often modelled on Mussolini's example (the British Fascisti, one of the earliest fascist groups in Italy, whose very name indicates indebtedness to Italy, offers a signal instance). What should be recognized, however, is that Pound's letter to the *Morning Post* exerted the impact it did just before a significant shift in political climate in the mid-1930s that affected British sentiment regarding Italy, which, in turn, affected fascists as well as other groups. By the time of Pound's correspondence with Nott, interest in Mussolini was waning – in part in response to Italy's ambitions in Abyssinia – and, among some British Fascist groups, attention to National Socialism was taking its place. At first, for instance, Leese had been an ardent supporter of Mussolini, but by 1931, he had turned away in response to what he perceived as Mussolini's weak position on the Jews. And while the BUF had originally been behind Italian Fascism and the ideal of the Corporate State, and while it was significantly funded by Mussolini's government in the mid-1930s (Thurlow, *Fascism in Britain*, xi), by the mid-1930s, in response to Italian aggression in Abyssinia, the relationship had cooled (Linehan 105). Viscount Lymington's movement, the English Array, was also far more Nazi than Italian Fascist in its leanings (Stone, "English Mistery, 345). Accordingly, while Pound's interest in Mussolini initially catalyzed his correspondence with members of these groups, established his credibility with them, and spurred his interest in them, and while connections with these groups may well have strengthened his investment in Mussolini, his ties to Mussolini were not the major factor in his ability to sustain a relationship with these British Fascists over time. Instead, it was his economic views that chiefly fuelled conversation with them.

Pound's involvement in Social Credit circles afforded him access to several figures linked to British Fascist groups; and this, along with his eagerness to address economic issues, made for substantive exchange with them of a kind that satisfied his hunger for connection. Further, these exchanges convinced him of his impact and contribution, his participation in what he conceived of as a kind of "committee of correspondence" akin to those he associated with the nascent United States in the eighteenth century (see Essay 3). As Finlay notes, British Fascists were often significantly receptive to Social Credit ideas, if not entirely in agreement with them. Mosley, for example, had been sympathetic to Social Credit for many years, long before his turn to fascism and the formation of the BUF in 1932. He had been in favour of an economic program similar to that recommended by Social Credit as early as 1925, when he was rising to prominence within the Independent Labour Party.[44] And once having formed the BUF in 1932, Mosley continued to press for policies akin to those recommended by Social Credit. A letter to Pound from Alexander Raven Thomson from April 1934 – a response to a letter that Pound had sent him in reaction to a piece of his in the *NEW* – underscores the affinities between the economic policies being developed by the BUF at this juncture and those of the Social Crediters.[45] Finlay notes that also participating in *NEW* circles and open to Social Credit were figures of the non-Mosleyite British Fascist Right, including Leese (210–11); Viscount Lymington (Gerald Wallop); the Marquis of Tavistock (Hastings William Sackville Russell), who published one of the items in Nott's Pamphlets on the New Economics series; and Anthony Ludovici, a "Nietzchean extremist" (175–6) involved in the English Mistery (Ludovici's work often appeared in the pages of the *NEW*). Thus a significant factor in Pound's swift passage to connections with key players within British Fascist circles in the 1930s was his involvement in Social Credit groups.

One note from the Pound/Nott correspondence indicating that Pound is linking these British Fascist groups with Social Credit, and in fact associating with them chiefly because of this Social Credit connection rather than because of the link to Mussolini, is that, after invoking both the BUF and the NSL, Pound notes with surprising impartiality: "Both lots have 'accepted Douglas analysis'" (Letter 98). This suggests that he is considering both groups as equals, eliding the schism between them and the reasons for it, bypassing the NSL's violent antisemitism and pro-Nazism, recognizing only their shared (as he perceives it) interest in Social Credit. This in turn implies that investment in Social Credit was by this time paramount for Pound: it overrode other considerations and contributed to his apparent insensitivity to the political valences of these groups. If their "acceptance" of "Douglas analysis" was uppermost for him, this assumed acceptance likely fostered his belief that not only were Social Credit and fascism compatible but also that fascism offered a good route to Social Credit's achieving a position of official power – and that a congruent Italian Fascist acceptance of Social Credit was just around the corner.

Thus while Italian Fascism did not move significantly in the direction of Social Credit – indeed Pound seems to have been misled into this belief by Por and wishful thinking[46] – British Fascism, on the other hand, did. From his contacts in Britain, Pound would have had strong and consistent indications that fascist groups were interested in Social Credit measures. And although they disagreed with Douglas's tenets, the British Fascists with whom Pound corresponded did so in a way that accorded with Pound's own critiques of Douglasism – sometimes, as did Leigh Vaughan-Henry, suggesting "fusions" of the ideas of Douglas and those of others who were attractive to Pound, who himself consistently favoured such hybrids.[47] Accordingly, the BUF's clear receptivity to Social Credit ideas of the kind Pound supported may well have provided him with a major piece of evidence of the compatibility between fascism and Social Credit – a piece that had been missing from the puzzle. Accordingly, in response to Surette's be-musement about Pound's insistence that Social Credit and fascism would be "mutually supportive" (*Purgatory* 86), I would suggest that many sig-nals of Pound's British line of correspondence encouraged him to persist in "the belief that fascism was the political instrument that would bring about [the] economic reforms" he supported" (86).

DISTINGUISHING SOCIAL CREDIT FROM FASCISM

Although at this time, there was a significant contingent of British Fascists interested in economic reforms in the vicinity of Social Credit, this is not to say that Social Credit should itself be considered a fascist movement, as has sometimes been assumed. The problematic connections frequently drawn between Social Credit and British Fascism often derive from the interest shown in Social Credit by John Hargrave, leader of the Green Shirts, whose program adopted it in 1924. And it is the commitment Hargrave displayed to quasi-military spectacle that, not surprisingly, has prompted readers to interpret the Green Shirts as fascist.[48] Both Pound and Nott keenly admired Hargarve (see Essay 1). At this point, however, what was defining Brit-ish Fascism was not the pageantry of the kind paraded by the militaristic Green Shirts. While in its purism and commitment to "muck and mystery," Hargrave's group bore superficial similarities to British Fascist groups such as the English Mistery and the Array, to look to their "muck and mystery," or what Pound in a letter to Mosley referred to as the theatrical dimension of fascism, in the Green Shirts is to look to the wrong site both for the core of practices shared by various British Fascist groups of the time and for the substantive links between Social Credit and British Fascism.

Groups associated with fascism in Britain arose from a common reser-voir of disillusionment with liberal democracy, laissez-faire capitalism, and big finance, as well as with socialism. They emerged also from a conviction that degenerate tendencies within the culture had weakened British might and that reform was needed to purify and strengthen British society. That many sets of reformers in Britain at the time proceeded from this constel-lation of disenchantments and a hope for augmentation of British strength made for a great deal of solidarity among proximate groups – and, at times, strange bedfellows. As Linehan notes, while the allure of a negative def-inition of fascism is powerful, it is also important to identify the positive goals for which fascist groups were striving. In Britain, fascist groups were nationalistic, often suspicious of "aliens," and protectionist: many advo-cated economic self-sufficiency, or autarchy, within the Commonwealth.

Many sought a purer, cleaner society, rooted in careful husbandry and stewardship of the land; many groups strongly emphasized organicism and back-to-the-land efforts in their programs. Some played out their project for purity through ideals drawn from medieval England; others through mystical beliefs. Many, though not all, were antisemitic, and usually this antisemitism intertwined with their suspicion of international finance. Many believed in the efficacy of corporatism – a society organized into groups founded according to professions. And many were invested in a myth of an "elite," a community of strong men (and, depending on the fascist group, women) who could improve British society, along with the fit few individuals who could act as galvanizing leaders. Several recent commentaries, including that of Dan Stone and Martin Pugh, have underscored the "indigenousness" of British Fascism: indeed these groups were not, on the whole, merely seeking to imitate their Continental counterparts, though an openness to Continental examples formed a kind of British fascist signature.

At this time, then, many Social Crediters shared with British Fascists a suspicion of both liberalism and statist socialism as well as a tendency to hold banking culpable for the economic crises of the time and to demonize international finance, which led them towards antisemitism. All this brought them into contiguous, and sometimes even shared, territory. As Alexander Raven Thomson notes in a letter to Pound, however, what divided the fascists from the Social Crediters was different attitudes towards liberal individualism, which the Social Crediters generally favoured, and which the fascists markedly rejected. The fascists also took issue with the way the Social Crediters devalued the idea of work (see Finlay 213). Moreover, whereas the fascists committed themselves to the "Führerprinzip," Social Crediters, although they did trust that the state could, and should, handle the nation's finances, remained consistently resistant to a vision of society governed by one strong leader. And as Arnold Leese points out in a letter to Pound, Social Crediters were fighting for economic reform in order to ensure equality for all, whereas fascists, British or otherwise, were invested in a hierarchical view of society.

Several points in this account suggest that Pound's convictions were more in the neighbourhood of the British Fascists than in that of the Social Crediters: he tended to look to strong "leader" figures such as Mussolini as agents of historical change, and out of one strand of his convictions (which encouraged and was nourished by his study of Confucianism), he much preferred hierarchical to democratic systems of order.[49] But the compatibility between Pound's views and those of the British Fascists in the 1930s also importantly stemmed from the fact that these groups were interested in measures associated with Social Credit in the same critical ways as was he. Accordingly, correspondence with them reinforced his belief that his political and economic work was heading in a viable ideological direction. It also persuaded him that, if Social Credit reform of the kind to which he was committed was imminent in England, then a fruitful pairing between Social Credit–minded measures and fascism would soon appear in Italy as well. And for Pound, in all senses, this was greatly to Italy's credit.

POUND'S EPISTOLARY PRACTICE

Ezra Pound rightly holds a legendary status as one of the modernist period's most prolific correspondents: as Tim Redman notes, the volume of Pound's correspondence was massive, amounting to what has been estimated at close to 100,000 letters ("Review" 936).[1] This is generally the first point to strike readers' attention: the terrific avidity with which Pound exchanged letters with an astonishing number and variety of correspondents. As Forrest Read notes, while Pound wrote abundantly throughout his career, during the 1930s, out of a sharpened conviction of his responsibility to engage with the political and economic crises of the day, he intensified his epistolary production even further (Pound, *P/J*, 13). This indicates, in turn, the importance Pound placed on letter writing as a means of accomplishing crucial cultural work.

Over the past three decades, interest in Pound's letters has generated another kind of remarkably prolific output: more than twenty published editions of Pound's correspondences. Like the letters of other writers, Pound's have rightly been regarded as valuable because they provide vital records of a writer's mind in motion as well as background information that enriches understanding of literary production. However, letters form such an integral part of Pound's intellectual and artistic practice that they should be regarded not only as supportive material ancillary to understanding his poetry but also as comprising a significant branch of his work in their own right – a module of his corpus on par with his poetry and essays.

A. David Moody argues that what Pound asserts in his prose – Moody focuses on Pound's published essays, but what he argues pertains to Pound's letters as well – offers a merely polemical rendition of his ideas. This is inferior to the performance of these ideas as presented in his *Cantos*, in which the technique of counterpoint afforded by the hybrid genre Pound creates allows for a more nuanced delivery of ideas as well as a display of that which is to be celebrated in conjunction and in tension with that which is to be denounced – and thus a truer record of the subtleties of Pound's thought.[2]

As Moody notes, Pound himself at times characterized his prose as "merely stop-gap" (188). But I would resist both the implications of Pound's own off-hand remarks and the claim that Pound at his subtlest is the truest Pound – the one to whom we should pay most attention. What Pound perceived as the pull of his times, in his view, demanded polemics – as Moody puts it, "agitprop" – and while Pound at times expressed misgivings about having to enter the zone of pamphleteering, the fact remains that he did enter that domain, copiously and vigorously. As a result, the epistolary dimension of his corpus deserves as much status as do other aspects thereof.

To privilege the work of the *Cantos*, and the modes of expression exhibited there, is to fail to do justice to the impressive volume of Pound's output in prose, letters included, and, more relevant for this project, to the great importance that Pound accorded letter-writing as a practice that served significant cultural activity and reform. Moreover, beyond the position Pound himself assigned letters in his repertoire, they form an indispensable part of his cultural work. And I would argue that, more than merely recording work that goes on elsewhere, off the page, the letters themselves participate in that work.

In part, then, Pound's correspondence with Nott provides important testimony to his thought and projects as well as to the cultural debates and work of this moment more generally. Specifically, it illuminates aspects of the development of Pound's thought during the 1930s in the spheres of economics and politics that require further analysis. It sheds light especially on the conditions that stimulated and sustained Pound's confidence in his new identity as political and economic commentator, his continuing belief in the value of collaborative endeavour, and what I term his theory of epistolary knowledge: a set of epistemological convictions both revealed and carried out through his epistolary practice. Again, here and elsewhere, Pound's letters not only register work done off the epistolary page but also themselves effect a form of labour, thus forming an infrastructure through which Pound sought to accomplish cultural work.

THE CULTURAL WORK OF POUND'S LETTERS

From early in his career, Ezra Pound conceived of his letters as documents like those circulated by the American founding fathers in their "committees of correspondence" (Redman, *Italian Fascism*, 106). Convened by local governments in the American colonies to facilitate communication of information and colonial responses to British actions, these committees were also sites for planning and organizing towards collective action. Raised in

Philadelphia, Pound was surrounded from an early age by monuments to and lore about America's founders: the city had been the site for meetings of the Second Continental Congress in the 1770s, the location of the signing of the Declaration of Independence and the adoption of the US Constitution, and the nation's first capital.

This climate exerted a lifelong impact on how Pound regarded the work of letters. In his view, at their best, letters would foster exchanges like those enabled by the committees of correspondence: interchanges through which crucial cultural information was transmitted, actions planned and carried out, and decisions arrived at collaboratively – as Pound saw it, among an informed and thoughtful elite of the kind that had led the American Revolution. Pound's epistolary conduct was thus shaped by the desire to foster, through letters, significant cultural labour akin to that in which Jefferson, the Adamses, and other leading political figures had engaged during the formative years of the United States. Pound might even be said to have regarded himself as participating through his letters in endeavours comparable to nation-building, although the imagined communities that Pound sought to construct were supranational – composed of kindred minds aspiring to improve the state of the arts and, later, intellectual and cultural practice more broadly. For Pound, letters played an indispensable role in this constructive process.

Pound reflects these convictions about the power of letters when, in Cantos 8–11, he evinces a fascination with the letters of Sigismundo Malatesta, the Renaissance soldier and patron of the arts whose combination of warrior prowess and artistic commitments Pound admired.[3] In Canto 9 especially, he focuses on what the Sienese were able to seize from the "postbag" they captured from Malatesta's forces. In his research for the Malatesta Cantos, Pound consulted letters in various archives during his trip through Italy in early 1923 (Rainey, *Monument*, 68, 230); and, as the dominance of these letters in Cantos 8–11 indicates, he clearly displayed the contents of this "post-bag" in his *Cantos* as evidence of Malatesta's strength and merit. It was not only the content but also the volume of these letters that compelled Pound: that Malatesta had engaged in such a rich and varied correspondence with relatives, friends, and artists who were sustained by his patronage evidenced for Pound both Malatesta's status as a vibrant cultural motive force and the vitality of the Renaissance culture he had inhabited. As Pound indicates in Canto 41, he admired both the man who believed that "you must work day and night / to keep up with your letters" (C 203) and the milieu from which such a man arose: such an individual was obviously immersed in what Pound read as a cultural vortex of activity, himself laudably contributing to that vortex. Rendered in the second person, these lines from the *Cantos* read as an instructive imperative from Pound.

POUND'S THEORY OF COLLABORATIVE KNOWLEDGE

If epistolary exchange both evidenced and promoted cultural vitality for Pound, it also served as an epistemological strategy, a cherished collaborative method of gaining and fostering knowledge. Pound's fierce commitment to letters indicates not only his belief that correspondence offered a vital means of catalyzing collective action towards justice but also an epistemological conviction that knowledge was best won from a dialogical process of interchange. Rather than articulate this principle explicitly, he demonstrates it through his sustained commitment to various forms of interchange and collaborative work. Richard Badenhausen observes that, out of a combination of personality traits, psychological needs, and values, T.S. Eliot was given to diverse forms of collaboration; in a similar spirit, I would maintain that Pound, spurred by a blend of temperament, psychological needs, and social and political ideals, likewise invested deeply in collaboration as a way of getting things done. For him, letters formed a pivotal site for collaboration with others towards the development of both his own knowledge and the larger cultural reservoir of knowledge. To adapt a term from Social Credit, letters could contribute crucially to a society's "cultural heritage."[4]

Significant here as well is that the American committees of correspondence that shaped Pound's perspective on epistolary practice were formed out of revolutionary crisis: they were initially struck to disseminate a colonial critique of the British government's conduct – to articulate and strengthen the cause against the adversary. A similar spirit of revolution informed Pound's letters. Deliberately placing himself as an avant-gardist revolutionary, Pound sought to advance what he saw as a cultural revolution, enlisting letters to send news past the sentries of the establishment to ears more sympathetic to his rebel's cause. This is what distinguishes the vector of Pound's career from those of other modernists who were equally receptive to collaboration but who proceeded more out of a Renaissance notion of what Wendy Wall calls a "poetics of exchange,"[5] which involved interchange of literary work within a coterie. Like Pound, moderns such as Eliot, Stein, and Woolf clearly believed that exchange and conversation could stimulate and fertilize literary creation. But generally, their ideals were more those of the salon than of the political committee, focused chiefly on the arts rather than on culture more broadly; and their work, while undoubtedly politically committed, was not animated by the revolutionary fervour of Pound's. Long after the heady days of the avant-guerre moment, when he was involved in Imagism and Vorticism, Pound still believed that such collaborative exchange, among like-minded men of an intelligent elite – as he put it in Canto 11, "conversation between intelligent men" (C 51) – could revolutionize a society.

But while zeal and scope may have differentiated Pound from compatriots, his ardour for "conversation between intelligent men" he shared with many other modernists. As Richard Badenhausen notes, Eliot likewise celebrated robust conversation as necessary to the production of good literature. In one essay, Eliot conceived of journals as at best creating virtual "drawing rooms" (Badenhausen 58) – fora that encouraged such conversation.[6] Eliot notes that the artist who is fortunate enough to talk with others will be more likely to flourish: "I believe that to write well it is necessary to converse a great deal ... [T]here are two types of good writers: those who talk a great deal to others, and those, perhaps less fortunate, who talk a great deal to themselves" (Selected Essays 500; qtd. Badenhausen 75). Badenhausen rightly observes that Eliot shared Pound's profound commitment to the cultural formation of modernism as essentially collaborative (75). In part, this collaborative tendency arose out of solidarity among writers and artists who regarded themselves as kindred marginalized figures in a literary climate that was often inhospitable to their experiments. Beyond this, however, they promoted collaborative work among groups out of a conviction that members of collectives could both help one another build reputations and foster one another's development through the exchange of ideas. Pound likewise believed in the benefits of such conversation – the turning back and forth of claims in an alembic process. And more than his fellow writers, he believed that the yield of such ample conversation could be not just literary and artistic but also cultural in a wider sense.

During the 1930s, Pound's own conditions altered, such that he often did end up talking to himself – by virtue of his geographical and cultural isolation, the psychological changes he had sustained, and the new directions of his work and thought – even as he continued to seek (and believed, often misguidedly, that he was engaged with) conversational partners.[7] But while, in reality, environmental and psychological factors rendered it increasingly difficult for Pound to participate in exchanges rather than in mere monologues, his ideal of cultural conversation remained intact – the force behind his lifelong, committed, aggressive epistolary conduct.

Although he wrote to an astonishing range of recipients, Pound depended on some correspondents more than others, seeing them as special conversationalists who could engage incisively with his ideas and provide him with good advice. Generally, Pound positioned himself far more often as advice-giver than as seeker of advice. But he certainly relied on the epistolary dyad that he and Nott created over time: it provided a space in which to work out his concerns and convictions about, and plans for, the cultural project of the "New Economics"; and it enabled him to build his new identity as a political and economic commentator. In his analysis of Eliot's collaborations, Badenhausen refers to a "psychology of collaboration" that was equally relevant to Pound. Pound certainly responded favourably to the climate that Nott provided him; to adapt Badenhausen's words, Nott "played· the key role of sensitive auditor and responder, giving [Pound] a specific audience for which to write and from whom he could expect significant practical feedback."[8]

Letters that Pound exchanged with others were thus vital to him as a means of accomplishing cultural work, of gleaning and giving knowledge, of developing the knowledge base of a culture, and of fostering a climate that could generate creative work. Accordingly, his beliefs about letter-writing, together with his demonstrated epistolary conduct, implicitly advance a theory of knowledge.

LETTERS AS RECORD OF HISTORICAL STRUGGLE

In his guise as historical archaeologist, sifting through the archives of culture and the letters of others from other times, Pound also attributed another significance to letters, which I use to read his own correspondence. He interpreted letters as vital historical documents, fugitive textual productions that could catch a historical figure in motion as he dashed off obiter dicta. Such letters seized Pound's attention more than did seamless written productions crafted in retrospect and tranquility: he indicates his interest in letters both in his Malatesta Cantos, in which he features correspondence from Sigismundo; and in Cantos 31–41, in which he highlights exchanges among figures such as Jefferson, Adams, and Washington as they navigate through problems of the country in formation, ranging in their observations from the lofty to the homely, the sweepingly philosophical to the minutely detailed. In one of his essays, Pound praises the letters between Jefferson and Adams as a "shrine and a monument" and advocates that contemporary readers revisit them for a vibrant understanding of the struggle, labour, and issues involved in the American Revolution.[9]

When working with letters from bygone eras, Pound regarded epistolary practice as providing an authentic, breathing record of individuals negotiating challenging times: letters witnessed history on the boil, an understanding of which, for Pound, was crucial to recover. His loyalty to letters' fugitive status – in this, he implies, resides their honesty and their fidelity to the chaotic real – he demonstrates through the way he exhibits letters in his *Cantos*.[10] He displays them in fragments, ragged pieces torn off the newswire, incorporating them into his textual montage as though to underscore the speed and haste with which they were written. And he thereby suggests the dynamic cast of mind from which these missives arose: not from a serene cognitive condition in which all was settled, enabling suave pronouncements, but rather from a mental condition streaked with thought on the fly. Through his techniques of inclusion (his "documentary method" in the *Cantos*, which presents documents with ragged edges), Pound suggests that it is the rough and tumble process of negotiation, the sudden quick turnabouts, the untidiness of daily living in a moment of crisis that characterized the American Revolutionary period, Malatesta's life, and, from Pound's perspective, the lives of individuals who put their convictions courageously on the line and their ideas into action. For Pound, jaggedness of expression implied energy, urgency, and commitment; torn edges betokened the attitudinal "edge" and dynamism he favoured.

Moreover, for him, such roughness was the mark of real historical access, the "muse in tatters" (as Hugh Kenner famously notes of Pound's response to Sappho),[11] all the more convincingly the muse for being in tatters. For Pound, the quicksilver quality implied by rough-edged materials suggested, and provided access to, the quick of history: it was through fragmented documents born of intensely dynamic, and thus transient, states of mind and feeling that one reached a conceptual and cultural vortex – and thus for Pound, historical truth.

Furthermore, beyond his vitalist search for rushing energy, Pound's moral perspective was such that he believed that, unless historical agents got down in the dust and wrestled their victories out of turmoil and resistance, out of the vortex, the grappling necessary to real historical achievement and progress had not occurred. This points to Pound's signature American stance, given his conception of the American approach: in many contexts, especially overtly political ones, Pound favoured the rag-tag militia over the well suited and comported redcoat. Raggedness of dress, like raggedness of document, indicated sincerity and drive.

POUND'S EPISTOLARY IDIOM

Pound's language in general, of course, is famously heterodox. But the language of his letters is usually more maverick still, bent even further away from linguistic norms than that which he constructs in other genres. Pound's distinctive epistolary idiom is characterized by renegade spellings, Joycean word deformations and neologisms, metamorphosis of morphemes, typographical mischief à la E.E. Cummings, unconventional spacing, elliptical explications, nearly altogether private references to names and places, and such wrenchings away from ordinary syntax that it seems apt to coin the term "Poundese." The compressed telegraphic and typical postcard communication styles prevalent in the early twentieth century seem to resonate with, and perhaps influence, Pound's characteristic epistolary delivery as well.[12] Editors of Pound's other correspondences have offered a range of observations about Pound's "idiosyncratic" epistolary style: in *Pound/Laughlin*, David Gordon notes that "The reader must face ... Pound's intentional misspellings and puns that run throughout his letters." In *Pound/Ford*, Brita Lindberg-Seyersted notes Pound's "eccentricities of spelling, punctuation, line arrangement, indentation ... They were part of a highly individual style which seems to have developed gradually during his London years and which may be identified as a conscious way of composing around 1920 or a little later."

Pound's deformations of ordinary words and syntax, I would offer, grow from drives similar to those animating the early twentieth-century Italian Futurist effort to revolutionize spelling and writing – to create what the leader of the Futurists, F.T. Marinetti, called "parole in libertà," or "words in freedom." Although Pound's practice cannot be neatly aligned with Marinetti's, Marinetti's avant-guerre theorizations of words in liberty provide a point of departure for understanding the implications of Pound's epistolary gestures. Although Italian Futurism faded with the advent of the First World War, Pound indicates that he is still enlisting Marinetti's avant-guerre concept of "parole in libertà" as a category of understanding in the 1930s: in a 1935 letter, Pound uses the phrase "paroles en liberté" to capture Carlo Dazzi's reaction to Guido Cavalcanti's "modernity" – at a point at which Pound has been working on a translation of Cavalcanti (*L* 274). For readers, the two Italian names invoked in the letter's sentence transform "paroles en liberté," rendered playfully in French, into "parole in libertà." Significant here also is that Pound enlists such "paroles en liberté" as indicative of "modernity." Although Marinetti theorizes *parole in libertà* in 1913, the idea still connotes modernity to Pound as late as 1935.[13]

The many similarities between Pound's idiom and Marinetti's are illuminating: like Marinetti's ideal revolutionary language, Pound's epistolary idiom evinces "Love of speed, abbreviation, and the summary" (Marinetti, "Destruction of Syntax," 98); like Marinetti, Pound renounces the "confused verbalisms of the professors" (98) with an idiom implicitly designed to debunk academic pedantry; and, like Marinetti, Pound associates destruction of ordinary syntax with a "zone of intense life" (98). Someone in such a zone, the implication runs, "wastes no time in building sentences." Marinetti could be describing Pound's epistolary modus operandi when he notes of the Futurist poet who will write this new idiom into being: "He will despise subtleties and nuances of language ... The rush of steam-emotion will burst the sentence's steampipe, the valves of punctuation, and the adjectival clamp. Fistfuls of essential words in no conventional order. Preoccupation of the narrator, to render every vibration of his being" (98). In his letters, Pound demonstrates the "urgent laconicism" (98) that Marinetti describes – or, to put it another way, a laconicism born of urgency. For Marinetti, this mode of delivery, in turn, suggests "laws of speed that govern us" (98): the speed characteristic of modern culture. For Pound, this approach primarily implies another kind of speed, mental speed, born both of quickness of mind and the urgency of the moment, and thus signalling both.

Letter 3 from Pound to Nott provides an especially good example of the distinctive features of Pound's epistolary idiom. This communiqué falls at the outset of their correspondence, before Pound knows Nott well enough to engage in the elliptical and heterodox modes of expression he will later adopt. (In the 1930s, the eccentricity of Pound's idiom still depends to a significant degree on how well he knows the correspondent in question; later, he will use the eccentric idiom no matter his relation to the recipient.) Nonetheless, in this letter of early 1935, he already uses the typical markers of his epistolary style – and does so in a letter that, because it explains to Nott his pamphlet style, performs the style to which he refers: in self-reflexive comments on his pamphlet style, he highlights important components of his epistolary idiom. He distinguishes his approach to pamphlets from the "cold and technical stuff" he associates with C.H. Douglas: as he notes, "I have of set purpose done the thing hot and molten." This description of pamphlet style, suggesting motion born of passion, is just as applicable to the language characteristic of Pound's letters. He also wants Nott to understand that his unconventionality arises from deliberate strategy: "This is merely to say that there is reason behind the heat," he says; in offhand terms, he establishes an important point with an interlocutor not yet familiar with his rough-cut idiom.

He opens the letter with the abbreviation "wd," characteristic of his letters; both it and other comparable compressions in the letter (such as "yr") suggest speed. As he says elsewhere of abbreviations in his *Cantos*, they "save *eye* effort. Also show speed in mind of original character supposed to be uttering" – and here, it is the speed of Pound's own mind (*L* 322). Evident also in Letter 3 is the forward slash that in Pound's epistolary idiom often takes the place of other punctuation marks; it corresponds to, and replaces, no one other specific mark but rather indicates a pause or break in thought that merits a boundary. It also signals a desire to avoid the precision implied by conventional punctuation (to avoid, as it were, putting a "fine point" on his expressive phrases). The Poundian slash suggests a jazzier scattering of ideas, implying that they emerge from a conceptual jam session appropriate to a relaxed setting in which he trusts recipients to understand, and make an effort to understand, where he is coming from and where he is going.

In Letter 3, Pound also evinces his typical bent for unorthodox spacing and layout, along with a characteristic use of capital letters and underscore. In part, these techniques emerged from the reigning technology on which Pound depended: as Forrest Read notes, "Pound was one of the early users of the typewriter for composing both poems and letters" (Pound, *P/J*, 13). Through the typewriter, as Marinetti puts it in his comments on the "typographical revolution" the Futurists advanced, Pound sought to "impress on the words (already free, dynamic, and torpedo-like) every velocity of the stars, the clouds, aeroplanes, trains, waves, explosives, globules of seafoam, molecules, and atoms" (Marinetti 105). Furthermore, Pound also uses typewriter techniques to suggest what he termed "relative emphasis." Capital letters and underscorings Pound conceived of as roughly equivalent in effect; about his *ABC of Economics*, for instance, Pound noted that using either capitals or underscoring for rendering his stress markers was fine with him – as long as the "relative emphasis" that both signs suggested was preserved: "ANY change that wd/ tend to obscure relative emphasis, (emphases) or the articulation, or the proportion of the ABC wd. I think diminish the impact."[14] (In this letter, Pound demonstrates the phenomenon to which he refers with the all-capitals rendering of "ANY.") In Letter 3 to Nott, the key words and thus concepts upon which Pound lands with particular gusto, indicated by majuscules, include "INTELLIGENT," "AT LEAST," "LOCALLY," and "HIGH visibility."

For Pound, however, as important an effect of such stress marks was the construction of a voice audible to an inner ear. Lindberg-Seyersted recognizes that Pound's approach to typography was intended to suggest sound as well as a pattern of emphasis: "His unorthodox paragraphing and in-dentation were no doubt part of a rhythmic and intonational pattern of composition" (Pound, *P/F*, xviii). Timothy Materer likewise observes that Pound composed letters "to strike both the eye and the ear" (Pound, *P/WL*, vii). As Pound noted in a letter in a descriptive passage about the *Cantos* that, again, pertains equally here, "ALL typographic disposition, placings of words *on* the page, is intended to facilitate the reader's intonation" (*L* 322). Or, as he put it elsewhere in this letter, his techniques indicate "vari-ous colourings and degrees of importance or emphasis attributed by the protagonist of the moment" (*L* 322) – and, in the letters, the "protagonist of the moment" is Pound himself in various epistolary guises. "Degrees of importance" are once again accented in these statements, but so are "in-tonation" and "various colourings": through his typographical markings in his letters, as he does in his poetry, Pound implies attitude; he constructs a stance or posture, a character sketched in thumbnail form. In a letter from the 1930s to W.H.D. Rouse about Rouse's translation-in-progress of the *Odyssey*, Pound notes that Homer was a master at providing "indication" of not only "speeds of utterance" but also "of tone of voice" (*L* 298).

Later, Pound's conception of "tones of voice" appropriate to the moods and attitudes he wishes to convey would form an important part of his radio broadcasts, which he delivered for listeners in a bewildering array of voices. Charles Norman suggests that, by this point in the early 1940s, such adoption of different voices had become a standard feature of Pound's con-versational style: "He spoke with many voices. In the midst of expositions in a flat, pedantic, and occasionally scolding tone, he would lapse into ex-aggerated Western drawls, Yankee twangings, feet-on-the-cracker-barrel pipings, and as suddenly switch to upper-class British sibilants and even Cockney growls" (Norman 5). In an off-hand fashion, Norman connects Pound's "odd and loosely spaced typing style, which was full of his own ab-breviations and punctuation of his own devising" to his "voices," observing that "His way of talking was just as odd as his way of typing" (5). To put a finer point on this connection, Pound's "odd way" of typing was designed to suggest and even create a "way of talking" – to generate the "many voices" that gave voice to the multiplicity of imaginative stances through which, à la Browning, Pound's thought and judgments took shape.

Worth noting in Letter 3 as well is Pound's mischievous transforma-tions of words reminiscent of the work of Joyce in *Finnegans Wake* – per-mutations and deformations that signify. In part, these might be read as instances of what Marinetti called "free expressive orthography," but for a couple of reasons, this term doesn't quite suit: first, Pound's politically significant incorrectness deliberately rejects the kind of "correctness" connoted by the term "orthography," whose etymology points to the Greek for "correct." Moreover, Pound generally deviates from a common linguistic practice towards a replacement that bears a specific significance beyond mere "expressiveness." As James Laughlin suggests, Pound's marked departures from ordinary language signal his effort to move beyond the limitations of ordinary language, encrusted with habit, towards renewed forms of language that will promote clarity and cultural health. Nothing in Pound's idiosyncratic prose, he says, "is accidental":

> The staccato paragraphing, the rough diction, the sound effects, the distorted spelling, the typographic stunts, the anecdotes & allusions, the shouting & swearing are all there for a purpose: to shatter the reader's mental slumber and *make* him absorb the content.
>
> ... The arteries of English, especially ideologic English, are badly hardened. Bad habits have done it, habits of verbal association. And now the blood of meaning flows too slowly to keep the body politic (and the bodies poetic & philosophic) in health. So Pound has invented his own pressure pump.[15]

As Laughlin's Orwellian comments suggest – the critique of "ideologic English" resonates with that of "Politics and the English Language" – Pound's unconventional, rough-and-ready idiom provides a "pressure pump" for the sclerotic arteries of the bodies "poetic," "philosophic," and "politic."

Pound's deformations of particular words often carry even more specific significances. In Letter 3, for instance, he notes that he hasn't yet "untangle[d]" the "complexities of Social Credit organ(or disorgani)ZATION in London. Don't make out who sees or speaks to who(M)." Here Pound refers playfully to the intricacies and internal divisions of Social Credit circles, demonstrating skilful control over his ludic gestures and subtly indicating the precise grammatical knowledge he possesses ("who(M)") but from which he often deliberately lapses to evoke a casual voice or colloquial swing (as Norman astutely puts it, "feet-on-the-cracker-barrel pipings"). In the same letter, Pound stresses that he'd rather "historians or economists" review his Cantos 31–41 than the "snoops of bloomsbuggy letteratets." Here, the word deformations indicate his disdain for the Bloomsbury set but, more specifically, for forms of sexual perversity he associates with the group and considers distasteful (Pound uses "buggy" to connote not only loopiness but also "buggery") as well as for what he regards as their prurience and voyeurism ("snoops"). He also suggests his dismissal of their "literary" credentials by bastardizing "literati" into "letteratets" in order to suggest the diminutive status of their authority (the sound of "letteratets" suggests "ettes").

At other times, Pound's word transmutations in this letter, such as "colly/ borate," seem designed not to point to any one connotation but, rather, simply to undercut conventional earnestness and to suggest vigour born of irreverence, a high-spirited Tom-Sawyerish mangling of terms indicating maverick energy, critical spirit, and insouciance. As Timothy Materer notes, when such misspelling is visited on proper names, this often indicates how well Pound knew the people in question and/or how much he disliked them (Pound, *P/WL*, viii). I would emphasize also that these misspellings, especially when they are insulting pejorations, often point to specific qualities he associated with individuals. John Middleton Murry, for instance, becomes, scatalogically, "Muddleton Mudshits": this indicates Pound's connection between Murry and indecisiveness, lack of vital flow, and a condition of being mired in muck.

In general, Pound always went further than Marinetti in using such heterodox strategies not only to suggest speed, energy, directed will, and an impatient hunger for modernity but also to control the rhythm and emphasis of his discourse, the connotations of his words, and his relationship to his audience. Moreover, while Pound's approach recalled that of Marinetti's *parole in libertà*, the political activity in which he engaged was more specifically politically valenced than the scattershot Futurist linguistic experiments meant to signify general defiance, novelty, and freedom. Marinetti's manifestoes announced a revolution in linguistic practice tied to a broad and vague cultural program of liberation and cultural renewal. Pound, meanwhile, enlists linguistic play in the service of specific revolutionary ideals: he saw himself as engaged in a cultural revolution at a moment of crisis, and he wrote letters accordingly. Especially during the 1930s, his letters were typically written out of, and so as to suggest, the haste of a mind straining under pressure.

Moreover, Pound's idiom indicates a cultural, philosophical, and attitudinal stance. Above I suggest that, through his epistolary practice, Pound advances a theory of knowledge by implying that knowledge is best gained through collaborative interchange. Through his unorthodox style, Pound also implies that this kind of epistemological process, this way towards valuable cultural knowledge, should be informed by certain attitudes towards the powers that be. One mood dominant in Pound's epistolary repertoire is *ira* – the wrathful indignation of the jeremiac figure.[16] The wrath provides the Marinettian steam bursting the pipe of the sentence, and, in

Pound's case, this steam is *not* merely, in Marinettian terms, "intoxication"; instead his energy suggests a rage born out of a desire to redress injustice, the superego rather than the id, a sense of mission.[17]

Even more prominent in his letters is a note of irreverence that Pound both inscribes and encourages through his ludic linguistic gestures. This is not mere foolery on Pound's part: that he forges this idiosyncratic idiom for his letters – one distinct from, and more renegade than, the language he uses elsewhere – suggests the specific political implications of his incorrectness. Pound used such linguistic tricksterdom to establish himself in his letters as a certain kind of wise man, what I would call, adapting theatre parlance, a "raked sage." He sought a stance akin to that of Victorian "sages" such as Ruskin and Arnold but rakishly so, standing at an angle from norms of wisdom and sagacity, thumbing his nose at traditional academic practice. Pound famously thought little of university environments, which he dismissively called "the beaneries" to capture their penchant for what he perceived as bean-counting (*GK* 219). He wanted readers to notice the roguishness running through his discourse – one signalling impatience with traditional pedantry and a defiant assertion of forms of erudition liberated from dutiful obedience to ordinary procedure.[18] One could say that, in his discourse, he sought to defy gravity, in order to achieve a new, more convincing, kind of seriousness – one both laced with, and created through, irony about the sedulousness of experts and scholarly folk. Pound aspired to the kind of authority gained from standing outside intellectual practice, politics, and economics-as-usual.

Pound's characteristic subversive playfulness is also enlisted to create a rapport with his correspondents, to invite them into a world of private, informal, mischievous exchange as though letting them in on an inside joke, departing from decorum and sparring in a way that only intimates can. That Pound doesn't often explain himself fully in his letters, that he uses word abbreviations and telegraphic style, suggests that he believes his interlocutors both astute enough and close enough to him to decipher his half-formulated language. Marinetti's description from "Words in Freedom" of the relationship between "poet and audience" illuminates the relationship between Pound and the letter's recipient, whom Pound uses his idiom both to signal and to foster. "The same rapport exists," Marinetti observes, "as between two old friends. They can make themselves understood with half a word, a gesture, a glance. So the poet's imagination must weave together distant things *with no connecting strings*, by means of essential *free* words" (98). Accordingly, Pound's method curtails full explanation out of an assumed sympathetic reception and familiarity. The chief signal is that Pound trusts his auditors to complete his sentences for him.

One can also regard Pound's letters as written in a kind of cipher, reminiscent of the coded language, or "trobar clus," of the medieval troubadours whom Pound featured in his early work, who had to hide their heretical beliefs from the authorities, reserving their words for those in the know. In Canto 31, which features the American Revolutionary period, Pound features an instance of a letter from James Madison written in cipher: "This country is really supposed to be on the eve of a XTZBK49HT" (C 154). To imbue one's writing with this kind of mystique is to imply that it is under suspicion by reigning authorities, that there is an attendant necessity for secrecy, and that, by virtue of this cultural position, it carries revolutionary potential.

This, then, is another significant way in which Pound signalled a component of his theory of knowledge – his reading of how to gain the most effective and "live" kind of cultural knowledge, for which he famously articulates a desire in Canto 7. Not only is such knowledge circulated, and arrived at collaboratively, through exchanges of "intelligent men," but gaining it also necessitates a posture of dissidence, scepticism and irony, sometimes anger, towards the powers that be. One might even call to mind a Wildean irreverence about being "earnest." This, Pound suggests, provides the way toward what he calls in *Guide to Kulchur* "real knowledge" (GK 99, 107).

As Forrest Read observes, in the 1920s, Pound was "much more conscious of *le mot juste* than he was in his letters of the 1930s, when he became one of the century's most prolific correspondents" (Pound, P/J, 13) Again, out of Pound's sense of urgency, and the association in his mind between urgency and the need for a blast of untidy energy, his epistolary style evolved towards a far less carefully crafted mode, towards a style whose bibliographic code was conspicuously unruly, sprawling, resistant, intractable, and difficult of access. As Lindberg-Seyersted notes, Pound's letters show an "unusual mixture of conscious composition and hasty improvisation" (Pound, P/F, xix). Forrest Read characterizes this, likewise, as Pound's "combined spontaneity and care" (Pound, P/J, 13).

Reviewing Pound's letters and prose, it is easy to feel that his control over the style wanes over the years, that what begins as conscious strategy gradually deteriorates into habit, even sometimes mere tic. But as true as this might be in part – Pound did seem increasingly to lose the ability to pitch appropriately for specific recipients and occasions – much of what Pound created in the style of his letters emerged from profound commitments. These commitments may have been sustained out of inertia after originally being forged out of principle, but his letters, even during the later periods, continue to indicate them nonetheless. Thus whatever his degree of local control over specific gestures, Pound's playfulness signals a general attitude of resolutely maintained disdain for obedience to conventional practices: it suggests, importantly, a form of political dissidence.

DIPLOMATIC EDITING

Even if, over time, Pound became less acutely conscious of the significance and potential impact of his mischievous gestures, even if these ossified into habit, they still deserve editorial treatment faithful to the original inscriptions, so as to foster understanding of the cast of mind from which they arose. As David Gordon notes of Pound: "Picture Ludwig van Beethoven behind a typewriter ... [H]is epistolary vehemence left one typewriter constantly in the repair shop ... No reader of Pound's letters will remain long in doubt about his moods, ranging from deepest depression to fiery ebullience" (Pound, *E/L*, xxi). In the name of intellectual biography, it is the quicksilver changes of mood and mind that this edition aims to preserve. As a result, rather than lament the orneriness of Pound's epistolary idiom, this edition uses it to offer thick description of and rich information about the turns and twists of Pound's thought as it developed in the 1930s. It also captures Pound's efforts – in retrospect, deeply misguided – at communication and diplomacy towards forging the "committees of correspondence" he saw as necessary for what he construed as a revolutionary moment. Pound's "idiosyncratic typing, composition, and writing habits," insofar as they "do not conform to typographical conventions," may "test the transcriber's and editor's mettle" (*P/A*, xxvi). But more important – and this claim emerges from a spirit similar to that which animated Pound's own fascination with letters from history – they provide a crucial record of Pound's work during these years, of his mind in motion. This is a dimension of his "struggle" not inscribed elsewhere.

The editorial approach here is therefore documentary, or, as it is sometimes termed, diplomatic.[19] There is of course an irony in this, as one of the many troublesome features of Pound's letters is that they show precisely the deterioration of his ability to exercise diplomacy, to suit his style to the attitudes and values of his recipients and write in a way that would be genuinely persuasive to them. But this breakdown in diplomacy – the ability to communicate with those around him – constitutes a phenomenon in Pound's development that itself needs to be placed on record, given the importance of both the reasons for it and its effects. These letters contribute importantly towards enriching its record.

In September of 1935, Stanley Nott observed to Ezra Pound that, by the end of the upcoming month, his firm would have published "43 books and pamphlets" in "about 19 months" (Letter 62). As this comment indicates, Stanley Nott Ltd. had been up and running since early 1934. The achievement was clearly a source of satisfaction, as Nott repeated the same figure in a letter written ten days later, nearly verbatim (Letter 63). At this juncture, Nott affirmed that the publishing work was not only "going very well" but was also "intensely interesting." In his memoirs, Nott observes, "Our small firm was regarded as one of the most progressive of the younger publishers. All kinds of people came into the tiny office." He notes that both young aspiring writers and well-known writers sent their work to his firm (*Further Teachings* 51) – and recalls that Dylan Thomas and surrealist David Gascoygne stopped by with their poems.

What this doesn't capture, however, is that between 1934 and 1935 Stanley Nott Ltd. was principally known for publishing work on economic radicalism, and especially on Social Credit. By December 1935, the journal *New Democracy*, edited by Gorham Munson, which formed the American counterpart to the British *New English Weekly*, was describing Stanley Nott Ltd. as "the largest Social Credit publisher in the world."[1] Nott's correspondence with Pound began just after the foundation of the publishing house and lasted beyond it, registering the firm's successes, accomplishments, vicissitudes, and eventual demise. By the summer of 1937, the firm had folded, like many small publishers in the 1930s, in part as a result of the Depression.

And of course it was the economic distress of England during the 1930s, as well as of North America and the United Kingdom more generally, that the Social Credit literature published by Stanley Nott was meant to address. Nott's lists did not consist exclusively of Social Credit literature: as

Nott observed to Pound, in order to remain solvent, the firm had to publish books on such subjects as wine, art, music, travel, and cuisine (Letter 2).[2] At one point, Nott even suggested that he deliberately diversified his publications in order to achieve range and balance in his lists rather than simply to remain afloat: "It's not good to publish only S. C." (Letter 53). But from the first, Nott saw his publications on Social Credit as the "foundation" (Letter 2) and chief purpose of the firm.

It was about one series of these publications, the Pamphlets on the New Economics (see Appendix 2), that Nott first approached Pound. At Nott's invitation, Pound contributed two pamphlets to the series – no. 8 (*Social Credit: An Impact*) and no. 9 (*Alfred Venison's Poems*) – the latter collecting satirical poems on economics Pound had contributed to the *NEW* between February and August 1934. These pamphlets, providing a wide variety of commentary on Social Credit, were published between 1934 and 1936, numbering nineteen in total, and sold for an affordable sixpence – in the late 1930s in England, the price of a pint of beer or a cheap movie ticket.[3] The writers of the pamphlets ranged from C.H. Douglas and A.R. Orage to Storm Jameson and Edwin Muir. As Nott commented in an October 1935 volume in which he compiled a subset of the pamphlets:

> The idea of the pamphlets arose out of a conversation with A.R. Orage and ourselves and the editorial staff of the *New English Weekly*. The idea was that pamphleteering ought to be revived, but that it should be based on a need; and the need was the interest of the average man in the present economic situation. The series comprises the opinions of all sorts of thinking men and women. The pamphlets are being bought and read by all sorts and conditions of people in every part of the world. (*Social Credit Pamphleteer*, frontispiece)

Nott's phrasing here ("all sorts of thinking men and women") indicated that he courted diverse perspectives on the "New Economics" – his name for the range of radical economic thought related to Social Credit – from not only the "leading money heretics" of the time (such as those featured in one of his other publications, *To-Morrow's Money*)[4] but also from a variety of artists and writers. Nott welcomed, even cultivated, a mixture of viewpoints on Social Credit, initially issuing Douglas's texts,[5] but then purposely not confining the roster of pamphlet writers to orthodox Douglasite Social Crediters.

That Nott featured the Pamphlets on the New Economics series as a cornerstone of his publishing lists – it was often advertised in the leading Social Credit-related publications such as the *NEW* and *New Democracy* – indicates Nott's self-fashioning as a kind of heretic among money heretics, a position that he often signals to Pound. In their correspondence, Nott notes his impatience with the internal divisions of the Social Credit movement: "Confidential," he writes: "I hate almost all Social Creditors" (Letter 11). Here, Nott's resistance to "Social Creditors" seems to stem from his dislike of the interpersonal conflicts typical of the movement and his desire to avoid "petty jealousies" (Letter 11) rather than from doctrinal quarrels with other Social Crediters. But Nott's exchanges with Pound also suggest his recognition that the internecine strife of the movement was related to the hidebound viewpoints of many adherents. And while his firm's overt mission was to educate a wide body of readers about Social Credit, an ulterior project appears to have been to counter this tendency towards doctrinaire entrenchment. Through his publications, he would seek to engender debate about Social Credit, raise questions, guard against dogmatism, and enliven the movement by fostering a "symposium" on its ideas – committed to the symposium's connotations of free exchange of ideas – which featured commentators approaching Social Credit from various perspectives.[6]

Accordingly, although Stanley Nott Ltd. constituted one of the era's principal sources for Social Credit literature, in the profile and body of work it developed, Nott's firm neither hewed sedulously to Douglas's teachings nor confined itself to publishing the views of a group of authoritative commentators who had arrived at a consensus about Social Credit thought. Douglas's books were among its lists, and the importance of Douglas's work is stressed in the firm's advertisements; but Nott's commitment to Douglas's ideas did not result in uncritical deference to the Major's views. Nott evidently conceived of the Social Credit movement as a phenomenon in process, and he dedicated his work to helping it to evolve. And in Nott's vision, this evolution required an abundance of different voices – which the genre of the pamphlet series showcased especially well – offering commentary on various facets of the movement, sometimes from positions markedly alternative to main-line Douglasite thought. For instance, while Douglasite Social Credit opposed communism and socialism, communist Hewlett Johnson, the "Red" Dean of Canterbury, authored one of the contributions to Pamphlets on the New Economics, as did Herbert Read, whose pamphlet was entitled *Essential Communism* and supported Social Credit from a "Communist point of view" (31). Also represented in the series was G.D.H. Cole, who remained a Guild Socialist into the 1930s after Social Credit had distanced itself from Guild Socialism per se; and, of course, featured prominently was Pound, whose allegiance to Italian Fascism was clear and whose dedication to the work of economic reformer Silvio Gesell never met with Douglas's approval. Nott's choices about the pamphlet series' content suggest a belief that the movement's health depended on the degree to which it resisted intransigence – of any kind, not just Douglasite – and fostered dialogue among adherents of various perspectives. Notably, Nott began the Pamphlets on the New Economics series in 1934, at just the time that worry was rising about Major Douglas's Secretariat and its dogmatic tendencies (Finlay 137). Nott expresses this concern to Pound in June 1935: "Douglas Secretariat seem chiefly to be concerned with establishing a dictatorship" (Letter 51).

Nott's chosen role as facilitator of salutary debate helps to account for his affinities for Pound's eccentric, provocative economic diatribes as well as for his active efforts to recruit Pound for his pamphlet series. Similarly, Pound, although ardently interested in Social Credit, refused to toe a party line, Douglasite or otherwise, displaying his usual eclecticism by insisting on the relevance to Social Credit of both Mussolini and economic radical Silvio Gesell as well as celebrating the work of maverick Social Crediter John Hargrave, who fell from Douglas's grace in the mid-1930s. Pound gave voice to, and put into print, a spirit of energetic contention, transferring to the domain of economics the poetic notion of "tenzone," or contest, that, in artistic contexts, he had championed from his early career onward.[7] Moreover, Nott was impressed by Pound's drive and verve. Behind Nott's preference for stimulating debate, and thus for provocative writers who could spark such debate, was a regret at what he regarded as an inability to demonstrate emotion typical of British Social Crediters. He complained to Pound that most Social Crediters he knew "lacked *passion*" (Letter 9).[8] In contrast, Pound possessed ardour in abundance (he noted to Nott about his pamphlet entitled *Social Credit*: "I have of set purpose done the thing hot and molten" [Letter 3]), as did John Hargrave, whom both Nott and Pound admired as a "live wire" (Letter 46).

Also bound up in, and fuelling, Nott's appreciation for stimulating debate ("stimulating" is a word Nott employs frequently in his memoirs) was his belief that it was often well to resist the prevalent trends of the age. Nott's tendency to maintain detachment from dominant cultural currents becomes evident when he explains his willingness to publish Pound's *Jefferson and/or Mussolini*. When Nott announced to Pound his firm's accomplishments of the past eighteen months, the firm had just recently published the book, and Pound was expressing gratitude: he recognized Nott as a "virtuous publr" who had the "GUTS" to print *Jefferson and/or Mussolini* when, Pound noted, it was not favoured by the "Keynses" – that is, by orthodox economists.[9]

Evidencing Nott's receptivity to active debate is the fact that he was willing to publish the book even as he himself disagreed with Pound's position on Mussolini. Nott was no supporter of the political left, and certainly not of communism, as he repeatedly notes in his memoirs.[10] But, as his reminiscences make equally clear, he was also keenly opposed to fascist dictators on the rise throughout Europe.[11] And by the fall of 1935, like many in England, Nott opposed Italy on grounds of Mussolini's imperialistic designs on Abyssinia, which had reached the point of full-fledged invasion by October 1935, turning British sentiment markedly against Italy and drawing sanctions from the League of Nations. Commenting to Pound on *Jefferson and/or Mussolini*, Nott evinces his resolve to remain a disinterested publisher above partisan politics:

> The book is the one stem against the flood of anti-Italian sentiment here. Feeling is strong against Mussolini. People have to vent their resentment against life on someone - it has turned from Germany to Italy. And though I myself think that Italy's excuses are an insult to any half intelligent person, and that the invasion is [sic] belongs to gone and dead 19th century Imperialism, one must not go altogether with the tide. For that reason I am interested in pushing J/M.
> (Letter 63)

Elsewhere, Nott likewise justifies his decision to publish on the basis of the book's quality, topicality, and likely impact, calling *Jefferson and/or Mussolini* "an important book" (Letter 53). He notes, using his favoured adjective, "[A]s I said, it is one of the most stimulating things I've ever read. And it belongs to just this age" (Letter 29). By way of his decision to publish *Jefferson and/or Mussolini*, and his assertions about both its quality and importance during an intensely anti-Italian moment in Britain,[12] Nott shows (1) his admiration for Pound's perspective; (2) more generally, that, as he decides on publications, a writer's drive and ability to "stimulate" debate carry more weight for him than whether or not he agrees with the writer's positions; and (3) that, as a publisher, he is politically committed to "not" going "altogether" with what he considers the prevailing cultural "tide." Nott's delicate phrasing here suggests that he will not oppose the tide entirely, in contrarian fashion, but rather that he will remain wary of capitulating to the most powerful beliefs and assumptions of his milieu.

NOTT'S PUBLISHING PHILOSOPHY

In the London of this moment, "tide" was a word that would have resonated, as attested by the name of one of Britain's leading weeklies of the era, *Time and Tide*. In this environment, to "catch the tide" was to be au courant. One of Nott's fellow publishers in London at the time, the well known Victor Gollancz, observed in a letter to Daphne Du Maurier that "the essence of publishing is to 'take the tide.'"[13] This is not to suggest that Stanley Nott's work issued from a philosophy antithetical to Gollancz's: of course much depends on which "tide" is being referred to in the expressions concerned. Nott's and Gollancz's publishing houses in fact shared a commitment to resisting some cultural tides and following others. Like Gollancz's firm, which rode the wave of the popularity of its bestselling authors and then the demand for its "Left Book Club," Nott's rode a wave of interest in the burgeoning movement of Social Credit. Moreover, both Gollancz's and Nott's firms committed themselves to publishing literature from non-dominant political viewpoints that they deemed important.[14]

But these points of convergence aside, signal differences in the emphases and goals of the two publishers highlight the distinctive features of Nott's venture. Gollancz was far more invested than Nott in coupling an endeavour to disseminate left-wing literature with an effort to attain large-scale commercial success; in Gollancz's view, the latter would support the former. It was because of the great success of Gollancz's major authors – such as Dorothy Sayers and Daphne Du Maurier – that, by the 1930s, Gollancz could afford to undertake the overtly political Left Book Club, where the heart of his political interests lay. In contrast, while Nott did his utmost to remain solvent so as to continue to publish, he was out for no more success than would allow him to do just this: to keep the firm going and support a family. Unlike the commercially savvy Gollancz, Nott readily admitted that he was no "business man" (Letter 100); and although at moments he displayed sensitivity on this point, at other times he expressed satisfaction that this allowed him to avoid what he read as crass commercialism.[15] Finally, as Nott's telling comment to Pound indicates, unlike Gollancz, who was dedicated to the dissemination of leftist literature, Nott was deliberately non-partisan in political commitments, devoted to fostering constructive controversy.

Nott's idealistic approach, so little concerned with the bottom line, although at first glance surprising in someone so focused on economic reform, in fact accorded with the leading principles of Social Credit. Like many idealistic movements of the interwar period, Social Credit was known for its anti-materialism.[16] While Social Crediters asserted that purchasing power and economic comfort were necessary for all, and strove for economic justice, this was not in the name of material gain but rather to establish conditions under which people would be sufficiently provided for so as to be able to focus on the more important (and for most Social Crediters, this equated to non-material) aspects of their lives. Nott's commitment to publishing out of this attitude deeply impressed Pound, for whom, given his long-standing avant-gardist perspective, idealism in publishing was tantamount to virtue.[17] Accordingly, for Pound, Stanley Nott Ltd. deserved to be classified among the admirably pure independent publishers that, for decades, he had praised, supported, and courted for modernism.

In fact, as Gregory Barnhisel notes, Pound initially regarded Nott as occupying the same niche with respect to publishing his important cutting-edge work as did James Laughlin a few years later. (Laughlin, largely through Pound's tutelage, likewise came to sympathize with Social Credit.) Had Nott been able to continue as a publisher into the 1940s, he might well have been approached by Pound to assume the role of Laughlin's counterpart in England.[18] Laughlin launched his own publishing firm, New Directions Books, in 1936, as Stanley Nott Ltd. was moving towards demise – and devoted a career to the rehabilitation of Pound's image, the dissemination of his work, and more generally to the promotion of modernist literary work. Like Nott, Laughlin was committed to avoiding publishing-as-usual. With a polemical bravura reminiscent of Pound, he once asserted: "It is time I think to damn the book publisher as hard as you can ... They're traitors and enemies of the people. They have made of literature a business" (qtd. Barnhisel 64). Laughlin and Nott thus shared the idealistic motives Pound admired. But whereas Laughlin had the luxury of losing financially on book lists whose items likely would make little money, Nott never did. And whereas Laughlin became increasingly committed to literature as an agent of social change, Nott remained dedicated to non-literary work as necessary propaganda towards social change and justice and, thus, remained far more receptive than did Laughlin to Pound's economic and political work. In fact, Laughlin increasingly saw Pound as doing himself a disservice through his non-literary work, angering readers with controversial writing and heading himself into a cul-de-sac that would destroy his audience. Accordingly, Laughlin would deliberately steer his firm away from the category of the "political," despite intense pressure from Pound to do otherwise, both because he took issue with Pound's fascism – as Barnhisel notes, "in order to keep New Directions free of the taint of fascism, Laughlin would refuse Pound the bully pulpit he craved" (77) – and because he read Pound's politics as precisely what would prevent his work from circulating. Repair of Pound's damaged image, Laughlin believed, could only be achieved by the promotion of Pound's chiefly literary, and usually earlier, work.

In dramatic contrast, during the 1930s, Nott was willing to take a chance on Pound's politically charged economic writing. Again, this willingness derived in part from respect for Pound; in part from Nott's and Pound's shared adherence to, and impatience with, the factionalism and partisanship of Social Credit; and partly from Nott's preference for controversial and thus stimulating work as well as for work that moved against the grain of ordinary political commentary. But importantly, it was also born of Nott's distinctive detachment about political matters, which, in turn, issued from another of Nott's commitments: to the mystical teachings of G.I. Gurdjieff.

NOTT AND GURDJIEFF

Nott's passion for the thought of this Russian-Armenian guru animated, but also outlasted and overrode, both his allegiances to publishing and to Social Credit. In his correspondence with Pound, Nott mentions Gurdjieff only once (Letter 1), but, as he attests, it was his work with Gurdjieff's thought that left the deepest imprint on his life and that guided his major decisions. Like many intellectually and literarily inclined middle-class Britons of his generation, Nott was drawn to Gurdjieff out of spiritual needs after the devastation of the Great War, in which Nott had served.[19] As Nott puts it, although in his youth he had been a "'God-fearing' young man" and even a Sunday-school teacher, after the war, he noted, "organized religion now had no content for me, nor could it give me a satisfying answer to the questions that arose in me as a consequence of the disillusionment resulting from the war" (*Teachings* xii). Moreover, even before his experience in the trenches, Nott suggests that, from his youth onward, he had suffered from a profound dissatisfaction with ordinary life, never finding what seemed genuinely important to him. After Nott's many years of travel all over the world (to such places as the United States, Japan, China, Burma, India, Egypt, Italy, and Russia) and engagement in many different arenas, Gurdjieff's work reached him in the early 1920s in a way that never left him. He notes that, once he had found Gurdjieff's "teachings," he felt that he had achieved the end of his search: "from that time to this, never has any doubt assailed me" (*Teachings* 12). These teachings arrived through A.R. Orage, who, as a new disciple of Gurdjieff, came to lecture in New York in 1923 at the "Sunwise Turn," a bookstore frequented by the leading literary lights of the day and at which Nott was working at the time. The relationship between Orage and Nott would quicken into the close, long-standing friendship that lasted until Orage's premature death in November 1934.

At the beginning of the first of two journals Nott devoted to his work with Gurdjieff, he summarizes Gurdjieff's thought: "Briefly, the Gurdjieff system comprises writings; sacred dances, movements, and exercises; music; and the inner teaching" (*Teachings* x). John Carswell, commenting sceptically on Gurdjieff, notes that, when the guru arrived in London in 1920, he was more dancing-master than mystic, principally concerned with the physical world, and only later evolved into a teacher focused on interiority and spiritual life. But Carswell implies, debatably, that Gurdjieff's work with dance stood apart from his engagement with spirituality. Nott instead stresses the continuity between the two, noting that Gurdjieff focused on the spiritual insight afforded by the discipline of sacred dances from around the world. Nott observes that the "inner teaching" that Gurdjieff espoused, whose overarching goal was bringing into harmony the three "centres" into which he analyzed the individual – the intellectual, the emotional, and the instinctual (*Teachings* 3) – was frowned upon in both the intellectual and leftist activist circles in which he moved: the intellectuals derided Gurdjieff as an uneducated mountebank, while activists judged his focus on the interior life to be self-indulgent when there was crucial work to be done in the external world. In response to such charges, Nott readily admits that, as Carswell notes, "Gurdjieff was not an intellectual" (Carswell 185) – and appreciates this: for Nott, Gurdjieff's insistence on living and teaching from all three centres of his being importantly countered the tendency of many around him to locate in, and live from, their minds only.[20] And in response to the second accusation, Nott was content to place himself apart from the ruling assumptions, methods, and convictions of the political left, lamenting what he termed the "disease" of communism (*Teachings* 49). He agreed with Gurdjieff that the most effective way to achieve lasting improvement in the exterior world was to go within – for each individual to work on himself.

The niche Nott carved out in the world of publishing in the 1930s was unquestionably shaped by his Gurdjieffian allegiances. When he turned to publishing in the 1930s after years of close work with Gurdjieff, Nott realized that, for him, publishing was a profession that enabled him to call into play all three centres of his being simultaneously (*Further Teachings* 43) – in Gurdjieffian terms, to lead a robust life. More surprisingly, the way Nott inhabited his role as publisher was affected by an earlier conclusion he had drawn through his work with Gurdjieff: that his youthful passion for books as artefacts, which had driven many of his early ambitions, was a harmful attachment from which he had to wean himself. Nott acknowledges that distancing himself from books meant surrendering a tie to a legacy from his family: such a love of books, he notes, "may have been inherited from my ancestor, William Nott, a bookseller in St. Paul's Churchyard in the seventeenth century" (*Further Teachings* 37). In 1926, when Nott was obliged to give up a bookseller's business he had run for a couple of years, he realized that this had freed him of a burden:

> In the late autumn of 1926 I was again in New York. In December
> an offer was made for my book business; and in a few weeks it was
> sold and passed out of my hands. With some surprise I recalled that
> less than four years previously I had been afraid that if I became
> interested in the Gurdjieff system I might not be able to carry out
> the project that then seemed so dear to me; and now it had slipped
> away with not only no regret but even with relief. I saw how that
> from my childhood I had been so identified with books that I had
> almost worshipped them. I had been a bibliolatrist, a bibliomane, a
> bibliophile, a bibliopolist, and even a bibliotaphist. Now, a feeling of
> thankfulness pervaded me for having been cured of the book disease.
> (*Teachings* 117)

Nott addresses his epiphany through a description of an encounter with Holbrook Jackson, whom he had once idolized as a kindred book-lover: "Like myself, from a child he had been devoted to books and book knowledge ... Even at school, it seems, we had the same feeling about books: the smell of the paper, the binding, and even the names of publishers on the title page were surrounded by an atmosphere of romance" (*Further Teachings* 36). But Nott's work with Gurdjieff shocked him into conviction that his love of books was a form of idolatry from which he had to detach: "The lunch and talk with Holbrook Jackson coincided with the last gasp of my life-disease of bibliophily, the love of books for themselves" (36). The Gurdjieffian interpretation that Nott brings to bear here is that love of books in themselves is, as he twice says, a "disease" – a pathology that, he believed, often indicated misdirections of sexual energy of the kind that Gurdjieffian teachings aimed to redress.

> I had begun to discover, in the course of my business and my connexion with the First Edition Club in London, that there is an association between the identification with books – book-collecting, book-hoarding, and book-stealing – and sexual maladjustments. Identification with books, even stealing books, is only one of the many manifestations of the diversion of sex energy from its real purpose, that of normal sex relations and its use in inner development. Yet a man can still have ordinary sex relations with women and at the same time be too passive, especially if the feminine creative part of himself is strong. As I have said, Gurdjieff and his teaching developed the masculine in men and the feminine in women. (*Teachings* 118)

Apropos of this, Nott comments that, in the "oak-panelled" library at the Prieuré, where Gurdjieff and his disciples gathered, there was not a single book (*Teachings* 102).

It would seem to follow that, after breaking his old tie with books, Nott would have given up on books altogether. But instead, in the early 1930s, he turned to publishing, and his memoirs indicate nothing about this move constituting a violation of his new resolution.[21] The implication here is that Nott had now developed a new relationship with books, one that no longer involved worshipping them as things in themselves. Insofar as the books Nott was publishing were a means to an end – economic reform – work with them did not involve a lapse back into a fetishistic relationship. Again, Nott observes of the work of the small publisher that "he ha[d] to use all three centres" (*Further Teachings* 43): in Nott's view, this new line of work accorded with a Gurdjieffian way of life.

In view of the attention Nott pays to avoiding the fetishization of books, his decisions about the layout and typeface of the books he published come across as part of a principled commitment to the ends these books were designed to serve. Nott's comments in both memoirs and letters indicate that, even after leaving behind his first love of books, he still focused a great deal on "lay-out, type-faces, paper, binding, reproduction of illustrations and so on" – and found such work very "satisfying" (*Further Teachings* 43).

When planning the Pamphlets on the New Economics series, for instance, he noted: "The series should be typographically interesting as well as intel-lectually. *Each booklet will be done in a different face of type.* We want to make them a well-printed series" (Letter 40).

In general, the bibliographic code of the books Nott published is conspicuously plain. The typefaces tend to be simple, unadorned, sans-serif; book covers are likewise simple, with either no design or one that remains subtle. Colours are dark, often brown, tan, or rust. The effect of the physical books' features is so regular, so consonant with dominant practices, as to be almost invisible – so as to let the attention move directly to the matter of the book. At one point, Nott observes: "We have a range of 12 types to work from ... all the accepted faces" (Letter 42). The goal, then, appears to have been to keep to faces and semiotics that were "accepted" in this cultural climate so as to avoid decisions that would call attention to themselves. These books were dressed modestly, signalling a restraint suitable for serious purposes and times.

The muted bibliographic codes Stanley Nott featured accorded both with a style prevalent in the 1930s and one typical of books and pamphlets such as these, which were intended to be instructive about urgent topical matters. This was an approach to bibliographic code that Pound came to favour as well: coinciding with Pound's shift towards work on politics and economics in the 1930s was a turn towards publishing his work in plainer editions that were preferable both because they could be offered to a public more inexpensively (and thus reach a wider readership than more ornate, costly editions) and because their very visual signals suggested engagement and gravitas.[22] Nott likewise committed to both these justifications for plain format. Moreover, in light of Nott's own turnabout, the plain typefaces and notably understated book designs also suggest his own project – one that forms part of his narrative of spiritual advancement – of refraining from showy visuals that would either express or invite idolatry of the book-as-artefact.

Nott's own preferences about visual features, and especially typeface, are guided by Gurdjieffian values in yet another sense. Referring to the NEW, he suggests that it ought to be "reorganized, typographically," because it "doesn't look important enough – too feminine." This suggests that Nott also favoured plain typefaces because, for him, they connoted masculinity and importance – in his reading, they suggested importance because they suggested masculinity. This line of thought aligned with Gurdjieff's argument that, as Nott explains, proper masculinity involved dominance and command.[23]

Gurdjieffian work also influenced Nott's approach to publishing in another regard, as it was Orage who played a significant role in Nott's decision to turn to Social Credit. Although Nott's observations about needless poverty in Britain and America suggest that his own convictions steered him towards Social Credit,[24] clearly his intimate friendship with Orage, who had been so dedicated to Social Credit before his departure for Fontainebleau and who decided that he would return to economic reform after parting from Gurdjieff, also exerted considerable influence over Nott's decision to commit himself to the cause. Suggesting Orage's role in Nott's choice to pledge allegiance to Social Credit is the fact that Nott's turn to the movement coincided chronologically with Orage's return to England, at which point Orage sought to resume work with Social Credit and devote a new magazine to it. In Nott's words, the journal would "formulate the causes of the breakdown of the financial system and ... outline a possible cure" (*Further Teachings* 29). Nott remembers having offered to be of service to Orage as he re-entered England and having embarked on the journal with him (8).[25] From 1932 until 1933, Nott would act as manager for the *NEW*.

But Nott's retrospective descriptions of having done this, which never directly articulate support for Social Credit, suggest that his commitment to the periodical initially issued more from loyalty to Orage than to Social Credit per se. And Nott's closeness to Orage, in turn, was intertwined with their mutual dedication to Gurdjieff: at one point, as the *NEW* got under way, Nott even suggested to Orage that Social Credit was merely Orage's "secondary interest," while his devotion to Gurdjieffian work remained primary. Orage admitted that the Social Credit work was merely a "pseudo-interest" (*Further Teachings* 30). While Carswell reads this as implying that Orage's connection to economic reform was mere posturing, in context, this indicates the hierarchy by which both Orage and Nott lived: Gurdjieffian principles held the privileged place, and other life-projects were subordinate to, and ideally served, these. As Orage had a significant hand in Nott's link to Social Credit, and as Nott suggested to Orage the possibility that his interest in Social Credit was "secondary," Nott likely adopted a similar attitude.

Such a Gurdjieffian perspective on Social Credit, reinforced through Orage's acting as Nott's significant transmitter of Social Credit ideas, would accord with, even account for, Nott's detachment from partisan loyalties within the Social Credit movement. As he noted to Pound about the various groups of Social Crediters, "I do better staying out and keeping in touch with them all" (Letter 11). An additional factor guiding Nott to such a stance was the example of Orage's own approach to Social Credit: as

John Finlay notes, Orage "conceived of his role apart from the hurly-burly of practical politics and decision-making and of himself as *au dessus de la mêlée*" (65) – above the fray.

Nott's close work with Gurdjieff also likely rendered him receptive to Pound's personality and style. By the early 1930s, after nearly a decade of intense interaction with the enigmatic and imperious Gurdjieff, Nott was not only well prepared to work with someone of Pound's comparably forceful, volatile temperament, but also likely even favoured Pound for his eccentricities. Admiringly, Nott describes Gurdjieff's magnetic, charismatic personality; his gift for emphatic pronouncement; his demanding and capricious ways; his severe treatment of disciples, often tantamount to verbal and psychological bullying; his gnomic sayings; his tendency to evade questions with indirect, mysterious, or apparently irrelevant responses; his sense of mischief; his idiosyncratic use of language and, above all, his ability to promote growth in his students by shocking them into awareness.[26] For Nott, this constellation of characteristics made him a superb teacher, able to effect profound transformations in others. This roster of qualities is one that could easily likewise be attributed to Pound, and it is safe to suggest that this was not lost on Nott, whether or not he was consciously aware of it. Nott was not only accustomed to reckoning with someone like Pound and schooled in tolerating it, but he also favoured interchanges with such personalities as catalysts to vibrancy and development.

PAMPHLETS

Given his Gurdjieffian approach to publishing, which subordinated both the physical artefacts of the book and the work of publishing to a greater cause, Nott was particularly invested in publishing pamphlets – the publication format that rose to prominence in the 1930s out of the era's spirit of political reform. As Nott observes, it was a conversation with Orage and the staff of the *NEW* that inspired the idea that "pamphleteering," as a genre associated with earlier eras (such as the revolutionary period in England in the seventeenth century or the eighteenth century in England, the United States, and France), "ought to be revived" in response to a clear contemporary need: "the interest of the average man in the present economic situation." As a publication medium, the "pamphlet" forms the visual, bibliographic correlative to the genre of *pamphleteering* – writing dashed off, as Pound puts it, while ideas are "molten," to meet an urgent political need. It is also the suitable physical instantiation for the mode of discourse associated with this genre, which Marc Angenot calls *la parole pamphletaire*:

polemical writing in response to a current controversy, news that has to reach readers quickly about a topical matter.[27]

Writing of the 1930s, which often stressed a cultural moment of crisis, frequently used a traditional bibliographic marriage between writing of political moment that could answer an immediate need and pamphlet format – the physical pamphlet, inexpensive, housed in paper covers, usually fastened (with staples) rather than bound. The pamphlet *format*, then, signalled to prospective readers the *genre* of the pamphlet: that is, that what was within its covers was politically topical, politically charged, and part of an ongoing political debate. Used in connection with Social Credit, the pamphlet also carried the valence of a "primer": the semiotics of the slim, inexpensive format implied an educational purpose related to political activism – i.e., the efficient dissemination of important information to prepare readers for informed action. Accordingly, Stanley Nott's Pamphlets on the New Economics series, through its packaging and advertising, connoted educational usefulness, participation in important arguments, and topicality.

Nott's observations to Pound in these letters make clear that the decision to publish in pamphlet form was strategic, designed to set a certain tone. He did not choose to publish pamphlets only because the manuscripts he was receiving could be best delivered through them: the idea of pamphlets preceded – and superseded – the material that they were to address. Nott, in other words, commissioned the items in the "pamphlet series" on the "New Economics," and as he indicates through exchanges with Pound, he also sought out texts that could be brought out in pamphlet form. Indicating that the image of the pamphlets may have been just as, if not more, important than their practicality, Nott noted that it would actually cost him as much to publish in pamphlet form as in book form (Letter 57). He thus indicated his recognition of the attraction of pamphlets for conveying the sense of urgently topical ideas-in-progress that would appeal to the Social Credit readership.

In her review of theoretical work on the pamphlet and the manifesto, Alice Kaplan suggests that the mode of discourse associated with pamphleteering often precludes self-awareness of its own underlying assumptions and self-critical thought: justified by the urgent need that its writing can meet, the pamphlet's characteristic rhetoric proceeds unreflectively, pronouncing with the resolution and unequivocality needed to raise awareness and galvanize action.[28] But again, with his pamphlet series, Nott sought to counter this tendency of the pamphleteering mode by assembling a group of writers with diverse perspectives, whose commentaries, if taken in aggregate (and Nott encourages such a reading by publishing a volume containing ten of the pamphlets),[29] would display a range of views. In some cases, these views even contend with one another, creating out of their friction productive debate and mutual interrogation. When Nott publishes the volume that consolidates these pamphlets, he stresses in the subtitle that they are by "various hands." As Nott describes the Pamphlets on the New Economics series, he emphasizes not only the diversity but also the thoughtfulness of the contributors. It "comprises the opinions of all sorts of thinking men and women." Here, the word "thinking" exerts pressure on the common assumption that pamphleteering involves unthinking partisan commentary: the implication is that the diversity of the "various hands" fosters such "thinking."

Taken as a whole, Nott's Pamphlets on the New Economics implies a line of conviction that is suggested both by his comments to Pound throughout their correspondence and by his body of work more generally: that the free play of ideas, born of intellectual contention, promotes political health. It was just such salutary intellectual contention, issuing from those able to destabilize settled positions and to incite debate, that Nott associated with, and valued in, Ezra Pound.

APPENDIX I: GLOSSARY

Alfred Venison's Poems: Social Credit Themes, by the Poet of Titchfield Street. Published in 1935 as no. 9 in the Pamphlets on the New Economics series, this pamphlet collected eighteen poems EP wrote under the pseudonym "Alfred Venison," each originally appearing in the *NEW* and introduced by A.R. Orage with a brief letter between February and November 1934. Two more poems and two more letters would appear under the pseudonym in the *NEW*, three between March and June 1935 (C1169, C1189, C1217) and one more in December 1936 (C1386). The pamphlet is dedicated to "S.C.N." (Stanley Charles Nott).

Baker, Jacob (1895–1967). Administrator in the US Federal Emergency Relief Administration and later the Works Progress Administration/Federal Art Project designed to create jobs for artists. In his letter to the *Morning Post* (6 December 1934), "Gesell's 'Natural Economic Order'" (C1123), EP notes that Baker had urged the Vanguard Press of New York "to publish a condensation of 'The Natural Economic Order,' ... and that they would have done so, but that Gesell refused, and that the disciples regarded the work as that of a holy prophet whose every syllable was inspired" (*P&P* VI 223). EP corresponded with Baker in the late 1930s.

Bird, Otto A. (1914–2009). Bird initially corresponded with EP while a graduate student. (Bird's dissertation on Cavalcanti is referred to in a footnote in *Guide to Kulchur* 55.) Bird later became a professor of philosophy and general director of liberal studies at Notre Dame University. The Otto A. Bird Correspondence with Ezra Pound is housed at the University of Arkansas, Fayetteville. Otto Bird is not to be confused with William Augustus Bird, American journalist and proprietor of the Three Mountains Press.

Brenton, Arthur (dates unknown). Editor of *Credit Power,* author of Social Credit pamphlets such as *The Veil of Finance* (1926) and *Through Consumption to Prosperity* (1924) as well as an outline of C.H. Douglas's credit proposals reprinted from the *New Age*, Brenton took over the editorship of the *New Age* (1923–38) following Orage's departure and Arthur Moore's retirement. Preda suggests that his work considerably influenced John Hargrave (*Ezra Pound's Economic Correspondence* 259). As Finlay notes, Brenton's relationship with the Social Credit Secretariat grew increasingly strained in the 1930s. In Letter 14, EP characterizes Brenton as the "forgotten man" of the Social Credit movement.

Butchart, Montgomery (dates unknown). Canadian writer and commentator on economics. Butchart thanked EP in his anthology, *Money: Selected Passages Presenting the Concepts of Money in the English Tradition, 1640–1935* (Nott 1935) as the one "who first aroused my interest in economics and whose suggestions have been a constant provocation to clarity" (5). Butchart later worked with Ronald Duncan on the *Townsman*. The correspondence between EP and Butchart during the 1930s is considerable. In 1936, Nott published two further books edited by Butchart: *To-Morrow's Money, by Seven of Today's Leading Monetary Heretics* and a collection of Orage's work, *Political and Economic Writings: From the* New English Weekly, *1932–1934*.

The Chandos Group. Founded in the late 1920s, inspired by Dimitri Mitrinovic (pseudonym M.M. Cosmoi), who originally convened the meetings from which the Chandos Group emerged, this informal London group of intellectuals, named for the restaurant in which they met, included members such as Maurice Reckitt, W. Travers Symons, Philip Mairet, Alan Porter, Albert Newsome, V.A. Demant, and Hilderic Cousens. G.D.H. Cole, Lewis Mumford, and T.S. Eliot also attended several meetings. The group discussed issues of the day, often from a Social Credit perspective, but without full advocacy of Social Credit principles. The Chandos Group provided A.R. Orage with what Hutchinson and Burkitt call a "reservoir of willing contributors" when he founded the *New English Weekly* in 1932 (158).

Chesterton, Gilbert Keith (1874–1936). British writer, poet, and editor. With Hilaire Belloc, G.K. Chesterton theorized the economic theory of Distributism (see entry in this appendix and Essay 1). With help from the Distributist League, Chesterton founded, financed, and edited *G.K.'s Weekly* (1925–37), organ of the Distributist movement, until his death in 1936. Chesterton interviewed Benito Mussolini, and his views became increasingly favourable to Italy in the 1930s.

The Chinese Written Character as a Medium for Poetry. Pound discovered this essay by Ernest Fenollosa among the papers of this American sinologist, given him by Fenollosa's widow in 1913. EP used Fenollosa's notes and translations of Chinese poems to develop his volume *Cathay* (1915), then sought to publish Fenollosa's commentary on the significance of the Chinese character as an *ars poetica*. Fenollosa's reading of the Chinese ideogram would particularly influence EP's thought.

EP initially serialized the *Chinese Written Character* in the *Little Review* in 1919; edited by EP, it was then published in 1920 as part of EP's *Instigations*. Stanley Nott published the first separate edition of it in March 1936: the text is reprinted from *Instigations* with a few minor changes and the addition of a "Foreword" in which EP draws an explicit link between it and C.K. Ogden's work. The CWC was positioned as no. 1 in the Ideogrammic series.

Colbourne, Maurice Dale (1894–1965). British thespian and author of several key texts in the Social Credit library, including *Unemployment or War* (1928) – revised as *Economic Nationalism* (1933), revised again as *The Meaning of Social Credit* (1935) – and the pamphlet *The Sanity of Social Credit* (1935), which Nott published as no. 11 in the Pamphlets on the New Economics series. Montgomery Butchart reviewed the pamphlet in the *NEW* 7, 17 (5 September 1935), 335–6. Colbourne advised Butchart on the edition of Orage's *Political and Economic Writings* (Nott 1936) and is credited with introducing Douglas's system into Alberta via William Aberhart, who read *Unemployment or War* in 1932 (Hesketh 44). Pound corresponded with him in the late 1930s.

Cole, George Douglas Howard (1889–1959). British writer, political theorist, and economist, G.D.H. Cole was an early Guild Socialist and long-standing member of the Fabian Society who contributed to the *New Age*. Cole helped to found the National Guilds League in 1915 and set out his early theories in *The World of Labour* (1913). Cole became Labour correspondent for the *Manchester Guardian* and historian of the British Labour movement. During the interwar years, Cole wrote *The Intelligent Man's Guide through World Chaos* (1930) on economics; he appears in Montgomery Butchart's anthology, *To-Morrow's Money* (1936); and Nott published his *Fifty Propositions about Money and Production* (1936) as no. 18 in the Pamphlets on the New Economics series.

Coughlin, Father Charles Edward (1891–1979). Roman Catholic "radio priest" who preached economic reform over the airwaves during the 1930s, Coughlin was critical of Roosevelt's New Deal and founded the National Union for Social Justice based largely on principles receptive to Social Credit. EP corresponded with him and often mentioned him in his *NEW* columns. Surette argues that Coughlin influenced EP's drift towards "conspiracy theory and anti-Semitism" (*Purgatory* 262).

Cousens, Hilderic Edwin (dates unknown). Cambridge educated, Cousens wrote for the *New Age*, in which he was sometimes critical of Major Douglas, and for the *NEW*, in which he provided Social Credit commentaries under the pseudonym Pontifex II. In 1921, he published *A New Policy for Labour: An Essay on the Relevance of Credit Control*, which introduced the social and economic ideas of C.H. Douglas.

The *Criterion* (1922–39). Prominent periodical edited by T.S. Eliot. Seeking to maintain "international standards" and display what Eliot called in his essay "Tradition and the Individual Talent" the "mind of Europe," the *Criterion* featured creative work, reviews, and essays – the latter ranging widely through artistic, cultural, and political topics. Much of the work was modernist in bent. Contributors included W.H. Auden, Jean Cocteau, Ford Madox Ford, Herman Hesse, Aldous Huxley, James Joyce, D.H. Lawrence, Wyndham Lewis, Marianne Moore, Marcel Proust, I.A. Richards, May Sinclair, and Gertrude Stein. Eliot sought to include both more established and newer writers, to introduce English-speaking readers to new foreign writers, and to provide space for more sustained reviews than was possible in other magazines. EP published more than twenty articles and letters in the *Criterion* between 1923 and 1939.

Distributism. A group of social and political theories that coalesced into a program in the 1920s, emerging from a vision of an agrarian society and small land ownership, advocating equitable distribution of property (Distributists regarded property ownership as essential to liberty and security); worker control of commerce, agriculture, and industry; and a return to medieval guilds. Distributists opposed both modern monopolistic capitalism and socialism. Its most prominent theorists and advocates were G.K. Chesterton and Hilaire Belloc; its ideas were influenced by the work of A.J. Penty and Montague Fordham; and it was also associated with Eric Gill and Maurice Reckitt. Distributists often informed their socio-political commitments with Roman Catholic theology. Vigorous opponents of state control and the industrial factory system, Distributists differed from the Guild Socialists on the function of guilds and the degree of worker control within society: while Guild Socialists sought to blend syndicalism with socialism, creating, as A.R. Orage noted, a partnership between guilds and the state, and graft a national guild system on to the existing industrial structure, Distributists sought both to eradicate the existing factory structure and to eliminate state control. See Essay 1.

Douglas, Major Clifford Hugh (1879–1952). British engineer and economist, considered the founder of Social Credit, although some accounts credit A.R. Orage with collaborating with him on the creation of the movement (see Essay 1). Douglas's theories proceed from the premise that there was insufficient purchasing power to consume what was produced in economies in North America and Europe, thereby leading to economic depression and war. According to Douglas, the state could alleviate the problem by increasing the purchasing power of its members, such as by the use of a National Dividend. In *Social Credit: An Impact*, EP defends this measure against the criticism that it is essentially inflationary by quoting Orage's pronouncement: "'Would you call it inflation to print tickets for every seat in a theatre, regardless of the fact that the house had hitherto been always two thirds empty *simply because* no tickets had been printed for the greater number of seats?'" (17). Nott published several books and pamphlets by Douglas (see Appendix 2).

Drummond, John (1900–82). British correspondent and friend of EP who lived in Rapallo during the 1930s; supporter of Social Credit and Fascism (Preda, *Economic Correspondence* 265). Drummond helped EP to proofread and index GK (1938). He also translated into English Pound's money pamphlets written in Italian during the Second World War, some of which were written in support of the Nazi puppet Republic of Salò, led by Mussolini after German forces rescued Mussolini from Italian arrest in 1943 (*EPE* 192). Surette (*Pound in Purgatory* 246) suggests that Drummond played a significant role in the intensification of EP's antisemitism. See Essays 1 and 2.

Dyson, William Henry (1880–1938). Australian-born illustrator and cartoonist. Dyson's artwork appeared in such publications as *Vanity Fair*, the *Daily Herald*, and the *New Age*. He served as official Australian artist on the front during the First World War; publications from the war period include *Kultur Cartoons* (1915) and *Australia at War* (1918). He contributed both writing and artwork to the *NEW*. Dyson's *Artist among the Bankers*, reflecting his interest in Social Credit, was published by Nott in 1933.

Eleven New Cantos: XXXI–XLI. This instalment of EP's *Cantos* was published through Farrar and Rinehart (New York) in October 1934 and Faber and Faber (London) in May 1935. Stephen Adams notes of the volume: "Pound was writing as economic reformer carrying the banner of Social Credit, as American patriot, and as ardent supporter of Mussolini" just prior to his "virulent anti-Semitic turn" and Mussolini's invasion of Abyssinia (*EPE* 30–1). The three reviews gathered in *Ezra Pound: The Critical Heritage* all cite – some negatively – EP's radical revision of the "boundaries of subject in poetry" (298), as the English poet George Barker puts it in his favourable review for the *Criterion* (July 1935). See Letter 26, in which EP expresses his desire that the volume be reviewed alongside *Alfred Venison's Poems*.

The *European Quarterly* (1934–35). "A Review of Modern Literature, Art and Life," this quarterly periodical was created by its two editors, Edwin Muir and Janko Lavrin, and Stanley Nott. The magazine sought to bridge England and the Continent, positioning itself in the second issue (August 1934) as "a valuable link between the culture of the Anglo-Saxon world and of Europe" (qtd. in Sullivan 174). Though the magazine only ran four issues, it featured work by such writers as Franz Kafka and Federico García Lorca, and it helped bring the work of the Danish philosopher Søren Kierkegaard to the English reading public.

Faber and Faber. Faber and Faber became one of the premiere publishing houses in Britain during the 1930s. Established in 1929 under that name, the firm had its roots in the early twentieth century at the Scientific Press. Under Geoffrey Faber's chairmanship, the editorial board in 1929 included T.S. Eliot, Richard de la

Mare, Charles Stewart, and Frank Morley. The firm published Eliot's journal the *Criterion*.

Fack, Hugo R. (?–1954). German-American physician, Gesellite economic reformer, editor, and publisher (Free Economy Publishing Company, San Antonio, Texas). Fack published the first American edition of the English translation of Silvio Gesell's *The Natural Economic Order* (two vols., 1934 and 1936). Out of San Antonio, Texas, Fack also edited *The Way Out*, a monthly Gesellite organ dedicated to economic issues, and brought out a series of pamphlets called the Neo-Economic Series of Freedom and Plenty. Fack was investigated by the FBI for his antisemitism and Nazi sympathies. Preda notes that the Pound/Fack correspondence of the 1930s addressed combining Social Credit with Gesellite theory (*Ezra Pound's Economic Correspondence* 267).

Fenollosa, Ernest Francisco (1853–1908). American sinologist, specializing in Far Eastern art and literature, whose papers were entrusted to EP by Fenollosa's widow in 1913. EP arranged for the posthumous publication of Fenollosa's *The Chinese Written Character as a Medium for Poetry*. EP originally serialized Fenollosa's CWC in the *Little Review* between September and December 1919 and reprinted it in *Instigations* (1920) with a few minor changes. Nott published the text with a foreword and notes by EP as no. 1 in the Ideogrammic series.

Fisher, Irving (1867–1947). American mathematician and economist known for contributions to economic theory. Awarded a PhD from Yale in 1891, he remained as a professor at Yale until 1935 – first of mathematics, later of political economy. Fisher's numerous and wide-ranging publications include *The Theory of Interest* (1930) and *Stamp Scrip* (1933), the latter of which featured the theory of stamp scrip associated with Silvio Gesell; focused on experiments with it that were under way around the world, including in the United States; addressed a bill recently introduced before the US Congress to implement stamp scrip (the Bankhead-Pettingill bill of 1933); and advocated that Americans take greater note of it. Drawn to Fisher because of his interest in stamp scrip, EP reviewed and commented on him on five occasions in the *NEW* (C981, C990, C1244, C1495, C1497): in his review of Fisher's *Stamp Scrip* (26 October 1933), EP suggested that "Douglasites ought to reach out a friendly hand" to Fisher (31). Pound corresponded with Fisher in the mid-1930s.

Fox, Douglas Claughton (1906–?). Leo Frobenius's assistant and proponent of his work, Fox facilitated a correspondence between EP and Frobenius in the 1930s (*EPE* 126). Fox wrote the Introduction to Frobenius's *African Genesis* (1937), and his "Frobenius' Paideuma as a Philosophy of Culture" was serialized in the *NEW* (September–October 1936).

Frobenius, Leo (1873–1938). German anthropologist and ethnologist whose work focused on Africa. In research expeditions to Africa between 1904 and the mid-1930s, Frobenius collected a wide range of ethnographic and historical data, cultural objects and materials, paintings, and oral records. Frobenius's seven-volume *Erlebte Erdteile* greatly influenced EP, who first encountered Frobenius's work in the late 1920s. EP often refers to Frobenius in the *Cantos* and *Guide to Kulchur* and makes considerable use of his concepts of *paideuma* (which refers to how culture imprints itself on humans [*EPE* 126] and which EP famously interpreted as "the gristly roots of ideas that are in action" [*GK* 57–8]) and *sagetrieb* (which Hugh Kenner defines in *The Pound Era* as "saying-force" [534]).

Gesell, Silvio (1862–1930). German businessman and economist who spent considerable time in Argentina, Gesell was a devout monetary reformer and advocate of stamped paper money, or "stamp scrip" (in German, *Freigeld*, or *Schwundgeld*). EP was significantly influenced by Gesell's theories. To encourage spending and consumption, currency in Gesell's scheme would have to be stamped at certain time intervals in order to maintain its original value; this was intended to discourage hoarding. This scheme had worked in the Austrian town of Wörgl from 1932 to 1933 until the nation's central bank halted the experiment. EP refers to stamp scrip in Cantos 41, 74, and 78. Gesell's theories are best outlined in his most influential work, *Die Natürliche Wirtschaftsordnung durch Freiland und Freigeld* (1916). Translated into English in 1929 as *The Natural Economic Order*, the book was reprinted in two volumes by Hugo Fack in 1934 and 1936.

Guild Socialism. Social and economic program developed by G.D.H. Cole and S.G. Hobson, influenced by the thought of A.J. Penty, supported by A.R. Orage in the pages of the *New Age*. Guild Socialism rose to prominence earlier than Distributism, with which it is often compared. Orage construed Guild Socialism as a hybrid of syndicalism and socialism: like syndicalism and Distributism, it advocated the formation of guilds and worker control of commerce, agriculture, and industry; but, unlike Distributism, Guild Socialism recommended that guilds share management with the state. Guild Socialism also differed from Distributism in that Guild Socialists sought to integrate guilds into the existing industrial factory system, whereas the Distributists sought to eradicate this system. See Essay 1.

Gurdjieff, George Ivanovitch (1866/72/77?–1949). As biographer James Moore notes, G.I. Gurdjieff's provenance is shrouded in mystery: "Gurdjieff was born in four different countries on three different dates" (Moore 19). Born in Alexandropol, Gurdjieff was educated in Russia and travelled to various parts of Europe, Africa, the Middle East, and Asia in search of "secret" knowledge. Gurdjieff returned to teach in Russia about 1913 but left again during the Russian Revolution. Taking his mystical teachings and spiritual wisdom to the West, Gurdjieff established the Institute for the Harmonious Development of Man in 1922 in Fontainebleau-Avon, south of Paris. His system focused on self-awareness and the attainment of spiritual balance through breathing, meditation, and dance. Considered by many to be occultist and esoteric, Gurdjieff's work continues under his name in London, Paris, and New York. Stanley Nott later wrote and published two books on his experiences with Gurdjieff and Orage: *Teachings of Gurdjieff: A Pupil's Journey* (1961) and *Journey Through This World: The Second Journal of a Pupil* (1969).

Hargrave, John Gordon (1894–1982). British writer and cartoonist, Hargrave was also an inventor, political activist, and leader of the Social Credit Party of Great Britain. In 1920, Hargrave founded the Kindred of the Kibbo Kift out of disillusionment with the ultra-patriotism and militarism of Baden-Powell's Boy Scouts, to which he had belonged. The Kibbo Kift was a movement that focused on woodcraft and the revival of folk traditions in England, known for elaborate rituals and committed to national regeneration and world peace. In the 1930s, Hargrave became leader of the Green Shirts, a militant wing of the Social Credit movement. In the mid-1930s, Hargrave and EP began a correspondence that lasted until 1939, when Hargrave could no longer accept EP's support of fascism and Mussolini (*P/C* 213). EP reviewed Hargrave's novel *Summer Time Ends* in the *NEW* (28 November 1935).

Heap, Jane (1883–1964). American artist, writer, and, with Margaret Anderson, co-editor of the *Little Review* (1914–29). Heap studied with G.I. Gurdjieff in France during the 1920s and 1930s after witnessing a performance in New York of sacred dances by pupils of Gurdjieff and attending an explanatory lecture by A.R. Orage. Heap signed her work in the *Little Review* with the lower-case "jh" (see EP's reference, Letter 89).

Ideogrammic series. Only two numbers of Nott's and Pound's planned Ideogrammic series (sometimes spelled with one "m" in the correspondence) were published (see Appendix 2). The "Ideogramic Series, Edited by Ezra Pound," led off with *The Chinese Written Character as a Medium for Poetry* (March 1936 [5s.]) and was followed by *Ta Hio, The Great Learning* (May 1936 [2s.]), nos. 1 and 2, respectively. The third number in the series was to have been William Carlos Williams's *In the American Grain: Seven Essays*; however, as Gallup notes, "Nott ceased his publishing activities before the book could be printed. Pound's editing of the later numbers in the series was to have been confined to his selecting and securing the manuscripts for inclusion" (160).

Jameson, Margaret Storm (1891–1986). English writer, critic, and political activist, Jameson became a leading member of International PEN (Poets, Essaysts, and Novelists). Her novels include two trilogies about Yorkshire shipbuilders, *The Triumph of Time* (1927–31) and *The Mirror in Darkness* (1934–36). Jameson often contributed to the *NEW* and wrote *The Soul of Man in the Age of Reason* (1935), no. 13 in the Pamphlets on the New Economics series.

Jefferson and/or Mussolini (1935). Written in 1933, this treatise was EP's effort to praise Mussolini and fascist Italy through a comparison between the Italian leader and American founder Thomas Jefferson. Gallup reports that Nott published a special edition (thirty copies) in July 1935 and the standard edition in August 1935. Liveright published the first American edition in January 1936. Superficial differences aside, EP asserted that Jefferson and Mussolini shared a bent for astute political opportunism, an ability to read the needs of their respective lands, an advocacy of government that did not interfere with the rights and freedoms of the individual, and what Pound called, drawing from Dante, the "directio voluntatis" – the will directed towards justice. When Stanley Nott published the book in 1935, a prefatory note by EP noted that "forty publishers" had refused it. As the Pound/Nott correspondence indicates, EP pressed to get the book into print, as he felt it encapsulated much of what he had to convey as an economic and political commentator. See Introduction.

Johnson, Hewlett (1874–1966). A Christian Marxist and outspoken supporter of the Soviet regime, Johnson was Dean of Canterbury Cathedral from 1931 to 1963 and known as the "Red Dean." His pamphlet *Social Credit and the War on Poverty* (1935) was published as no. 6 in the Pamphlets on the New Economics series.

Lansbury, George (1859–1940). British politician, socialist, and Christian pacifist who supported the guild movement. Early in his career, Lansbury had ties first with the British Liberal Party and then with the Marxist Social Democratic Federation, but early in the twentieth century he joined the nascent Labour Party. As of 1910, he served as MP until a conflict with Prime Minister Asquith over women's suffrage, which Lansbury supported, led to his ten-year departure from Parliament; he would return in the early 1920s. During his decade-long hiatus, as of 1912, he helped to found the *Daily Herald*, a populist leftist newspaper; there, as proprietor and then editor and manager, Lansbury worked closely with Will Dyson, Hilaire Belloc, G.D.H. Cole, and H.G. Wells. Lansbury would later serve as leader of the Parliamentary Labour Party from 1932 to 1935.

Larkin, James Crate (1878–1947). Businessman and monetary reformer, Larkin published *From Debt to Prosperity: An Introduction to the Proposals of Social Credit* through the New Economics Group of New York in 1934. John Drummond summarized a series of his articles in the *NEW* (14 February 1935). EP and Larkin corresponded in the mid-1930s. EP mentions him in his American Notes for the *NEW* (24 January 1934) as "president of the Larkin Co. of Buffalo, N.Y., one of America's clearest Social Credit writers" and notes that "the Larkin Co. is one of those which asserted the ancient right of Industrial Companies to issue their own money. This the Larkin Co. did in the form of 'merchandise bonds' ... This money was good money and functioned, until it was outlawed by political intrigue" (*NEW* 6, 15: 310–11).

Laughlin, James (1914–97). American poet and founder of New Directions Books in 1936, Laughlin befriended EP in 1933 when an undergraduate at Harvard University and visited him in Rapallo in 1933 and 1934. At EP's suggestion, Laughlin returned to the United States to begin a career in publishing. Influenced by Pound, Laughlin would become sympathetic to the cause of Social Credit and publish in Gorham Munson's Social Credit–focused journal *New Democracy* in the 1930s. Laughlin coordinated Pound's legal defence when Pound was facing charges of treason in the United States for his broadcasts over Rome Radio during the Second World War (*P/W* 330). Laughlin authored *Pound as Wuz: Essays and Lectures on Ezra Pound* (1987). Pound and Laughlin would engage in a considerable correspondence, which David M. Gordon has edited as *Ezra Pound and James Laughlin: Selected Letters* (1994). New Directions continues to publish EP's works today. See Barnhisel, *James Laughlin, New Directions and the Remaking of Ezra Pound* (2005).

Lavrin, Janko (1887–1986). Slovenian-born journalist, academic, and contributor to the *New Age*, Lavrin joined University College, Nottingham, as a lecturer in 1918, where he became the leading figure in Slavic and Russian studies until his retirement in 1952. Lavrin wrote several studies of Russian and European literatures. Nott published Lavrin's *Aspects of Modernism: From Wilde to Pirandello* (1935) and his wife Nora's *Jugoslav Scenes. Dry Points* (1935).

Leese, Arnold Spencer (1878–1956). Veterinarian known as an expert on camels; British Fascist. A virulent antisemite, Leese founded the Imperial Fascist League in 1928. Members dressed in black shirts and adopted the swastika as an emblem. Leese published numerous books and pamphlets and was imprisoned for six months in 1936 for libelling Jews in the IFL's monthly paper, the *Fascist: The Organ of Racial Fascism* (1929–39). EP and Leese corresponded in the mid-1930s. See Essay 2.

Long, Huey Pierce (1893–1935). Governor of Louisiana (1928–32) and later Democratic senator (1932–35), Long was a radical populist known as "the Kingfish." Long fought for the redistribution of wealth in his "Share Our Wealth" campaign, and he announced his candidacy for the Democratic presidential nomination in August 1935. He was assassinated the following month.

Mairet, Philip (1886–1975). British writer and journalist who assumed principal editorial control of the *NEW* following Orage's death and remained with the paper until it ceased publication in 1949. Mairet was an original member of the Chandos Group. His books include *Aristocracy and the Meaning of Class Rule* (1931); *The Douglas Manual* (1934), which was published by Nott; and *A.R. Orage: A Memoir*

(1936), which was introduced by G.K. Chesterton. Pound corresponded with Mairet during the 1930s.

Mark, Jeffrey (1898–?). British commentator on economics and history. Mark's arguments for monetary reform in *The Modern Idolatry* (1934) are expanded upon in *Analysis of Usury* (1935). R.L. Northridge's review of *The Modern Idolatry* in the *NEW* (24 January 1935) suggests that, while Mark disagrees with Douglas, the book supports Social Credit in principle. Mark is also one of the "monetary heretics" to appear in Montgomery Butchart's anthology *To-Morrow's Money* (see Appendix 2).

Money, Sir Leo George Chiozza (1870–1944). Born in Genoa (as Leone Giorgio Chiozza; name changed in 1903) and knighted in 1915, Money rose to prominence as a British journalist and politician who served as a Liberal MP (1906–10, 1910–18) before migrating to the Labour Party over the issue of nationalization and redistribution of wealth via taxation. He was known for statistical analysis. A supporter of free trade, Money published several books on economics and economic policy, such as *British Trade and the Zollverein Issue (1902), Elements of the Fiscal Problem* (1903), and *Riches and Poverty* (1905). EP and Money corresponded in the late 1930s.

Muir, Edwin (1887–1959). Scottish-born poet, critic, and novelist. Nott published Muir's *Social Credit and the Labour Party* (1935) as no. 15 in the Pamphlets on the New Economics series. In the early 1920s, Muir was a frequent contributor to the *New Age*, where he was assistant to A.R. Orage, and later co-edited the *European Quarterly* (1934–35) with Janko Lavrin.

Munson, Gorham B. (1896–1969). American writer and editor, Munson became involved with Social Credit, largely due to the influence of A.R. Orage, and served as the *NEW*'s representative in New York. In 1933, Munson began editing *New Democracy*. Munson founded the American Social Credit Movement in 1938. EP and Munson corresponded from the late 1920s until about 1940.

Murry, John Middleton (1889–1957). British critic and editor (*Rhythm, Athenaeum, The Adelphi, The New Adelphi*). Murry published widely on Shakespeare, Swift, Keats, Blake, and D.H. Lawrence. Spouse of Katherine Mansfield (1888–1923), who was involved with the Ouspensky-Gurdjieff circle, Murry turned to questions of Marxism and politics in the 1930s, contributing chapters to *Marxism* (1935) and publishing *The Fallacy of Economics* (1932) pamphlet in the Criterion Miscellany series.

National Socialist League. Formed March 1937 out of a schism with the British Union of Fascists, the NSL was a minor British fascist group founded by William Joyce (later known as "Lord Haw Haw" for his radio broadcasts for a Nazi propaganda organization in Britain), John Beckett, and Angus McNab. The NSL was imperialist, pro-German, pro-Nazi, and intensely antisemitic. Although approximately sixty people split with the BUF in 1937 to join Joyce, Beckett, and McNab, by the time of the group's demise in 1939, the membership had diminished to about twenty (Linehan 139).

The *New Age* (1894–1938). Weekly publication (issues from 1907 to 1922 available online through the *Modernist Journals Project*) that, under A.R. Orage's editorship, became one of the most influential periodicals of its time. Renowned for excellence in literary and social criticism, the magazine was the first to champion Major C.H. Douglas's theory of Social Credit. Arthur Brenton took over from Orage as editor in 1922 and remained in that position until the final issue, though the popularity of the *New Age* declined following Orage's departure. The paper merged with the *NEW* in 1939.

New Democracy (New York, 1933–39). "A Review of National Economy and the Arts," *ND* was a Social Credit journal published by the New Economics Group of New York, the organization that handled Nott's Pamphlets on the New Economics series in the United States. Gorham Munson edited *ND* between 1933 and 1939. The periodical went through several changes in frequency and had close ties with *Controversy* (San Francisco) and *Beacon* (Winnipeg).

The *New English Weekly* (1932–49). "A Review of Public Affairs, Literature, and the Arts," the *NEW* was edited by A.R. Orage until his death in 1934, after which time the magazine was edited by Philip Mairet and Albert Newsome, with assistance by other members of the Chandos Group such as Will Dyson and Maurice Reckitt. According to Preda, both T.S. Eliot and EP were invited to join the editorial board, but both declined (Preda, *Ezra Pound's Economic Correspondence*, 134). Orage's wife Jessie assumed control until it ceased publication in 1949. Although EP published about sixty pieces in the paper prior to the Orage memorial issue (15 November 1934), he published more than a hundred more by June 1940, when his last appeared. EP's somewhat irregular column "American Notes" ran from January 1935 until April 1936.

Newsome, Albert (dates unknown). Member of the Chandos Group and an editor of the *NEW* along with Philip Mairet, Newsome wrote sections of the regular Credit Forum under the pseudonym "Pontifex" as well as on drama and cinema under the name "Paul Banks." Newsome published *People versus Bankers* (1931) with C.M. Grieve (Hugh MacDiarmid) under the name Paul Banks. EP corresponded with Newsome in the mid-1930s.

Ogden, Charles Kay (1889–1957). Cambridge-trained psychologist and linguist; founded and edited *Cambridge Magazine* (1912–22); founded and, for a time, served as president of the Cambridge Heretics Society; and, in 1920, helped to found and edit the international journal *Psyche* (1920–52), which focused on psychology. In the late 1920s, Ogden originated BASIC (British American Scientific International Commercial), a language system that reduced English to 850 common words, and he founded the Orthological Institute at Cambridge. Ogden's books include *The Meaning of Meaning* (1923, co-authored with I.A. Richards); *The ABC of Psychology* (1930); *Debabelization* (1931); and *The Basic Words* (1932). EP wrote to Ogden that, with fifty more words, he could make BASIC "into a real licherary and mule-drivin' language ... You watch ole Ez do a basic Canto" (qtd. in Carpenter 505).

Orage, Alfred Richard (1873–1934). Editor of the *New Age* (1907–22) and later the *New English Weekly* (1932–34), Orage wrote on matters economic, social, and political during the 1910s, leaving England for France to study with G.I. Gurdjieff in 1922. After spending time in the United States raising interest in Social Credit and moving in Gurdjieffian circles, Orage returned to London to run the *NEW* until his sudden death on 6 November 1934. Orage gave Social Credit theories a voice in England and, according to Redman, was one of the chief influences on EP's changing view of the public intellectual and of the place of economics in contemporary government and thought. Orage published EP's *Alfred Venison's Poems* in the *NEW* in 1934.

Pamphlets on the New Economics. This pamphlet series published by Stanley Nott focused on Social Credit and consisted of nineteen pamphlets published between 1934 and 1936. Nott's invitation to Pound to contribute to the series inaugurated their correspondence in 1934. See Appendix 2 and Essay 4.

Pellizzi, Camillo (1896–1979). Friend of EP and professor of Italian at University College, London (1920–39). Pellizzi was president of the National Institute of Fascist Culture in Italy (1940–43). He published *Italy* in 1939 and *Oro e lavoro nella nuova economia* in a series sponsored by the National Institute of Fascist Culture. Pellizzi and EP corresponded during the late 1930s and early 1940s.

Por, Odon (1883–?). Hungarian-Italian journalist and economist, Por was a member of the *New Age* circle in London during the First World War. His *Guilds and Co-operatives* and *Fascism in Italy* (the latter an early book defending Mussolini's policies) were translated into English in 1923. A Guild Socialist, Por eventually turned to Social Credit and fascist syndicalism. Por served as propagandist for the fascist regime in Italy and as London correspondent for *Avanti* when Mussolini edited the periodical in Milan. He held a minor position in Mussolini's government (*P/A* 283). In *Ezra Pound and Italian Fascism*, Redman notes Por's influence in convincing EP that Mussolini was likely to implement economic policies akin to those advocated by the Social Credit movement.

Pound, Thaddeus Coleman (1832–1914). Pound's grandfather, Coleman was a lumber baron and railway magnate. Pound often emphasized his issuing paper money to his employees at the Union Lumbering Company of Chippewa Falls, Wisconsin. The legend on the money stated that it would "pay to the bearer on demand ... in merchandise or lumber"' (*Pound/Cummings* 28). T.C. Pound served as Republican assemblyman, speaker of the state assembly, lieutenant governor, and acting governor of Wisconsin. Pound tended to elevate his grandfather into a larger-than-life hero and align his politics with his own (*P/C* 4–5). He is mentioned several times in the *Cantos* (e.g., *Cantos* 21, 22, 97, 99) as a pioneer figure who "'sweat blood/ to put through that railway'" (*Canto* 22).

Read, Sir Herbert (1893–1968). British poet and critic of modern art and literature. With Frank Rutter, he founded the journal *Art and Letters* (1917–20) and contributed to the *New Age* and Eliot's *Criterion*. In the 1930s, he became art critic for the *Listener*, edited the *Burlington Magazine*, and co-organized the London International Surrealist Exhibition in 1936. His books include *Art Now* (1933), *Art and Society* (1937), *Education through Art* (1943), *Modern Painting* (1959), and *Modern Sculpture* (1964). Read contributed no. 12, *Essential Communism* (1935), to the Pamphlets on the New Economics series and, with Denis Saurat, co-edited *Selected Essays and Critical Writings of A.R. Orage*, which Nott also published in 1935. By 1937 Read had declared himself an anarchist. He was knighted for his services to literature in 1953.

Reckitt, Maurice Benington (1888–1980). Writer and Christian sociologist, member of the Christian Socialist League, member and unofficial chair of the Chandos Group, Reckitt contributed to the *New Age* and *G.K.'s Weekly*, on whose editorial board he served, and later the *NEW*, where he assumed an important editorial role (1934–49). A supporter of national guilds, Reckitt became a member of the Distributist League executive (Finlay 45), interested in synthesizing Distributist ideas with those of Social Credit (Corrin 130–1). He edited *Christendom: A Journal of Christian Sociology* from 1933 to 1950. Reckitt also co-authored *The Meaning of National Guilds* (1918) and wrote *Faith and Society* (1932). Reckitt's correspondence with EP is held at the University of Sussex.

Rouse, William Henry Denham (1863–1950). Renowned expert on Greek antiquity, Rouse was headmaster of the Perse School (Cambridge, England) for twenty-six years. Rouse's translation of Homer's *Odyssey* appeared in volumes 7–12 of the *NEW*, and his translation of the *Iliad* appeared in volume 12. Rouse's prose translation of the *Odyssey* (on which EP consulted) appeared in 1937.

Saurat, Denis (1890–1958). Anglo-French writer and contributor to the *New Age*, Saurat wrote on philosophy, psychology, literature, religion, and occultism. With Herbert Read, Saurat co-edited *Selected Essays and Critical Writings of A.R. Orage*, which Nott published in 1935. In 1935, Nott also reprinted Saurat's *The Three Conventions* (1926) and *Blake and Milton* (1926).

Social Credit (1934–39). A self-described "journal of economic democracy," the official organ of the Social Credit Secretariat based in London.

Social Credit: An Impact (1935). One of Pound's two contributions to the Pamphlets on the New Economics series. Written specifically for the series, it appeared as no. 8.

Swabey, Reverend Henry S. (1916–96?). Anglican minister and editor of the Social Credit paper *Voice* (*P/L* 343). Swabey published "From Just Price to Usury" in the *BUF Quarterly* and published *Christianity and World Government* in 1959. The manuscript "The Church of England and Usury" is attributed to Swabey in EP's papers at the Harry Ransom Humanities Research Center, the University of Texas, Austin, and has now been published on-line as *Usury and the Church of England/ Usury and the English Church* (http://historyofusury.blog.co.uk.). Swabey edited EP's unpublished book, "Money and Morals." Information at Yale University's Beinecke Rare Book and Manuscript Library indicates that Nott was considered as a possible publisher for this book as late as 1939.

Ta Hio: The Great Learning. EP's translation of a text by Confucius also known as *Da Xue*. Pound's translation was first published in 1928 as no. 14 in the University of Washington Chap-Book series, edited by Glenn Hughes. According to Mary Paterson Cheadle, EP produced three separate translations of the Confucian text (1928, 1942, 1947) and based his initial translation on a French version by Guillaume Pauthier rather than on a Chinese source (*EPE* 65). The philosophical tract "contains the basis of the Confucian order," both individual and imperial, and advances concepts such as self-discipline, verbal precision, revolution, wholeness, integrity, circulation of goods and money, and the importance of agriculture (66). *Ta Hio* is reprinted by Nott as no. 2 in the Ideogrammic series (1936).

Thomson, Alexander Raven (1899–1955). Principal intellectual and Director of Policy of the British Union of Fascists. In 1939, Thomson became editor of the BUF's weekly organ, *Action*, in which EP published twenty-six pieces between November 1937 and April 1940. Thomson wrote *Civilisation as Divine Superman* (1932) and *The Coming Corporate State* (1938), and he was largely responsible for bringing out EP's *What Is Money For?* (1939) with Greater Britain Publications, which published work by BUF members.

Time and Tide (1920–79). Influential London weekly. Originally left-wing and feminist in outlook, *Time and Tide* gradually became more conservative, but for most of its long run it remained one of the more influential periodicals in Britain. It was founded by Margaret Haig Thomas (Viscountess Rhondda) (1883–1958), British writer, editor, and feminist. Lady Rhondda took over as editor from Helen Archdale in 1926.

Wallop, Gerard Vernon (1898–1984), Viscount Lymington. Ninth earl of Portsmouth, Lymington was a politician, environmentalist, writer, and key figure in several right-leaning movements in Britain. Lymington directed the back-to-the-land organization English Mistery and its successor, English Array, in the 1930s; he also edited the pro-German, antisemitic *New Pioneer* between 1938 and 1940. His books include *Famine in England* (1938) and *Alternative to Death* (1943). He also contributed both to the *Criterion* and to the *NEW*.

Wilson, Robert McNair (1882–1963). British writer on history, biography, medicine, and economics, Wilson was a correspondent for the *London Times* from 1914 to 1942 and corresponded with EP from the mid-1930s to the late 1950s. Many of Wilson's works, such as *Monarchy or Money-Power* (1933); *Promise to Pay* (1934), which EP reviewed in the *Chicago Tribune* (2 April 1934); and *The Defeat of Debt* (1935), argued against the destructive force of money power. Wilson is another of the "monetary heretics" to appear in Montgomery Butchart's anthology *To-Morrow's Money* (Nott 1936).

Woodward, William E. (1874–1950). American historian, biographer, and journalist whom EP admired, Woodward served on several advisory boards and councils during Roosevelt's first term in office. EP and Woodward corresponded during the 1930s. EP quotes Woodward in Canto 86 on Roosevelt, and he published two short pieces on him in the *NEW* in February 1937 (C1391, C1392).

APPENDIX 2: WORKS PUBLISHED BY STANLEY NOTT LTD.

{PNE} = included in the Pamphlets on the New Economics series (see below)

Allen, Edgar Leonard. *Kierkegaard: His Life and Thought.* London: Stanley Nott, 1935. 210 pp.

Bennet, Charles Augustus Ker. Earl of Tankerville. *Poverty Amidst Plenty: A lecture given in Stockholm in May 1934.* London: Stanley Nott, 1934. Pamphlets on the New Economics series, no. 4., 22 pp. {PNE}

– *Poverty amidst Plenty.* London: Stanley Nott, 1934. 403 pp.

Björset, Brynjolf. *Distribute or Destroy! A survey of the world's glut of goods with a description of various proposals and practical experiments for its distribution.* Translated from the Norwegian by I.R. and E.S. de Maré. London: Stanley Nott, 1936. 188 pp.

Butchart, Montgomery. *Money. Selected passages presenting the concepts of money in the English tradition, 1640–1935.* Compiled by M. Butchart. London: Stanley Nott, 1935. 348 pp.

– *To-Morrow's Money. By seven of to-day's leading monetary heretics: F. Stuart Barr (Silvio Gesell), Arthur Kitson, Frederick Soddy, R. McNair Wilson, C.H. Douglas, G.D.H. Cole, and Jeffrey Mark.* Edited, with preface and concluding chapter, by Montgomery Butchart. London: Stanley Nott, 1936. 286 pp.

Cloud, Yvonne [later Yvonne Kapp], ed. *Beside the Seaside: Six Variations.* [Essays on sea-side resorts by various authors. With plates.] London: Stanley Nott, 1934. 264. + xi. pp.

Colbourne, Maurice Dale. *The Sanity of Social Credit.* London: Stanley Nott, 1935. Pamphlets on the New Economics series, no. 11. 32 pp. {PNE}

Cole, George Douglas Howard. *Fifty Propositions about Money and Production.* London: Stanley Nott, 1936. Pamphlets on the New Economics series, no. 18. 32 pp. {PNE}

Confucius. *Ta Hio. The Great Learning.* Newly rendered into the American language by Ezra Pound. London: Stanley Nott, 1936. Ideogramic series, II. 2. 32 pp. (May 1936).

Corke, Helen. *From Scarcity to Plenty. A short course in economic history, from the XVIIth century to the present day.* [Reprinted from "The Schoolmaster."]

London: Stanley Nott, 1935. 2nd ed. Pamphlets on the New Economics series, no. 10. 31 pp. {PNE}

Cumberland, Marten, and Raymond Harrison. *The New Economics*. 2nd ed. London: Stanley Nott, 1936. 119 pp.

Davis, John Irving. *A Beginner's Guide to Wines and Spirits*. With eight illustrations and six maps. London: Stanley Nott, 1934. 93 pp.

Day, Gerald William Langston. *What's Wrong with the World?* (Social Credit for everyman). London: Stanley Nott, 1935. 90 pp.

Dobrée, Bonamy. *An Open Letter to a Professional Man*. London: Stanley Nott, 1935. Pamphlets on the New Economics series, no. 14. 31 pp. {PNE}

Douglas, Clifford Hugh. *The Control and Distribution of Production*. 2nd ed., rev. and enlarged. London: Stanley Nott, 1934. 162 + vii pp.

– *Credit-Power and Democracy: With A Draft Scheme For The Mining Industry*. With a commentary on the included scheme by A.R. Orage. 4th ed., rev. and enlarged. London: Stanley Nott, 1934. 211. + xi pp.

– *The Douglas Manual. Being a recension of passages from the works of Major C.H. Douglas outlining social credit*. Compiled by Philip Mairet. London: Stanley Nott, 1934. 116 pp.

– *Economic Democracy*. 4th ed., revised and enlarged. London: Stanley Nott, 1934. 155 + xi. pp.

– *The Nature of Democracy: Speech made by Major C.H. Douglas at Buxton June 9th 1934 on his return from a tour round the world*. London: Stanley Nott, 1934. Pamphlets on the New Economics series, no. 2. 16 pp. {PNE}

– *The Nature of Democracy*. London: Stanley Nott, 1934. 279 pp.

– *The Use of Money*. London: Stanley Nott, 1934. 30 pp. Pamphlets on the New Economics series, no. 1. {PNE}

– *Warning Democracy*. 2nd ed., enlarged. London: Stanley Nott, 1934. 214 + vii pp.

Dunningham, Brian. *Christian Economics*. London: Stanley Nott, 1936. 89 pp.

Dyson, Will. *Artist Among the Bankers*. London: Stanley Nott, 1933. 244 pp.

Eluard, Paul [pseudonym Eugene Grindel]. *Thorns of Thunder. Selected poems*. Ed. George Reavey. With a drawing by Pablo Picasso. Translated from French by Samuel Beckett [and others]. London: Europa Press and Stanley Nott, 1936. 67 + x pp.

The European Quarterly: A Review of Modern Literature, Art and Life. London: Stanley Nott, 1934–35. One volume. Vol. 1, no. 1 (May 1934)–vol. 1, no. 4 (February 1935). Ed. Edwin Muir and Janko Lavrin.

Fenollosa, Ernest Francisco. *The Chinese Written Character as a Medium for Poetry*. With a foreword and notes by Ezra Pound. London: Stanley Nott, 1936. Ideogramic series, no. 1. 52 pp.

Freeston, Charles Lincoln. *The Roads of Spain. A 5000 miles' journey in the new touring paradise*. 2nd ed. London: Stanley Nott, 1936. 278 pp.

Gibson, Arthur Leslie. *What is this Social Credit?* London: Stanley Nott, 1935. Pamphlets on the New Economics series, no. 17. 31 pp. {PNE}

Gill, Eric. *And Who Wants Peace?* London: Published for the Council of Christian Pacifist Groups by S. Nott, 1937. Pax Pamphlets, No. 1. 12 pp.

Harrison, Raymond. *The Measure of Life. An introduction to the scientific study of astrology.* London: Stanley Nott, 1936. 297 + xix pp.

Henry, Leigh. *The Story of Music.* London: Stanley Nott, 1935. 200 pp.

Hobson, Samuel George. *Functional Socialism.* London: Stanley Nott, 1936. 178 pp.

Holter, E.S. *The A.B.C. of Social Credit.* London: Stanley Nott, 1934. 111 pp.

Hughes, Randolph. *The Republic Arraigned. An indiscreet enquiry into the principles and working of democracy.* London: Stanley Nott, 1936. 30 pp.

Jameson, Margaret Storm. *The Soul of Man in the Age of Leisure.* London: Stanley Nott, 1935. Pamphlets on the New Economics series, no. 13. 30 pp. {PNE}

Johnson, Hewlett. *Social Credit and the War on Poverty.* London: Stanley Nott, 1935. Pamphlets on the New Economics series, no. 6. 31 pp. {PNE}

Johnstone, William. *Creative Art in England: from the Earliest Times to the Present.* London: Stanley Nott, 1936. 276 pp.

Lavrin, Janko. *Aspects of Modernism: from Wilde to Pirandello.* London: Stanley Nott, 1935. 247 pp.

Lavrin, Nora. *Jugoslav Scenes. Dry points.* London: Stanley Nott, 1935. 45 pp.

Longinus, Dionysius Cassius. *A Treatise on the Sublime.* Trans. Frank Granger. London: Stanley Nott, 1935. 114 pp.

M., H.M. *The A + B Theorem.* London: Stanley Nott, 1935. Pamphlets on the New Economics series, No. 16. 35 pp. {PNE}

MacDiarmid, Hugh. *Second Hymn to Lenin, and Other Poems.* London: Stanley Nott, 1935. 77 pp.

– *At the Sign of the Thistle. A collection of essays.* London: Stanley Nott, 1934. 222 pp.

MacNiece, Louis. *Iceland: Lyrics from a Play.* London: Stanley Nott, 1936. 13 pp.

Makarenko, Anton Semenovich. *Road to Life.* Trans. Stephen Garry. London: Stanley Nott, 1936. 287 pp.

Mauduit, George, Viscount de. *Mauduit's Cookery Book. The Vicomte in the Kitchen.* London: Stanley Nott, 1934. 326 pp.

Mauduit, George, Viscount de. *The Vicomte in the Kitchenette.* London: Stanley Nott, 1934. 146 pp.

Muir, Edwin. *Social Credit & the Labour Party: an Appeal.* London: Stanley Nott, 1935. Pamphlets on the New Economics series, no. 15. 28 pp. {PNE}

Orage, Alfred Richard. *Political and Economic Writings. From the New English Weekly, 1932–1934, with a preliminary section from the New Age, 1912.* Arranged by Montgomery Butchart, with the advice of Maurice Colbourne, Hilderic Cousins, Will Dyson, and others. London: Stanley Nott, 1936. 268 pp.

– *Social Credit. Broadcast in the B.B.C. series, "Poverty in Plenty," on November 5th, 1934. And, The Fear of Leisure. An address to the Leisure Society.* London: Stanley Nott, 1935. Pamphlets on the New Economics series, no. 5. 32 pp. {PNE}

– Selected Essays and Critical Writings. Ed. Herbert Read and Denis Saurat. London: Stanley Nott, 1935. 216 pp.

The Social Credit Pamphleteer: By Various Hands, etc. [A reissue in one volume of nos. 1, 4–6, 8, 11–14 and no. 17 of Pamphlets on the New Economics series.] London: Stanley Nott, 1935. 10 pamphlets.

Pound, Ezra. *Jefferson and/or Mussolini.* London: Stanley Nott, 1935. 128 pp.

– Social Credit: an Impact. London: Stanley Nott, 1935. Pamphlets on the New Economics series, no. 8. 31 pp. {PNE}

Read, Sir Herbert Edward. *Essential Communism.* London: Stanley Nott, 1935. Pamphlets on the New Economics series, no. 12. 32 pp. {PNE}

Romanov, Panteleimon Sergeevich (1884–1938). *Diary of a Soviet Marriage.* Translated from the Russian by John Furnivall and Raymond Parmenter, with an introduction by Janko Lavrin. London: Stanley Nott, 1936. 143 pp.

Russell, Hastings William Sackville, Duke of Bedford, Marquis of Tavistock. *Short Papers on Money.* London: Stanley Nott, 1934. Pamphlets on the New Economics series, no. 3. 36 pp. {PNE}

– Short Papers on Money. London: Stanley Nott, 1934. 285 pp.

Saurat, Denis. *Blake and Milton.* London: Stanley Nott, 1935. 159 pp.

– The Three Conventions, etc. London: Stanley Nott, 1935. 155 pp.

Selver, Percy Paul. *A Baker's Dozen of Tin Trumpets, and two others of different metal.* London: Stanley Nott, 1936. 30 pp.

Sequeira, Horace. *The Pageant Rehearsal, and other monologues & duologues for women, etc.* London: Stanley Nott, 1936. 80 pp.

Shakespeare, William. *Gatherings from Shakespeare.* By H. Colborne-Smith. London: Stanley Nott, 1936. 206 pp.

Soames, Jane. *The English Press: Newspapers and News.* Preface by Hilaire Belloc. London: Stanley Nott, 1936. 178 + xi pp.

Solovyev, Vladimir Sergeevich. *Plato.* Translated from the Russian by Richard Gill, with a note on Solovyev by Janko Lavrin and a portrait by Nora Lavrin. London: Stanley Nott, 1935. 83 pp.

Venison, Alfred [Ezra Pound]. *Alfred Venison's Poems: Social credit themes, by the Poet of Titchfield Street.* [Reprinted from the *New English Weekly.*] London: Stanley Nott, 1935. Pamphlets on the New Economics series, no. 9. 32 pp. {PNE}

Vickers, Vincent Cartwright. *Finance in the Melting Pot: Reform or revolution? The petition to His Majesty the King.* London: Stanley Nott, 1936. Pamphlets on the New Economics series, no. 19. 31 pp. {PNE}

Ward, William, ed. *The National Dividend: The Instrument for the Abolition of Poverty.* [By various authors.] Summary and conclusion by Montgomery Butchart, with an epilogue by Philip McDevitt. London: Stanley Nott, 1935. Pamphlets on the New Economics series, no. 7. 48 pp. {PNE}

Wien-Claudi, Franz. *Austrian Theories of Capital, Interest, and the Trade-Cycle.* London: Stanley Nott, 1936. 176 pp.

Wintringham, Thomas Henry. *Mutiny: Being a Survey of Mutinies from Spartacus to Invergordon*. London: Stanley Nott, 1936. 355 pp.

PAMPHLETS ON THE NEW ECONOMICS SERIES

1. Douglas, C.H. *The Use of Money*. London: Stanley Nott, 1934. 30 pp. Appeared with the subtitle "An Address delivered by Major Douglas in St. James' Theatre, Christchurch, New Zealand on Feb. 13th, 1934."
2. – *The Nature of Democracy. Speech made by Major C.H. Douglas at Buxton June 9th 1934 on his return from a tour round the world*. London: Stanley Nott, 1934. 16 pp.
3. Russell, Hastings William Sackville, Duke of Bedford, Marquis of Tavistock. *Short Papers on Money*. London: Stanley Nott, 1934. 36 pp.
4. Bennet, Charles Augustus Ker. Earl of Tankerville. *Poverty Amidst Plenty: A lecture given in Stockholm in May 1934*. London: Stanley Nott, 1934. 22 pp.
5. Orage, A.R. *Social Credit. Broadcast in the B.B.C. series, "Poverty in Plenty," on November 5th, 1934. And, The Fear of Leisure. An address to the Leisure Society*. London: Stanley Nott, 1935. 32 pp.
6. Johnson, Hewlett. *Social Credit and the War on Poverty*. London: Stanley Nott, 1935. 31 pp.
7. Ward, William, ed. *The National Dividend: The Instrument for the Abolition of Poverty*. [By various authors.] Summary and conclusion by Montgomery Butchart, and an epilogue by Philip McDevitt. London: Stanley Nott, 1935. 48 pp.
8. Pound, Ezra. *Social Credit: an Impact*. London: Stanley Nott, 1935. 31 pp.
9. Venison, Alfred [Ezra Pound]. *Alfred Venison's Poems: Social credit themes, by the Poet of Titchfield Street*. [Reprinted from "The New English Weekly."] London: Stanley Nott, 1935. 32 pp.
10. Corke, Helen. *From Scarcity to Plenty. A short course in economic history, from the XVIIth century to the present day*. [Reprinted from "The Schoolmaster."] London: Stanley Nott, 1935. 2nd Edition. 31 pp.
11. Colbourne, Maurice Dale. *The Sanity of Social Credit*. London: Stanley Nott, 1935. 32 pp.
12. Read, Sir Herbert Edward. *Essential Communism*. London: Stanley Nott, 1935. pp. 32.
13. Jameson, Margaret Storm. *The Soul of Man in the Age of Leisure*. London: Stanley Nott, 1935. 30 pp.
14. Dobrée, Bonamy. *An Open Letter to a Professional Man*. London: Stanley Nott, 1935. 31 pp.
15. Muir, Edwin. *Social Credit & the Labour Party: an Appeal*. London: Stanley Nott, 1935. 28 pp.
16. M., H.M. *The A + B Theorem*. London: Stanley Nott, 1935. 35 pp.

17. Gibson, Arthur Leslie. *What is this Social Credit?* London: Stanley Nott, 1935. 31 pp.
18. Cole, George Douglas Howard. *Fifty Propositions about Money and Production.* London: Stanley Nott, 1936. 32 pp.
19. Vickers, Vincent Cartwright. *Finance in the Melting Pot. Reform or revolution? The petition to His Majesty the King.* London: Stanley Nott, 1936. 31 pp.

INTRODUCTION

1 For detailed commentary on Pound's interest in Jeffersonian thought, see Marsh, *Money and Modernity*.
2 For an extensive account of Joyce's position, see Farndale, *Haw-Haw*.
3 As Redman, *Italian Fascism*, 89–90, notes, during the 1930s, through his correspondence with a cluster of American senators and congressmen – such as Congressman Tinkham of Massachusetts, Senator Borah of Idaho, and Senator Cutting of New Mexico – Pound was led to the mistaken belief that he was exercising considerable influence in American political affairs. That he was convinced of this also indicates his desire to wield such influence. Pound was disabused of this illusion when he visited Washington, DC, in 1939. See also Barnhisel's account of the disappointments of Pound's 1939 visit (Barnhisel, *James Laughlin*, 76–7).
4 Barnhisel, *James Laughlin*, points out that publisher Laughlin played a crucial role in rehabilitating Pound's reputation after the Second World War, such that, by the 1960s and 1970s, "scholars published more on Ezra Pound than on any other modernist writer" (2). Laughlin "managed and directed the transformation of Pound's public image and literary reputation in America from the mid-1930s, when he became known as a profascist, anti-Semitic crank, to the close of the 1960s, when for a brief time he was seen as the most important and accomplished writer of the modernist period. Laughlin was the most important force in the shaping of Pound's reputation in America" (3).
5 See, for instance, Chace, *Political Identities*; Jameson, *Fables of Aggression*; Morrison, *Poetics of Fascism*; Cullingford, *Yeats, Ireland, and Fascism*; and Sherry, *Ezra Pound*.
6 The approach of this edition emerges from a commitment to Geertzian "thick description" of instances of interwar support of fascism, along the lines advocated by historian of fascism George Mosse and modernist scholar Lawrence Rainey. For bringing this position into focus, I am indebted to Griffin, "Primacy of Culture."
7 Jameson, *Fables of Aggression*, 120, notes Pound's "manifestly hero-worshipping celebrations of Mussolini."

8 As Pound remarked to Gorham Munson in 1934, "I don't think one can settle down to vie licheraires UNTIL the econ/mess is cleared up" (Harry Ransom Humanities Research Center, the University of Texas at Austin, Pound Collection, series 2, box 7, folder 14; Postcard 26 February 1934).

9 For commentary on Pound's dwindling public and the suspicion of his work on economics, see Redman, *Italian Fascism,* chap 6; and Whittier-Ferguson, *Framing Pieces,* chap. 4, esp. 133–41.

10 As Surette, *Purgatory,* 10, notes, "From 1931 to 1945 his poetry took a back seat to his activities as an economic reformer and propagandist for the corporate state."

11 This appears in Pound's review of *Credit Power and Democracy,* sometimes attributed to both C.H. Douglas and A.R. Orage, *Contact* 4 (1921): 1. Here Pound also observes, indicating the principled reluctance with which he enters the economic arena at this point:

> Don't imagine that I think economics Interesting – not as Botticelli or Picasso is interesting. But at present they, as the reality under political camouflage, are interesting as a gun muzzle aimed at one's own head is "interesting," when one can hardly see the face of the gun holder and is wholly uncertain as to his temperament and intention.

A similar statement from Pound appears in "Regional xvii," *New Age,* 13 November 1919, 32. Here, Pound critiques the "symbolist error of detachment"; while the "man of letters," he says, need not "'go down into the forum' ... or take up a detailed answer to all the editorials in the Press," he must nonetheless "have some concern for public affairs."

12 See Redman, *Italian Fascism,* 84. For him, the claims of Pound's *ABC of Reading* (1934), which evolve out of "How to Read," 1929, mark the volta.

13 In "Murder By Capital" (1933), Pound recognizes his own drastic change in direction by posing the question: "What drives, or what can drive a man interested almost exclusively in the arts into social theory or into a study of the 'gross material aspects' viledicet economic aspects of the present?" He goes on to explain a focus on economics as the responsibility of any "thoughtful man" (*SP* 228). As he would put it in 1936, "A man who is too stubborn or silly to learn economics IN OUR time has no moral value whatsod/never." (qtd. Redman, *Italian Fascism,* 172).

14 The pamphlets published through Nott were *Social Credit: An Impact* (1935) and *Alfred Venison's Poems* (1935) (Gallup A39 and A40). *Ta Hio,* published through Nott in 1936, had also appeared in an American edition through the University of Washington Bookstore in 1928 (Gallup A28); *The Chinese Written Character as a Medium for Poetry* had appeared previously as part of *Instigations* (New York: Boni and Liveright, 1920) (Gallup A18).

15 Editions of Pound's letters upon which this research has drawn include *Pound/ Lewis,* ed. Timothy Materer; *Pound/Williams,* ed. Hugh Witemeyer; *Pound/Zukofsky,* ed. Barry Ahearn; *Ezra Pound and Senator Bronson Cutting: A Political Correspondence,* ed. E.P. Walkiewicz and Hugh Witemeyer; *Ezra Pound and James Laugh-*

lin, ed. David Gordon; *Ezra and Dorothy Pound: Letters in Captivity, 1945–46*, eds. Robert Spoo and Omar Pound; and *"I Cease Not to Yowl": Ezra Pound's letter to Olivia Rossetti Agresti*, eds. Demetres P. Tryphonopoulos and Leon Surette. The last two especially have provided models for the editorial work of this edition.

16 Where Casillo, *Genealogy of Demons*, 13–15, characterizes Pound's antisemitism as "not only economic" but also "essentialist, racial, and biological," Surette, in *Purgatory* 240, describes it as chiefly economically based. Evidence from the Pound/Nott correspondence suggests that it is both: that what begins as economically based antisemitism evolves during the 1930s into racially based antisemitism, in part as a result of Pound's engagement with racist antisemites such as Leese.

17 Whereas Preda, *Ezra Pound's Economic Correspondence*, 4, argues that Pound's relationship with Social Crediters in the 1930s was "not satisfactory at all" because his attempts at a synthesis between Douglasite and Gesellite thought deflected so many, I claim that this bent of Pound's solidified ties with certain Social Crediters in the New Age circle such as Nott, who were receptive to such combinatory efforts.

18 As Redman, *Italian Fascism*, 98, notes, as Pound reckoned with doubt about both his abilities in these new realms and his capacity to exert an impact, he "needed to be convinced of the success of his efforts." I argue that Pound's extensive work with Nott during the 1930s contributed significantly to convincing him of this. Apt for capturing Nott's role with respect to Pound's work and thought is Badenhausen's sensitive description of Martin Browne's relationship to T.S. Eliot, which he characterizes as collaborative (*T.S. Eliot* 152). Browne, he notes, "played the key role of sensitive auditor and responder, giving Eliot a specific audience for which to write and from whom he could expect significant practical feedback ... Browne positions himself beyond the edges of the text and his collaboration is most often centered upon issues other than the language of the drama. As a result, Browne's assistance rarely appears ... for all to see, but tends to surface instead in verbal support more difficult to reconstruct."

19 The publication in question was probably not the "first" item in Nott's Pamphlets on the New Economics series – C.H. Douglas's *The Use of Money* – but, rather, Pound's own "first" contribution to the series, *Social Credit: An Impact* (1935). This can be inferred from the fact that, in this letter, the book to which Pound refers is *Jefferson and/or Mussolini*, which would have little to do with Douglas's text but a great deal to do with *Social Credit*, which was published in April 1935, the month in which this letter was written.

20 Pound himself recognized that his notoriety as a renegade might at points jeopardize the stability of the firm, and accordingly he wished not to harm Nott's enterprise: "I sure do NOT want to bust the firm of S/N in its promising egg ... Sales resist[a]nce to ME is supposed to be diminishing, but FAR from non-extant" (Letter 14). At the same time, however, he believed that he could benefit the firm if he were able successfully and credibly to change shape: "sooner I get a grand reputation as a kneeconymist, the better fer the firm of NOTT" (Letter 30).

21 One major factor encouraging Nott's receptivity to Pound was the good opinion of Nott's mentor and intimate friend, A.R. Orage, Pound's close associate. However, Nott also appears to have formed an independent admiration for Pound's energy, drive, and irreverence. This independence is evidenced particularly by Nott's hospitality to Pound's writing on Social Credit, which Orage, though an ardent Social Crediter, generally sought to discourage, believing Pound better suited to commentary on aesthetics than on work on economics and capable of making better contributions in poetry than in prose. See Surette, *Purgatory*, 52.

22 This statement appears in a review of *Jefferson and/or Mussolini* 16 (August–September 1935): 18–20, by a commentator identified only as "A. M."

23 Williams's favourable review of *J/M* appeared in *New Democracy*, 15 October 1935, 61–2. Williams lauds Pound's comparative approach as a "legitimate method of thought" and suggests that, especially given the way that, in his reading, the communist emphasis on action is impeding the free play of thought in the United States, Pound's book is welcome because of its ability to spur mental activity: "There is room for such work as this by Ezra Pound – plenty of room in America ... Pound has in *Jefferson and/or Mussolini* written a good and extremely useful book." Writing in *New Democracy*, an American periodical whose purpose was to promulgate the ideas of Social Credit, Williams also praises Pound's emphasis on the need to respond to current crises from the "economic angle" and celebrates Pound's Social Credit–minded recognition of the need for wide and equitable distribution of credit to solve current problems before the "widely-touted professional economists" have realized it. This review appears the fall following the spring in which, in a letter of 25 March 1935, Williams criticizes Pound for asserting himself as an expert on economics when he has little experience in this realm (*P/W* 171). This strengthens the impression of Williams's review as a genuinely supportive response to the book.

24 As Pound notes in *Guide to Kulchur*, 99, "Real knowledge goes into natural man in titbits. A scrap here, a scrap there, always pertinent."

25 I am indebted to Lindberg, *Reading Pound Reading*, for "unsystematic" as a descriptor of Pound's rhetoric.

26 See review, *New Democracy*, 15 October 1935. Williams's advocacy of writing, such as poetry, that proceeds according to principles other than those of reason and logic encouraged by the domains of "Science and Philosophy" is captured in his notes of 1928–30, published posthumously as Williams, *Embodiment of Knowledge*.

27 As Surette, *Purgatory*, 153, notes: "[Pound] seems to have been incapable of seeing how disjointed and cryptic his prose frequently appeared to others."

28 *Jefferson and/or Mussolini* was published the next year by Liveright in New York. It was the recommendation of well-reputed American historian W.E. Woodward, a correspondent of Pound's, that enabled the publication.

29 For commentary on the sympathy of a significant contingent of American liberals of the time for Mussolini, see John P. Diggins, "Flirtation with Fascism." Part of

Mussolini's significant popularity in the United States of the 1920s, Diggins explains, was attributable to the way that a "middle-class, property-conscious nation, confronted by the towering antithetical figures of Lenin and Mussolini, would naturally turn to the charismatic Italian who paraded as the savior of capitalism." Moreover, a "nation of churchgoers, faced with a crisis in moral values, would understandably respond to the image of Mussolini as the redeemer who turned back the tide of materialism and anticlericalism in Italy. And a nationalistic people, reacting to Wilsonian internationalism, could readily applaud Mussolini's scorn for the League of Nations and praise the Fascist virtue of patriotism" (487). Beyond this, however, Diggins goes on to note that Mussolini received praise from such a diversity of American communities as to "defy ideological analysis" and attest to the use of Mussolini as a projection screen for the desires of a bewildering array of different constituencies. This, in turn, points to how Italian Fascism's doctrinal ambiguity left it susceptible to supportive appropriation by observers of many different perspectives and political stripes: the business set lauded Mussolini's rejection of Bolshevism; Southern Agrarians celebrated Mussolini's perceived resistance to modern technologies; philosopher George Santayana read Mussolini as the champion of hierarchy, order, and the rule of the aristocracy. Diggins focuses on how some liberals of the time supported Mussolini on the basis of perceived affinities between Il Duce's approach and the American pragmatic tradition associated with figures such as William James and John Dewey.

30 For commentary on the favourable, if superficial, press that Mussolini received among conservative British newspapers between the period of the March on Rome and the year before the invasion of Abyssinia, see Bosworth, "British Press." Pound notes of Italian fascism in Letter 10, "Brit. Tories like it."

31 As Nott comments appreciatively in response to Pound's pamphlet, *Social Credit: An Impact*, which was written for the Pamphlets on the New Economics series: "It's refreshing to have passion in economics. So many of the SC's lack *passion*. Its not good form in England—except at an anti-vivesectionist meeting" (Letter 9).

32 See Redman, *Italian Fascism*, chap. 1. In Redman, "Ezra Pound and American Populism," Redman argues that Pound's formative years in Hailey, Idaho, where his father served as registrar for the Federal Land Office, put him in early contact with American populist discourse about money and that this paved the way for his later economic interests. The more substantive and immediately affecting and relevant "education," however, derived from Pound's work with Orage and the *New Age*.

33 See Nott, *Further Teachings of Gurdjieff*, 29, 37, 43, 51.

34 Redman does not go so far as to explicitly assert that Orage was a cause of Pound's shift to work with economics, but the timing certainly suggests this.

35 This was likely facilitated in part through his long-standing connection with T.S. Eliot, who had become an influential editor at Faber and Faber (see *P/W* 134) and who was also interested in Social Credit. For an account of Eliot's links to Social Credit, see Bradshaw, "T.S. Eliot and the Major."

36 The typographic and lexical mischief here encodes simultaneously both his desire to establish legitimacy and his effort to remain apart from the economic establishment per se.

37 By 1939, Pound was ready to bestow on himself the title of "Poeta Economista" (Redman, *Italian Fascism*, 186); but during the years before this, his confidence in his status was not so settled.

38 As Patricia Cockram notes, "To his grandson Ezra, Thaddeus was a model of the American pioneer spirit and a warrior in the struggle against corruption and usury" (*EPE* 240). T.C. Pound borrowed against the script that he had issued to establish a railway company, which failed against the competition of the more powerful Northern Pacific line.

39 *The Chinese Written Character as a Medium for Poetry* (1936) (Pound's first separate edition of Ernest Fenollosa's work, which had originally been published as part of Pound's *Instigations* [1920]) and a re-issue of Pound's *Ta Hio* (Pound's translation of the first of the Chinese Four Books) became the first two and, ultimately, the only texts that Nott published under the aegis of this series.

40 The plan anticipates those Pound would later draw up with more pointed didacticism in the 1950s, when he began a phase of advocating the development of textbooks for adequate cultural education. See Hickman, "Pamphlets and Blue China."

41 Pound mocks such experts in this vein through his send up in Canto 22 of "Mr. Bukos," an "orthodox/Economist," standing for John Maynard Keynes, whose views Pound despised. In this canto, Bukos can make no good sense of the high cost of living, attributing it to "lack of labour" when, says the canto's more perceptive narrator, there are plainly "two millions of men out of work" (*C* 101–2).

42 Pound clearly favoured economists working outside of orthodox academic circles. In "The Individual in His Milieu," devoted to praising Silvio Gesell, he commented that "Gesell was right in thanking his destiny that he had begun his study of money unclogged by university training" (*SP* 273).

43 Gorham Munson, likewise a Social Crediter and, through Orage, a devotee of Gurdjieff, would offer space for Pound's economic writing in his short-lived American periodical *New Democracy*; however, Pound published fewer articles for *New Democracy* than he did for the *New English Weekly*. Moreover, while he supported the efforts of the *New English Weekly*, Pound considered *New Democracy* "pale and ineffectual" (Preda, "Social Credit in America," 218).

44 Flory, *American Ezra Pound*, credits Pound with a distinctive "American jeremiac" perspective born out of the American Puritan heritage, kindred to that of such leading nineteenth-century American intellectuals and artists as Emerson, Thoreau, Whitman, and Melville. For her theorization of this phenomenon, Flory draws on the work of Sacvan Bercovitch, whose *The American Jeremiad* "shows how the jeremiad of the Puritans, which castigated so that it might hasten the inevitable progress of American society toward its predestined ideal state, established ways

of thinking which far outlasted the influence of the Puritan church and decisively shaped middle-class thinking about American society" (5).

45 See Hickman, "To Facilitate the Traffic."

46 For sustained praise from Pound of the heroic efforts of such little magazines and similar ventures, see Pound, "Small Magazines."

47 The demographics of the readership of Stanley Nott's publications are difficult to ascertain, but it was likely composed of subsets of those reading Social Credit journals such as the *New English Weekly* in England and *New Democracy* in the United States, both of which advertised Nott's publications. According to Finlay, Social Crediters were a group of largely middle-class reformers, many of them intellectuals, of varying political stripes who sought to revise capitalism away from its contemporary laissez-faire form (which, as Social Credit saw it, was dominated by international finance) so as to increase purchasing power for consumers. They welcomed Social Credit as offering a third political way that could avoid what they perceived as the dangers of both liberal democracy and statist socialism.

ESSAY I

1 See Surette, *Purgatory*, 13; Redman, *Italian Fascism*, 51.

2 To counter the general view that Pound's work in economics was initially spurred by the meeting with Douglas, Kadlec points to the influence exerted on Pound by the work of economic reformer Arthur Kitson, whose work Pound was reading in 1913 in the pages of the *New Freewoman*, as well as the exchanges about economics with Dora Marsden, editor of the *New Freewoman*, in the years just before the outbreak of the Great War. As Kadlec notes: "Despite the consensus among Pound scholars that the poet's introduction to economics did not take place until the end of World War I, it was at this pre-war moment, [through] this body of pre-war writings, that radical economic theory began to shape modern poetry" (58). While Kadlec's archival information is persuasive, I would differentiate between the way Pound responded to economic thought before the First World War (i.e., with some attention) and the way he responded upon meeting Douglas (with enthusiasm verging on zeal) and, thus, still mark the most significant point for Pound's turn to economics as 1918.

3 Surette credits Massimo Baciagalupo, Robert Casillo, William Chace, and John Lauber with such views (*Purgatory* 37).

4 See Finlay; Surette; Redman; Desai.

5 In Hutchinson and Burkitt, "An Economic Silence," 321, the authors refer to the "alternative economics" of C.H. Douglas and A.R. Orage.

6 Contemporary commentators such as Frances Hutchinson and Brian Burkitt, engaged in a socialist feminist critique of classical economics, suggest that such movements as Social Credit were offering important ideas from which today's

economists would do well to learn: "In view of the persistent failure of neoclassical economics to incorporate environmental values and forms of work undertaken by women, the Douglas/*New Age* texts offer a framework for a sustainable economics of socialism" (2). See Hutchinson and Burkitt, *Political Economy of Social Credit*.

7 For further biographical detail on Douglas, see Hughes. Even Hughes acknowledges, however, that, because of Douglas's characteristic reticence about divulging information about his private life, material on him remains scant.

8 See Gallup C555, C620a, and C622: "Economic Democracy," *Little Review* 6, 2 (1920): 39–42; "Ouvrages recues," *Action* (Paris) I.7 (1921): 56 (on *Credit Power and Democracy*); and Rev. of *Credit Power and Democracy, Contact* (New York) 4 (1921): 1. Pound reminisces about his writing on economics from this period in Letter 106.

9 See, for instance, the review in the *Daily Telegraph*, 26 August 1936, of Philip Mairet's *A.R. Orage: A Memoir* (1936), which suggests that Orage's "versatility of enthusiasm misled many people into the conclusion that he possessed a volatile, and, as such, a superficial mind." The review is taped into Pound's copy of Orage's pamphlet, *Social Credit. Broadcast in the B.B.C. series, "Poverty in Plenty" ... and The Fear of Leisure. An address to the Leisure Society* (London: Stanley Nott, 1935), Pamphlets on the New Economics series, no. 5, housed at the Harry Ransom Humanities Research Library, the University of Texas at Austin.

10 Marsden's the *New Freewoman*, later renamed the *Egoist*, weighed in on the "economic problem," as Marsden put it (Kadlec 55), through both her own commentaries and the work of Arthur Kitson, who wrote a series for the journal. Marsden regarded her journal as advancing a critique of capitalism.

11 Accordingly, much commentary on the *New Age* emphasizes the challenge of categorizing the journal, given the diversity of topics and political perspectives for which it provided a forum. See, for instance, Robert Scholes's remarks in his introduction to the *New Age* on-line in the *Modernist Journals Project* (available at http://dl.lib.brown.edu/mjp/), which features the *New Age* as one of the most influential journals of the modernist period. Finlay, writing in 1972, likewise contends that the *New Age* was "hard to categorize" (83) and laments the lack of scholarly attention accorded it. Work such as that of Ann Ardis and that of the *Modernist Journals Project* have gone a significant way towards redressing the "neglect" Finlay observes. While the journal's circulation spiked to more than 23,000 during 1908, when a controversy about socialist independent political candidate Victor Grayson erupted in England and the *New Age* backed him (Finlay 64, 68), generally, while the figures were kept secret, its circulation has been estimated to have been much lower, often running less than three thousand (Martin 10). By the time the journal was disseminating the ideas of Social Credit, only 2,250 copies were printed weekly (Finlay 64).

12 Contributors to the *New Age* included G.B. Shaw, Cecil Chesterton, G.D.H. Cole, Havelock Ellis, T.E. Hulme, Wyndham Lewis, Katherine Mansfield, J.M. Murray, Ezra Pound, Herbert Read, Walter Sickert, and J.C. Squire.

13 Ardis, while taking issue with the failure to recognize one kind of diversity in the pages of the *New Age*, overlooks another: deploring the recent habit of characterizing the *New Age* as "modernist" at the expense of recognizing its anti-modernist elements, she nonetheless characterizes it as an organ devoted to the promulgation of Guild Socialism, which does an injustice to the other points of view and movements represented in its pages (see Ardis chap. 5).

14 The rightist reformers of this circle followed Ruskin, Carlyle, and Morris; were often Catholic; advocated rights of individuals over rights of the collective; sought to protect private property; and tended to be anti-democratic.

15 According to Philip Mairet, later a close associate of Orage's, only one other editor in London besides Orage, Austin Harrison of the *English Review*, welcomed Douglas at first (Mairet 74).

16 For this line of thought, I am indebted to the work of Anurag Jain, whose Master's research paper, "The Toys of Desperation: Ezra Pound's Remembrance and Vengeance for the Death of Gaudier-Brzeska" (McGill University, 2004), traces the effects of Pound's grief about Gaudier-Brzeska's death on his later thought. I am persuaded by Jain's work that Gaudier-Brzeska served a role in Pound's imagination comparable to that which Jean Verdenal played in T.S. Eliot's.

17 For a discussion of Pound's bent for transforming the subjective and personal into the objective, as expressed in his early commitment to the dramatic monologue, see Grieve, *Ezra Pound's Early Poetry and Poetics*.

18 See Poggioli, *Theory of the Avant-Garde*, for an elaboration of the oppositional stance characteristic of the avant-garde figures of the late nineteenth and early twentieth centuries.

19 See Redman, *Italian Fascism*, 70; Surette, *Purgatory*, 58.

20 Keynes: "Since the war there has been a spate of heretical theories of underconsumption, of which those of Major Douglas are the most famous. The strength of Major Douglas's advocacy has, of course, largely depended on orthodoxy having no valid reply to much of his destructive criticism ... Major Douglas is entitled to claim, as against some of his orthodox adversaries, that he at least has not been wholly oblivious of the outstanding problem of our economic system. Yet he has scarcely established an equal claim to rank – a private, perhaps, but not a major in the brave army of heretics – with Mandeville, Malthus, Gesell and Hobson" (370–1).

21 For further information on the rise of Social Credit in Alberta, see Hesketh, *Major Douglas and Alberta Social Credit*.

22 An 11 June 1954 letter to Pound biographer Noel Stock, located among the Ezra Pound Papers at the Harry Ransom Humanities Research Center, the University of Texas at Austin, issues from the government of the Province of Alberta, Department of Economic Affairs, evidently in reply to a query from Stock about what Canadian constitutional barriers prevented Alberta from carrying out its Social Credit plans. The representative from the Department of Economic Affairs admits

that Alberta's hands had been tied, as had been the hands of its neighbouring province, British Columbia, which had likewise sought to put Social Credit measures into effect (series 2, box 11, folder 7). For a detailed account of how Aberhart's efforts were thwarted by the Canadian federal government, see Hesketh, *Major Douglas and Alberta Social Credit*, chap. 9. Countering interpretations of Albertan Social Credit that read it as having diverged from Douglas's model, Hesketh maintains that in fact it was founded in Douglas's ideas. The Canadian official writing the letter to Noel Stock seeks, defensively, to do likewise and to assert complete identity between Social Credit in Alberta and Douglas's Social Credit.

23 See Hesketh, chap. 3, "The Popular Appeal of Alberta Social Credit."

24 For additional discussion of the relationship between Distributism and Social Credit, see Stone, *Responses to Nazism in Britain*, 122–32.

25 For a rich account of the development of Distributism, see Corrin, *G.K. Chesterton and Hilaire Belloc*.

26 The events of the Russian Revolution in fact revealed disagreements within Guild Socialism regarding how much control the state should exert – that is, regarding how "socialist" it actually was. Accordingly, Guild Socialists divided on what attitude to adopt towards the revolution, and this split weakened movement (Finlay 81–3). In this conflict, those on the political right among the Guild Socialists tended to side with the anti-statist Distributists, while those on the left channelled their efforts into the program of Social Credit. In general, when the Guild Socialist movement foundered on the "rocks of communism" (Finlay 120) and many former adherents sought alternatives, Social Credit, strongly recommended by Orage, seemed to offer a promising route into a new phase. The Distributists, meanwhile, offered the chance in the early 1920s to adopt the Social Credit program (some of their members, such as Maurice Reckitt, were staunch advocates of Social Credit), ultimately voted to reject it because, in their view, Social Credit would "require a massive bureaucracy and too much state intervention in economic affairs" (Corrin 135).

27 Addressing the movement in England, James Webb places Social Credit among what he terms an "idealistic Underground," a collection of interwar British reform movements emerging from a desire for cultural healing and improvement. He interprets their common premise as holding that "something was drastically wrong with society," and he reads them as sharing a desire for a "Garden of Eden" (Webb 135). His taxonomy implicitly characterizes Social Credit as idealistic; concerned with spiritual health; and, ironically, despite its focus on economics, anti-materialist.

28 It thus misrepresents Social Credit to call it, as Surette does, merely a "technologized version of Belloc's distributism" (*Purgatory* 29). The Distributists were significantly more wary of the state than were either the Social Crediters or the Guild Socialists.

29 Webb's account places Social Credit among such developments as the Woodcraft movement, John Hargrave's Kibbo Kift movement, and the many back-to-the-land

efforts that were emerging around England at the time and that propagated a blend of what was popularly and jocularly termed "Muck and Mysticism" (Webb 103).

30 Douglas's scheme, of course, took into consideration neither the fact that those earning an "A" in one factory might be able to pay for the goods from another nor the fact that the "B" payments would make for purchasing power for some individuals. But these were among many counter-arguments to the "A + B Theorem" that fell on deaf ears among the converted.

31 As Surette notes, after 1931, "*The Cantos* began to serve Pound's economic and political agenda rather than merely being informed by it" (*Purgatory* 2). That Pound featured Douglas's theorem in his Canto, and published it through Orage in the *NEW*, indicates both his keen commitment to these ideas at the time and a shift in his strategies. In the Pound/Nott correspondence, Pound indicates this new standpoint, one that licenses using his literature in the service of economic and political commentary as well as his concomitant preference that his poetry be evaluated by standards from the fields of economics or history:

> Of course my damn CANTOS are a store house of ammunition. I
> dunno when people are going to begin to realise this ....WD/much
> rather have historians or economists comment of Cantos , esp.
> 31/41 than the snoops of bloosmbuggy letteratets... (Letter 3)

32 See Douglas, *Social Credit*, 146–7.

33 As Surette (*Purgatory* 236–7) notes, by the 1940s Pound was recommending the *Protocols*, which he had been sent by Arthur Kitson in the 1930s, to his correspondent Odon Por.

34 One of the most notorious and influential promulgators of conspiracy theory of the time was Nesta Webster, member of the British Fascist organization known as the British Fascisti and author of several books on how secret societies of Jews, in alliance with other groups, were exerting concealed influence over the workings of world society and were responsible for "all the ills of the modern world, from the threats of the British Empire through to the nudity movement" (Thurlow, *Fascism in Britain*, 58). Webster's work was, like Douglas's, deeply informed by the *Protocols*.

35 On Manning's effort, see Hesketh, chap 12, "Social Credit in the Postwar Era."

36 Another factor rendering Albertan Social Credit susceptible to the line of antisemitic thought associated with Social Credit's underlying logic was the form of Christianity prevalent among supporters of Aberhart, who was himself an evangelical preacher. This style of populist Christianity, much like the populism to which Pound would have been exposed at any early age, emphasized evicting the money-changers from the Temple (Hesketh chap 2, esp. 41–55). This conceptual pattern created yet another conduit for the spread of antisemitism within the system of the Albertan variety of Social Credit.

37 On Pound's relationship to American Populism, though to its economic rather than religious thought, see Redman, "Ezra Pound and American Populism." Redman usefully points to other sources on the roots of Pound's thought in Amer-

ican Populism: Ferkiss, "Ezra Pound and American Fascism"; and Flory, *American Ezra Pound*. In the third volume in his Age of Roosevelt series, Arthur M. Schlesinger dismissively refers to Pound as "springing" from a line of "monetary cranks," his grandfather, Wisconsin Congressman Thaddeus Coleman, being a monetary reformer who issued his own scrip when head of the Chippewa Lumbering Company, and his father being an employee for the US Mint who harboured "monetary delusions" (Schlesinger 72). While I would read Pound's lineage as more maverick than "crank," all this certainly indicates a familial context in which there was much talk of monetary reform.

38 Pound was originally sent the Pelley article by poet Louis Zukofsky, who expected him to recognize the absurdity of it, only to find that Pound was persuaded by its arguments (Surette, *Purgatory*, 242; *P/Z* 158–9). William Dudley Pelley was founder of the antisemitic Silvershirt Legion, an American fascist organization (Preda, *Ezra Pound's Economic Correspondence*, 278).

39 Richard Thurlow deems Webster the "grand dame of British conspiracy theory" (see Thurlow, *Fascism in Britain*, 57–61. Thurlow notes elsewhere that, in research on British fascist ideology, "the most glaring gap is a serious consideration of the ideas and influence of conspiracy theorist Nesta Webster" (Lunn and Thurlow, *British Fascism*, 16). As Surette notes, Pound also had in his library a copy of one of Nesta Webster's other books, *World Revolution: The Plot against Civilization*, which had also originally been Drummond's copy (Surette, *Purgatory*, 246).

40 Drummond worked closely with Pound in Rapallo as the latter was writing *Guide to Kulchur* between February 1937 and January 1938. And, as thanks in a note in GK indicate, it was Drummond who helped to proof GK and to develop its index (GK 379). Surette contends that work with Drummond played a crucial role in Pound's pronounced move after 1934 into antisemitism (*Purgatory* 246).

41 On 20 August 1934, Leigh Vaughan-Henry, an associate of Pound's from *New Age* days who was involved in the British Union of Fascists, wrote from the organization's "Policy Department" that neither he nor the man considered the BUF's leading intellectual, Alexander Raven Thomson, could accept Douglas's ideas but that they were interested in Social Credit. He hoped that Pound could create a "fusion" of Gesell's and Douglas's ideas to remedy the flaws he saw in the latter: "Meanwhile, since neither I nor Raven can swallow A plus B in Dougl/ if you, (your statement/) care to forward considrd/ ideas offering some fusion Dougl/ (minus A plus B or substitute theory therefore), Gesell and Woergl, I think I can promise courteous receptn" (Beinecke Rare Book and Manuscript Library, Ezra Pound Papers, YCAL MSS 43, series 1, box 5, folder 250).

42 "Stamp scrip," as it came to be called, designates currency that depreciates at an established rate, forcing the possessor to affix a stamp on the note in order to retain its value. In the Wörgl experiment, notes devaluated at 1 percent monthly, and the velocity of circulation accordingly increased greatly. Irving Fisher's book, *Stamp Scrip* (1933), documents the experiment and provided EP initial access to Gesell's ideas. As Roxana Preda notes, EP found common ground between Social

Credit and Gesell and regarded "stamp scrip as a good corrective for the Douglasite scheme: as a mechanism for the cancellation of credit, it could prevent inflation" (Preda, "Social Credit in America," 207).

43 Surette, *Light from Eleusis*, 167.

44 On Pound's preference for swift circulation, see Hickman, *Geometry of Modernism*, 126.

45 "Toward an Orthological Economy," *Rassegna Monetaria* 9–10 (September–October, 1937): 1103 (trans. Redman, *Italian Fascism*, 139). Pound might have been drawing this idea from Colbourne, *Meaning of Social Credit*, 156, in which Colbourne asserts: "Money, like blood, flows." However, Colbourne goes on to debunk the myth that increased circulation of money increases purchasing power.

46 Orage "conceived of his role apart from the hurly burly of practical politics and decision-making and of himself as *au dessus de la mêlée*" (Finlay 65).

ESSAY 2

1 As Surette notes: "Fascio is an innocent Italian word meaning *bundle* or *group*, and – before Mussolini adopted it for his movement – was used for any association, such as a club. (It was only later that Fascist ideologues stressed the connection with the Roman *fasces*, a bundle of sticks symbolizing the power to inflict corporal punishment)" (*Purgatory* 16).

2 For a survey of developments in fascist studies since the 1970s, see Griffin, "Primacy of Culture."

3 See, for instance, Surette's comments on the "rag-tag" and "ad hoc" nature of Fascist ideology (*Purgatory* 19), and Jeffrey Schnapp on the way that fascism compensated for an "ever unstable ideological core" with "aesthetic *overproduction*" ("Epic Demonstrations" 3).

4 See Mann, *Fascists*.

5 On this point, see also Rainey: "We err ... in urging that [Pound's] adherence [to fascism] had its basis in reasoned examination of competing economic theories or a sustained comparison of Mussolini's programs with those of guild socialism or revolutionary syndicalism" (*Institutions of Modernism* 145).

6 See North, *Reading 1922*.

7 "The indifferent have never made history" – (*Gli indifferenti non hanno mai fatto la storia*" (GK 195) – Pound maintained, such that deserving a place in his pantheon were those who, not indifferent, *could* make history.

8 See Beltramelli, *L'uomo nuovo* (1923). As Lawrence Rainey notes, "Not surprisingly, when Beltramelli sought to establish forerunners" for Mussolini, "he dwelled on figures from the house of Malatesta" as they hailed from the province of Romagna, as did Beltramelli himself (*Monument* 46).

9 See also Slatin, "History of Pound's Cantos I–XVI."

10 Here I think of the way Pound uses this concept in *Gaudier-Brzeska* (1916), in which he characterizes what he was doing in his early poetry involving personae,

or Browningesque masks, as a "search for the real" outside the boundaries of what one assumes to be the ordinary individual self. Pound notes here that he continued this search for the "real" in his translations, "which were but more elaborate masks" (*G-B* 85). I would contend that Pound is constantly driven onward by this idea of the "real" that always eludes him, that accrues different significances for him as years pass, and that, in the late 1920s and 1930s, comes to point to the realm of "econ/ and politics."

11 See Introduction for a discussion of the receptivity, in both Britain and the United States, to Mussolini at this time. For the reception of Mussolini in Britain, see Bosworth, "The British Press"; and on the support of many groups in the United States for Mussolini, see Diggins: "Flirtation with Fascism."

12 While others such as Beltramelli were, like Pound, interpreting Mussolini as the return of the heroic spirit associated with the magnificent figures of ancient Rome and Renaissance Italy, the American accent of Pound's thought placed his veneration in a distinct category.

13 See Surette, *Pound in Purgatory*, chap. 3.

14 For references to Por's book, see *P/Z* 232; for Por's disavowal of being fascist, see Redman, *Italian Fascism*, 160; for Por's government post, see *P/A* 283.

15 The fascist "axe and faggot" insignia – fasces and an axe – was on BUF letterhead at this time.

16 See the *NEW* for 8, 15, and 22 February and for 1 March 1934.

17 See Finlay, 211; Linehan, 90.

18 See 6 September 1934, 392–4.

19 See Gorham Munson, "The Douglasites," *The Commonweal*, 13 October 1933, 551–3.

20 See also Pound's letter to the *NEW*, 24 May 1934, in which he likewise complains about British ignorance, and misrepresentation, of what is happening in Italy.

21 See letter to Pound from G.A. Pfister, 20 March 1934, Beinecke Rare Book and Manuscript Library, Yale University, Ezra Pound Papers, YCAL MSS 43, series 1, box 5, folder 250.

22 See Leigh Vaughan-Henry to Pound, 20 August 1934, Beinecke Rare Book and Manuscript Library, Yale University, Ezra Pound Papers, YCAL MSS 43, series 1, box 5, folder 250.

23 For the BUF official, see Beinecke Rare Book and Manuscript Library, Yale University, Ezra Pound Papers, YCAL MSS 43, series 1, box 5, folder 251, 5 April 1934; for Leese, see YCAL MSS 43, series 1, box 29, folder 1229, 31 October 1934.

24 See Linehan, 74; Finlay, 210–11.

25 See Stone, "English Mistery."

26 See also Morell, "Arnold Leese and the Imperial Fascist League."

27 See also Thurlow's discussion of Leese in *Fascism in Britain*, 70–6. Thurlow notes that "Leese's virulent antisemitism and racial fascist beliefs made him the nearest equivalent in outlook to an English Hitler" (71).

28 In this letter of 31 October 1934, Leese notes: "I have sent you some literature for your donation, & have entered your name as a subscriber to 'The Fascist' for 1 year from October ... Yes, as far as I remember, I sent you the Fascist as a result of seeing your letter in the M. Post" (Beinecke Rare Book and Manuscript Library, Yale University, Ezra Pound Papers, YCAL MSS 43, series 1, box 29, folder 1229).

29 Surette notes that, ironically, it was the Jewish poet Louis Zukofsky who sent this article to him from the periodical the *Liberator*, in order to feature the "excesses of anticommunism and antisemitism," but Pound, to Zukofsky's surprise, took Pelley's charges seriously (Surette, *Purgatory*, 242). See Essay 1, note 38.

30 As Leese's letters to Pound indicate, Leese was in close touch with Kitson. Kitson, a member of the antisemitic and fascist group known as the Britons (which Thurlow credits with a "crude and obsessional antisemitism" (*Fascism in Britain* 66), was also affiliated with Leese's IFL.

31 In a 3 January 1935 letter to John Hargrave, Pound acknowledges the small size of the IFL: "(I don't know whether there are more than six imperial fascists???)" (Preda, *Ezra Pound's Economic Correspondence*, 129).

32 See Thurlow, *Fascism in Britain*, 63–4 (on small numbers) and 75 (on impact).

33 See Thurlow, "Developing British Fascist Interpretation of Race."

34 See EP to Leese, 2–3 November 1934, Beinecke Rare Book and Manuscript Library, Yale University, Ezra Pound Papers, YCAL MSS 43, series 1, box 29, folder 1229.

35 In a letter of 7 November 1934, Leese counters Pound's stress on the precedence of economic problems with his own emphasis on race: "I agree that when Money is free, the Jew power is gone; but they still copulate. That is the point. RACE BEFORE ECONOMICS!" (Beinecke Rare Book and Manuscript Library, Yale University, Ezra Pound Papers, YCAL MSS 43, series 1, box 29, folder 1229.

36 See EP to Leese, 2–3 November 1934, Beinecke Rare Book and Manuscript Library, Yale University, Ezra Pound Papers YCAL MSS 43, series 1, box 29, folder 1229.

37 The issue of the *Fascist* that Pound praises in a letter to Nott, June 1935, indicates disapproval of Italy's designs on Abyssinia. The byline for the piece is "HHL," or H.H. Lockwood, one of the members of the IFL.

38 See Stone, "English Mistery," 346.

39 Ibid., esp. 343–4.

40 In fact, in a letter of January 1935 to Hargrave, Pound indicates that he is inclined to steer away from Mosley and to side with those who "attack" him (Preda, *Ezra Pound's Economic Correspondence*, 129).

41 See Pound's correspondence with Olivia Rossetti Agresti (*"I Cease Not to Yowl"*). Pound tended to read Hitler as a "lunatic" but displayed sympathy toward him in letters such as 70 and 71, in which he recommends that Agresti read Hitler's *Table Talk*.

42 In her note on Alexander Raven Thomson, Preda notes that "Pound had an extended correspondence with T. first in 1934, when they discussed a rapprochement between SC and fascism" (*Ezra Pound's Economic Correspondence* 283).

43 Pound's work for the bulletin was initiated by Camagna, who wrote for both the *Morning Post* and the *British-Italian Bulletin* and had been recommended to Pound by a mutual friend, Robert Hield.

44 Finlay, 206; Linehan, 87.

45 In this letter of 3 April 1934, which responds to Pound's reply to a piece Thomson published in the *NEW* about BUF economic policy, Thomson notes both similarities and divergences between Social Credit thought and the economic thought of the BUF. "Undoubtedly there is a great deal in what you say regarding the resemblance between the economics of Douglas Social Credit and ourselves ... There is, however, more difference of opinion between us than you might suspect ... Apparently, many Social Credit men regard the dividend as a means of assuring economic independence for the individual. They thus tend towards Liberal ideas of individual freedom, which are obviously contrary to Fascist principles. I fear it is upon this point that divergence of opinion will arise between us when we do meet. However, as our agreement on economic matters is so deep, possibly this difficulty may be successfully overcome" (Beinecke Rare Book and Manuscript Library, Yale University, Ezra Pound Papers, YCAL MSS 43, box 52, folder 2338).

46 See Redman, *Italian Fascism*, 123; Davis, 157.

47 See letters to Pound from Alexander Raven Thompson (3 April 1934) and Leigh Vaughan-Henry (8 August, 20 August, and 28 August 1934), which indicate the BUF's interest in Social Credit measures, though, as Vaughan-Henry stresses, not their acceptance of Douglas's ideas "in toto" (20 August 1934). See Beinecke Rare Book and Manuscript Library, Yale University, Ezra Pound Papers, series 1, box 5, folder 250 for Vaughan-Henry; and YCAL MSS 43 box 52, folder 2338 for Raven Thomson.

48 As Finlay observes, "those who discerned a fascist streak" in the group might be "pardoned": "the uniforms, the marching, the drums, the notion of an elite" (162) all read to many as the trappings associated with fascism.

49 I am struck here by the compatibility between what Roger Griffin has termed fascism's tendency to conceptualize efforts as leading towards "palingenesis," a form of cultural rebirth, and the pattern in Pound's thought, revealed inter alia through the structure and preoccupations of his *Cantos*, with palingenesis. For the argument about Pound's work and palingenesis, I am indebted to Demetres Tryphonopoulos's *The Celestial Tradition*.

ESSAY 3

1 Redman, Review of Ira B. Nadel's *Ezra Pound: A Literary Life*. *Modernism/modernity* 13.1 (January 2006): 935–6.

2 See Moody, "Directio Voluntatis."

3 The name of Malatesta (1417–1468) is sometimes also spelled "Sigismondo," but in Pound's lexicon, it is "Sigismundo."

4 C.H. Douglas theorized the "cultural heritage" as all the resources, natural, human-made, physical, or knowledge-based that a community had developed over time and to which the members of a community were accordingly entitled: Douglas believed that "natural resources are common property, and the means of exploitation should also be common property"; because "the industrial machine is ... the result of the labours of generations of people whose names are for the most part forgotten"; it is a "common heritage" (Douglas, *Credit Power and Democracy*, 18, 31–2).

5 Wall, 31.

6 This points to the infrastructure of little magazines that came to be characteristic of, and crucial to the development of, modernist cultural work, an infrastructure that Pound did much to found and foster – which allowed for conversational exchange within the chatrooms formed by their pages. As such commentators as Marek (*Women Editing Modernism*), Rainey *(Institutions of Modernism)*, and Morrisson (*The Public Face of Modernism*) have observed, little magazines were both engines for the literary output of modernism – their very existence and standing welcome to modernist writers helped to inspire new work – and an important mechanism for the endowment of that work with modernist status. Little magazines facilitated the recognition of individual texts and their integration into the wider cultural movement that modernism came to be. But more than this, the very nature of the genre of magazines, in contrast to the small presses that the moderns likewise used as important outlets, favoured multivocality and conversation; and this capacity, favoured within modernist circles, points to modernism's bent for collaboration.

7 As John Whittier-Ferguson notes in *Framing Pieces*, Pound's words in the 1930s and 1940s "increasingly sound like the words of a man talking to himself" (147). In *Wireless Writing in the Age of Marconi*, Timothy Campbell draws attention to a reading of Pound's mental condition from the late 1960s, from Dr Cornelio Fazio of the University of Genoa. Fazio diagnosed Pound as "suffering from 'an extreme autistic situation'": "It seemed as if the personality had always been on the autistic side, with a prevailing phantasmatic attitude and insufficient contact with reality" (qtd. Campbell 125–6). See also Wendy Flory on what was diagnosed at St Elizabeths as Pound's "Delusional Disorder." "Throughout Pound's years at St. Elizabeths," she notes, "political or economic topics invariably precipitated a psychotic response" (Flory 291).

8 See Badenhausen (152) on the role played by Martin Browne in the development of Eliot's work.

9 See "The Jefferson-Adams Letters as a Shrine and a Monument" (*SP* 147–58).

10 See Campbell, *Wireless Writing*, on Pound's assumed linkage between fragmentary utterance and the "Real" (127–8).

11 See Kenner, *The Pound Era*, chap. 4, 54–75, "The Muse in Tatters."

12　For this claim, I am indebted to Bradley Clissold's work-in-progress on the impact of early twentieth-century postcards on modernist idioms.

13　Pound's reunion with Marinetti in the 1930s might also have exerted some influence on his tendency to invoke a Marinettian vocabulary here. For Pound's reawakened interest in and admiration for Marinetti in the 1930s, see Hickman, *Geometry of Modernism*, 102–3.

14　See Pound's letter to Eugene Davidson of Yale University Press, 1934 (no month given), Beinecke Rare Book and Manuscript Library, Yale University Library, Ezra Pound Papers, YCAL MSS 43, series 1, box 24, folder 1059.

15　This metaphor resonates noticeably with the Marinettian notion of the "steam" of revolutionary impulse bursting the "steam-pipe" of language, though Marinetti figures language through the pipe, while Laughlin figures a civilization through the image of arteries. See *New Democracy* (1 December 1935): 120 for Laughlin's brief piece, "New Directions: Pound's Prose" which prefaces Pound's "Who Gets It?" (120–2).

16　For commentary on Pound as "American jeremiah," see Flory's *American Ezra Pound* (5). She notes that "the Social Credit vision fulfilled exactly the requirements of the jeremiac imperative which Pound had carried with him as an ineradicable part of his heritage" (49).

17　Like the Futurists, though from different motives, Pound also seeks to depersonalize and dehumanize, to get beyond the ego and the merely personal to larger matters, to move to the building of a culture. Like the Futurists, he wants to transcend the mere lyrical "I" in favour of another kind of energy – a new lyricism not dependent upon, not based in, the traditional "I." His letters, I would offer, register an attempt at this new kind of lyricism.

18　For theorization of the Victorian sage figure, see Holloway, *Victorian Sage*. The stance as cultural commentator connoted by "Pound-ese" might also be read as that of the jester: but Pound is not quite so given to subversive puncturing of nonsense as this implies. What does hold about the parallel is his insistence on standing outside the limits that conventional serious discourse is supposed to confer on him in order to signal that he possesses greater insight than those on the inside.

19　William Proctor Williams and Craig Abbott note that "Documentary (or diplomatic) editing aims to reproduce a manuscript or printed text as a historical artefact. It presents a text as it was available at a particular time in a particular document" (Williams and Abbott 55). Lawrence Rainey traces the practice of "diplomatics" back to its "foundations" among Benedictine monks who "were assembling a documentary collection not only of legal documents, but of materials related to French writers, the *Historiae Francorum scriptores coetanei*" (*Monument* 64). Rainey notes the "romantic sensibility" to which such diplomatics can appeal: "For original documents offered a special *frisson*, a magical sense of vivacity or spontaneity undiluted by narrative conventions" (65). Pound himself, of course, was moved by such a *frisson*, like Charles Yriarte, whose work he consulted, investing in the belief that "the true elements of history" (qtd. Rainey, *Monument*, 65) were available in original documents, unedited. Not entirely disavowing such a "romantic sensibility," I likewise maintain that dimensions of history not otherwise available are accessible through the careful diplomatic transcription of Pound's epistolary conduct.

ESSAY 4

1   See "Literature Headquarters," *New Democracy*, 15 December 1935, 136.
2   These titles included Leigh Henry, *The Story of Music* (1935); George Mauduit, *The Vicomte in the Kitchenette* (1934); Charles Freeston, *The Roads of Spain*; Nora Lavrin, *Jugoslav Scenes: Dry Points* (1935); and William Johnstone, *Creative Art in England* (1936). See Appendix 2.
3   See Stevenson, 396.
4   Included in this collection, edited by Montgomery Butchart, were J. Stuart Barr (a pseudonym for Silvio Gesell), Arthur Kitson, Frederick Soddy, R. McNair Wilson, C.H. Douglas, G.D.H. Cole, and Jeffrey Mark. Douglas and Cole were also featured in the Pamphlets on the New Economics series.
5   Nos. 1 and 2 of the series were Douglas's *The Use of Money* and *The Nature of Democracy*, respectively.
6   Indicating that he was thinking in terms of "symposia," one of the pamphlets in Nott's series includes the term "symposium" in its title. This was no. 7, edited by William Ward and entitled *The National Dividend: A Symposium by 16 Public Men*. It included contributions by Orage, Douglas, Will Dyson, Harold Bowden, W.T. Symons, Clive Kenrick, Philip McDevitt, the Earl of Tankerville, the Dean of Canterbury, the Marquis of Tavistock, Thomas Johnston, C. Marshall Hattersley, Maurice Colbourne, A.L. Gibson, and Montgomery Butchart. Beyond this, Nott also seemed to be trying to create a "symposium" by way of the Pamphlets on the New Economics series as a whole.
7   In the poetic sequence *Contemporania*, published in *Poetry* magazine in 1913, Pound entitles one of his poems "Tenzone," reflecting his interest in the notion of poetic contest engaged in by the troubadour poets of medieval France, whose poetry inspired much of Pound's early work.
8   In his memoirs, Nott continues this lament: "Why are the English so afraid of showing emotion? Up to the end of the eighteenth century the English were not ashamed to weep when deeply moved" (*Further Teachings* 13).
9   By invoking Keynes, Pound positioned *Jefferson and/or Mussolini* as a publication focused on economic issues, as he likewise attempted to do by subtitling it "Volitionist Economics." This is a misrepresentation – likely stemming from Pound's wish to establish himself as an economic commentator. Although at moments the book focuses on economic issues, featured principally is its forthright celebration of Mussolini's political achievements.
10 At one point in his memoirs, Nott notes that Hugh McDiarmid suffered from "that strange disease, communism" (*Further Teachings* 49).

11 As Nott recalls of the early 1930s, "Each day we opened our newspapers in trepidation to see what Hitler and Mussolini were saying or what they threatened to do. Life went on – it could do no other – but it began to be rather like living on the slopes of Vesuvius when the rumbles of an eruption are heard, with the weak hope that it may not take place. Gradually the attention of everyone in Europe was drawn towards those two tremendous puppets, Hitler and Mussolini, who, for some reason or other, had been impelled by events into the centre of the world-stage" (*Further Teachings* 33).

12 By fall of 1935, Montgomery Butchart, seeking to offer a favourable review of *Jefferson and/or Mussolini*, deliberately soft-pedalled Mussolini's crucial role in the book's arguments, indicating the disfavour into which the Italian regime had fallen by that juncture. See review in the *Criterion* 15, 59 (1936): 323–6.

13 See Hodges, epigraphs. Gollancz is almost a direct contemporary of Nott's, and one of the firms occupying, with some of its publications, a structural niche comparable to Nott's in the field of British publishing. Gollancz, like Nott, conceived of his work as politically committed – in Gollancz's case, as activist publishing designed to promote the ideas of the political left.

14 Through the work of his Left Book Club, Gollancz came to represent what was termed by publisher Cass Canfield the "responsible Left." See Hodges, 122.

15 In March of 1936, for instance, when Pound notes that John O'Hara Cosgrave, who had served as literary editor of the *New York World* and editor of *Everybody's Magazine*, which published sensational journalism for a mass readership, thinks that Nott hasn't any business sense, Nott retorts that he "should consider [him]self a bad business man" if he published as Cosgrave did. For Nott, one kind of "business sense" is clearly "bad."

16 See Webb, chap. 2, in *Occult Establishment*, which places Social Credit among the idealistic movements of the "Progressive Underground" of the interwar years, characterized by anti-materialism.

17 In Letter 85, commenting on the quality of Nott's publishing and his lack of capital, Pound notes, "I spose you'll git yr/ reward in heaven."

18 Describing the moment of the beginning of Pound's relationship to Laughlin, Barnhisel notes this linkage: "At this time, Pound was also trying to cultivate a similar relationship with the Englishman Stanley Nott, a book distributor who published his political works in England in the 1930s. Because of the limited appeal of such works as *Jefferson and/or Mussolini* and the 'Money Pamphlets,' though, and because of Nott's significantly smaller financial resources, he could never fulfill the role that Pound then assigned to Laughlin" (215).

19 Other figures of this time drawn by Gurdjieff included Katherine Mansfield, Jean Toomer, Frank Lloyd Wright, Margaret Anderson, and Jane Heap.

20 Nott's praise of Orage reflects his preference for those who don't proceed solely by intellect: "Orage's mind stimulated one's own; it was alive, very different from the minds of the rigid 'intellectuals' I had mixed with at the 1917 Club in London … Orage felt as well as thought" (*Teachings* 93).

21 In *Further Teachings*, Nott reminisces about the beginnings of the firm: "For some time the idea of starting a publishing business had been in my mind; and very soon I started with a hundred pounds capital, though after the first book was published two other men joined the firm. It was the worst possible time to start, for the first thing the public gives up buying in times of depression is books. Yet a small publishing business, in which the publisher has to do almost everything himself, is an interesting way of making a living ... In the hat business I was out of my element, in publishing I was at home" (43).

22 See Hickman, "To Facilitate the Traffic."

23 Nott observes that Gurdjieff taught that "a man should not be dominated by a wife or mistress ... Part of Gurdjieff's training consisted of ... developing the active part of his men pupils, and the passive in women; it brought out the masculine in men and the feminine in women" (*Teachings* 98).

24 In his memoirs, Nott recalls the outrage at economic conditions – poverty in the midst of plenty – that fuelled his commitment to Social Credit: "The present state was a blinding example of how life is organized by the power-possessing beings on the planet. In America alone twenty million people were going hungry while food was being destroyed. Wheat was being used as fuel, fruit dumped into the sea by thousands of tons a week. Farmers were being paid not to produce wheat and pigs, and all because there were not enough dollar bills, printed pieces of paper, being distributed with which to buy them. The big banks were bursting with money, while the small banks failed right and left" (*Further Teachings* 25).

25 Of the foundation of the *New English Weekly*, Nott remarks: "The journal saw the light of day on April 21st 1932. From the first it was a success, not in circulation but in that it accomplished the task Orage had set himself: to expound the ideas of Major C.H. Douglas, who had discovered the cause of the financial breakdown and had formulated it in language so turgid that few could understand it. Everyone agreed that only Orage could make the muddy waters clear" (*Further Teachings* 29).

26 When a pupil learning about Gurdjieff's thought from Orage once asked Orage why Gurdjieff claimed he didn't know what the textbook he himself had written was about, Orage replied: "To shock you, of course. To make you ponder" (*Further Teachings* 23).

27 See Angenot, *La Parole Pamphlétaire*.

28 See Kaplan, "Recent Theoretical Work."

29 See Nott, *Social Credit Pamphleteer*.

BIBLIOGRAPHY

Angenot, Marc. *La Parole Pamphlétaire: Contribution à La Typologie Des Discours Moderne.* Paris: Payot, 1982.

Ardis, Ann. *Modernism and Cultural Conflict, 1880–1922.* Cambridge: Cambridge University Press, 2002.

Badenhausen, Richard. *T.S. Eliot and the Art of Collaboration.* New York: Cambridge University Press, 2004.

Barnhisel, Gregory. *James Laughlin: New Directions and the Remaking of Ezra Pound.* Amherst: University of Massachusetts Press, 2005.

Bornstein, George. *Material Modernism: The Politics of the Page.* Cambridge: Cambridge University Press, 2001.

Bosworth, R.J.B. "The British Press, the Conservatives, and Mussolini, 1920–1934." *Journal of Contemporary History* 5, 2 (1970): 163–82.

Bradshaw, David, "T.S. Eliot and the Major." *Times Literary Supplement,* 5 July 1996, 14–16.

Campbell, Timothy. *Wireless Writing in the Age of Marconi.* Minneapolis: University of Minnesota Press, 2006.

Cannistraro, Philip V., and Brian R. Sullivan. *Il Duce's Other Woman: The Untold Story of Margarita Sarfatti, Mussolini's Jewish Mistress, and How She Helped Him Come to Power.* New York: William Morrow and Co., 1993.

Carpenter, Humphrey. *A Serious Character: The Life of Ezra Pound.* Boston: Houghton Mifflin, 1988.

Carswell, John. *Lives and Letters: A.R. Orage, Beatrice Hastings, Katherine Mansfield, John Middleton Murry, S.S. Koteliansky.* London: Faber and Faber, 1978.

Carter, John. *A B C for Book Collectors.* London: Rupert Hart-Davis, 1967.

Casillo, Robert. *The Genealogy of Demons.* Evanston, IL: Northwestern University Press, 1988.

Chace, William. *The Political Identities of Ezra Pound and T.S. Eliot.* Stanford: Stanford University Press, 1973.

Colbourne, Maurice. *The Meaning of Social Credit.* London: Figurehead, 1933.

Corrin, Jay P. *G.K. Chesterton and Hilaire Belloc: The Battle against Modernity.* London: Ohio University Press, 1981.

Cullingford, Elizabeth. *Yeats, Ireland, and Fascism*. New York: New York University Press, 1981.

Davis, Earle. *Vision Fugitive: Ezra Pound and Economics*. Lawrence, KS: University Press of Kansas, 1968.

Desai, Meghnad. *The Route of All Evil: The Political Economy of Ezra Pound*. London: Faber and Faber, 2006.

Diggins, John P. "Flirtation with Fascism: American Pragmatic Liberals and Mussolini's Italy." *American Historical Review* 71 (1966): 487–506.

Doob, Leonard, ed. *"Ezra Pound Speaking": Radio Speeches of WWII*. Westport, CT: Greenwood Press, 1978.

Douglas, C.H. *The Approach to Reality: Address to Social Crediters at Westminster on March 7, 1936, Together with Answers to Questions*. London: K.R.P. Publications, 1958.

– *Credit Power and Democracy*. London: C. Palmer, 1920.

– *Social Credit*. 1924. London: Eyre and Spottiswoode, 1937.

Eliot, T.S. *Selected Essays*. New York: Harcourt Brace, 1964.

Farndale, Nigel. *Haw-Haw: The Tragedy of William and Margaret Joyce*. London: Macmillan, 2005.

Ferkiss, Victor, C. "Ezra Pound and American Fascism." *Journal of Politics* 17 (1955): 173–97.

Finlay, John. *Social Credit: The English Origins*. London: McGill-Queen's University Press, 1972.

Flory, Wendy. *The American Ezra Pound*. New Haven: Yale University Press, 1989.

– "Pound and Antisemitism." In *The Cambridge Companion to Ezra Pound*, ed. Ira B. Nadel, 284–300. Cambridge: Cambridge University Press, 1999.

Foucault, Michel. "Power and Strategies." In *Power/Knowledge: Selected Interviews and Other Writings 1972–1977*, ed. Colin Gordon, 135–65. New York: Pantheon, 1980.

Gallup, Donald. *A Bibliography of Ezra Pound*. London: R. Hart-Davis, 1969.

Gaskell, Philip. *A New Introduction to Bibliography*. New York: Oxford University Press, 1972.

Grieve, Thomas G. *Ezra Pound's Early Poetry and Poetics*. Columbia: University of Missouri Press, 1997.

Griffin, Roger. "The Primacy of Culture: The Current Growth (or Manufacture) of Consensus within Fascist Studies." *Journal of Contemporary History* 37, 1 (2002): 21–43.

Harding, Jason. *The Criterion: Cultural Politics and Periodical Networks in Inter-War Britain*. Oxford: Oxford University Press, 2002.

Hesketh, Bob. *Major Douglas and Alberta Social Credit*. Toronto: University of Toronto Press, 1997.

Hickman, Miranda B. "'To Facilitate the Traffic': Ezra Pound's Turn from the Deluxe." *Paideuma* 28, 2–3 (1999): 173–92.

– *The Geometry of Modernism*. Austin, TX: University of Texas Press, 2005.

– "Pamphlets and Blue China: Ezra Pound's Preference for Plainness in the 1950s." *Paideuma* 26, 2–3 (1997): 165–79.

Hindle, Wilfrid. *The Morning Post, 1772–1937: Portrait of a Newspaper.* Westport, CT: Greenwood Press, 1974.

Hodges, Sheila. *Gollancz: The Story of a Publishing House, 1928–1978.* London: Gollancz, 1978.

Holloway, John. *The Victorian Sage: Studies in Argument.* London: Macmillan, 1953.

Homberger, Eric, ed. *Ezra Pound: The Critical Heritage.* Boston: Routledge and Kegan Paul, 1972.

Hughes, John W. *Major Douglas: The Policy of a Philosophy.* Glasgow: Wedderspoon Associates, 2002.

Hutchison, Frances, and Brian Burkitt. "An Economic Silence": Women and Social Credit," *Women's Studies International Forum* 20, 2 (1997): 321–7.

– *The Political Economy of Social Credit and Guild Socialism.* New York: Routledge, 1997.

Hynes, Samuel. *The Auden Generation: Literature and Politics in England in the 1930s.* Toronto: The Bodley Head, 1976.

Jameson, Fredric. *Fables of Aggression: Wyndham Lewis, the Modernist as Fascist.* Berkeley: University of California Press, 1979.

John-Steiner, Vera. *Creative Collaboration.* Oxford: Oxford University Press, 2000.

Kadlec, David. *Mosaic Modernism: Anarchism, Pragmatism, Culture.* Baltimore: Johns Hopkins University Press, 2000.

Kaplan, Alice Yaeger. "Recent Theoretical Work with Pamphlets and Manifestoes." *Esprit Createur* 23, 4 (1983): 74–82.

Kenner, Hugh. *The Pound Era.* Berkeley and Los Angeles: University of California Press, 1971.

Kermode, Frank. *The Sense of an Ending: Studies in the Theory of Fiction.* New York: Oxford University Press, 1968 [1966].

Keynes, John Maynard. *The General Theory of Employment, Interest, and Money.* London: Macmillan and Company, Ltd., 1951 [1936].

Levenson, Michael. *A Genealogy of Modernism: A Study of English Literary Doctrine, 1908–1922.* Cambridge: Cambridge University Press, 1984.

Lewis, Wyndham. *The Letters of Wyndham Lewis.* Ed. W.K. Rose. London: Methuen, 1963.

Lindberg, Katheryne V. *Reading Pound Reading: Modernism After Nietzsche.* New York: Oxford University Press, 1987.

Linehan, Thomas. *British Fascism, 1918–1939: Parties, Ideology, and Culture.* New York: Manchester University Press, 2000.

Lunn, Kenneth, and Richard C. Thurlow, eds. *British Fascism: Essays on the Radical Right in Inter-War Britain.* New York: St. Martin's Press, 1980.

Mairet, Philip. *A.R. Orage: A Memoir.* New Hyde Park, New York: University Books, 1966.

Mann, Michael. *Fascists*. Cambridge: Cambridge University Press, 2004.

Marinetti, F.T.M. "Destruction of Syntax – Imagination without Strings – Words in Freedom 1913." In *Futurist Manifestoes*, ed. Umbro Apollonio, 95–106. Boston: MFA Publications, 1970.

Martin, Kingsley. "British Opinion and the Abyssinian Dispute: A Survey of the Daily Papers During the Second Half of August, 1935." *Political Quarterly* 6, 4 (1935): 583–90.

Martin, Wallace. *The New Age under Orage: Chapters in English Cultural History*. Manchester: Manchester University Press, 1967.

Marsh, Alec. *Money and Modernity: Pound, Williams, and the Spirit of Jefferson*. Tuscaloosa, AL: University of Alabama Press, 1998.

McGann, Jerome. *The Textual Condition*. Princeton: Princeton University Press, 1991.

Moody, David. "Directio Voluntatis: Pound's Economics in the Economy of the Cantos." *Paideuma* 32, 1 (2003): 187–203.

Moore-Colyer, Richard. "Towards 'Mother Earth': Jorian Jenks, Organicism, the Right and the British Union of Fascists." *Journal of Contemporary History* 39, 3 (2004): 353–71.

Moore, James. *Gurdjieff: Anatomy of a Myth*. Rockport, MA: Element, 1991.

Morell, John. "Arnold Leese and the Imperial Fascist League: The Impact of Racial Fascism." In Lunn and Thurlow, 57–76.

Morrison, Paul. *The Poetics of Fascism: Ezra Pound, T.S. Eliot, and Paul de Man*. New York: Oxford University Press, 1996.

Norman, Charles. *The Case of Ezra Pound*. New York: Funk and Wagnalls, 1968.

North, Michael. *The Political Aesthetic of Yeats, Eliot, and Pound*. Cambridge: Cambridge University Press, 1991.

– *Reading 1922: A Return to the Scene of the Modern*. New York: Oxford University Press, 1999

Nott, Charles Stanley. *Further Teachings of Gurdjieff: Journey through This World*. New York: Samuel Weiser, Inc., 1969.

– *The Social Credit Pamphleteer by Various Hands*. London: Stanley Nott, 1935.

– *Teachings of Gurdjieff*. London: Routledge and Kegan Paul, 1961.

Poggioli, Renato. *Theory of the Avant-Garde*. Cambridge, MA: Harvard University Press, 1968.

Pound, Ezra. *The Cantos*. New York: New Directions, 1987.

– *Ezra and Dorothy Pound: Letters in Captivity, 1945–46*. Ed. Robert Spoo and Omar Pound. New York: Oxford University Press, 1999.

– *Ezra Pound and James Laughlin: Selected Letters*. Ed. David Gordon. New York: W.W. Norton, 1994.

– *Ezra Pound and Senator Bronson Cutting: A Political Correspondence, 1930–1935*. Ed. E.P. Walkiewicz and Hugh Witemeyer. Albuquerque: University of New Mexico Press, 1995.

– *Ezra Pound's Poetry and Prose: Contributions to Periodicals.* Ed. Lea Baechler, A. Walton Litz, and James Longerbach. 10 vols. New York: Garland, 1991.
– *Gaudier-Brzeska.* New York: New Directions, 1970 [1916].
– *Guide to Kulchur.* New York: New Directions, 1970 [1938].
– *"I Cease Not to Yowl": Ezra Pound's Letters to Olivia Rossetti Agresti.* Ed. Demetres P. Tryphonopoulos and Leon Surette. Urbana-Campaign: University of Illinois Press, 1998.
– "The Individual in His Milieu." *Criterion* 15, 58 (1935): 30–45.
– *Jefferson and/or Mussolini.* London: Stanley Nott, 1935.
– *Letters to Ibbotson.* Ed. Vittoria I. Mondolfo and Margaret Hurley. Orono, M E: National Poetry Foundation, 1979.
– *Literary Essays.* Ed. T.S. Eliot. Norfolk, C T: New Directions, 1958.
– *Pound/Cummings: The Correspondence of Ezra Pound and E.E. Cummings.* Ed. Barry Ahearn. Ann Arbor: University of Michigan Press, 1996.
– *Pound/Ford: The Story of a Literary Friendship.* Ed. Brita Lindberg-Seyersted. New York: New Directions, 1982.
– *Pound/Joyce: The Letters of Ezra Pound to James Joyce.* Ed. and with commentary by Forrest Read. New York: New Directions, 1967.
– *Pound/Lewis: The Letters of Ezra Pound and Wyndham Lewis.* Ed. Timothy Materer. New York: New Directions, 1985.
– *Pound/The Little Review: The Letters of Ezra Pound to Margaret Anderson.* Ed. Thomas L. Scott, Melvin J. Friedman, and Jackson R. Bryer. New York: New Directions, 1988.
– *Pound/Williams: Selected Letters of Ezra Pound and William Carlos Williams.* Ed. Hugh Witemeyer. New York: New Directions, 1986.
– *Pound/Zukofsky: Selected Letters of Ezra Pound and Louis Zukofsky.* Ed. Barry Ahearn. New York: New Directions, 1987.
– *Selected Letters of Ezra Pound, 1907–1941.* Ed. D.D. Paige. London: Faber and Faber, 1951.
– *Selected Poems.* Ed. and with an introduction by T.S. Eliot. London: Faber and Faber, 1959.
– *Selected Prose, 1909–1965.* Ed. with an introduction by William Cookson. New York: New Directions, 1973.
– "Small Magazines." *English Journal* 19, 9 (1930): 689–704.
Preda, Roxana. *Ezra Pound's Economic Correspondence, 1933–1940.* Gainsville: University of Florida Press, 2007.
– "Social Credit in America: A View from Ezra Pound's Economic Correspondence, 1933–1940." *Paideuma* 34, 2–3 (2005): 201–27.
Rainey, Lawrence. *Ezra Pound and the Monument of Culture: Text, History, and the Malatesta Cantos.* Chicago: University of Chicago Press, 1991.
– *Institutions of Modernism: Literary Elites and Public Culture.* New Haven, C T: Yale University Press, 1998.

– "The Letters and the Spirit: Pound's Correspondence and the Concept of Modernism." *Text* 7 (1994): 365–96.

Redman, Tim. "Ezra Pound and American Populism." *Paideuma* 34, 2 and 3 (2005): 14–36

– *Ezra Pound and Italian Fascism*. Cambridge: Cambridge University Press, 1991.

– "Review of Ira B. Nadel's *Ezra Pound: A Literary Life*." *Modernism/ modernity* 13, 1 (2006): 935–6.

Roberts, Michael, ed. *The Faber Book of Modern Verse*. 1936. Faber and Faber, 1983.

Schlesinger, Arthur, M. *The Politics of Upheaval, 1935–1936*. Vol. 3 in the Age of Roosevelt series. Boston: Houghton Mifflin, 1960.

Schnapp, Jeffrey. "Epic Demonstrations: Fascist Modernity and the 1932 Exhibition of the Fascist Revolution." In *Fascism, Aesthetics, and Culture*, ed. Richard J. Golsan, 1–32. Hanover, NH: University Press of New England, 1992.

Selver, Paul. *Orage and the New Age Circle: Reminiscences and Reflections*. London: Allen and Unwin, 1959.

Sherry, Vincent. *Ezra Pound, Wyndham Lewis, and Radical Modernism*. New York: Oxford University Press, 1993.

Slatin, Myles. "A History of Pound's Cantos I–XVI, 1915–1925." *American Literature* 35, 2 (1965): 183–95.

Sternhell, Zeev. *The Birth of Fascist Ideology*. Princeton, NJ: Princeton University Press, 1994.

Stevenson, John. *British Society, 1914–1945*. London: Penguin Books, 1984.

Stingel, Janine. *Social Discredit: Anti-Semitism, Social Credit, and the Jewish Response*. Montreal: McGill-Queen's University Press, 2000.

Stock, Noel. *The Life of Ezra Pound*. NY: Pantheon Books, 1970.

Stone, Dan. "The English Mistery, the BUF, and the Dilemmas of British Fascism." *Journal of Modern History* 75 (2003): 336–58.

– *Responses to Nazism in Britain, 1933–1939*. Basingstoke: Palgrave Macmillan, 2003.

Stough, Christina C. "The Skirmish of Pound and Eliot in the *New English Weekly*: A Glimpse at Their Later Literary Relationship." *Journal of Modern Literature* 10, 2 (1983): 231–46.

Sullivan, Alvin, ed. *British Literary Magazines: The Modern Age, 1914–1984*, Vol. 4. Westport, CT: Greenwood Press, 1983.

Surette, Leon. *A Light from Eleusis: A Study of Ezra Pound's Cantos*. New York: Oxford University Press, 1991.

– *Pound in Purgatory: From Economic Radicalism to Anti-Semitism*. Chicago: University of Illinois Press, 1999.

Terrell, Carroll F. *A Companion to the Cantos of Ezra Pound*. Berkeley: University of California Press, 1980.

Thurlow, Richard C. "The Developing British Fascist Interpretation of Race, Culture, and Evolution." In *The Culture of Fascism: Visions of the Far Right in Brit-*

ain, ed. Julie V. Gottlieb and Thomas P. Linehan, 66–82. New York: I.B. Tauris, 2000.

— "The Return of Jeremiah: The Rejected Knowledge of Sir Oswald Mosley in the 1930s." In Lunn and Thurlow, 100–13.

— *Fascism in Britain: A History, 1918–1985*. Oxford: Basil Blackwell, 1987.

Tryphonopoulos, Demetres. *The Celestial Tradition: A Study of Ezra Pound's* The Cantos. Waterloo, ON: Wilfrid Laurier Press, 1991.

Tryphonopoulos, Demetres, and Stephen J. Adams, eds. *The Ezra Pound Encyclopedia*. Westport, CT: Greenwood Press, 2005.

Wall, Wendy. *The Imprint of Gender: Authorship and Publication in the English Renaissance*. Ithaca, NY: Cornell University Press, 1993.

Weaver, Mike. *William Carlos Williams: The American Background*. Cambridge: Cambridge University Press, 1971.

Webb, James. *The Occult Establishment*. La Salle, IL: Open Court Publishing Co., 1976.

Webber, G.C. *The Ideology of the British Right, 1918–1939*. New York: St Martin's Press, 1986.

Whittier-Ferguson, John. *Framing Pieces: Designs of the Gloss in Joyce, Woolf, and Pound*. New York: Oxford University Press, 1996.

Williams, Carlos Williams. *The Embodiment of Knowledge*. New York: New Directions, 1974.

Williams, William Proctor, and Craig Abbott. *An Introduction to Bibliographical and Textual Studies*. 2nd ed. New York: Modern Language Association, 1985.

Boldfaced entries refer to items included in Appendix 1. EP in index refers to Ezra Pound.

American Mercury, 99, 99n8

American Revolution, xxxiv, 294, 301–2, 304, 305, 313, 328

Anderson, Margaret, xxiv, xxxv, 31n12, 42, 42n21, 338, 372n19

Angell, Norman: biographical sketch of, 108n19, 122n5; EP's first letter to, published in *Time and Tide*, 117, 117n4, 122, 122n4, 128–34, 128n2, 132n8, 132n11, 136, 141n1; EP's second letter to, 131n6, 133, 134, 134n20, 141, 141n1, 149, 149n3, 152, 152n2; pacifism of, 108n19, 131n3; "Seraph" referring to, 132, 132n10; and Union for Democratic Control (UDC), 108n19

Angenot, Marc, 328–9

Angold, John Penrose, 145n13, 169, 169nn2–3, 249, 249n12

Antheil, George, 124, 124n4

Antheil and the Treatise on Harmony (Pound), 124, 124n3

antisemitism: in Alberta, Canada, 271–2, 363n36; and *American Mercury*, 99, 99n8; in Britain, 271, 290; and British Fascism, xxi, 297; on critical climate, 35, 35n19; of Douglas, 269–72; of Drummond, 113n6, 273, 290, 335, 364n40; economically based antisemitism, xix, 269–72, 355n16; of EP, xv, xvii, xix, xxi, 259, 260, 272–4, 289–91, 333, 355n16, 367n29; of EP's radio broadcasts, xv; of Fack, 92n3, 273, 290, 336; in *Fascist: The Organ of Racial Fascism*, 146–8, 146n2, 147nn6–11, 290, 340; on Jubilee celebration of George V's reign, 90, 90n29; of Kitson, 273, 290, 363n33, 367n30; of Leese, xix, 273–4, 289–91, 355n16, 366n27, 367n35; of Mussolini, 92n6; of National Socialist League (NSL), 292, 295, 341–2; and Nazism, 271; of Pelley, 273, 290, 364n38, 367n29; racially based antisemitism, xix, 355n16; and Social Credit, xxi, 259, 260, 269–72, 297; of Nesta Webster, 273, 363n34, 364n39

"anti-storico," 211, 211n5

The Approach to Reality (Douglas), 268

Archdale, Helen, 346

Ardis, Ann, 262, 360n11, 361n13

Are These Things So?, 273

Aristotle, 28, 28n31, 60, 163n6, 232, 232n17

Arnold, Matthew, 205n19, 312

Array. *See* English Array

Arrow Editions: and William Carlos Williams, 177, 177n5; and *The Chinese Written Character as a Medium for Poetry*, 71n9, 177, 177n4, 197–9, 197nn1–2, 198n2, 199n1, 211, 211n3, 219, 219n2, 220n5, 226, 226n13; EP's question on, 220; and Ideogrammic series, 71n9, 177, 177n5; and *Ta Hio*, 199. *See also* Codman, Florence

Aryan Path, 229, 229n1

aspidistra, 82, 82n3

Associated Press, 171, 171n8

Athanasian Creed, 36, 36n22

Auden, W.H., 161n3, 334

Australia, xix, 229, 229n2, 265

Austria, 12, 217n18, 275, 278, 337

avant-garde code, xxxiii–xxxiv

L'Avvenire d'Italia, 87n6

Axe and Faggot, 61, 71, 71n10, 81, 82, 287, 366n15

Axis, 229, 229n5

Baciagalupo, Massimo, 359n3

Background to Chinese Art (Porteus), 36n23

Bacon, Francis, 60, 60n30

Badenhausen, Richard, 302, 303, 355n18, 369n8

Bailey Bros., 235, 240n1, 242n1

Baker, Augustus, 6, 6n8

Baker, Jacob, 6, 6n8, 331

A Baker's Dozen of Tin Trumpets (Selver), 111n5

Baldwin, Stanley, 23n3

banks: Bank of England, 94n14, 122n4, 129, 132, 132n8, 133, 133n17, 134n19; Butchart's book on banking, 165, 165n15; Douglas on, 269–71; EP on types of, 7n3; EP's suspicion of, 272; international banks, 44, 44n2, 45n7;

in Italy, 7, 7n3, 12; and Jackson, 20, 20nn10–11; Laughlin on Roman banking, 232n20, 233; Nott on, 373n24; Por's article on bankers, 208; Second Bank of the United States, 20n11; and Social Credit, 260

Bardsley, William L., 203–4, 203n6

Barker, George, 335

Barnhisel, Gregory, 321, 322, 353nn3–4, 372n18

Barr, J. Stuart. *See* Gesell, Silvio

Barry, Iris, 336

BASIC English, 25, 25nn9–10, 27n25, 33, 33n9, 44, 44n4, 60, 60n29, 343

The B.B.C. Speech and the Fear of Leisure (Orage), 4n11, 126n20

Beckett, John Warburton, 231n5, 292, 342

Beevers, John Leonard, 136, 136n11, 152, 152n2

Belloc, Hilaire: and Distributism, 94n15, 107n12, 267, 332, 334, 362n28; identification of, 107n12; and Lansbury, 339; and *New Age*, 262; and Soames, 194n5; and *Social Credit: An Impact* by EP, 107

Beltramelli, Antonio, 282, 365n8, 366n12

Bennet, Charles Augustus Kerr (Eighth Earl of Tankerville), 126, 126n21, 371n6

Bercovitch, Sacvan, 358n44

Berkeley, George, 60, 60n30

Better Money, 114n8

Biddle, Nicholas, 20n11

Binyon, Robert Laurence, 125, 125n13

Biosophical Review, 46, 46n16

Bird, Otto A., 56n13, 60, 60n28, 331

Bird, William Augustus, 331

Black, Hugo LaFayette, 112, 112n11

BLAST, 35n18, 143, 143n10

Bloomsbury Group: and *Cantos* by EP, 9, 76, 76n17; criticism of Squire by, 47n20; EP on, 9, 9n8, 76, 201, 310–11; and EP's literary criticism, 43; and Ideogrammic series, 81, 81n3; and Lady Morrell, 106n6; sexuality of members of, 9, 9n8, 310

Blue Moon Press, 215n11

Bombay Theosophy Company, 229n1

Bone, Homer Truett, 112, 112n10

Bonner and Company, 254n9

Books Abroad, 111–2, 111n3

boot licking, 130, 133, 134

Borah, William Edgar, 88, 88n15, 353n3

Bornstein, George, xiv

Bosanquet, Theodora, 109, 109n31

Bosworth, R.J.B., 24n5, 357n30

Bottai, Giuseppe, 32n2

Bourdieu, Pierre, xxxiii, 264

Bowden, Harold, 371n6

Bradshaw, David, 18n5

The Breakdown of Money (Hollis), 231, 231n10

Brenton, Arthur: biographical sketch of, 331–2; and Dyson, 41; and EP, 57, 169, 248; EP's and Nott's interest in publishing collection of works by, 161, 161n5, 169, 169n5, 248, 248n8; EP's question about literature and, 47; and Mairet and Newsome, 41, 51, 57, 57n16; as *New Age* editor, xxix, 51, 51n13, 57n16, 248n2, 332, 342; and Nott, 171, 171n5; and Social Credit, 51n14, 331–2

Breton, André, 225n6

Bridson, D.G., 131n4

Britain: antisemitism in, 271, 290; antiwar movement in, 108n19; boot licking in, 130, 133, 134; courageous men in, 135, 135n22; decline of Social Credit in, 224, 230, 230n2; EP on British "blackout" on Mussolini, 287–8, 366n20; general election (November 1935) in, 23, 23n3, 54–5, 55n7, 136n3; Jewish aristocracy in, 146n2, 147–8, 147nn7–10; Labour Party in, 24, 30, 30n4, 180n5, 249, 294, 333, 339, 341; lapse of, from Edenic state of ignorance, 207, 207n5; markets for EP's writing in, 41–2; Nott on nature of the English, 38, 40, 371n8; reading public of, 125, 134, 137, 137n12, 201; sales of EP's works in, 58, 58n18; Social Credit Party of, 32n1, 117n1, 136n3, 164n9, 224n8, 338. *See also* British Fascism; Social Credit

British Fascism: and antisemitism, xxi, 297; and EP, xix, xxi, xxxvi–xxxvii, 195, 196n10, 286–98; and Fascio di Londra,

195, 195n4, 197, 197n3, 199, 293; goals of, 296–7; and Italian Fascism, xix, xxi, 288–94; and *Jefferson and/or Mussolini* by EP, 196, 196n10, 197, 197n3, 199; and Leese, 288–94; and Mosley, xxxvi, 81n1, 82n2, 287, 294, 367n40; Munro on, 24; and Pellizzi, 195n4; pro-Nazi factions of, 289–94; and Social Credit, xxi, xxxvi–xxxvii, 231, 231n7, 286, 287, 288–9, 293–8, 368n45, 368nn47–48; and Nesta Webster, 364n39. *See also* British Union of Fascists (BUF); Imperial Fascist League (IFL)

British Fascisti, 363n34

British-Italian Bulletin, 182n5, 195–6, 195n5, 196n7, 196n11, 205, 205n14, 293, 368n43

British People's Party, 126n22

British Union of Fascists (BUF): "axe and faggot" insignia on letterhead of, 366n15; and EP, 288; founding of, xxxvi, 294; and Italian Fascism, 294; Leese on, 289; and Mosley, xxxvi, 81n1, 82n2, 287, 294; and *New English Weekly*, 287; publication of EP's *What Is Money For?*, 170n13, 171n9, 202n4, 206n4, 249n10, 252, 345; and Social Credit, 274, 288–9, 295–6, 364n41; split in, 231, 231n5, 249, 249n10, 292, 341–2; and Thomson, 252n4, 287, 288, 345, 364n41, 367–8n42. *See also* British Fascism

British Union Quarterly, 220n2, 230, 230n4, 249–50, 249n15, 251n24, 292, 345

Britons (organization), 367n30

Brown, Robert Carleton, 87, 87n9, 109, 109n33

Browne, Martin, 355n18, 369n8

Bryher. *See* Ellerman, Annie Winifred

Buchan, John, 166, 166n21

BUF. *See* British Union of Fascists (BUF)

Bunting, Basil, 59, 59n24, 99, 99n9, 145

Burkitt, Brian, 332, 359nn5–6

business sense, 209–10, 238, 320, 372n15

Butchart, Montgomery: on Aristotle, 60; biographical sketch and identification

of, 4n12, 232n12, 332; as bridge between Hargrave and Chandos Group, 164, 164n14; EP on, 139, 163, 164, 204; and EP's article on Frobenius, 198; EP's influence on, 163n4, 332; and *Jefferson and/or Mussolini*, 169–70, 170n8, 372n12; and *New English Weekly*, 10, 10n2, 60; and Nott after demise of Stanley Nott Ltd., 245; and Orage's writings, 4, 4n11, 192n1; and Pamphlets on the New Economics, 371n6; and Por's writings, 220; as reader of *Jefferson and/or Mussolini* and *Social Credit: An Impact* manuscripts, 81, 97, 97n8; review of Colbourne's *Sanity of Social Credit* by, 333; and *Townsman*, 244, 244n6, 332. *See also Money* (Butchart); *To-Morrow's Money* (Butchart)

Butchart, Mrs. Montgomery, 220, 220n2, 251, 251n24

Butler, Nicholas Murray, 130, 131, 131n3, 132, 146

"buzzards" (derogatory term), 26, 26n17, 33, 33n6, 83, 124, 159

Byrne, L.D., 270

"The Cabinet of a Dream, and Congress Should Go on the Air" (Pound), 255n8

Caico, Lina, 86, 86n6

Cairoli, Luigi Pasquale, 233, 233n22

Calvert, Bruce T., 95, 95n22

Camagna, Carlo, 195n5, 196, 196n11, 368n43

Campbell, Jane Allen, 106, 106n7

Campbell, Timothy, 369n7, 369n10

Canada, 217, 224, 224n8, 231, 231n8, 265–6, 271–2, 276, 333, 361n22, 363n36

Canada Reconstructed (Woodward), 92n4

Canfield, Cass, 372n14

Cannistraro, xxvii

Canterbury, Dean of. *See* Johnson, Hewlett (Dean of Canterbury)

Canto 7 (Pound), 45n8, 313

Canto 8 (Pound), 264

Canto 11 (Pound), 303

Canto 22 (Pound), 358n41

Canto 31 (Pound), 20, 313

Canto 37 (Pound), 20, 20n10

Canto 38 (Pound), xxix, 9, 9n10, 269

Canto 41 (Pound), 9, 9n10, 20, 282, 301–2, 337

Canto 45 (Pound), 40n9

Canto 74 (Pound), 337

Canto 78 (Pound), 337

Canto 86 (Pound), 346·

Canto 95 (Pound), 43n22

Cantos (Pound): abbreviations in, 308; compared with EP's prose, 299–300; and Criterion, 213, 213n4; "documentary method" in, 305; Douglas in, 9n10; Faber and Faber as publisher of, 232, 232n15; Frobenius in, 337; Gesell in, 9n10; "ideogrammic method" of, xxv; Jefferson in, 9n10, 20; letters in, 304, 305; as magnum opus, xv; Malatesta Cantos, 281, 283–4, 301, 304; and modernism, 280; and Mussolini, 9n10, 282; in New English Weekly, 269, 363n31; and palingenesis, 368n49; on Thaddeus Pound, 344; "rag bag" form of, 279; review of, in Time and Tide, 131n4; and Social Credit, 8–9; and tones of voice, 309; typography of, 309; Zaharoff in, as Sir Zenos Metevsky, 98n3. See also Eleven New Cantos: XXXI–XLI (Pound); and specific Cantos

capitalism, 261, 263–4, 265, 266, 285. See also economics

Capitol Daily, 255, 255n2

Carlyle, Thomas, 361n14

Carnegie Endowment for International Peace, 131n3, 146

Carpenter, Humphrey, 252n5, 255n1

Carswell, John, xxiii, 323, 327

Casillo, Robert, 290, 355n16, 359n3

Caslon, William, 121n10

Cassell and Company publishers, 245–6, 245n6

Cathay (Pound): compared with Ta Hio, 26, 36, 41; cover of, 109, 109n30, 187, 187n5, 189; description of, 26n15, 332; publishers of different editions of, 187n5, 199n3

Catholic Church. See Roman Catholic Church

"The Causes of War: 'Why Do Pacifists Evade Them?'" (Pound), 131n3

Cavalcanti, Guido, 187n9, 306, 331 ·

Cerio, F. Ferruccio, 282

Chace, William, 359n3

The Challenge of Economic Freedom (Gesell), 92n4

Chamberlain, Arthur Neville, 133, 133n12, 134

The Chandos Group: Butchart as bridge between Hargrave and, 164, 164n14; description of, 332; EP's response to questionnaire by, 122, 122n7; and EP's second letter to Angell, 131, 131n6, 136, 136n9; members of, 332, 340, 344; and New English Weekly, 332, 342; and Social Credit: An Impact by EP, 108

Cheadle, Mary Paterson, 345

Chesterton, Gilbert Keith: biographical sketch of, 332; and Distributism, 94n15, 107n12, 263, 266–7, 332, 334; EP on getting answers from, 108; and EP's economics, 140; and G.K.'s Weekly, 94n15, 108, 332; and New Age, 262, 360n12

Cheveaux de Diomede (Gourmont), 59

"A Child's Guide to Economics" (Pound), 94n15

The Chinese Written Character as a Medium for Poetry (Fenollosa): and Allen and Unwin publisher, 240, 240n4, 242, 242n3; American edition of, from Arrow Editions, 71n9, 177, 177n5, 197, 197nn1–2, 198, 198n2, 199, 199n1, 211, 211n3, 219, 219n2, 220n5; announcements of, 91; binding of, 194n4; book jacket for, 194, 194n4; copyright concerns about, 178, 178nn1–2, 197, 197n2; description of, 332–3, 336; discrepancy in British and American spellings in, 190, 190n8; EP's interest in combining BASIC English with, 33, 33n10, 60, 60n29; and Faber and Faber, 25, 238, 240n4, 242n3; foreword of, 132, 132n9, 333; in Ideogrammic series, xviii, 26, 26n19, 58, 59, 99, 102,

corporatism, 297

correspondence. *See* epistolary practice; Pound/Nott correspondence

Corriere della Sera, 195, 195n3, 196

Cosgrave, John O'Hara, 209, 209n4, 210, 210n2, 372n15

Costigan, Edward Prentiss, 112, 112n9

Coughlin, Father Charles Edward, 145n15, 166, 166n25, 255n6, 333

Cousens, Hilderic Edwin, 4n11, 139, 139n12, 332, 333

Cox-McCormack, Nancy, 284

Creative Art in England (Johnstone), 225, 225n2, 227, 227n4, 229, 229n4, 371n2

Credit Power and Democracy (Douglas), xvii, 261, 263, 354n11, 360n8, 369n4

The Criterion: advertising for Ideogrammic series in, 27, 27n26; and *Cantos* by EP, 213, 213n4, 335; contributors to, 334, 344; description of, 334; Eliot as editor of, 19n3, 36, 36n23, 213n4, 214, 250n16, 334; end of, 250n16; EP as contributor to, 15n10, 19, 19n3, 40n11, 77n21, 78, 168n1, 216n14, 334; EP on, 250; EP's memoriam for Orage in, 77n21, 78, 101, 101n19, 125, 125n10; EP's writings from, for Yale University Press publication, 124; focus of, 334; review of, in *New English Weekly*, 21n13; review of EP's *Jefferson and/or Mussolini* in, 372n12; Social Credit monthly magazine compared with, 35; subscription cost for, 21, 21n13

Critica Fascista, 32, 32n2

cultural heritage, 302, 369n4

Culture and Anarchy (Arnold), 205n19

Cummings, E.E.: as contributor to *Townsman*, 244n6; and Fox, 336; and Ideogrammic series, 27, 58, 58n22, 59, 59n27, 61, 70, 72, 72n12, 99, 99n12, 102, 119, 120–1, 144; and literary policy of *New English Weekly*, 56n13, 57, 57n14; and New Deal, 59, 59n27; Nott's interest in publishing poetry by, 70, 70n4, 72, 72n12, 110, 111, 111n1, 113–15, 119, 119n9; poems by, published in *New English Weekly*, 70n4; poems by, sent to

EP, 110, 110n36; popular view of works by, 43; review copies of EP's writings sent to, 110; sexually explicit poems by, 58, 72, 72n11; "typographical curiosities" in poetry by, 115, 121, 121n11, 306

Cunard, Lady Maud Emerald, 106, 106n5

Cunard, Nancy, 87n9

Curtis Browne Literary Agency, 18, 18n3

Cutting, Bronson Murray, 87, 87n14, 111n2, 353n3

Daily Herald, 335, 339

Dali, Salvador, 225n6

Dante, 34, 272, 280, 339

Davidson, Eugene, 77n18, 370n14

Davis, Joseph, 5n3

Dazzi, Carlo, 306

Dearborn (Mich.) Independent, 270

Debabelization (Ogden), 25n10, 343

"Debabelization and Ogden" (Pound), 25n10, 42n20, 44, 44n4

From Debt to Prosperity (Larkin), 89n21, 339

De Kruif, Paul Henry, 88, 88n20, 127, 127n27

De la Mare, Richard, 336

Delphian Quarterly, 85, 85n9, 87

Demant, V.A., 332

"Demarcations" (Pound), 230n4

Depression. *See* Great Depression

Desai, Meghnad, xvi, 276

Dewey, John, 127, 127n25, 356n29

Dial, 35n17

Diggins, John P., 356n29

diplomatic editing, 314, 370n19

Distributism: and Chesterton, 94n15, 107n12, 263, 266–7, 332, 334; compared with Guild Socialism, 267, 334, 337; description of, 334; Finlay on, 344; and *New Age*, 107n12, 267; and *New English Weekly*, xxxvi; and Reckitt, 334, 344, 362n26; and Roman Catholic Church, 267, 334; and Social Credit, 266–7, 362n26, 362n28

Dobrée, Bonamy, 112, 112n6

Dole & Morss publishers, 245

Dollfuss, Engelbert, 278

Douglas, Major Clifford Hugh: "A + B Theorem" of, 196n9, 269, 276, 363nn30–31, 364n41; antisemitism of, 269–72; biographical sketch of, 260–1, 334, 360n7; and Brenton, 51, 51n14; and British Fascism, 231, 231n7; Cousens on, 333; on cultural heritage, 369n4; as engineer/old guard, 16, 40n11; in EP's *Cantos*, 9n10; EP's first meeting with, 259, 274, 359n2; EP's reference to, 217; EP's synthesis of Gesell's economic reforms with Social Credit of, xxi, 15n10, 92n3, 273, 274–5, 288–9, 318, 355n17, 364n41; EP's writings on, 204n10, 250–1, 250n21; and *Fig Tree*, 217n21, 270; Fisher's *Stamp Scrip* on, xxix, 15n9; Gesell compared with, 16; and Hargrave, 276, 318; Keynes on, 196n9, 265, 361n20; and National Dividend, 40n9, 231n9, 334; opposition of, to fascism, xxxvi; and Orage, 260–1, 361n15; in Pamphlets on the New Economics series, 126n19, 316, 371nn4–6; and plan for Social Credit monthly magazine, 31, 31n11; and royalties, 210; and Social Credit, xvii, 6n7, 259–64, 266, 268, 274–7, 334, 354n11, 361n20; and Social Credit Secretariat, 76n12, 150, 204n10, 318; writings by, xvii, 6, 6n6, 86n2, 126n19, 164n8, 204n10, 232n13, 261, 263, 268, 316, 317, 334, 354n11, 355n19, 371nn4–6; writing style of, 264, 307. *See also* Social Credit

The Douglas Manual (Mairet), 7, 7n1, 340

Drummond, John: antisemitism of, 113n6, 273, 290, 335, 364n40; biographical sketch of, 335; on Cummings, 113; and "Ezra Pound on Gold, War, and National Money," 255; and *Guide to Kulchur* by EP, 255n3, 335, 364n40; influence of Nesta Webster on, 364n39; and Larkin, 339; and *Westminster Magazine*, 87n10

Drummond, Lindsay, 161n3

Duckworth, Gerald, 64, 220, 220n8, 221

Duffy, Francis Ryan, 95, 95n27

Du Maurier, Daphne, 320

Duncan, Ethel M., 89, 89n25

Duncan, Ronald Frederick Henry, 244, 244n6, 244n8, 249, 249n14, 332

Dyson, William Henry: biographical sketch and identification of, 3n5, 335; and Brenton, 41; EP's letters to, 138, 150; and Lansbury, 339; and merger of *New Age* and *New English Weekly*, 51, 51n12, 56n12, 138n3, 139, 150n8; and *New English Weekly*, 37, 246n9, 342; Nott on writing by, xxx, 29, 150; Nott's relationship with, 151; and Orage's writings, 4n11; and Pamphlets on the New Economics series, xxix, 3, 371n6; personality of, 150

An Early Martyr and Other Poems (Williams), 119n12

Economic Democracy (Douglas), 204n10, 261, 263, 264, 360n8

Economic Reform Club and Institute, 253–4, 253n8

economics: *Alfred Venison's Poems* as satirical poetry on, xxix, xxxii, 18, 316, 331, 354n14; capitalism, 261, 263–4, 265, 266, 285; classical equilibrium theory of, 261; death of Scarcity Economics in Italy, 19n3; early twentieth-century economic radicalism, 260, 261, 265–7; EP as commentator on generally, xvi–xvii, xx–xxiv, xxix–xxxiii, xxxvii, 354n8, 354nn10–13; EP's and Nott's economic heresies, 317–20; EP's lack of formal training in, xxxi, xxxii, 356n23; EP's linking of economic conditions to start of the arts, 40n9; EP's need to establish himself as authority on, xxii–xxiv, xxx–xxxiii, xxxv–xxxvi, 14n8, 84–5, 355n18, 358nn36–37, 371n9; EP's passion regarding and focus on, 7, 22, 22n3, 213, 213n3, 357n31; EP's reluctance about, 354n11; EP's turn to "econ/ and politics," xvii–xviii, xxxiii, 259–64, 283, 359n2, 366n10; EP's writings on generally, published by Stanley Nott Ltd., xviii, xxii–xxiii, xxiv, xxxi–xxxii,

xxxvi, 240, 322, 354n14; influences on
EP's interest in, xvii–xviii, xxix, 259–
64, 359n2; Johnson's passion regarding,
22, 22n22; *Morning Post* letters by EP
on, 12, 15n10, 19, 20n12; Orage's opinion of EP's writings on economics,
356n21; proposed collected edition of
EP's economic writings to be published by Yale University Press, 77–8,
77nn18–21, 80, 82–5, 83n3, 87n12, 96,
100–1, 100n16, 101n19; socialist feminist critique of classical economics,
359n6; underconsumptionist theory in,
261, 264, 265, 361n20; Williams on EP's
lack of expertise in, xxxi, 356n23. *See
also* Pamphlets on the New Economics;
Social Credit; Stanley Nott Ltd.; *and
specific economists*
Economics in the Middle Ages
(Featherstone), 108n22
"Economics Reference Library," 172,
172n10
Les Écris Noveaux, 250, 250n21
Eden, (Sir Robert) Anthony, 207, 207n5
"Eeldrop and Appleplex" (Eliot), 135,
135n25, 137n14, 143n9
Egoist, 248, 248n6, 360n10
Egoist Press, 250, 250n17
Eleven New Cantos: XXXI–XLI (Pound),
8–9, 76, 76nn16–17, 131, 131n4, 304, 310,
335. *See also Cantos* (Pound)
Eliot, T.S.: Browne's relationship to,
355n18, 369n8; and Chandos Group,
332; and collaboration, 302–4; as contributor to *New English Weekly*, 178; as
Criterion editor, 19n3, 36, 36n23, 213n4,
214, 334; on EP as critic, 212, 214n5;
EP on getting answers from, 108, 120,
135; and EP's involvement in *The Waste
Land*, 280; as Faber and Faber editor,
42n18, 214n6, 235n1, 243, 335–6, 357n35;
and fascism, xvi; friendship between
EP and, xxxv; and Heap, 212; and Ideogrammic series, 27, 30, 30n8, 58, 58n22,
59, 59n25, 64, 71, 99, 99n12, 102, 118,
118n4, 120, 122, 135, 137, 137n14, 143,
143n9, 144; and literary policy of *New*

English Weekly, 57, 57n14; on *London
Mercury*, 47n20; and *New English
Weekly*, 10n6, 342; Nott on, 210; and
Nott's Pamphlets on the New Econom-
ics series, 18, 38, 59, 59n25, 64, 99n12;
and plan for Social Credit monthly
magazine, 31, 31n11; Quinn as patron
of, 216n12; snubbing of Nott by, 243n3,
245; and Social Credit, 18n5, 357n35;
support for Mussolini by, 285; and
Verdenal, 361n16; writings by, 280
Ellerman, Annie Winifred, 147n10
Ellerman, Sir John Reeves, first baronet,
147, 147n9
Ellerman, Sir John Reeves, second
baronet, 147, 147n9
Ellis, Havelock, 360n12
Emerson, Ralph Waldo, 358n44
England. *See* Britain; British Fascism
English Array, 292, 294, 296, 346
English Mistery, 292, 294, 295, 296, 346
The English Press: Newspapers and News
(Soames), 194n5, 199, 199n6, 202, 202n1,
241, 241n8
English Review, 205, 205n15, 261, 361n15
Enlightenment, 278–9
epistolary idiom, xiv, xix–xx, xxiii,
305–14
epistolary practice: abbreviations in, 308;
cipher and coded language in, 313;
cultural work of EP's letters, xxi–xxii,
xxxiii–xxxvi, 300–2; deformations of
ordinary syntax by EP, 306–7; and diplomatic editing, 314, 370n19; epistolary
corpus of EP, xviii, 299, 354n15; epistolary idiom of EP, xiv, xix–xx, xxiii,
305–14; importance of EP's letters
generally, 299–300; and *ira* (wrathful
indignation), 311–2, 370n15; irreverence
and playfulness in, 312–13, 370n18;
letters as record of historical struggle,
304–5; Lewis on style of EP's letters,
xiv; Marinetti compared with EP,
306–12, 370n13, 370n15; in Pound/Nott
correspondence, 307–8, 310–11; published editions of EP's letters, xx–xxii,
299, 355n17; punctuation marks in, 308;

spacing and layout in, 308; and theory
of collaborative knowledge, 302–4, 311;
and tones of voice, 308–9; typography
of EP's letters, 308–9; "urgent laconicism" of, 307–8; word deformations
and neologisms in, 306, 309–11
Esquire, 94n20
Essential Communism (Read), 55n11,
161n3, 318
Ethiopia, 226n12. *See also* Abyssinia
The European Quarterly: and *Books
Abroad*, 111, 111n3; description of, 335;
editors of, 31, 31n13, 43n24, 48, 50n7,
52, 335, 341; EP critique of, 44, 46,
46n16, 48; EP's refusal to write article
for, 31, 34–5, 34n15; and Heap, 48, 57;
and Lavrin's foreign language expertise, 52, 57; Nott's publication of, 40,
40n6, 50, 138n6; number of issues of,
31n14; Selver as Polish translator in,
111n5; and Social Credit, 50, 50n7
Evans, Myfanwy, 229n5
Everybody's Magazine, 209n4, 210n2,
372n15
"Ezra Pound on Gold, War, and National
Money" (Pound), 255, 255n2

The Faber Book of Modern Verse, 214,
214nn6–7
Faber and Faber: *ABC of Economics* by
EP published by, xxxi, 13n3, 77, 77n19,
100; *Active Anthology* by EP published
by, 100n18; *Cantos* by EP published
by, 232, 232n15, 335; and *The Chinese
Written Character as a Medium for
Poetry*, 25, 238, 240n4, 242n3; and
demise of Stanley Nott Ltd., 238,
240n4, 242nn2–3, 243; description of,
335–6; Eliot as editor at, 42n18, 235,
235n1, 243, 335–6, 357n35; EP's poetry
published by, 58, 100n18; *Faber Book of
Modern Verse* published by, 214, 214n6;
Guide to Kulchur by EP published by,
232n16, 250n19; history of, 203n4, 335;
Make It New by EP published by, 77,
77n18, 109, 175n2; Morley as founding
director of, 100n18, 243n2; Morley at

generally, 235n1; Nott's exploration of
employment at, 235, 236, 236n2, 240,
243; Nott's relationship with Morley at,
over publishing matters, 100, 122, 156,
156n5; *Polite Essays* by EP published
by, 77n21, 83n3, 124n1; and proposed
collected edition of economic writings
by EP, 83, 85, 85n10, 96, 115, 115n2, 125,
125n14, 156n5; and sales of EP's works,
42, 58n18; and *Ta Hio*, 240n4, 242n2;
and *What Is Money For?* by EP, 203
Faber, Geoffrey, 203n4, 335
Fabian Society, 180n5, 263, 333
Fack, Hugo R.: antisemitism of, 92n3,
273, 290, 336; biographical sketch of,
336; EP's economic publications sent
to, 92; Gesell's *Natural Economic
Order* published by, 15n9, 337; and
Social Credit, 94, 95n16, 273, 274, 275;
support for Hitler by, 92n3; translation
of Gesell's *The Challenge of Economic
Freedom* by, 92n4
Fairbairn, Wingfield, and Wykes, 234n2,
240, 240n3, 253
Farrar and Rinehart, 335
Fascio di Londra, 195, 195n4, 197, 197n3,
199, 293
fascism: ambiguous meanings of, 278,
365n1; American attitude toward, in
1920s, 356n29; Douglas's opposition
to, xxxvi; European fascist dictators,
278, 319, 372n11; in interwar years, 278;
and modernist literature generally, xvi;
Nott's opposition to, xxxvi, xxxvii, 173,
319, 372n11; and palingenesis, 368n49;
perception of, during interwar years,
xxvi–xxvii; scholarship on, 278–9,
365n3; and Social Credit, xxxvi–xxxvii.
See also British Fascism; Italian
Fascism
Fascism (Por), 20n6
*Fascist Quarterly. See British Union
Quarterly*
Fascist: The Organ of Racial Fascism:
antisemitism in, 146–8, 146n2,
147nn6–11, 290, 340; copy of, sent
to EP, 273, 367n28; copy of, sent to

Tinkham, 146–7, 147n6; on Italian invasion of Abyssinia, 367n37; and Leese, 142–3, 142n7, 146–8, 146n2, 147n6, 288–90

Fazio, Cornelio, 369n7

Featherstone, Hammond, 108, 108n22

Fenollosa, Ernest Francisco: biographical sketch of, 336; EP's interest in combining BASIC English with Fenollosa's work on Chinese ideogram, 33, 33n10, 60, 60n29; influence of, on EP, xxv, 81n2; papers of, entrusted to EP, 25n11, 58n21, 336; as sinologist, xxv, 25n11, 58n21, 141n3, 336. *See also The Chinese Written Character as a Medium for Poetry* (Fenollosa)

The Fifth Decad of Cantos (Pound), 232, 232n15

Fig Tree, 204n13, 217, 217n21, 270

Financial Armageddon (Featherstone), 108n22

Findley, Timothy, xvi

Finlay, John: antisemitism, 271; on Brenton's relationship with Social Credit Secretariat, 51n14, 332; on British Fascism, 294, 295, 297; on Distributist League, 344; on Douglas and Social Credit Secretariat, 318; on Gould, 108n23; on Green Shirts, 368n48; on Guild Socialism, 267; on Hargrave, 276; on *New Age*, 360n11; on Orage, 328; on Social Credit, 260, 261, 294, 297, 359n47

Firdusi, 59

First World War. *See* World War I

Fisher, Irving, xxix, 15n9, 101n22, 127, 127n28, 274, 336, 364n42

Flory, Wendy, xxxiii, 358n44, 369n7, 370n16

Ford, Ford Madox, 205n16, 214, 214n5, 219, 220, 221, 221n9, 226, 334

Ford, Henry, 270

Fordham, Montague, 334

Fortune, 10, 10n5

Foucault, Michel, 278

The Foundations of Aesthetics (Ogden and Richards), 27n25

Fox, Douglas Claughton: in Africa, 60, 60n31; biographical sketch of, 336; and Frobenius, 26, 26nn20–21, 60, 60n31, 144n8, 201n4, 336; Frobenius booklet by, for Ideogrammic series, 26, 26n20, 144, 201, 201n4, 206, 207, 228n4, 229, 229n3

Franco, Francisco, 278

Franks, Rebecca, 147, 147n8

Free Economy Publishing Company, 15n9

Freeston, Charles, 371n2

Freytag-Loringhoven, Elsa, Baroness von, 43, 43n22

Frobenius, Leo: biographical sketch of, 337; EP's article on, 198, 198n4, 199; and Fox, 26, 26nn20–21, 60, 60n31, 144n8, 201n4, 336; Fox's booklet on, in Ideogrammic series, 26, 26n20, 144, 201, 201n4, 206, 207, 228, 228n4, 229, 229n3; influence of, on EP, 26n22, 337; and New English Weekly, 228, 228n4; popular view of works by, 43

Functional Socialism (Hobson), 163n6

Galbraith, John Kenneth, 260

Galeazzo, Ciano, 90, 90n28

Gallup, Donald: on *Alfred Venison's Poems* by EP, 136n6; on *British Union Quarterly* articles by EP, 230n4; on *The Chinese Written Character as a Medium for Poetry*, 52n19, 178n1, 194n4, 223n3, 242n3; on Ideogrammic series, 27n23, 52n19, 119n10, 338; on *Introductory Text Book E.P.*, 254n9; on *Jefferson and/or Mussolini* by EP, 153n1, 168n1, 175n3, 227n3, 339; on *Progrès civique*, 250n21; on *Rassegna Monetaria* by EP, 251n24; on *Social Credit: An Impact* by EP, 136n5; on *Ta Hio*, 41nn15–16, 52n19, 101n23, 242n2; on Williams's *In the Grain*, 27n23, 119n10, 338

García Lorca, Federico, 335

Gascoygne, David, 315

Gaudier-Brzeska, Henri, xvii, 263–4, 361n16

Gaudier-Brzeska (Pound), 225, 225n3, 248n5, 263, 365n10

Hallinan, Charles T., 171, 171n6

Hargrave, John Gordon: action-oriented approach of, 164, 164n14, 277; and *Attack!*, 117, 117n1; biographical sketch of, 338; and Brenton, 332; copy of *Social Credit: An Impact* sent to, 94; correspondence of, 32; and Douglas, 276; and EP, 39, 39n3, 40, 40n11, 46, 138n2, 139, 164, 296, 318, 338; and Green Shirts, 32n1, 117n1, 136n3, 164, 164n9, 164nn12–13, 172n10, 296, 338; and Kindred of the Kibbo Kift, 37, 37n1, 39, 39n3, 276, 338, 362n29; and Mairet, 35; and Mosley, 367n40; and *New Age*, 277; Nott on, 37–8, 39n3, 136, 277, 296, 318; novels by, 39; and Pamphlets on the New Economics series, 103; and size of Imperial Fascist League (IFL), 367n31; and Social Credit, 32n1, 39, 39n4, 46, 136n3, 268, 274, 276–7, 296, 318; and Social Credit Party, 32n1, 117n1, 136n3, 164n9, 338; writing style of, 103

Harmsworth, Desmond, 223, 223n5

Harrison, Austin, 361n15

Hastings, Beatrice, 215, 215n11

Hatry, Clarence Charles, 104, 104n2, 104n4

Hattersley, C. Marshall, 371n6

Hawkins, A. Desmond, 161n2

Heap, Jane: biographical sketch and identification of, 4n14, 338; and Eliot, 212; and EP, 34, 57, 211; and *European Quarterly*, 48; and Gurdjieff, xxiv, 4, 268, 338, 372n19; and *Little Review*, 4n14, 34n14, 42n21, 338; and new quarterly on art and literature (1936), 210–18, 210n3, 211n4, 215n9, 216n14, 222, 222n2, 224, 226; Nott on, 52, 57n15, 210; personality of, 31, 31n12, 38; refusal of, to publish EP's writings in *Little Review*, 42, 42n21

Hebdomeros (Chirico), 225, 225n7

Henry, Leigh, 371n2

Hesketh, Bob, 266, 269–70, 271, 362n22

Hesse, Herman, 334

Hield, Robert, 93, 93n9, 368n43

Higham (David) Associates, 202, 202n3, 206n4

Hitler, Adolf: compared with Douglas's National Dividend, 231, 231n9; EP on, 367n41; Fack's support of, 92n3; fascism associated with, 278; Leese's support of, 289–91; Mosley's preference for Mussolini over, 231n5; and Mussolini, xxv, xxvi, xxvii; and National Socialist League (NSL), 292; Nott on, 372n11; Nott's assistance to Czech refugees from Hitler's Germany, 255n5; *Table Talk* by, 367n41. *See also* Nazism

Hobson, S.G., 163n6, 267, 337, 361n20

Hodge, A., 179n5

Hogarth Press, 194n5, 214n7

Hogben, Lancelot, 246n10

Hollis, Christopher, 231, 231n10, 232

Holmes, 248

Holter, E.S., xliv, 164n8

Homage to Sextus Propertius (Pound), 41, 41n16

Homer. *See Iliad* (Homer); *Odyssey* (Homer)

Houseman, Alfred Edward, 125, 125n11

How to Read (Pound), 223n5, 354n12

Hughes, Glenn (Arthur), 201, 201n3, 345

Hughes, John W., 360n7

Hugh Selwyn Mauberley (Pound), 26, 26n18, 263

Hull, Merlin, 95, 95n25

Hulme, T.E., 262, 360n12

Hunt, Isabel Violet, 107, 107n14

Hutchinson, Frances, 332, 359nn5–6

Huxley, Aldous, 334

Hynes, Samuel, xxvi, xxxviii, 214n7

Ibbotson, Joseph, xiv

ideogram, definition of, 81n2

"ideogramic method," xxv

Ideogrammic series: advertising for, 27, 27n26, 117; announcements of, 91, 91n35; and Arrow Editions, 71n9, 177, 177n5; blurbs or announcements for, 113, 114, 120, 153, 154–5, 154n3, 194; and Cocteau, 13n5, 26, 26n20, 58, 58n20,

61, 100, 102–3, 144; compared with Pamphlets on the New Economics series, 52, 52n19, 57n17, 118; cover of, 109, 109n27, 118n6; description and purpose of, xxxi–xxxii, 43, 43n23, 139, 194, 338; editor's fee for, 65, 71; EP as editor of, xxxi–xxxii, 43, 52, 52n19, 61, 71n8; EP's cost for each booklet in, 93, 93n8, 106, 118, 118n3; imprint for, 118, 118n6; length of booklets in, 58, 64, 64n7, 119, 119n8, 123n10, 201; and Lowe, 187; and New English Weekly, 117; Nott's eagerness to resume production on, 161, 174, 174n6, 193, 226; Ogden's work distinguished from, 26, 26n19, 30n6, 33, 33n7, 113, 113n2, 114, 114n10; order of issuing booklets in, 61, 70–1, 118, 118n4, 119, 338; price of, 52, 52n19, 57, 57n17, 64, 64n6, 101, 118n5, 123, 152, 206; printing costs for, 52; proposed works for inclusion in, 13n5, 26–7, 26nn19–22, 27nn23–25, 33, 38, 58–61, 70–1, 99–100, 102–3, 193, 193n2, 194; royalties for, 71, 158; sales needed to break even on, 81; schedule for publication of, 200, 200n7, 229, 229n3; title of series, 61, 64, 71, 71n10, 81, 81nn1–3, 82; titles of works in, 25n14, 26, 26n19, 61, 70–1, 118, 118n4, 119, 144–5, 338, 358n39; typography and design of, 118, 119, 121, 121nn9–10, 121n12, 123, 123n13, 152, 156, 156n4. See also The Chinese Written Character as a Medium for Poetry (Fenollosa); Cummings, E.E.; Eliot, T.S.; Ta Hio: The Great Learning (Confucius); Williams, William Carlos; and specific authors
Idola Fori (Bacon), 60, 60n30
IFL. See Imperial Fascist League (IFL)
Iliad (Homer), 58n23, 102, 102n27, 120, 120n5, 121, 121n13, 144–5, 145n10, 344
imagined, supranational communities, xxxiv, 301
Imagism, xxv, 274, 303
Des Imagistes, 346
Imperial Fascist League (IFL), xxi, 142n7, 146n2, 273, 288–91, 340, 367n31

India, 108n19, 114n8, 229, 229n1
Indian Institute of World Culture, 229n1
L'Indice, 87n7, 90n27
"Individual in His Milieu" (Pound), xxxv, 15n10, 358n42
Instigations (Pound), 132, 132n9, 178n1, 190n8, 333, 336, 358n39
Insull, Samuel, 98, 98n4, 105n6
"Intellectual Money" (Pound), 230n4
International Cartels, Combines and Trusts (Liefmann), 171n6
The International Jew, 270
International PEN, 338
International Surrealism Exhibition, 225, 225n6
In the American Grain (Williams), 27, 119n10, 193n2, 194, 194n1, 233, 233n24, 338
"In the Wounds (Memoriam A.R. Orage)" (Pound), 77n21, 78, 101, 101n19, 125, 125n10
Introductory Text Book E.P., 254, 254n9
In What Hour (Rexroth), 145n17
ira (wrathful indignation), 311–12
Ishiguro, Kazuo, 126n22
Italian Fascism: British attitude toward, xxvi–xxvii, 357n30; and British Fascism, xix, xxi, 288–94; efficacy of, 283–4; EP's allegiance to Mussolini and, xv, xvi, xvii, xviii, xx, xxvi, xxxvii, 27n23, 40n11, 272, 279–86, 294, 297, 318, 353n7, 365n5, 366n12; EP's first encounters with, 280; EP's letter to Morning Post on, 287–8, 293–4; EP's radio broadcasts on, xv, xvi, 309, 340; and Guild Socialism, 20, 20n6, 51n11; and modernism, 280; Mussolini's book on, 194n5; Mussolini's coinage of term "fascismo," 278, 365n1; Nott on, xxxvii; and political left, 19, 19n4; and Social Credit, xxi, 277, 285–6, 293, 295, 343; sympathizers of, and New English Weekly, xxxvi. See also Mussolini, Benito
Italian Futurism, 306–8, 311, 370n17
Italia Nostra, 195n5, 293

Italy: annexation of Ethiopia by, 226n12; banks in, 7, 7n3, 12; death of Scarcity Economics in, 18n3; E P as expatriate in, xv, xvi, xxxv, xxxvii, 280, 281; invasion of Abyssinia by, xxvi, xxvii, 24nn5–6, 173, 173n4, 196n10, 294, 319, 367n37; land laws in, 104n5; lifting of sanctions against, 226n12, 227n5; lira policy of, 227, 227n5; Mussolini's policies and accomplishments in, 281; sanctions against, following invasion of Abyssinia, 90n31, 196n10, 319; S.P.Q.R. inscribed on civic buildings in, 172n12. *See also* Italian Fascism; Mussolini, Benito

"Jacataqua" (Williams), 30n7
Jackson, Andrew, 20nn10–11
Jackson, Holbrook, 324–5
Jain, Anurag, 361n16
James, Henry, 109n31
James, William, 356n29
Jameson, Fredric, 280, 353n7
Jameson, Margaret Storm, xxix, 3, 3n4, 316, 338
Japan, 216, 216n15, 217n17, 228
Jefferson, Thomas: in *Cantos* by E P, 9n10, 20, 304; Clark's book on, 159, 159n12; correspondence between Adams and, 304; E P's interest in generally, xv; quotations from, in E P's *Introductory Text Book E.P.*, 254n9. *See also Jefferson and/or Mussolini* (Pound)
Jefferson and/or Mussolini (Pound): American edition of, by Liveright, 19n3, 168, 168nn1–2, 170, 171, 171n3, 173, 175, 175n1, 177, 177n2, 211n5, 339, 356n28; Axe and Faggot ideograms in, 71n10; binding for, 23, 29, 39, 50; blurb for, 153, 154, 154n4; and British Fascists, 196, 196n10, 197, 197n3, 199; and Butchart, 169–70, 170n8; Butchart's view of, 97; on Confucius, 154; contract for, 65, 66, 67, 69, 73, 74, 79; design of, 153, 153n3, 154, 158–60, 158n10; E P's charges for copies of, 160, 160n2, 179, 179n1; E P's financial contribution to publica-

tion of, 39, 50, 54, 54n4, 55, 63, 74, 79, 232n14; E P's frustrations over difficulties in publishing, 19, 19n2, 23–4; E P's letter to *Criterion* in American edition of, 168n1; E P's literary agent for, 13, 18, 18n3; E P's reaction to and complaints about design of, 157, 158–60, 158n10, 159n11; E P's reference to Keynes regarding, 196, 319, 371n9; focus and theme of, xviii, xxiv–xxvi, 18n4, 281, 339, 371n9; Foreword of, 19n2; front matter for, 74, 74n5, 75; on fundamentals of state organization, 154–5; jacket copy for, 75; "Kung" chapter of, 71n10, 109, 109n27, 159, 160; lack of availability of, in U S, 356n28; leftover stock of, offered to E P at low price, 227, 227n3, 234, 234n2, 237, 238, 238n9, 240; "Letter" introducing Liveright edition of, 211n5; libel concerns about, 96, 98, 98n2, 98nn5–6, 104–5; line-spacing and chapter divisions in, 75, 75n7, 79; Mairet's view of, 96–7, 98n6, 99, 99n8; marketing contact for, 171; *Morning Post* letters by E P suggested for inclusion in, 20, 20n12, 21n13; negative public reaction to, 227; and *New English Weekly*, 122; Nott's positive reaction to, and decision to publish, 18, 29, 82, 136, 173, 319; number of copies of, for E P, 23; number of review copies of, 173; page proofs of, 149; price for sheets of, for Liveright's American edition of, 168, 168n2, 175, 175n1, 177n2; price of, 21n13, 42, 153, 153n1, 160n2; printer for, 62, 159n10; printing costs of, 20, 23, 29, 37–9, 42, 50, 50nn2–3, 62, 63; and printing delays, 49, 54–5, 82, 136; printing of Chinese characters for, 74, 74nn5–6, 75; proofs of, and E P's corrections, 63, 74–6, 79, 81; publication date of, 153n1; publication of, by Nott, xviii, xxiv–xxviii, xxxii–xxxiii, xxxvii, 125, 196, 319, 339, 355n19; publicity copies of, 157; qualities of Mussolini in, 281–2; recipients of review copies of, 87–90, 92, 159, 179; reference to *Ta Hio*

340, 370n15; on EP's prose and non-literary works, 310, 321–2, 370n15; and modernist literary works, 321; and New Directions Books, xxxvi, 232–3, 232n20, 233n25, 321–2, 340; as publisher of EP's writings, xxxvi, 321–2, 353n4; publishing philosophy of, 321–2; and rehabilitation of EP's reputation, 321–2; on Roman banking, 232n20, 233; and Social Credit movement, 321, 340; and Social Credit poetry, 56n13, 60, 60n28, 145; and treason charges against EP, 340

Social Credit, 341; on usury, 183, 183n6, 341

Marsden, Dora, 250n17, 262, 359n2, 360n10

Marsh, Alec, 259

Martin, John Jex, 145, 145n15

Martin, Kingsley, 161n2

Marx, Karl, 15, 26, 26n20, 45

Marxism, 279, 341

Masons, 148, 148n13

Masters, Edgar Lee, 20, 20n9

Materer, Timothy, 309, 354n15

Mathematics for the Million (Hogben), 246n10

Mathews, Charles Elkin, 187, 187n5

Mauduit, George, 5n3, 371n2

McCurdy, Edward B., 64, 64n5

McDevitt, Philip, 371n6

McEachran, F., 225n5

McGann, Jerome, xx

McLeod, John, 225n8

McNab, John Angus, 231n5, 342

The Meaning of Meaning (Ogden and Richards), 27n25, 343

Meaning of Social Credit (Colbourne), 333, 365n45

Melville, Herman, 358n44

microphoto, 243, 243n4, 246

Milan Lectures (1933), 61, 61n33

Mitrinovic, Dimitri, 332

The Modern Idolatry (Mark), 183, 341

modernism: and *Cantos* by EP, 280; of Cavalcanti, 306; and collaboration, 302–3; and *Criterion*, 213n4; and Italian Fascism, xvi, 280; and Lewis, 143n8; and little magazines, 369n6; and *New Age*, 360n11, 361n13; and postcards, 370n12; Quinn as patron of, 215n12; supranational nation, or imagined community of, xxxiv, 301; vagueness of term, 278. *See also specific authors*

Modernist Journals Project, 342, 360n11

Money, Sir Leo George Chiozza, 179, 179n3, 341

Money (Butchart): acknowledgement of EP in Preface to, 163n4, 332; advertise-

ment for, 163n6; and Allen and Unwin, 241; blurb for, 163, 163n6; EP's praise for, 163, 165, 171, 204; EP's reference to, 61; excerpts from EP's writings in, 165, 165n16; Nott as publisher of, 161, 161n4, 163n3, 169n7, 171n1, 204n8, 208, 237, 237n4, 332; possible serialization of, 204n13; recipients of review copies of, 166, 169–70, 170n10; sales potential of, 165

Money and Morals (Gill), 192n2

"Money and Morals" (Pound), 182n2, 183n5, 248, 248n7, 345

Monotti, Francesco, 87, 87n7

Monro, Harold, 55, 55n10, 125, 125n12

Monroe, Harriet, xxxv, 107n8

Moody, A. David, 299–300

Moore, Arthur, 332

Moore, James, 337

Moore, Marianne, 334

Moral Education League, 108n23

Morel, E.D., 108n19

Morley, Felix Muskett, 174, 174n7

Morley, Frank Vigor: brother of, 174n7; and EP's writings, 100n18, 122; as Faber and Faber editor, 336; as Faber and Faber founding director, 100n18, 243n2; at Faber and Faber generally, 235n1; Nott's exploration of employment with, at Faber and Faber, 235, 236, 236n2, 240, 243; Nott's relationship with, over publishing matters, 100, 122, 156, 156n5

Morning Post: Baker's letter to, on Gesell, 331; Camagna as contributor to, 368n43; EP on church and usury published in, 182n5; EP's letter on Italian Fascism in, 287–8, 293–4; EP's letter on pacifists in, 131n3; EP's letters on economics to, 12, 15n10, 19, 20, 20n12; Hield as assistant editor of, 93, 93n9; on Italy and Mussolini, 24, 24nn5–6; Munro as foreign correspondent for, 24, 24nn5–6; style of, 133

Morrell, Lady Ottoline, 106, 106n6

Morris, 361n14

Morrison, Mark, 369n6

Mosley, Oswald: and British Union of Fascists (BUF), xxxvi, 81n1, 82n2, 287, 294; dislike of, by various groups, 82; EP's lack of support for, 367n40; Munson on, 287; Nott on, 82, 82n3; preference of, for Mussolini over Hitler, 231n5

Mosse, George, 279, 353n6

"muck and mystery," 296, 363n29

Muir, Edwin: biographical sketch of, 341; and *Books Abroad*, 111, 111n3; EP's opinion of, 34, 43; as *European Quarterly* editor, 31, 31n13, 34n15, 48, 50, 335, 341; and literary policy of *New English Weekly*, 52–3; and *New Age*, 341; and Pamphlets on the New Economics series, 176, 176n4, 316; and plan for Social Credit monthly magazine, 31, 31n11

Mumford, Lewis, 332

Munro, Ion Smeaton, 24nn5–6

Munson, Gorham B.: biographical sketch of, 341; and EP on literature and "econ/mess," 354n8; and Gurdjieff, 358n43; and *Jefferson and/or Mussolini* by EP, 356–7n28; on Mosley Fascists, 287; as *New Democracy* editor, 164, 164n11, 166n20, 222n2, 315, 340, 341, 342, 358n43; and *New English Weekly*, 341; and Nott's economic publications, 165–6; and Orage, 166, 166n20; and Social Credit, 164n11, 341, 358n43

"Murder by Capital" (Pound), 354n13

Murdoch, Kenneth Ballard, 166, 166n22

Murry, John Middleton, 34n16, 43, 46, 311, 341, 360n12

Mussolini, Benito: accomplishments of, 281–2, 285; on all that is against historic process, 211n5; antisemitism of, 92n6; and artists, 282, 284, 285; Chesterton's interview with, 332; coinage of term "fascismo" by, 278, 365n1; copy of EP's *Jefferson and/or Mussolini* for, 157, 157n3; copy of EP's *Social Credit: An Impact* for, 93, 93n12; documentary on, 282; EP's allegiance to, xv, xvi, xvii, xviii, xx, xxvi, xxxvii, 27n23, 40n11, 272, 279–85, 294, 297, 318, 353n7, 365n5, 366n12; in EP's *Cantos*, 9n10; EP's interview with (1933), 75–6, 75n10, 76n13, 282; EP's *Morning Post* letter on, 287–8, 293–4; and Guild Socialism, 20, 20n6; and Hitler, xxv, xxvi, xxvii; Leese on, 291–2, 294; Malatesta compared with, 282, 284, 365n8; March on Rome (1922) by, 280; mistress of, 92n6; Mosley's preference for, over Hitler, 231n5; Munro's interview with, for *Morning Post*, 24n6; and Nazi puppet Republic of Salò, 335; Nott's opposition to, xxxvii, 173, 319, 372n11; perceptions of, during interwar years, xxvi–xxvii, 173, 294, 356n29; and political left, 19, 19n4; Por's admiration for, 286, 343; socialism of, during early political career, 19n4; and split in British Union of Fascists, 231n5; and S.P.Q.R. inscribed on civic buildings in Italy, 172n12; support for, in Britain and North America during early 1930s, xxvi–xxvii, 284–5, 356n29, 357n30; as syndicated columnist for Hearst newspapers, xxvii; translation of writings by, 194n5. *See also* Italian Fascism; Italy; *Jefferson and/or Mussolini* (Pound)

Le Mystère Laïc (Cocteau), 13, 13n5, 17, 22, 22n4, 26, 26n20, 58, 58n20, 100

mysticism. *See* Gurdjieff, George Ivanovitch

National Delphian Society, 85, 85n9

National Dividend, 40n9, 231n9, 262, 334

The National Dividend (Ward), 10n3, 52n23, 126, 126n17, 371n6

National Institute of Fascist Culture, 196n12, 343

National Social Credit Association, 94, 94n17

National Socialism. *See* Nazism

National Socialist League (NSL), 231, 231n5, 292, 295, 341–2

Natural Economic Order (Gesell), 15n9, 331, 336, 337

The Natural Philosophy of Love (Gourmont), 59n26

The Nature of Democracy (Douglas), 126n19, 371n5

Nazism: and antisemitism, 271; and British Fascism, 289–94; and Holocaust, xxvi; William Joyce's propaganda for, xv, 341; and Leese, 289–91; and Lymington, 292; and National Socialist League (NSL), 292, 295; sympathizers of, and *New English Weekly*, 36; in Turkey, 148n13. *See also* Hitler, Adolf

"The Neocratic Manifesto" (Woodward), 92n4

NEW. See The New English Weekly (NEW)

The New Age: Brenton as editor of, 51, 51n13, 248n2, 342; circulation of, 360n11; collaboration between *New English Weekly* and, 41, 41n14; contributors to, 38n5, 261, 285, 333, 340, 341, 344, 346, 360n12; description of, 342; and Distributism, 107n12, 267; Dyson's artwork in, 335; eclecticism of, 262, 360n11; end of, 41n14; EP as contributor to, xxviii, 9, 9n9, 215, 259, 262, 268, 272, 357n32, 360n12; foreign affairs column of, 11, 11n10; function of, 56, 56n12; and Guild Socialism, 262, 263, 267, 337, 361n13; and Hargrave, 277; merger of *New English Weekly* and, 28n29, 51, 51n12, 56n12, 138–9, 138n3, 138nn5–6, 150–1, 150n8, 342; as model for Nott and Heap's quarterly, 212, 215n9, 216n14; as modernist, 360n11, 361n13; and Muir, 341; online version of, 342, 360n11; and Orage, xxviii, xxix, 3n2, 259, 262, 342, 343; review section of, 138, 138n5, 150, 150n9; Shaw's financial support for, 45n6; and Social Credit, 51n14, 262, 342; typography of, 150–1, 326; and underconsumptionist theory, 264; as weekly paper, 31n11

New Country, 214n7

New Deal, 59, 59n27, 333

New Democracy: advertisements in, 317, 359n47; compared with *New English Weekly*, 315; description and identification of, 88n19, 164n7, 222n2, 342; EP as contributor to, 358n43; EP's critique of, 164, 358n43; Laughlin as contributor to, 340, 370n15; Munson as editor of, 164, 164n11, 166n20, 222n2, 315, 340, 341, 342; readership of, 359n47; review copy of *Jefferson and/or Mussolini* sent to, 88; and Social Credit, 166n20, 315, 340, 356n23, 358n43; on Stanley Nott Ltd., 315; Williams's review of *Jefferson and/or Mussolini* in, xxvi, 356n23

New Directions Books: beginning of, 232n20, 321; description of, 340; EP's works published by, xxxvi, 321–2, 340, 353n4; and *Guide to Kulchur*, 250n19; and Laughlin, xxxvi, 232–3, 232n20, 233n25, 321, 321–2, 340; publishing philosophy of, 321–2; and *Ta Hio*, 242n2; and Williams's *White Mule: A Novel*, 233n25

"The New Economics Library," 164, 164n8, 172n10

New Economics Publishing Co., 253–4

New Economics series. *See* Pamphlets on the New Economics

The New English Weekly (NEW): address of, 204n7; advertisements in, 39n4, 200, 200n8, 317, 359n47; advertising for Ideogrammic series in, 27, 27n26, 117; *Alfred Venison's Poems* by EP published in, xxix, xxxii, 5, 63, 316, 331, 343; "American Notes" column by EP in, 11, 11n8, 176n6, 342; and Brenton, 51; and British Fascism, 287, 295; and Butchart's wife, 220n2; *Canto 38* by EP in, 269, 363n31; and Chandos Group, 332, 342; collaboration between *New Age* and, 41, 41n14; conflicts in, 31, 35, 35n20; contributors to, 30, 30n7, 115, 115n5, 136n11, 209n4, 225n9, 336, 338; and demise of Stanley Nott Ltd., 245; and Dobrée, 112; editors of generally and editorial committee of, 3n2, 10–11n6, 342; end of, 340; EP as contributor to generally, xxiv, xxix–xxx, 176, 176n6, 288, 342; EP on and his suggestions for, 10–12, 40, 251; EP's article

on Cocteau in, 13, 13n5; EP's article on
Gesell in, 15n10; EP's article on Ogden
in, 25, 25n10, 42, 42n20, 44, 44n4; EP's
article on orthology in, 125, 125n8; EP's
article on Woodward in, 346; EP's articles on Douglas in, 204, 204n10; EP's
letter on Italian Fascism, 366n20; EP's
"Private Worlds" in, 125, 125n9; EP's
review of Hargrave's *Summer Time
Ends* in, 338; and EP's second letter
to Angell, 141; EP's writings from, for
Yale University Press publication, 125;
finances of, 139n13, 150, 150n6, 223,
246, 246n9; first issue of, 253, 253n6,
373n25; and Frobenius, 228, 228n4;
Jefferson and/or Mussolini reviewed in,
169, 169nn2–3; on Larkin, 339; literary
policy of, 34, 34n13, 47, 47n21, 52–3,
56–7, 56n12, 57n14; Mairet as editor of,
7n1, 32, 35, 35n20, 37, 41, 47, 47n21, 51,
340, 342; merger of *The New Age* and,
28n29, 51, 51n12, 56n12, 138–9, 138n3,
138nn5–6, 150–1, 150n8, 342; monthly
magazine on Social Credit compared
with, 31n11, 35; and Munson, 341; name
change for (1938), 41n14; Newsome as
editor of, 7n2, 31, 35, 35n20, 37, 41, 47,
51, 342; Nott as manager for, xxviii–
xxx, 4, 253, 327; Nott's comparison of
EP's writing with, 29; Nott's critique
of, 176; Nott's departure from, 31, 37;
and Nott's interest in pamphleteering,
328; on Objectivist Press, 220n6; and
Orage, xxiv, xxviii–xxx, 3n2, 4, 4n9,
30, 246, 253, 269, 332, 342, 343, 373n25;
and Pamphlets on the New Economics, 316, 317; poetry by Cummings in,
70n4; Por's article on bankers in, 208;
readership of, xxxvi, 359n47; Reckitt as
editor of, 344; review of *Criterion* by,
21n13; reviews in, xxix, 101n22, 127n28,
166, 169, 169nn2–3, 176, 333; sales and
influence of, 99, 99n8, 115; and Social
Credit, xxviii–xxx, xxxvi, 31, 44, 53, 56,
56n13, 269, 373n25
New Freewoman, 250n17, 262, 359n2,
360n10

New Signatures, 214n7
Newsome, Albert: and Brenton, 41, 51, 57,
57n16; and Chandos Group, 122, 122n7,
332, 342; and EP's article on Gesell,
15; and literary policy of *New English
Weekly*, 52–3; marriage of, 51, 57; as
New English Weekly editor, 7n2, 31, 35,
35n20, 37, 41, 47, 51, 342; and Nott, 31,
53; and *Social Credit: An Impact*, 7, 22;
writings by, in "The New Economics
Library," 164n8
*New Statesman/New Statesman and
Nation*, 161, 161n2
New Verse, xxiv, 161n3
New York Times, 255n7
New York World, 209n4, 372n15
Nichomachean Ethics (Aristotle), 232n17
Nietzsche, Friedrich, 84
"1934 in the Autumn" (Pound), 19n3
*"Noh" or Accomplishment: A Study of the
Classical Stage of Japan* (Fenollosa),
109, 109n30, 186, 186n4
Norman, Charles, 309
Norman, Sir Montague Collet, 94, 94n14,
134, 134n19
North, Michael, 279–80
Northridge, R.L., 341
No Thanks (Cummings), 110n36, 115n4,
119n9
"Nothing Is Without Efficient Cause,"
19n3
Nott, Rosemary Lillard, xxiv, 38, 38n7,
156, 241, 243, 245, 253, 256
Nott, Stanley: biographical sketch of,
xxiii–xxiv; business sense of, 209–10,
238, 320, 372n15; demise of publishing
house of, 234–42, 315; and development of EP's authority, xxii–xxiv,
xxxi, xxxv–xxxvi, 14, 14n8, 84–5, 304,
355n18; and economic heresies, 317–20;
employment of, after demise of Stanley Nott Ltd., 245–6, 254, 255n5; EP's
ideas for publishing venture with, after
demise of Stanley Nott Ltd., 248–51,
253–4, 253n3, 256; and EP's maverick
and independent thought, xxii, xxxvii,
328, 356n21, 357n31; and *European*

Quarterly, 40, 40n6, 50, 136n6; family background of, 324; and Gurdjieff, xxiv, xxviii, 4, 268, 322–8, 338; and Hargrave, 37–8, 39n3, 136, 277, 296; health problems of, 156, 192, 241, 254; initial contact between EP and, xxix–xxx, 3–4; on Italian invasion of Abyssinia and tensions preceding, xxvii, 173, 176, 176n10, 319; and love of books, 324–5; marriage and family of, xxiv, 38, 38n7, 156, 241, 243, 245, 253, 256; meetings between Dorothy Pound and, 136, 153, 153n2, 156, 156n3; mutual advantage in relationship between EP and, xxii–xxiv, xxvii, xxx, 75, 75n9, 84–5; and *New English Weekly*, xxviii–xxx, 4, 31, 37, 245, 253; and new quarterly on art and literature (1936), 210–18, 210n3, 211n4, 215n9, 216n14, 217n21, 222, 222n2, 224, 224n7, 226; on "not go[ing] altogether with the tide," xxii, xxvii, xxxvii, 173, 318–20; opposition to fascism and Mussolini by, xxxvi, xxxvii, 173, 319, 372n11; and Orage, xxiii–xxiv, xxviii–xxx, 4, 29, 241, 323, 327, 356n21; personality of, 138n2; on readers' resistance to EP's writings, 42, 51, 51n17, 184, 212; travels by, 253, 253n7, 322–3; in World War I, xxiii, 322. *See also* Pound/Nott correspondence; Social Credit; Stanley Nott Ltd.

Nott, William, 324
Nottingham University, 50, 50n8, 52
NSL. *See* National Socialist League (NSL)
Nursing Mirror, 203n4
Nyland, W.A., 166, 166n19

Objectivist Press, 211n3, 220n6
Odyssey (Homer), 58, 58n23, 73, 73n3, 102, 102n24, 103, 103n32, 120, 120n5, 144–5, 145n10, 309, 344
Ogden, Charles Kay: and BASIC English, 25, 25nn9–10, 27n25, 33, 33n9, 44, 44n4, 60, 60n29, 343; biographical sketch of, 342–3; correspondence between EP and, 34n12; EP's article on, 25, 25n10, 42, 42n20; EP's type of orthology

distinguished from, 164, 164n13; and Ideogrammic series, 60, 61, 81n3; Ideogrammic series distinguished from, 26, 26n19, 30n6, 33, 33n7, 113, 113n2, 114, 114n10; link between *The Chinese Written Character as a Medium for Poetry* and, 26, 26n19, 27, 27n25, 30n6, 33, 33n7, 333; and Nott, 30; and orthological institute at Cambridge, 25n12; and Psyche Miniatures series, 25n12, 60, 60n29, 114; and Richards, 27n25; as "stuck mentally," 33–4, 38, 38n4; writings by, 27n25, 343
The Old "New Age" – Orage and Others, 215n11
"The Only True Function of the State" (Pound), 14n6
An Open Letter to a Professional Man (Dobrée), 112n6
Open Road, 95, 95n22
Oppen, Goerge, 220n6
Orage, Alfred Richard: and *Alfred Venison's Poems* by EP, xxviii–xxx, 63; biographical sketch of, 343; and Chandos Group, 332; charisma of, 262, 360n9, 372n20; as critic, 212; death of, xxiv, xxix, 4, 4n9, 31, 150, 150n5, 342, 343; detachment of, from practical politics and decision making, 276, 327–8, 365n46; and Douglas, 260–2, 361n15; and EP, xxix–xxx, 259, 262, 356n21, 357n32, 357n34; EP's memoriam for, in *Criterion*, 77n21, 78, 101, 101n19, 125, 125n10; and EP's synthesis of Social Credit with Gesell's economic reforms, 275; EP's writings on, 125n10; and Guild Socialism, 262, 263, 267, 334, 337; and Gurdjieff, xxiii–xxiv, xxviii, 268, 323, 338, 343, 373n26; Beatrice Hastings as partner of, 215n11; and Munson, 166, 166n20; and *New Age*, xxviii, xxix, 3n2, 259, 342, 343; and *New English Weekly*, xxviii–xxx, 3n2, 4, 30, 246, 253, 269, 332, 342, 343, 373n25; and Nott, xxiii–xxiv, xxviii–xxx, 29, 241, 323, 327, 356n21, 372n20; and Nott's interest in pamphleteering, 328; and Pamphlets

on the New Economics series, xxix, 3, 5, 5n4, 126, 126n20, 316, 371n6; and Social Credit, xxiv, xxviii–xxix, 6n7, 15, 30, 150, 246, 260–2, 268, 274, 327–8, 343, 354n11, 356n21; writings by, 4, 4n11, 4n13, 38n5, 316

Orage, Jessie, 37, 150, 150n5, 151, 176, 176n9, 342

Orage and the New Age Circle (Selver), 111n5

orthography, 309–10

orthology: and *The Chinese Written Character as a Medium for Poetry* by EP, 99; definition of, 25n12, 114n10, 239n11; EP's article on, 125, 125n8; and Italians, 238, 239n11; need for economic orthology, 230n4, 251, 251n24, 251n25; and Ogden, 25, 25n12, 114, 164, 164n13, 343

Orwell, George, 82n3, 278, 310

"Our (American) Ragcademicians" (Williams), 30n7

Oxford University Press, 188, 188n10

pacifism, 129–30, 131n3

Pagany, 13, 13n4, 102, 102n29

paideuma, 337

Paige, D.D., xiv

paleography, 187, 187nn8–9

palingenesis, 368n49

pamphleteering, 328–30, 373n22. *See also* Pamphlets on the New Economics

Pamphlets on the New Economics: advertisements for, xliv, 86n2, 317, 329; authors proposed for, 6, 231–3; on church and usury, 182–4, 184n1; compared with Ideogrammic series, 52, 52n19, 57–8n17, 118; connotations of pamphlet format for, 329; covers of, 101n23; criticisms of vulgarity of EP's pamphlets in, 137, 138n15; dates of publication of, 316, 318; description of, 316, 343; distribution of, in US, 126n16, 342; diversity of perspectives in, 316–18, 329–30, 371n6; Douglas's writing for, 6, 6n6, 316, 355n19, 371nn4–6; and Eliot, 18, 38, 59, 59n25, 64, 99n12; EP's writ-

ings for, xxii–xxiii, xxix, xxxi, 3, 3n7, 4, 4n10, 14–15, 17, 18, 18n1, 184, 316, 318, 343, 355n19; EP's writing style for, 184, 307, 318; finances for, 230, 230n3; focus of, on Social Credit and economics, xxvii–xxix, 43, 43n23; length of, 232, 232n18; list of, 126, 126nn17–24, 351–2; mailing list for review copies of, 86–95, 101, 106–10, 146; Nott on focus of, 6, 316; number of, 3n1, 316, 343; and Orage, xxix, 3, 4n11, 5, 5n4, 316, 371n6; and Por, 180–1, 181n7; price of, 52n19, 118n5, 316; printing costs of, 329; publication dates of, 3n1, 230n3; readership for, 316; sale of, after demise of Stanley Nott Ltd., 250; sales of, 52, 81, 81n6; schedule for publication of, 14, 17; "symposium" approach to, 317, 371n6; typography of, 326; and Yale University Press, 126, 126n16. *See also Social Credit: An Impact* (Pound); *and specific authors*

parole in libertà, 306, 311

Partisan Review, 145n17

Pauthier, Guillaume, 345

Paxton, Robert, 279

Payne, Stanley, 279

Pelley, William, 273, 290, 364n38, 367n29

Pellizzi, Camillo, 32n2, 195nn3–4, 196, 196n12, 293, 343

Pelmanism, 142, 142n2

Penty, A.J., 261, 262, 334, 337

Personae (Pound), 187n5

Pettengill, Samuel Barrett, 89, 89n24

Pfister, G.A., 288

Phillimore, Lucy, 247

Pitter, Ruth, 115, 115n5

Plantin, Christophe, 121n10

Poems of People (Masters), 20n9

Poetics (Aristotle), 28n31

Poetry and Drama (Monro), 55n10

Poetry magazine, xxxv, 20n10, 107, 107n8, 371n7

Poetry Review, 55n10

Poggioli, Renato, xxxiii

Polite Essays (Pound), 77n21, 83, 83n3, 124n1

Political and Economic Writings (Orage), 4, 4n11, 192, 192n1, 332, 333

The Political and Social Doctrine of Fascism (Mussolini), 194n5

"Politics and the English Language" (Orwell), 278, 310

Pollinger, Laurence Edward, 13, 13n2, 122, 122n2, 251, 251n22

Polytechnical institute (London), 142, 142n3

"poor bloody public," 84, 101, 101n20

Pope, James Pinckney, 89, 89n23

Populism, 272, 357n32, 363nn36–37

Por, Odon: biographical sketch and identification of, 161n1, 343; and *British-Italian Bulletin*, 195n5; connections of, with Italian government, 180, 180n3, 182, 182n4; and *Critica Fascista*, 32n2; and EP's antisemitism, 363n33; EP's correspondence with, 286; EP's first contact with, 285; EP's interest in, 180–1, 182, 207–8, 221; and Guild Socialism, 285, 343; and *Jefferson and/or Mussolini* by EP, 195n3; and Mussolini government, 286; and *New Age*, 285, 343; Nott's interest in, 161, 179, 219, 220, 220n4, 221, 221n10, 226; and Pamphlets on the New Economics series, 180–1, 181n7; review copies of EP's economic writings to, 86; and Social Credit, 285–6, 295, 434; translations of writings by, 220n2, 230n4; writings by, 20n6, 51n11, 180–1, 180n4, 181n6, 207n4, 221, 221n10, 226, 230n4

Porter, Alan, 332

Porteus, Hugh Gordon, 36n23, 81, 81n5

Potocki, Count, 231n5

Pound, Dorothy Shakespear: birth and death dates of, 54n5; and EP's financial accounts with Nott, 54, 153n2, 157, 157n5, 160, 160n7; and meetings with Nott, 136, 153, 153n2, 156, 156n3; review of William Carlos Williams's poetry by, 135, 135n23, 144, 153n2

Pound, Ezra: and anxiety of influence, xvi, xxxiv–xxxv, xxxvi, 275, 353n3; and avant-garde code, xxxiii–xxxiv;

conversational style of, 309; daughter Mary of, 191n10; as economic and political commentator generally, xvi–xvii, xx–xxiv, xxix–xxxiii, xxxvii, 354n8, 354nn10–13; as expatriate in Italy, xv, xvi, xxxv, xxxvii, 280, 281; family background of, xxxi, 6n12, 252, 252n2, 344, 357n32, 358n38, 364n37; friendships of, during his early career, xxxv; hero worship by, xvi, 280–1, 285, 365n7; "ideogramic method" of rhetorical development of, xxv–xxvi, 356n27; and independent publishers generally, xxxv–xxxvi, 359n46; initial contact between Nott and, xxix–xxx, 3–4; irritable and impatient nature of, 27, 55; Italian travels by, in 1922–1923, 283–4; and Jeffersonian tradition, xv; "jeremiac" personality of, xxxiii, 311–12, 358n44, 370n16; as lecturer at Polytechnical institute in London, 142, 142n3; literary agent of, 13, 18, 18n3, 122, 122n2, 202, 202n3, 251, 251n22; marriage of, 54, 54n5, 135, 135n23, 136, 156, 191n10; mental condition of, in late 1960s, 369n7; Milan Lectures (1933) of, 61, 61n33; mutual advantage in relationship between Nott and, xxii–xxiv, xxvii, xxx, 75, 75n9, 84–5; newspapers read by, 11; Nott's contributions to development of authority of, xxii–xxiv, xxx–xxxiii, xxxv–xxxvi, 14, 14n8, 84–5, 304, 355n18; persistence of, 27; plain format for books by, 326; plays about, xvi; poetry writing by generally, 217, 217n20; professed ignorance by, of British public for literature, 16, 16n12; prose written in Italian by, 217, 217n16, 255n3; pseudonym of, as Alf Venison, xxix, xxxii, 331; publishers' relationship with generally, xxxv; Quinn as patron of, 216n12; radio broadcasts by, xv, xvi, 309, 340; readers' resistance to writings by, 42, 51, 51n17, 184, 212; rehabilitation of reputation of, after World War II, 321–2, 353n4; and Roman Catholic Church, 182n3; and Olga Rudge, 163n2,

191n10, 244n5; scholarship on, xvi, xviii, 353n4; in St Elizabeths Hospital for "criminally insane," xv–xvi, 369n7; teaching position of, at Wabash College, Indiana, 55, 55n8; temperamental habits of, 282–3, 292, 328; and textbooks for cultural education, 358n40; translations from Chinese poetry by, xxv, 358n39; translators of works by, 86n6, 87n7, 87n11, 220n2, 251, 251n24, 255n3, 335; travel to US by (1939), xvi, 252n5, 255n1, 353n3; treason charges against, xv, 340; typewriting techniques of, 308, 309; and US Congress members, xvi, 89, 89nn23–24, 95, 95nn23–27, 112, 112nn9–14, 146, 146n4, 159, 159n12, 166, 166nn23–24, 353n3; in Venice, 163, 163n2, 191n10; youth of, xxxiv, 272, 357n32, 363n36. *See also* antisemitism; British Fascism; epistolary practice; Italian Fascism; Pound/Nott correspondence; Social Credit; *and specific works*

Pound, Harve, 113, 113n4

Pound, Thaddeus Coleman, xxxi, 6n12, 252, 252n2, 344, 358n38, 364n37

Pound/Nott correspondence: beginning of, 286; diplomatic editing of, 314; editorial principles regarding, xiii–xiv, 314, 355n15; epistolary idiom in, 307–8, 310–11; and Nott's contributions to development of EP's authority, xxii–xxiv, xxx–xxxiii, xxxv–xxxvi, 14, 14n8, 84–5, 304, 355n18; number of letters and time span of, xvii; Preda's edition of EP's correspondence compared with, xx–xxii, 355n17; Rainey's influence on Hickman's edition of, xiii, 353n6; sample pages from, xxxix–xlii; significance of generally, xvii, xviii–xxii, xxxviii, 300; topics in generally, xvii, xviii. *See also* epistolary practice

poverty, 84, 96, 101, 261, 327, 373n24

Poverty amidst Plenty (Bennet), 126, 126n21

Preda, Roxana: on Brenton, 332; on *British Union Quarterly*, 292; on *Critica Fascista*, 32n2; on Drummond, 335; edition of EP's correspondence edited by, xx–xxii, 355n17; on EP's relationship with Social Crediters, 355n17; on Fack, 273, 336; on Imperial Fascist League (IFL), 367n31; on Mosley, 367n40; on *New Democracy*, 358n43; on *New English Weekly*, 342; on Pelley, 364n38; on review of EP's *Jefferson and/or Mussolini*, 195n3; on stamp scrip, 275, 364–5n42; on Thomson, 367–8n42

printing costs: of *The Chinese Written Character as a Medium for Poetry*, 160; of Ideogrammic series, 52; of *Jefferson and/or Mussolini*, 20, 23, 29, 37–9, 42, 50, 50nn2–3, 62, 63; of Pamphlets on the New Economics, 329; of *Ta Hio: The Great Learning*, 64

printing delays: and *Alfred Venison's Poems* by EP, 79, 79n6, 90n29; and *Jefferson and/or Mussolini* by EP, 49, 54–5, 82, 136; and Jubilee celebration of George V's reign, 79, 79n6, 82, 90n29; Nott on, 29; political reasons for, 39, 39n1; for small publications, 64; and *Social Credit: An Impact* by EP, 79, 79n6; and *Ta Hio*, 205n14, 207, 207n2

"Private Worlds" (Pound), 125n8

Programme, 179, 179n5

Progrès civique, 250, 250n21

Progress and Poverty (George), 15n11

propaganda, EP on, 44, 44n2

Protocols of the Learned Elders of Zion, 270–1, 273, 363nn33–34

Proudhon, Pierre, 261, 265

Proust, Marcel, 334

Psyche Miniatures series, 25n12, 60, 60n29, 114

publishers: EP's frustrations with, 83–5, 205; EP's relationship with generally, xxxv; and fiction, 172n12; and future of publishing, 243, 243n4, 246; and Gollancz on "tak[ing] the tide," xxxviii, 320; independent publishers, xxxv–xxxvi, 359n46; Laughlin's criticism of, 321; and microphoto technique, 243, 243n4, 246; Nott on moneymaking focus of, 210, 210n2; refusal of *Jefferson and/or Mussolini* by, xviii, xxiv, 19, 19n2, 356n28; and remainders, 237n7. *See also* Faber and Faber; printing costs; printing delays; Stanley Nott Ltd.; Yale University Press; *and other publishers*

Publisher's Weekly, 174, 174n8

Pugh, Martin, 297

Quinn, John, 214n8, 215, 215–16n12

racism. *See* antisemitism

radio broadcasts by EP, xv, xvi, 309, 340

"rag bag" and "rag-tag," 279, 365n3

Rainey, Lawrence: on diplomatic editing, 370n19; and editorial approach of Hickman's edition of Pound/Nott correspondence, xiii, 353n6; on EP's allegiance to Mussolini and Italian Fascism, 283–4, 365n5; on little magazines, 369n6; on Malatesta Cantos by EP, 281, 301; on Mussolini compared with Malatesta, 365n8; on significance of a text's sociomaterial "inscriptures," xiii

Random House, xxxv

Rassegna Monetaria (Pound), 220n2, 230n4, 251, 251n24, 275

Read, Forrest, 299, 308, 313

Read, Sir Herbert: biographical sketch and identification of, 3n3, 344; as contributor to *New Age*, 360n12; EP's opinion of, 34, 43, 55; and literary policy of *New English Weekly*, 52–3; Nott on, 50–1; Orage's writings co-edited by, 38n5, 344–5; and Pamphlets on the New Economics series, xxix, 3, 55n11, 318; and plan for Social Credit monthly magazine, 31, 31n11; and Surrealism, 225n6; and World War I, 50, 50n10; writings by, 55n11, 161n3, 318; writing style of, 55

"real," 283, 365–6n10, 369n10

"real knowledge," 313, 356n24

Reckitt, Maurice Benington: biographical sketch of, 344; and Chandos Group, 332, 344; and Distributism, 334, 344, 362n26; funding of *New English Weekly* by, 139n13, 150, 150n6; and merger of *New Age* and *New English Weekly*, 139; as *New English Weekly* editor, 10n6, 342; and Social Credit, 268, 362n26; *Social Credit: An Impact* by EP sent to, 108; writings by, 344

Redman, Tim: on *British-Italian Bulletin*, 195n5, 293; on EP as "Poeta Economista," 358n37; on EP's *ABC of Reading*, 354n12; on EP's allegiance to Italian Fascism, xviii, 283–5; on EP's antisemitism, 272; on EP's anxiety of influence, xxxv, 275, 353n3, 355n18; on EP's correspondence, 299, 300, 354n15; on EP's dwindling public and suspicion of his work on economics, 354n9; on EP's lack of formal training in economics, xxxii; on EP's turn to economic and political work, xvii–xviii, xxix, 354n13, 357n34; on EP's writings on economics, 260; on Gesell, 274, 275; on *New Age*, xxviii, 262, 272; on Orage, 343; on populism, 357n32, 363n37; on Por, 285–6, 343, 366n14; on Social Credit, 275; on youth of EP, xxxiv, 357n32

remainders, definition of, 237n7

Remains of the Day (Ishiguro), 126n22

Rexroth, Kenneth, 145n17

Reznikoff, Charles, 211n3, 220, 220n6

Rhondda, Lady. *See* Thomas, Margaret Haig (Lady Rhondda, Viscountess)

Rhys, Ernest, 109, 109n32

Richards, Ivor Armstrong, 27, 27n25, 343

Richards, L.A., 334

Roberts, Michael, 214, 214nn6–7

Roman Catholic Church: and Distributism, 267, 334; and Father Coughlin, 145n15, 166, 166n25, 255n6, 333; on usury, 182–4, 182n3, 184n1

Roosevelt, Anna Eleanor, 93, 93n10

Roosevelt, Franklin D., 333, 346

Rouse, William Henry Denham: biographical sketch of, 344; and Ideogrammic series, 58–9, 118, 118n2, 120,

51n14, 332; dogmatic tendencies of, 136, 136n2, 150, 318; and Douglas, 76n12, 150, 204n10, 318; and *Fig Tree*, 204n13, 217n21; function of, 76n12; and Gibson, 138n2; and *Jefferson and/or Mussolini* by EP, 76; *New Age* support cut off by, 51n14; and Nott, 136, 204, 204n9, 318; orthodox Social Credit of, 277; and *Social Credit* (weekly), 51n14, 345

Social Credit (weekly): Bardsley as editor of, 203n6; description of, 345; EP as contributor to, 14, 14n6, 182n3, 182n5; EP on periodicals focused on Social Credit, 28, 28n29, 31n11; as official organ of Social Credit Secretariat, 51n14, 345; possible serialization of EP's or Butchart's book on money in, 204, 204n13; on usury, 182n3, 182n5

socialism: dislike of Mosley by Socialists, 82; of Gollancz, 16n15; of Mussolini, 19n5; and *New Age*, 262, 360n11; and *New Statesman/New Statesman and Nation*, 161n2; Social Credit's distrust of, xxxvi, 263–6, 317. *See also* Fabian Society; Guild Socialism; National Socialist League (NSL)

Soddy, Frederick, 232, 232n13, 371n4

El Sol, 86n4

Spender, Stephen, 161n3

Spoo, Robert, xxxvi, 355n15

Spring and All (Williams), 119, 119n12, 123, 123n10, 135n23

Squire, J.C., 360n12

Squire, Sir John Collings, 47, 47n20

Stable Money; A History of the Movement (Fisher), 101n22

stamp scrip, 89n24, 217, 231n8, 275, 336, 337, 364n42

Stamp Scrip (Fisher), xxix, 15n9, 101n22, 274, 336, 364n42

Stanley Nott Ltd.: advertisements of, xliv, 86n2, 142, 200, 200n8, 317, 359n47; beginnings of, 253, 315, 373n21; and business sense of Nott, 209–10, 238, 320, 372n15; compared with Gollancz, 320–1, 372n13; contracts between authors and, 52, 54, 54n2, 65, 66, 67nn3–4,

69, 73, 74, 79, 237, 237n8; Cummings's poetry considered for publication by, 70, 70n4, 72, 72n12, 110, 111, 111n1, 113–14, 115, 119; decisions on books published by, 172, 172n12; demise of, 234–42, 250, 253, 315; and economic heresies of EP and Nott, 317–20; and "Economics Reference Library," 172, 172n10; and EP's *British Union Quarterly* articles, 230, 230n4; and EP's controversial reputation, 355n20; EP's financial accounts with, 54, 153n2, 157, 157n5, 160, 160n7, 179, 179n1, 219, 224, 235; EP's interest in his own leftover stock after demise of, 237–40, 238n9, 242; EP's praise for, xxxvi, 157, 194, 196, 200n9, 209, 209n5, 236–8, 319, 321, 372n17; EP's suggested authors for, 16, 231–3, 231nn10–11, 232nn12–13, 232nn19–20, 233nn21–22; EP's writings published by generally, xviii, xxxvi, 240, 322, 354n14; establishment of, xxix; and *European Quarterly*, 40, 40n6, 50, 138n6; finances of, xxxiii, 29, 30, 42, 65, 81, 162, 173–4, 188, 200, 200n9, 201, 201n5, 203, 207, 207n2, 210, 210n4, 211, 211n2, 223, 225, 226, 230, 230n2, 232, 232n14, 235, 241, 250, 250n18, 372n18, 373n21; and Gurdjieff, 322–8; leftover stock of, after demise of, 237–43; management staff of, 116, 116n6; mutual advantage in relationship between EP and, xxii–xxiv, xxvii, xxx, 75, 75n9, 84–5; "The New Economics Library" of, 164, 164n8, 172n10; and "not go[ing] altogether with the tide," xxii, xxvii, xxxvii, 173, 318–20; number of books published by, 172, 173, 223, 223n2, 315; Orage's writings published by, 4, 4n11, 4n13, 38n5, 192n1, 344–5; and pamphlet format, 206, 206n3, 328–30; and Por, 161, 179, 219, 220, 220n4, 226; and price for pamphlet versus booklet, 118, 118n5, 206, 206n3; printers for, 54n6; printing costs for, 20, 23, 29, 37–9, 42, 50, 50nn2–3, 52, 62, 63, 64, 160; and printing delays, 29, 39, 39n1, 49, 54–5, 64, 79,

79n6, 82, 90n29; publications of, 347–52; publishing philosophy of, 320–2, 330; readability of works published by, 164, 164n13, 165; readership of publications of, 41–2, 359n47; royalties paid by, 3, 54, 54nn3–4, 71, 158, 210, 227, 235, 237, 237n8; sales of, 5, 52, 81, 81n6, 151, 164, 164n13, 172n10, 240, 241; and sales of EP's works in Britain, 51, 58, 58n18, 240; and sales resistance to EP's works, 42, 51, 51n17; *The Social Credit Pamphleteer* published by, 126n16, 330; as Social Credit publisher, 315–20; and Surrealism, 225, 225nn7–9; and textbooks, 162, 162n7, 165, 172; trade publications by, 5, 5n3, 151, 173, 225, 225n2, 227, 229, 229n4, 316, 371n2; typography of publications of, 326; and *What Is Money For?* by EP, 202, 202n4, 203, 203n2, 206, 206n4. *See also* Ideogrammic series; Nott, Stanley; Pamphlets on the New Economics; *and specific authors and titles of publications*

statist socialism. *See* socialism

Stein, Gertrude, 87n9, 302–3, 306, 334

Sternhell, Zeev, 278–9

Stewart, Charles, 336

Stingel, Janine, 271

Stock, Noel, 361n22

Stone, Dan, 289, 297

Stoneking, Billy Marshall, xvi

Stravinksy, Igo Fyodorovich, 35, 35n17

Sullivan, Brian, xxvii

Summer Time Ends (Hargrave), 338

supranational imagined communities, xxxiv, 301

Surette, Leon: on antisemitism, 270; on *Cantos* by EP, 363n31; on Coughlin, 333; on Douglas, 261, 275–6; on Drummond, 113n6, 335, 364n40; on EP and Social Credit, 274, 275–6, 356n21, 359n3; on EP's allegiance to Italian Fascism, xviii, xxvi–xxvii, 283–6, 296; on EP's antisemitism, 113n6, 272, 273, 290, 335, 355n16, 364n38, 364n40; 367nn29–30; on EP's idiosyncratic typographical conventions, 314; on EP's library, 364n39; on EP's turn to economic and political work, xvii–xviii, xxxiii, 354n10; on EP's turn to Roman Catholic Church, 182n3; on EP's view of himself as "major player," xxxiii; on EP's writing style, 356n27; on fascism, 278, 279, 365n1, 365n3; on Gesell, 15n9; on *New Age*, 262, 263, 264, 268; on Pelley, 273, 290, 364n38; 367n29; on Por, 20n6, 51n11; on *Protocols of the Learned Elders of Zion*, 363n33; on Social Credit, 260, 261, 265, 274–6, 296, 362n28; on supranational nation, or imagined community, of modernism, xxxiv; on Webb's critique of Social Credit, 180n5

Surrealism, 225, 225nn6–7, 315, 344

Swabey, Rev. Henry S.: biographical sketch and identification of, 182n2, 345; EP on, 165; EP's letter to, 248; and EP's writings, 251; and "Money and Morals" by EP, 248n7, 345; and Nott, 250; and Pamphlets on the New Economics, 233; on usury, 182, 182n2, 183n5, 345

Sylander, Gordon, 145, 145n17

symbolist movement, xvii, 59n26, 354n11

Symons, W.T., 10n6, 332, 371n6

syndicalism, 267, 285, 337, 343

"Systems of Compensation" (Por), 230n4

Ta Hio: The Great Learning (Confucius): advertisement for, 205, 205n14; American edition (1928) of, 25n14, 41, 41n15, 201n3, 345, 354n14; announcements of, 91; and Arrow Editions, 199; binding for, 41, 101, 101n23, 242; compared with *Cathay*, 26, 36, 41; description of, 345; EP's interest in Nott's reprinting of, 25–6, 32–3; EP's receipt of copy of, 209, 209n2; EP's translations of, 345; and Faber and Faber, 240n4, 242n2; in Ideogrammic series, xviii, 25n14, 26, 26n19, 37, 49, 49n3, 58, 59, 99, 102, 118, 118n4, 144, 193, 193n1, 338, 345, 358n39; length of, 119n8; link between Ogden and, 26, 26n19, 30, 30n6, 33, 33n7; and New Directions Books, 242n2; number

plain format of EP's publications, 326;
of Stanley Nott Ltd. publications, 326;
of *Ta Hio*, 151, 152

Uberti, Ubaldo, 87, 87n11
UDC. *See* Union for Democratic Control
(UDC)
Ulmann, Max, 187n9
Ulysses (Joyce), 280
underconsumptionist theory, 261, 264,
265, 361n20
"Under the Greenwood Tree" (Williams),
30n7
Union for Democratic Control (UDC),
108, 108n19
United Press, 171, 171n8
United States: committees of correspondence in eighteenth-century America,
xxxiv, 294, 300–2, 314; EP's travel to,
in 1939, xvi, 252n5, 255n1, 353n3; New
Deal in, 59, 59n27; Nott on Americans
as immature, but with possibilities,
38, 40; populism in, 272, 357n32,
363nn36–37; poverty in, 373n24; Social
Credit movement in, xix, 164n11, 265,
341. *See also* Congress, US; *and specific
presidents*
University of Washington Chap-Book
series, 25n14, 41n15, 201n3, 345
Upward, Allen, 36n25, 40–1, 346
The Use of Money (Douglas), 6, 6n6,
126n19, 355n19, 371n5
usury: church's opposition to, 182–4,
182nn2–3, 182n5, 184nn1–2, 345; Dante
on, 272; definition needed for term, 251;
English tradition of, 167; EP on, 182n5,
272; Mark on, 183, 183n6, 341; opposition to, by Social Credit movement,
182n3, 260; Pamphlets on the New
Economics on, 182–4, 184n1; Thaddeus
Pound's opposition to, 358n38; Swabey
on, 182, 183n5, 345

Van Buren, Martin, 20, 20n7, 20nn9–11
Vaughan-Henry, Leigh, 287, 288–9, 295,
364n41, 368n47
Verdad, S., 11, 11n10

Verdenal, Jean, 361n16
Voice, 182n2, 345
Vorticism, 143n10, 303
Vou, 216, 216n15, 217n17, 228n2
"Vou Club [Introduction]" (Pound),
216n15
"Voyage to Africa," 225, 225n8

Wadia, Sophia, 229n1
Wagner, Robert Ferdinand, 112, 112n13
Walkiewicz, E.P., 355n15
Wall, Wendy, 302
Wallace, Henry Agard, 89, 89n22
Wallace, (Richard Horatio) Edgar, 201,
201n6
Wallop, Gerard Vernon, Viscount
Lymington, xxxvii, 249, 249n9, 292,
294, 295, 346
Warburg, Frederic John, 203, 203n3
Ward, William, 10, 10n3, 16, 16n13, 52,
52n23, 126, 126n17, 371n6
Washington, George, 304
Washington Post, 174n7
The Waste Land (Eliot), 280
Waugh, Evelyn, 108n18
The Way Out, 336
Weaver, Harriet Shaw, 250, 250n17
Webb, James, 268, 362n27, 362n29, 372n16
Webb, Sir Montagu de Pomeroy, 114,
114n8
Webb, Sidney, 180, 180n5
Webber, G.C., xxvii
Weber, Eugen, 279
Webster, Nesta, 273, 363n34, 364n39
Weekly Review, 94n15
Wells, Herbert George, 44, 45, 45n6,
107n12, 262, 263, 339
West, Rebecca, 107, 107n13
Westminster Magazine, 87n10
What Is Money For? (Pound): and EP's
proposed collected edition of eco-
nomic writings, 101n19; and Faber
and Faber, 203; Nott uninterested in
publishing, 202, 203n2, 206, 206n4;
possible serialization of, 204, 204n13;
publication of, by British Union of Fas-
cists, 170n13, 171n9, 202n4, 206n4, 292,

345; and Routledge and Kegan Paul
Ltd., 170, 170n14, 171, 171n9
What Is This Social Credit (Gibson),
138n2
Wheeler, Burton Kendall, 112, 112n12
White, Compton Ignatius, 95, 95n23
White Mule: A Novel (Williams), 233,
233n25
Whitman, Walt, 358n44
Whittier-Ferguson, John, 369n7
Wilde, Oscar, 313
Williams, Whythe, 255, 255n7
Williams, William Carlos: and Arrow
Editions, 177, 177n5; and EP's allegiance to Mussolini and Italian fascism, 27n23; on EP's lack of economic
expertise, xxxi, 356n23; friendship
between EP and, xxxv; and Ideogrammic series, 27, 27n23, 58, 58n22, 71, 100,
100n15, 102, 119, 119n10, 119n12, 121,
135n23, 144, 193, 193n2, 194, 194n1, 200,
229, 229n3, 233, 233n24, 338; literary
agent of, 100, 100n15, 119, 119n11; and
literary policy for *New English Weekly*,
57, 57n14; on maverick writing styles,
xxvi, 356n26; Dorothy Pound's reading
of poetry by, 135, 135n23, 144, 153n2;
in *Readies for Bob Brown's Machine*,
87n9; review of EP's *Jefferson and/or
Mussolini* by, xxv, xxvi, 356n23; and
Social Credit, xxxi, 27n23, 30n7; writings by, 27n23, 30, 30n7, 119n12, 233,
233n25. *See also specific works*
Williams, William Proctor, xiii, 370n19
Wilson, Robert McNair: biographical
sketch and identification of, 249n11,
346; in Butchart's *To-Morrow's Money*,
232n13, 346, 371n4; expertise of, 6n10,
346; and Ideogrammic series, 30; news-
letter by, 249; and Pamphlets on the
New Economics series, 6, 232; review
copy of *Social Credit: An Impact* sent
to, 107; writings by, 231, 231n11, 346
Wilson, Theodore Carl, 87, 87n10
Wilson, Woodrow, 45, 45n7, 356n29
"wipers/wypers" (derogatory term), 10,
10n4, 20, 20n8

Witemeyer, Hugh, 59n26, 354n15
Woodcraft movement, 362n29
Woodward, Eugene Sydney, 92n4, 94,
94n16, 275
Woodward, William E., 21, 21n14, 346,
356n28
Woolf, Virginia, 302–3
*World Revolution: The Plot against Civil-
ization* (Webster), 364n39
World War I: anti-war movement during,
108n19; Battle of Gallipoli during, 135,
135n22; and Dyson, 335; economic
motives for, 263; EP and devastation
of, xvii; and Nott, xxiii, 322; and Read,
50, 50n10
World War II. *See* Fascist Italy;
Mussolini, Benito; Nazism
Wright, Frank Lloyd, xxiv, 372n19
Wrigley Printing Co., 92

Yale University Press: *ABC of Reading*
published by, 46n12; and Butchart's
Money, 170; correspondence between
Nott and, 119, 120, 120n2, 122; EP's
frustrations with, 26n17, 82–5, 84n7,
124, 127; and EP's proposed collected
edition of economic writings, 77–8,
77n18, 77n20, 80, 82–5, 87n12, 96,
100–1, 100n16, 101n19, 115, 115n2,
124n1, 125, 125n14; and EP's proposed
writings on subjects other than economics, 124–5, 124n1; and *Jefferson
and/or Mussolini*, 170, 170n12, 171;
Make It New published by, 175, 175n2;
Nott's criticism of, 122; and Pamphlets
on the New Economics series, 126–7,
126n16; review copies of Pamphlets of
the New Economics sent to, 87
Yeats, W.B., xvi, 216n12, 285
Yriarte, Charles, 370n19

Zaharoff, Sir Basil, 98, 98n2
Zarathustra (Nietzsche), 84
Zionism, 270–1
Zukofsky, Louis, 220n6, 364n38, 367n29